Pro Tools® 11

IGNITE!

The Visual Guide for New Users

❈ ❈ ❈

Andrew Hagerman

CENGAGE
Learning®

Australia • Brazil • Japan • Korea • Mexico • Singapore • Spain • United Kingdom • United States

Pro Tools® 11 Ignite!
The Visual Guide for New Users
Andrew Hagerman

Publisher and General Manager,
Cengage Learning PTR:
Stacy L. Hiquet

Associate Director of Marketing:
Sarah Panella

Manager of Editorial Services:
Heather Talbot

Senior Marketing Manager:
Mark Hughes

Acquisitions Editor:
Orren Merton

Project Editor: Kate Shoup

Technical Reviewer: Brent Heber

Copy Editor: Kate Shoup

Interior Layout: Jill Flores

Cover Designer: Mike Tanamachi

Indexer: Larry D. Sweazy

Proofreader: Gene Redding

For product information and technology assistance, contact us at
Cengage Learning Customer & Sales Support, 1-800-354-9706

For permission to use material from this text or product,
submit all requests online at **cengage.com/permissions**
Further permissions questions can be emailed to
permissionrequest@cengage.com

Library of Congress Control Number: 2013942744

ISBN-13: 978-1-285-84821-1

ISBN-10: 1-285-84821-7

Cengage Learning PTR
20 Channel Center Street
Boston, MA 02210
USA

Cengage Learning is a leading provider of customized learning solutions with office locations around the globe, including Singapore, the United Kingdom, Australia, Mexico, Brazil, and Japan. Locate your local office at: **international.cengage.com/region**

Cengage Learning products are represented in Canada by Nelson Education, Ltd. For your lifelong learning solutions, visit **cengageptr.com**

Visit our corporate website at **cengage.com**

Printed in the United States of America
1 2 3 4 5 6 7 15 14 13

This book is dedicated to my beloved bride Junko, to our beautiful daughter Sachiko, and all who fight the good fight for art's sake.

Acknowledgments

Your humble scribe Andy Hagerman here. Mine is the name on the front cover of the book, and although you might infer from that that it's *my* book, you'd be wrong. Truth is, this book is was a team effort, and there are a lot of names besides mine that deserve to be on that cover. Unfortunately, that'd look cluttered and strange, so allow me to give them a shout out here!

First and foremost, the team at Cengage Learning deserves a hand. This is my 10th book with them, and this title finds some of my favorite Cengage folks helping to bring this to you. Leading the pack is Kate Shoup—trust me, her editing makes me sound a lot smarter than I actually am! Working beside her was tech editor Brent Heber, a former Avid colleague who's making his mark in the Australian audio post-production scene. Thanks Brent, for keeping me honest on the technical bits!

I'm honored to be able to work closely with Avid (the people who have over the years made Pro Tools the powerful tool that it is today). Although it's a small company in relation to its industry prominence, Avid is composed of a crack team whose dedication to excellence really shows. Special thanks to Vicky Moreno, AJ Steffenberg, Andy and Claudia Cook, and Tim Mynett, and all my colleagues in the Avid Training department. Also, thanks to the team at the Avid Japan office, especially Tsukasa Tokiwano and Kazumi Mihashi, and Daisuke Naito (who was always on the spot in answering some very silly questions!).

This book's exercises are derived from some projects I've worked on recently, and thanks go out to the dedicated musicians who have graciously allowed me to share their work.

- "Listen" was a song that I wrote for a trade show in Japan (and yes, that language you hear in the track is Japanese). Special thanks to Tsukasa Tokiwano (guitar), and to Kazumi Mihashi and Sachiko Hagerman for the help with the Japanese lyrics.
- "Shady Grove" is a traditional American Folk song performed by a group named Under the Radar. They are Paul McCaskill (vocals and guitar), Jason Thomas (fiddle), Lamont Goff (mandolin), and Jessica Goff (bass).
- "Maybe Meagan" is a song written by American composer William Brooks. Special thanks to William for sharing his vocals and guitars, and for allowing me to flesh out an arrangement using MIDI within Pro Tools.

Last, but certainly not least, my thanks goes to my family and friends, without whose faith I'd never have started writing in the first place. My wife Junko and our daughter Sachiko are the best writing partners a guy could ask for. In this book, Sachiko even helped with the writing of "Listen" and is even at eight years old showing a very sharp ear for music.

About the Author

Andrew Hagerman has been a professional musician and teacher for the majority of his nearly 50 (gasp!) years. Beginning his musical life at the early age of eight as an aspiring tubist, Andy continued his studies at the prestigious Northwestern University in Chicago. During his time there, MIDI and computer music were in their infancy, and Andy recognized the usefulness of music technology in aiding the creative process. Hagerman had the opportunity to learn these new technological tools of the trade as they were being invented and refined, and his quest for the best in audio and music technology ultimately spurred him to use and teach Avid's Pro Tools.

As a performer and arranger, Hagerman has worked with numerous ensembles of all types, including many years of playing at Disneyland, Walt Disney World, and Tokyo Disneyland. With a passion for teaching, Hagerman has also worked as the Associate Course Director of Advanced Audio Workstations at Full Sail Real World University in Winter Park, Florida, and has authored 10 books on the topics of audio production and Pro Tools. As a composer and producer, he's active in the U.S. and Japan, where he currently lives. Hagerman currently works with Avid's Asia-Pacific Training Partner Program, working with excellent educational institutions throughout the region to offer the highest level of audio and video training to the next generation of creative professionals.

} Contents

CONTENTS }

❋ ❋ ❋

CONTENTS }

X

❁ ❁ ❁

CONTENTS }

Introduction

First of all, congratulations on becoming a Pro Tools user, and welcome (or welcome *back*, if you're already using Pro Tools and upgrading to Pro Tools 11)! When Avid says its powerful digital audio workstation (DAW) is the industry standard, you can believe it. You'll find Pro Tools at all levels of the business, from modest software-only systems all the way up to high-end HD/HDX systems, hard at work in every facet of audio and musical production. It's a serious, professional product, and your decision to buy it (and learn it well) is a step in the right direction.

The Chinese philosopher Lao-Tsu once said, "A journey of a thousand miles begins with a single step." That's where this book comes in—it's that critical first step. Gaining a solid fundamental understanding of the basics of Pro Tools will help ensure that your journey starts off without a hitch and pointed in the right direction. In this book, you'll learn the basic techniques of composing, recording, editing, and mixing digital audio and MIDI (Musical Instrument Digital Interface). You'll learn how to harness the power of Pro Tools' impressive array of features, from software effects, to virtual instruments, to mixes that are automated and edited with some of the best tools you'll find anywhere.

This is my seventh book about Pro Tools. The first covered version 6 of the software, followed with titles on Pro Tools 7, 7.4, 8, 9, and 10. The book you're holding stands on the shoulders of those previous books and includes some of the same material as those earlier titles. It also covers exciting new features of Pro Tools 11. Even if you're a long-time Pro Tools user, I think you'll find that the new improvements—things like its 64-bit rebuild and offline bounce—represent a new level of flexibility and power. These new features, combined with the solid design of Pro Tools in general, make Pro Tools 11 a quite exciting release indeed!

If your aim is to create and produce audio, Pro Tools is an excellent choice. *Pro Tools 11 Ignite!* will be your companion during those critical first steps on the road of discovery!

Who Should Read This Book?

Essentially, this book is geared toward beginners, and assumes little or no experience in working with a DAW. You'll find that this book's highly visual and plainly worded style makes it easy to follow. Nearly every step in the processes discussed is accompanied by clear illustrations, so you won't have to spend your time hunting around the screen for tools and menus. (What fun is *that*?) Once you're finished with the chapters and exercises, this book will be a valuable reference later on as well.

Don't worry if you're not a formally trained musician or if you haven't really dealt with digital audio before. The beauty of Pro Tools—and computer music in general—is that even untrained (but creative) musicians can enjoy great success in this kind of environment. Of course, any general music or audio knowledge you bring to the table is an added advantage, but it is certainly not a *requirement* for this book.

With that being said, there's no denying that Pro Tools is a *deep* program. Even those of us who have been using it for years still find new tidbits now and then. For that reason, I can't dedicate any of the limited space I have in this book to covering basic computer operations. That means it's up to you to understand the most basic ins and outs of your particular platform (either Mac or PC). Don't worry too much, though—the general computer knowledge required to use Pro Tools is pretty basic. If you can locate, launch, and close programs, you're probably in fine shape.

How to Use This Book

At its heart, music (and audio) production is a progressive process. From creation to performance, it's the result of many small steps taken in order. A solid mastery of Pro Tools works much the same way. This book is laid out to mirror the creative process, from setup, through the recording process, editing, mixing, and putting on the final touches. The first sections of the book also include a bit of information about the nature of DAWs in general so you understand the basic building blocks of digital audio and can work most efficiently. If you're just beginning with DAWs, you'll find this information valuable in the long run.

Because this book is arranged sequentially according to the production process, you'll be able to follow along from the very start of a project through its completion. However, if you're interested in some areas more than others (which is pretty common with more experienced users), feel free to take the book out of order and just concentrate on those sections first; this book will work that way as well.

You'll find that most of this book is laid out in a tutorial-style format, with exercise files downloadable from the publisher's companion website, at www.cengageptr. com/downloads, that you can use side by side with the book's examples. Of course, you can also employ this book as a targeted training source, using the clear, illustrated style of this format to your advantage as you locate information on specific functions.

Last but not least, you'll note that peppered throughout this book are notes, tips, and sidebars. Take a look at these to find additional ways to increase your efficiency, additional information on key functions, and even warnings that point out common pitfalls and how to avoid them.

Finally, a Little Background...

For nearly 30 years, Avid (formerly Digidesign) has been a leader in digital audio workstation technology, and the professional community has chosen Pro Tools as the clear industry standard. Over the years, many different configurations for Pro Tools have arisen, making choosing a Pro Tools system a bit complex. Never fear, though—these can all be broken down into a couple of simple groups. Let's start out with the software itself:

❋ **Pro Tools HD 11.** Short for Pro Tools *high definition*, this version of Pro Tools has all the bells and whistles that Pro Tools can offer. This includes advanced editing and mixing features, surround-sound support, and the ability to operate in either a DSP- or Native-based environment (I'll discuss that in just a moment).

❋ **Pro Tools 11.** This is your basic Pro Tools system, and although some features present in the HD version are missing in the basic version, it is still more than adequate for many professionals. It is on this version that this book will focus.

In addition to the software itself, there are two different modes in which Pro Tools can operate—either as a *hardware-based* or *host-based* DAW:

❋ **Hardware-based (or DSP) systems.** These Pro Tools systems rely on dedicated computer cards (called HDX cards) and audio interfaces specifically designed to work with Pro Tools. The HDX cards are responsible for Pro Tools 11's most important functions, including input-output management, mixing, and plug-in processing. The audio interfaces used by these hardware-based systems are designed to connect directly to the HDX cards. Only Pro Tools HD software can operate in a hardware-based mode.

Hardware-based Pro Tools systems have specific advantages in the number of inputs and outputs (I/O) that the system can manage, the processing power of the system, and overall system stability. These systems are commonly found in high-end professional facilities that demand the highest standards of scalability and performance.

❋ **Host-based (or Native) systems.** When we refer to a DAW as being *host*-based, we mean that the system relies on the computer's CPU to accomplish all essential Pro Tools processes (things like signal management, mixing, plug-in processing, and more). Host-based systems generally cost less than their hardware-based alternatives, but with the ever-increasing power of computer CPUs, are finding a place in more and more professional facilities. Basic Pro Tools 11 software operates only as a host-based DAW, while Pro Tools HD software can operate as either a host-based or hardware-based DAW (depending on the hardware setup of the system).

In terms of audio interfaces, host-based systems will operate with any audio interface that has an ASIO or Core Audio driver. Of course, the recommended combination is an Avid interface paired with Pro Tools 11, but it is no longer the only choice available to users.

> ❋ **PRO TOOLS|HD NATIVE**
>
> HD|native is a relatively new mid-range product that brings powerful aspects of both a hardware-based and host-based system together. With a single hardware card or thunderbolt device paired with HD interfaces, users operate Pro Tools as a host-based DAW, while at the same time getting the high fidelity of Avid's top-of-the-line audio interfaces.

The good news—and it's great news, really—is that regardless of your particular Pro Tools configuration, the software environment in which you work is nearly identical. That means you can take advantage of one of the most powerful and well-developed user interfaces on the market without breaking the bank. What's more, if you're a Pro Tools 11 user, when it comes time for you to step up to a Pro Tools HD or HD|Native system, you'll be ready to hit the ground running.

Adding to its already impressive arsenal of features, Pro Tools 11 is a highly anticipated release, bringing users some very important improvements. These include the following:

- ❋ **64-bit architecture.** Typically, when a version of software is updated, new features are added to existing computer code. That's not the case with Pro Tools 11. This is a complete 64-bit rebuild of the software. As a 64-bit application, Pro Tools 11 can utilize more system RAM than could previous 32-bit versions. (32-bit programs can access only up to 4 GB of system RAM.) This can radically improve the performance of your Pro Tools system.

- ❋ **Redesigned audio engine.** In line with the overall rebuild of Pro Tools, the previous audio engine (called the Digidesign Audio Engine, or DAE) has been replaced with the Avid Audio Engine (AAE). This new engine provides for more complex mixes and more plug-in power than has been possible in previous versions.

- ❋ **Offline (faster than real time) "bounce."** In previous versions of Pro Tools, mix-downs (commonly called "bounces") needed to be done in real time. In other words, the production of a three-minute song included budgeting three minutes in which to create a final mix. In Pro Tools 11, you now have the option of bouncing your final mix faster than real time (based on the processing power of your computer's CPU).

If a lot of this sounds like Greek right now, don't worry—we'll cover it in the chapters to come. Ready? Let's go!

Setting Up Your Sessions

Throughout *Pro Tools 11 Ignite!*, you'll have the option of using session files and other downloadable tutorial sessions and audio material so that you can follow along with the specific steps outlined in the chapters. These files will allow the tutorial sessions to play in their entirety. Generally speaking, you'll have no trouble downloading these materials to your hard drive.

1 **Go to www.cengageptr.com/downloads.** The Cengage Learning online companion website will open.

2 In the Companion Search field, **type Pro Tools 11 Ignite**, as shown here.

3 **Click** on the **Search button**. The search results will appear.

4 **Click** on the **book title link** (in this case, **Pro Tools 11 Ignite**). The companion site for the book will appear.

Online Companions:

MUSIC TECHNOLOGY

- Pro Tools 11 Ignite
  Author: Andy Hagerman

5 In the Companion Contents section, **click** on the **link** for the chapter whose material you want to download. You'll be directed to a page dedicated to the materials used in that chapter.

Companion Contents:

Appendix A

Chapter 01

Chapter 02

Chapter 03

6 **Click** the **link** for the material you want to download. You'll be prompted to enter a destination for your downloaded file, which will vary based upon your platform (Mac or PC) and the browser software you are using.

7 The file that will be downloaded is a ZIP file. You'll need to **extract** the **contents** before you can use the session. Again, this can vary depending on your platform.

The folder that will be extracted contains the session and other material for the chapter. You're all set to launch the session! After launching, you may see a Session Notes window appear. This may contain a number of messages, including the following:

❋ **Your I/O setup has changed since the last time this session was saved. Check the I/O Setups window to see what's changed.** Fundamentally, all this message is saying is that this session was created on a different setup from yours.

Session Notes

Your I/O setup has changed since the last time this session was saved. Check the I/O Setups window to see what's changed.

Some paths were made inactive because they could not be assigned to existing path definitions.

Would you like to save a detailed report?

No   Yes

❋ **Some paths were made inactive because they could not be assigned to existing path definitions.** This indicates that the inputs and outputs of the system upon which the session was created don't match the system with which the session is now being launched. Here again, if you can't hear everything you should, go to the I/O Setup window and adjust your input and output paths accordingly (covered in Chapter 3, "Getting Started with Audio").

❋ In any of these cases, you typically won't need to see a detailed report, so click on the No button.

Your session will continue loading, and in the vast majority of cases, you will be ready to go.

If you've already read Chapter 1, "Welcome to Pro Tools 11," you know that Pro Tools is a *pointer-based* application, which basically means that a session file—which is really the cornerstone of your project—refers to other files (such as audio files) to do its work. To do this, your session needs to know the location of the audio files it needs. In rare instances, however, you may see a dialog box that states that a number of audio and/or fade files cannot be found. No problem; you can tell the session where to look for these files.

1 **Click** on the **Manually Find & Relink option button**.

2 **Click** on the **OK button**. The Relink window will appear.

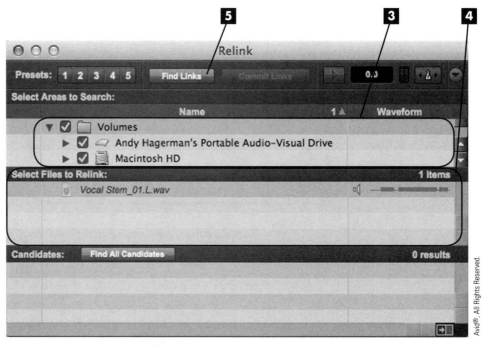

3 In the top section of the Relink window, **click** on the **hard drive** in which your session and audio files reside. Drives and folders that will be included in the search process will be indicated with a checkmark.

4 In the middle section of the Relink window, you'll see a list of filenames in italic print; these are your missing files. **Select them all.**

5 **Click** on the **Find Links button** at the top of the window. The Linking Options dialog box will appear.

6 **Click** on the **Find By File ID option button** and the **Match Format** and **Match Duration checkboxes** to select them.

7 **Click** on the **OK button**. The search for your missing audio files will begin.

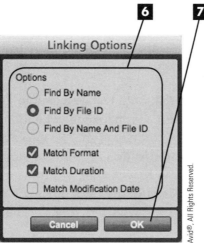

❄ ❄ ❄

❈ When a missing file is found, a small icon will appear next to the appropriate filenames, indicating that the file has been located by Pro Tools. When all files show these symbols, you're ready to proceed.

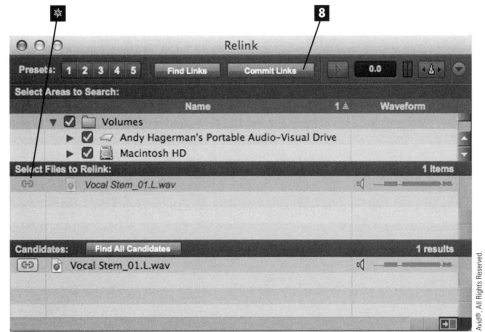

8 **Click** on the **Commit Links button** at the top of the Relink window.

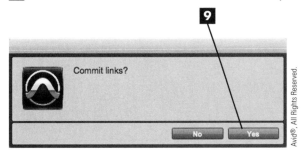

9 A final dialog box will appear, asking you if you want to commit links. Click on the Yes button.

❈ AUTOMATIC FIND AND RELINK

In the Missing Files dialog box, you'll see an Automatically Find & Relink option button. It does just what you'd guess: It searches your entire system for missing files. If you aren't sure where your audio files are, this might be a good route to take. But beware: Searching through all your attached hard drives might take a long time!

❈ UNIQUE FILE IDS

Pro Tools assigns a unique file ID to every file it uses, which is its proprietary tag for that file. You'll note that you can choose to find files that match by name, file ID, or both. Although it's quite common to find matching names, those names (including the file extension) must match perfectly. Filenames and extensions can vary from platform to platform; for this reason, searching by file ID only (as described) is sometimes a good way to make sure your files are found in this case.

That's it! You can now close the Relink window and continue working. Remember to save your session when you're finished to avoid having to do this a second time!

1 } Welcome to Pro Tools 11

Congratulations, and welcome to the world of Pro Tools! Throughout Digidesign's and Avid's nearly 30-year history, Pro Tools has established itself at the forefront of the digital audio workstation (DAW) community. Version 11 represents a major new release, particularly in terms of system performance and mixing workflows.

Pro Tools 11 can be found in virtually every facet of the audio industry, from music production for CDs to surround sound for movie soundtracks. Now, armed with Pro Tools' powerful array of functions and features, you'll be able to tap into this world of digital audio for yourself to realize your own creative vision. Welcome to the party!

The first step in the process is to set up your system and to master the essential functions of Pro Tools. In this chapter, you'll learn how to do the following:

* Identify the hardware and software components of your Pro Tools system and configure your audio engine.
* Organize sessions and data in Pro Tools.
* Use Pro Tools' most basic functions.
* Create, open, play, and close a session.

What Makes Up a Pro Tools System?

In the introduction, you learned that there are two different versions of Pro Tools software (Pro Tools 11 HD and Pro Tools 11), and two different hardware configurations in which Pro Tools can run (hardware-based or host-based).

For the purposes of this book, I'll limit this discussions to basic Pro Tools 11 systems (using Pro Tools 11 software and operating as a host-based DAW), but the skills you learn here can be applied to any level of Pro Tools system.

The Heart of Your DAW: The Computer

Your computer is the cornerstone of your Pro Tools system. The computer, particularly its central processing unit (CPU), will be called upon to do everything from mixing and automation to effects processing and more. That means the more power your CPU has, the more powerful your Pro Tools software will be. The host computer can be either a PC or a Mac.

In addition to CPU speed, your computer's random access memory (RAM) plays an important role in how your digital audio workstation will perform. It probably comes as no surprise to learn that the more RAM your computer has, the better. More RAM will enable your Pro Tools session to run more real-time processes and will make for an overall more powerful DAW. Avid recommends a minimum of 8 GB of RAM to run Pro Tools 11.

Ideally, your DAW computer should be dedicated solely to music- and audio-related tasks. Other applications running (or even installed) on your system can steal from your computer's overall efficiency when running Pro Tools. Recording and playing back digital audio can be demanding on your computer's CPU, and other programs interrupting the steady stream of data to and from your hard drive can cause major problems. Of course, having such a dedicated computer can be impractical for many users. If you're not able to devote your computer exclusively to Pro Tools, you should avoid running other programs during your Pro Tools sessions.

Audio Interface

All DAWs, regardless of brand, require some sort of audio interface to record and play back audio (also referred to as input/output, or I/O for short). Interfaces can vary from professional-quality devices used at large professional facilities (these facilities often use multiple interfaces together) down to the built-in microphone and headphone outputs of a laptop computer. Across this spectrum, different manufacturers have created a wide range of products featuring various numbers of channels and different levels of audio quality.

Your audio interface is the doorway for audio going to and coming from your computer. Generally speaking, your computer will connect directly to the audio interface, and your various audio devices (mixing boards, keyboards, and microphones) will connect to the interface's available audio inputs. To listen to your work, you should connect the main audio outputs of your interface to an amplifier, and from there to monitor speakers. If you're using powered monitors (those that have built-in amplifiers), you can connect the outputs of your interface directly to the inputs of the speakers.

In past versions of Pro Tools, the Pro Tools software has been unbreakably linked to Avid audio interfaces. For example, to run Pro Tools 8 LE, you needed to have a connected Avid interface (such as an Mbox), or the Pro Tools software would not launch. Possibly the most significant change in Pro Tools 9 was the breaking of this dependence on Avid hardware. Pro Tools 11 continues to be independent of specific hardware requirements, and is compatible with any interface with ASIO (Windows) or Core Audio (Mac) drivers. That means you can use Avid interfaces, a third party's, or even the built-in I/O of your computer.

Hard Drive(s)

Just as traditional tape-based recording studios rely on magnetic tape as a storage medium, Pro Tools relies on hard drives for the recording and playback of its digital audio. The drives can be IDE/ATA, SATA, eSATA, FireWire, SSD, or USB 2.0.

It is important to remember two factors when choosing a hard drive for Pro Tools: size and speed. First, a larger-capacity drive will enable you to store more audio data. This will translate into more minutes of audio that you can store, higher-resolution digital audio, or both. A fast drive will allow for more efficient transfer of data (also called throughput) when you are recording and/or playing back audio. This can translate into higher track counts and more reliability when working with complex sessions.

Using a Dedicated Audio Hard Drive

Adding a second drive dedicated to the storage of your Pro Tools sessions and audio files will greatly increase your Pro Tools system's performance, whether your system is used solely for Pro Tools or is more of a general-purpose machine. You'll still want to install the Pro Tools application on your computer's system drive, but when you create your sessions (something I'll get into later in this chapter), you can put them on your second "audio" drive. That way, you'll have one hard drive occupied with the nominal tasks of your computer and another separate drive, with its own read/write head and throughput, dealing only with your Pro Tools session and audio.

> ### ❋ PARTITIONING YOUR HARD DRIVE
>
> If you're wondering whether partitioning your system hard drive will do the trick, the short answer is no. Partitioning a single hard drive may give the outward appearance of creating a second drive, but in reality, there is still only one physical hardware device and only one throughput path. Although partitioning can be a convenient way of organizing your data, partitioning doesn't add another physical drive with its own read/write head, so it won't give Pro Tools the same benefit with real-time tasks as a second physical drive would.

Great Resources: Avid's Compatibility Documents, Knowledge Base, and In-Application Help

You might have noticed that although I've talked about desirable qualities in a DAW system, I haven't mentioned many specific details about what kind of hardware you should be using (things such as minimum CPU speed and chipset types). I apologize if I seem evasive on the subject, but the truth is that the landscape of computer-based products transforms and grows so rapidly that any specs I quote here might well be out of date by the time you read this. Don't despair, though! Avid has provided the help you need to build the Pro Tools system you want in the form of an up-to-date list of compatible hardware. You can find this list on Avid's website, at the following URL: http://avid.force.com/pkb/articles/faq/compatibility.

To view more technical information and alerts, you can also take a look at the Avid Knowledge Base. Although it takes a few steps to get there, it's well worth the trip. On the top of the Avid home page (www.avid.com), click on the Support and Services link. Then, on the Support and Services page, click on the Support Resources tab. On the Support Resources page, click the Find Answers link and choose Knowledge Base—Audio from the list that appears. Once you're in the Knowledge Base, you can search in a number of ways, including by product or keyword. Whether you're designing a Pro Tools system or troubleshooting one, the Knowledge Base is a trove of technical tidbits!

If that seems like too much work, don't fret. You don't even need to leave the application! Let's take a look at two more places you can go to get answers you need:

※ The top section of the Help menu includes links to online support resources, including Pro Tools Help, the Knowledge Base, and online user forums.

※ The Marketplace drop-down menu allows you to quickly access your Avid account, go to a plug-in purchasing website, purchase support, or buy and upgrade.

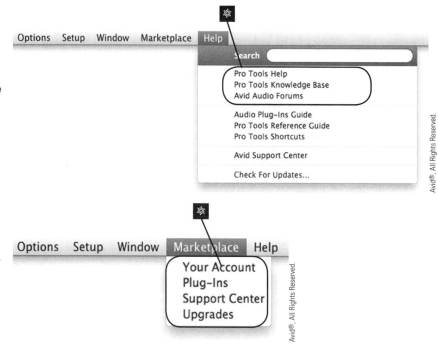

A Word About Installation

The installation process is basically broken down into two easy steps:

1 Install the Pro Tools software.

2 Install the appropriate drivers (ASIO or Core Audio) for the interface(s) that you will use with your system. Drivers for Avid interfaces are included with your Pro Tools 11 installation materials.

❄ IMPORTANT OPERATING SYSTEM NOTE

Because Pro Tools 11 is a 64-bit application, it can only run on 64-bit operating systems (such as Windows 8 or Mac OS X 10.8.4). Pro Tools 11 will not launch on any 32-bit operating system.

❄ CAN IT BE THIS EASY?!?

In previous versions of Pro Tools, the installation process was, if not onerous, certainly a bit time consuming. With Pro Tools 11 on a Mac computer, those headaches are a thing of the past. Pro Tools now sports a simple drag-and-drop installation method. Just drag the Pro Tools application into the Applications folder, and you're ready to launch Pro Tools!

❄ PRO TOOLS 11 AND PRO TOOLS 10 CO-INSTALLATIONS

If you're a Pro Tools user already and aren't quite ready to let go of your 32-bit plug-ins, take heart! Pro Tools 11 and Pro Tools 10 (version 10.3.6 or later) can be installed on the same machine. It's worth mentioning, though, that only one version of Pro Tools can be launched at a time.

Finding Installation Information

The documentation you received with your Pro Tools software and hardware is the first place to look for information on installation. In the ever-changing world of computers, though, that documentation could quickly become out of date. Once again, the Avid website is an invaluable resource. Just go to the Pro Tools Updates page in the Avid Knowledge Base (http://avid.force.com/pkb/articles/en_US/download/en355241) to see a comprehensive list of all Pro Tools versions dating back to version 5!

The documentation that came with your Pro Tools product, combined with a little Net surfing (if needed), should enable you to successfully install and configure your Pro Tools system. Once that's finished, you're ready to move on.

Checking for Software Updates

Wouldn't it be great if there were a way for Pro Tools to help you out with software updates? Good news: Pro Tools 11 includes exactly that functionality. It can search for any updates, bug fixes, and so on that are relevant to your system. Better yet, Pro Tools 11 can also check to see whether there are any updates

5

needed or available for your installed plug-ins. How cool is that? Pro Tools 11 even differentiates between paid and non-paid updates, so you can choose to make the larger version leaps at your discretion.

Using this new feature is very easy—so easy, in fact, that there's virtually nothing you need to do. By default, Pro Tools will quickly check for updates when you launch the program. All you need to do is make sure your computer is connected to the Internet, and this will happen automatically. (Don't worry. This check is very quick and doesn't add too much time to the Pro Tools launch.)

If you want to do an update check manually, you can do that as well. It's also a simple process:

1 Once Pro Tools is launched (something I'll go into later in this chapter), **click** on **Help**. The Help menu will appear.

2 **Choose Check for Updates.** The Software Update progress window will appear.

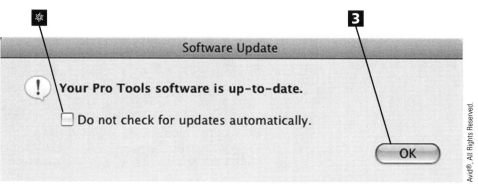

3 If there are updates to be installed, you will be directed to a website with links for the appropriate download(s). If you are up to date, you'll see the dialog box shown here. **Click** on the **OK button** to finish the process.

❄ If you don't wish for Pro Tools to perform automatic update searches upon startup in the future, just click on the Do Not Check for Updates Automatically checkbox.

iLok Protection

Long-time Pro Tools users should be familiar with the iLok method of copyright protection. It's been widely used for plug-in authorizations by many manufacturers (including Avid). For those who are new to the term iLok, think of it as a key that unlocks your software and enables it to run. Starting with Pro Tools 9, all versions of Pro Tools now rely upon this method of protection.

❋ A second-generation iLok (left),
along with an original iLok
(right). Pro Tools 11 requires a
second-generation iLok to run.

Pro Tools 11 requires a second-generation iLok—a hardware device that is rough-ly the size of a small USB flash drive. It can hold a large number of software licenses. In fact, this iLok can store more than 500 licenses. When you purchase Pro Tools 11, a second-generation iLok is included in the box. This iLok comes pre-loaded with the Pro Tools 11 license, so all you need to do is plug it into an available USB port or a USB hub attached to your computer, and you're ready to launch Pro Tools.

Your iLok hardware can be used for more than just your Pro Tools licenses, though. If you go to www.ilok.com, you can create an account into which you can deposit additional software licenses. With the convenience of the iLok copy-protection system, you can even have Pro Tools installed on multiple computers (though of course, you'll only be able to run Pro Tools when the iLok is physically attached)!

Choosing an Audio Engine

As discussed, the open design of Pro Tools 11 enables users to employ a wide variety of devices for audio I/O—in fact, any audio interface that includes an ASIO or Core Audio driver. To make the most of this new feature, though, you'll need to know how to choose the audio engine that works best in any given situa-tion. To get this fundamental control over Pro Tools, you'll make use of Pro Tools' Playback Engine dialog box.

1 **Click** on Setup. The Setup menu opens.

2 **Choose Playback Engine.** The Playback Engine dialog box will appear.

3 **Click** on the **Playback Engine** selector. A menu of available hardware options opens.

4 **Choose** the **interface** that you want Pro Tools to use for recording and playback of audio. In this image, I've chosen my trusty Mbox Pro.

5 **Click** on the **OK button.**

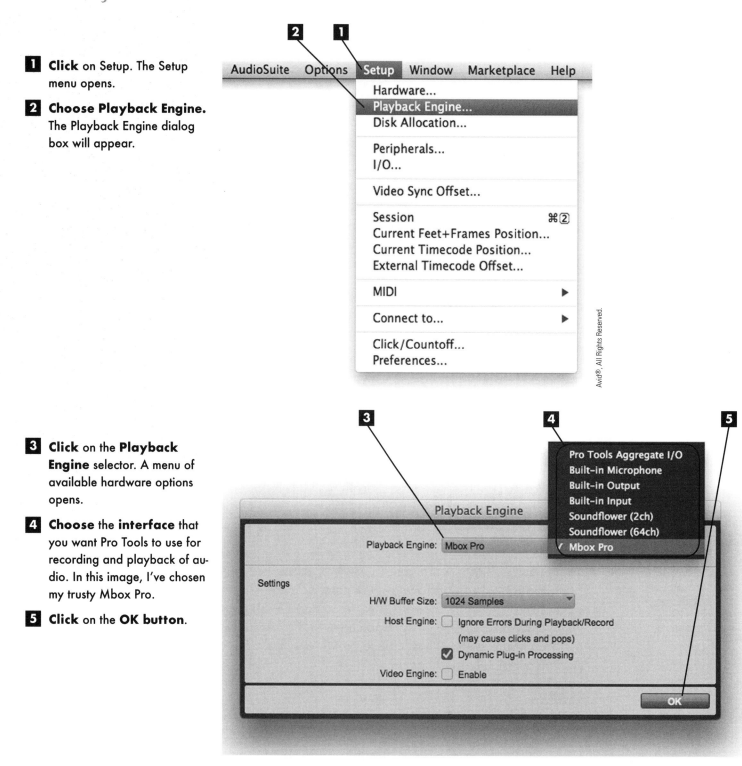

Avid®, All Rights Reserved.

Tips on Choosing an Audio Engine

If there's a downside to this new flexibility, it's that it's sometimes hard to make a choice! Of course, convenience is a factor. Here are some other things to keep in mind:

❄ When it comes to audio quality, one of the biggest factors in terms of clarity and stereo-imagery width is jitter—the lower the better. Jitter specs for audio gear are often printed on product documentation, and are readily available for professional interfaces on the Internet. Look for the interface with lowest jitter, and choose that one for your audio interface in the Playback Engine dialog box. If your audio interface's documentation doesn't include specific information about jitter, it's a safe bet that an external interface will have lower jitter than your computer's built-in I/O.

❄ If your computer has built-in sound capabilities (most do), you'll see some degree of built-in input or output options listed in the Playback Engine menu. Take care—they mean what they say! For example, if you choose Built-In Output, you'll have no input capabilities in your Pro Tools system. If you choose Built-In Input, you'll have no output! If you want to more fully use your Mac computer's built-in audio hardware, choose Pro Tools Aggregate I/O. (I'll talk more about that a little later in this chapter.)

❄ If you have a Pro Tools session open and you change your audio engine, Pro Tools will automatically save and close your session. Click on the OK button to relaunch the session with the new audio engine. If you don't want to overwrite your session file, choose the Save As option before making your audio engine changes. (I'll talk about the Save As option at the end of this chapter.)

Setting Up Your Hardware

After you've chosen an audio engine, you might want to tweak it a bit, configuring the various options that are included with your audio interface. That's where the Hardware Setup dialog box comes in. It's the second stage in the process of getting your audio hardware properly configured for use with Pro Tools.

1 **Click** on **Setup**. The Setup menu will appear.

2 **Choose Hardware.** The Hardware Setup dialog box will appear.

AudioSuite	Options	Setup	Window	Marketplace	Help

Hardware...
Playback Engine...
Disk Allocation...

Peripherals...
I/O...

Video Sync Offset...

Session ⌘②
Current Feet+Frames Position...
Current Timecode Position...
External Timecode Offset...

MIDI ▶

Connect to... ▶

Click/Countoff...
Preferences...

The Hardware Setup dialog box displays information related to the audio engine that you chose in the Playback Engine dialog box. If you change audio engines, the information displayed in the Hardware Setup dialog box will change accordingly. There are a few aspects that are commonly seen in this dialog box (this example shows the Hardware Setup dialog box that you would see with the Mbox Pro):

* On the lower-left side, you can choose a sample rate and clock source.

* Depending on the device, you'll see different options in the center of the Hardware Setup dialog box. In this case, you have the ability to configure the Mbox Pro's Multi-Button.

* Many interfaces allow further customization through a dedicated Control Panel. In this case, if you click on the Launch Control Panel button, you'll see the device's dedicated mixer.

Although the appearance of the Control Panel will vary from device to device (shown here is the Mbox Pro Control Panel), it is here that you'll gain a deeper level of control over your audio interface.

The Pro Tools Aggregate I/O

For the most part, Pro Tools is identical whether you're using a PC or a Mac. However, there is an interesting feature that is currently available only on Mac computers: the Pro Tools Aggregate I/O. Using the Aggregate I/O, you can simultaneously use multiple interfaces. For example, you can use an external audio interface, plus your computer's built-in inputs and outputs. Let's take a look:

1 **Click** on **Setup**. The Setup menu will appear.

2 **Choose Playback Engine.** The Playback Engine dialog box will appear.

3 **Click** on **Playback Engine**. A menu of available hardware options will appear.

4 **Choose Pro Tools Aggregate I/O**.

5 **Click** on the **OK button** to close the Playback Engine dialog box.

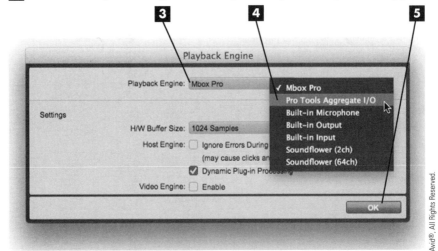

Avid®, All Rights Reserved.

Now, let's go back to the Hardware Setup dialog box:

1 **Click** on **Setup**. The Setup menu will appear.

2 **Choose Hardware.** The Hardware Setup dialog box will appear.

3 **Click** on the **Launch Setup App** button. The Audio Devices dialog box of the Mac Audio MIDI setup dialog box will appear.

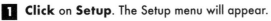

Avid®, All Rights Reserved.

❅ ❅ ❅

The Audio Devices dialog box lists not only individual audio devices that are attached (or built in) to your computer, but also a collection (or aggregate) of devices that can be used collectively. There are a few essential elements of this dialog box that will help you get the most out of your system:

* To reveal a list of all the devices included in the Pro Tools Aggregate I/O, click on the triangle icon to the left of the Aggregate icon.

* Click on the Pro Tools Aggregate I/O menu item to manage the aggregate devices. (These devices appear in the right section of the Audio Devices dialog box, as shown here.)

* The first thing you'll want to do is to choose a clock source for your aggregate devices. Because the Pro Tools Aggregate is intended for use with your Mac's built-in I/O, Avid recommends using the default clock settings.

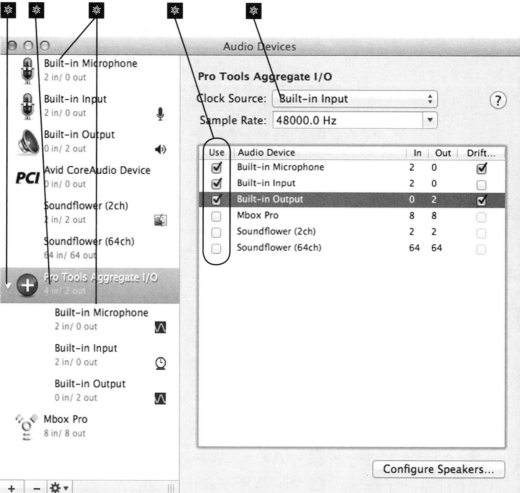

* To add or remove devices from your aggregate, click on the checkboxes in the Use column. As you might expect, checked boxes indicate that the device is an active part of the aggregate. (Once again, please remember that the Pro Tools Aggregate I/O was designed with only your built-in I/O in mind.)

* Individual devices often include some level of configurability—things like volume control, audio source, and so on. Click on the device you want to tweak, and you'll see the setup options in the right section of the Audio Devices dialog box. (You can select a device either within the aggregate list or outside the aggregate.)

❋ **DISCLAIMER**
The Aggregate I/O opens up a huge variety of configurations, and there isn't enough time or resources for Avid to test and qualify every possible permutation of devices. With that in mind, it's worth noting that Avid officially supports only the aggregation of a Mac's built-in I/O.

❊ **MAXIMUM I/O**

When dealing with multiple interfaces, you can really start adding up channels of I/O. But is there any limitation? Actually, yes. With Pro Tools 11 (the basic standalone software version), you'll have up to 32 channels of inputs and outputs. That's often just fine for smaller facilities, but if you need more, consider Pro Tools|HD Native, which supports up to 64 channels of I/O, or Pro Tools|HDX, which maxes out at a whopping 192 channels of I/O!

❊ **DRIFT**

The Drift checkbox allows you to enable individual members of the Pro Tools Aggregate I/O that aren't connected via word clock connections to resample their outputs as needed. As a general rule, click the checkbox for any non-word clock devices except the device chosen as a clock source.

Understanding Sessions and Files

Now you've gotten Pro Tools installed, and your system is set up (at least from a hardware perspective). Before you get any deeper into the world of Pro Tools, you should take a moment to understand the general principles behind this powerful digital audio workstation. An understanding of Pro Tools' overall architecture and how different elements work together is important fundamental knowledge as you continue to grow as a Pro Tools user.

Pro Tools Is a Pointer-Based Application

It's common to refer to a cursor as a pointer. But when discussing a pointer-based application like Pro Tools, we're referring to the way the program deals with digital audio data. In Pro Tools' case, this pointer-based structure can be broken down to three basic interdependent elements: session files, folders, and audio files. In this context, the term *pointer* refers to the way your Pro Tools session file will access (or point to) other files on your hard drive as your session plays.

A session folder is created when you create a new session. It contains the following items (as needed):

❊ **Session file.** The session file, which bears the project's name and has a file extension of .ptx, is at the top of the Pro Tools hierarchy. This is the file created by Pro Tools when you create a new session, and it's the file you open to return to a session you've already created. Although this file is relatively small, it is the master of all your session elements. Session files have a .ptx extension and contain the following session elements:

  ❊ The names, types, and arrangement of all tracks in your session

  ❊ All MIDI data

  ❊ Essential settings, such as inputs and outputs

  ❊ All edits, fades, and automation data

❊❊❊

❋ SESSIONS AND AUDIO

It might appear as if the only thing you need is a session file, but that's usually not the case. Although session files contain all the important aspects of a project, they don't actually contain any audio. Instead, a session file refers (or points) to audio files located in dedicated folders within your session folder.

❋ **Audio Files folder.** As soon as audio is recorded, it's stored in an Audio Files folder within the session folder. Different takes are stored in this folder as individual audio files. When you play a session, Pro Tools accesses, or points to, the audio files in this folder.

❋ HOW DO AUDIO FILES GET THEIR NAMES?

When you record audio in Pro Tools, the name of the file you create follows the name of the track on which it was recorded. For example, if you record onto a mono (one-channel) Audio track named Bass, the files created by Pro Tools in the Audio Files folder will be named Bass_01, Bass_02, and so on as you record takes on this track. In the case of stereo Audio tracks, two mono files (one for the left side and one for the right) are usually created. For example, if you record onto a stereo Audio track named Drums, two files, named Drums_01.L and Drums_01.R, will typically be created.

There are additional folders that can be created by Pro Tools as needed:

❋ **Clip Groups folder.** Pro Tools enables you to select multiple clips (something I'll talk about later in this chapter) and link them together in a single clip group. Digital audio, MIDI, and video clips can be grouped together, making editing much faster and easier. You'll learn more about clip groups later; for now, just know that groups you create are stored in this folder. (If you don't create any clip groups in a given session, a folder won't be created.)

❋ **Rendered Files folder.** Pro Tools 7.4 introduced a great feature called Elastic Audio. This was a very cool addition indeed, and one you'll learn about in Chapter 10, "Moving to the Next Level: Tips and Tricks." For now, all you need to know is that when you work with Elastic Audio, you have the option of rendering your elasticized audio to an audio file—and when you do, it will be stored in this folder.

❋ **Session File Backups folder.** Depending on your preference settings, Pro Tools can automatically create backups of your sessions and store them in this folder. By default, a new session backup is created every five minutes, and the folder keeps the last 10 backup files. This is highly recommended, particularly for new Pro Tools users; it can help you recover quickly if you encounter technical trouble.

❋ **Plug-in Settings folder.** In Pro Tools, you have the option of using plug-ins, which are programs designed to work within the Pro Tools environment and function as virtual effects. (You'll learn more about plug-ins in Chapter 8, "Basic Mixing.") When you create specific plug-in presets, you have the option of saving them in this session subfolder.

❋ **Video Files folder.** When your session calls for a video track, you can save it in this session subfolder.

❋ **WHAT ABOUT THE WAVECACHE?**

There's one more file you'll often find in your session folder that I haven't talked about yet. It's a small file named WaveCache.wfm, and it stores all the waveform overviews for any audio in your session. Waveform overview is a fancy way of describing the visual representation of audio waves that you might see on an Audio track. This small file is automatically created and updated, so there's nothing you need to worry about with it!

Clips Versus Files

Given the fact that Pro Tools records audio to individual files on your hard drive, how do you later access these files? Simply put, when audio is recorded to an Audio track (or even MIDI data to a MIDI track), Pro Tools creates an object called a clip in the Edit window. In the case of Audio tracks, these clips refer (or point) to files on your hard drive, triggering them to sound as your session plays.

Here's a close-up of the Pro Tools Edit window. There are three Audio tracks in this session (Vocal 1, Vocal 2, and Vocal 3), and a single clip on the Vocal 2 track.

Working with clips has many advantages. One of the first you'll discover is that you have the ability to move them earlier or later on the session's timeline, enabling you to position the clips precisely in time. An environment like this, in which you have the ability to manipulate elements independently on the timeline, is commonly described as nonlinear. In addition to moving clips earlier or later in time, you have the option of moving them to other similar tracks. (In other words, you can move a clip on a mono Audio track to another mono Audio track, and so on.)

Nondestructive Editing

Another great advantage of pointer-based editing is that you can nondestructively trim or split the clip—meaning no audio data is lost, so you can always undo what you've done. This can be a tricky concept, so let's take a look.

In this example, let's assume that the clip named Vocal Comp is playing an audio file of the same name in the Audio Files subfolder. What if you don't want to use the whole file in your session? No problem! You can just adjust the start or end point of that clip, effectively taking the unwanted bits of audio out of your session.

Does this mean you've changed the file on your hard drive? No! You've only changed the clip that is pointing to that file, so only a portion of that file will be heard in the session. Don't worry; because you haven't changed the audio file (only the clip that is pointing to it), you can always drag the clip boundaries back out if you change your mind later!

In addition to being able to trim data, there are other situations in which nondestructive editing can aid you in your production work, and you'll discover them as this book proceeds. The bottom line is that a nonlinear, pointer-based environment coupled with nondestructive recording and editing gives an educated Pro Tools user a huge amount of flexibility and power, and the ability to undo changes and operations when needed.

Basic Pro Tools Operation

It's the end of the beginning. You've set up your system efficiently, taken some time to understand the way Pro Tools works, and now, based on that understanding, you're ready to start working.

The Quick Start Dialog Box

The Quick Start dialog box will appear when you launch Pro Tools and will give you a number of useful options for creating or opening a session. Let's run through them one by one.

To create a session by choosing a template, follow these steps:

1 **Click** on the **Pro Tools program icon** to launch the Pro Tools application.

2 **Click** on the **Create Session from Template option button** in the Quick Start dialog box. A list of template categories and template files will appear to the right of the option button cluster.

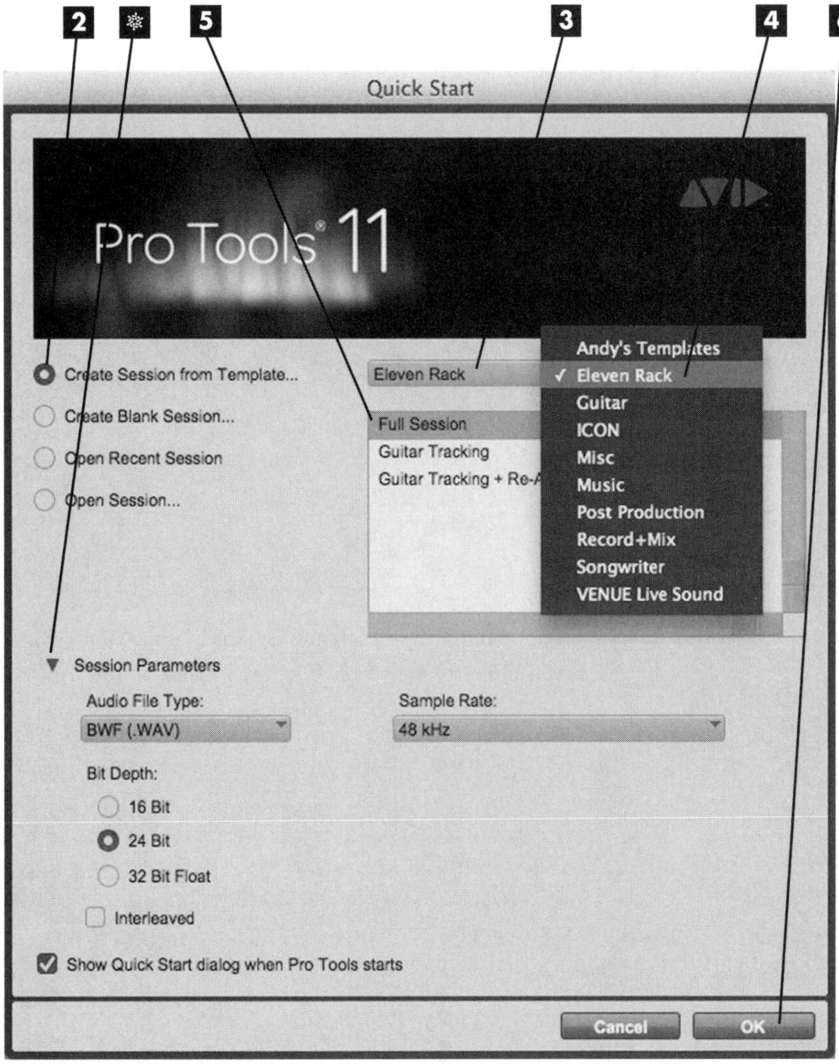

WHAT'S A TEMPLATE?

What's a template? I'll get into that later in this chapter and book. For now, just know that opening a template session will create a new session, complete with basic tracks, plug-ins, and so on, so that you can get straight to work.

3 **Click** on the **Template Category menu** to reveal a list of categories. (Note that you can organize your template list into different categories. You'll learn how later in this chapter.)

4 **Choose** a **category**. The list below the menu will be populated by the templates in that category.

5 **Click** on the **template** you want to load.

❖ Click the Session Parameters triangle to reveal details about the session you're about to create. If you want to change any aspect of the session, such as the sample rate or bit depth (aspects I'll talk about later in this chapter), you can do it here.

6 **Click** on the **OK button** to create the session. (Clicking on the Cancel button will bypass the Quick Start dialog box.)

Alternatively, you can create or open a session by performing one of the following actions in the Quick Start dialog box:

* Click on the Create Blank Session option button to create a session from scratch. I'll go through the details of creating a new session later in this chapter. Then click on the OK button.

* Click on the Open Recent Session option button to choose from a list of your most recently opened sessions (the list will appear to the right of the option buttons). Then click on the OK button.

Avid®, All Rights Reserved.

* Click on the Open Session option button, then click on the OK button to launch a standard File Open dialog box. This is the same dialog box you can access from the File menu in Pro Tools, which I'll go through in the next section.

※ BYPASSING THE QUICK START DIALOG BOX

If you don't want to see the Quick Start dialog box when you start Pro Tools (in which case you'd go directly to Pro Tools with no session loaded), just click on the Show Quick Start Dialog When Pro Tools Starts checkbox to remove the checkmark (this box is checked by default), then click on the OK button.

You can also prevent the Quick Start dialog box from being displayed when Pro Tools starts using the Preferences dialog box (which you'll learn quite a bit about as this book progresses). To do so, open the Pro Tools Setup menu and choose Preferences. The Preferences dialog box will open; click on the Show Quick Start Dialog When Pro Tools Starts checkbox in the lower-right corner of the Display tab to remove the checkmark. Then click on the OK button.

Opening a Session When Pro Tools Is Running

Suppose Pro Tools is already running, and you've already gone past the Quick Start dialog box. Here's how to open a session:

※ THE CHAPTER 1 EXERCISE SESSION

At this stage, you might not have a pre-existing Pro Tools session to work with. No problem. Included with the online support materials for this book is a number of exercise sessions for you to practice with. You can download these sessions from www.cengageptr.com/downloads. For information on downloading this book's exercise materials, please refer to the "Setting Up Your Session" section of the introduction.

The session that this chapter will use is a little piece called "Listen"—the exercise session is named "Chapter 01 Exercise Session (Listen)." I originally composed and produced this for an audio/video tradeshow in Japan, with the help of Avid Technology's own Tsukasa Tokiwano and Kazumi Mihashi. Also, special thanks go to my dear daughter, Sachiko Hagerman, for helping me with the Japanese! Note that the exercise materials are for educational use only, and not to be used for any commercial purposes.

1 **Click** on **File**. The File menu will appear.

2 **Click** on **Open Session**. A standard File Open dialog box will appear.

| Pro Tools | File | Edit | View | Track | Clip | Event |

New Session...   ⌘N
Open Session...   ⌘O
Open Recent   ▶
Close Session   ⇧⌘W

Save   ⌘S
Save As...
Save Copy In...
Save As Template...
Revert to Saved...

Send To...   ▶

Bounce to   ▶
Import   ▶
Export   ▶

Get Info...

Score Setup...
Print Score...   ⌘P

Avid®, All Rights Reserved.

✳ **YOUR FIRST SHORTCUT**

Pro Tools includes shortcut keys that enable you to work more efficiently. The shortcut for Open Session (Command+O on a Mac and Ctrl+O in Windows) is very useful—and easy to remember as well!

---

3 Using the navigation conventions of your computer's operating system, **select** the **drive**, **folder**, and **subfolder** (if necessary) in which your session folder resides. Remember that the session folder is named after the name of the session, so if you're using the tutorial material, the folder you're looking for is named "Chapter 01 Exercise Session (Listen)."

4 Once the session folder is created, open the folder to display its contents.

✳ ✳ ✳

5 **Click** on the desired **session file**. The file will be selected.

6 **Click** on the **Open button**. The session will be loaded into Pro Tools.

5   **6**

	Open
	Choose a session:
◀ ▶	📁 Chapter 01 Exercise S... ⬍ 🔍
FAVORITES	**Name**
📁 Dropbox	WaveCache.wfm
🖥 All My Files	Chapter 01 Exercise Session (Listen).ptx
🖥 Desktop	▶ 📁 Audio Files
📁 Data	
📁 Avid-Related	
🏠 andy	
🗂 Documents	
SHARED	
🖥 junko-san	
New Folder	Cancel Open

Avid®, All Rights Reserved.

❋ OPEN RECENT SESSIONS

The ability to select a recently opened file from a list is fairly common in the software world, and most users will be familiar with this idea from other applications. You've already seen the Open Recent Session option in the Quick Start dialog box, but you also have this available in Pro Tools itself. The Open Recent command can be found immediately below the Open Session command in the File menu. Simply click on Open Recent, and you will see a list of up to 10 of your most recently opened sessions.

Opening a Session When Pro Tools Is Not Yet Launched

In this case, suppose Pro Tools is not yet launched. To open a session, follow these steps:

1 Using the navigation conventions of your computer's operating system, **select** the **drive**, **folder**, and **subfolder** (if necessary) in which your session folder resides. Remember that the session folder is named after the name of the session, so if you're using the tutorial material, the folder you're looking for is named "Chapter 01 Exercise Session (Listen)."

2 **Open** the **folder** that contains the session file. The contents of the folder will be displayed.

3 **Double-click** on the desired **session file**. Pro Tools will launch automatically, and the session will be loaded.

Creating a New Session

Now let's take a closer look at the important process of creating a blank new session. (Many of these topics also apply to opening template sessions.) Once you've gotten your system together and everything working, your next step may

❋ ❋ ❋

be to create a new session (as opposed to opening a pre-existing session, as you did in the previous section of this chapter). The earlier discussion of how Pro Tools works will come in handy here.

Starting the Process

Earlier, you learned that you can create a blank new session from the Quick Start dialog box, but you can also create a new session from within Pro Tools itself.

1 With Pro Tools running, **click** on the **File menu**.

2 **Click** on **New Session**. The New Session dialog box will open. In a sense, it is a smaller version of the Quick Start dialog box.

❊ MORE SHORTCUTS!

As you explore Pro Tools further, you'll notice that many functions have shortcut keys associated with them. These shortcut key combinations are often displayed to the right of their functions, such as the shortcut for creating a new session—Command +N (Mac) or Ctrl+N (PC). Although there are far too many shortcuts to learn them all at once, learning the combinations for popular functions, such as opening or creating a session, can help you work more efficiently.

3a **Click** on the **Create Session from Template option button** to gain access to your session templates, just as you did in the Quick Start dialog box.

OR

3b **Click** on the **Create Blank Session option button** to create a new session, just as you can do in the Quick Start dialog box. For now, select this button.

New Session

○ Create Session from Template...

◉ Create Blank Session...

Session Parameters

Audio File Type:
BWF (.WAV)

Sample Rate:
48 kHz

Bit Depth:
○ 16 Bit
◉ 24 Bit
○ 32 Bit Float
☐ Interleaved

I/O Settings:
Last Used

Cancel   OK

Choosing Session Parameters

Whether you're creating a new session from the Quick Start dialog box or from the File menu, your next task is to choose your session parameters.

1 **Click** on the **Audio File Type selector**. A menu will appear.

2 **Choose** a **file type** from the following options:

(New Session dialog box showing Session Parameters with Audio File Type: BWF (.WAV), Sample Rate: 48 kHz, Bit Depth: 16 Bit / 24 Bit (selected) / 32 Bit Float, I/O Settings: Last Used, Interleaved checkbox, Cancel and OK buttons. Callouts labeled 5, 1, and 3.)

Avid®, All Rights Reserved.

❋ **BWF (.WAV).** A WAV file is a Windows standard file, and the Broadcast Wave Format (BWF) is a version of this file type that is particularly suited to television and film production. (The file extension is still .wav.) This is a good format choice for session files that will be used in both Mac and Windows systems.

❋ **AIFF.** This was originally the standard file format for Mac computers.

❋ CHOOSING A FILE FORMAT

Pro Tools' default file format is BWF (.WAV). This generally works well in most situations. If you are planning to share files between Mac and Windows systems, this is the preferred file format. There is no difference in audio quality between BWF (.WAV) and AIFF.

3 **Click** on the **Sample Rate selector**. A menu will appear, showing the sample rates supported by your audio interface.

4 **Select** a **sample rate** for your session.

5 **Select 16 Bit**, **24 Bit**, or **32 Bit Float** as the bit depth for your session.

❋ 32 BIT FLOAT AUDIO

For some, the idea of 32-bit floating-point audio is something new, as it is virtually unused outside of DAW production environments. Very simply put, using 32-bit floating-point audio will give you a larger dynamic (volume) range, which can greatly simplify the mixing process (especially in complex sessions using plug-in effects). On the other hand, 32-bit audio will require more hard-disk storage space and processing power, and using 32-bit audio may result in lower track counts (especially if you're using a slow hard drive).

❋ SUPPORT FOR INTERLEAVED FILES

An interleaved audio file is a single file that has multiple channels (e.g., stereo) combined into a single file. A good example of this would be the tracks on an audio CD. If you look at the files, there's only one per track, although you'll hear a stereo output. That's because they're interleaved.

❋ ❋ ❋

❄ To set up your session to use interleaved audio files, select the Interleaved checkbox.

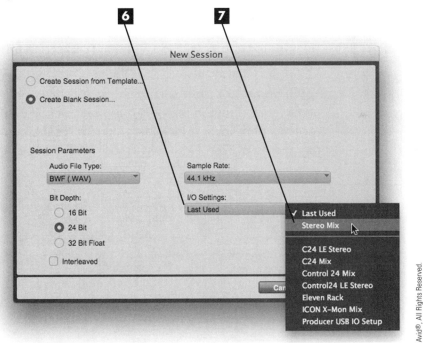

If you don't choose to use interleaved files, then any interleaved files that are imported (audio CD track files, for example) will be split into individual mono files. (In the case of an audio CD track, it would be split into a left channel file and a right channel file.)

6 **Click** on the **I/O Settings selector**. The I/O Settings menu will appear.

7 **Select** your **I/O (Input/ Output) settings** for this session. For now, choose Stereo Mix. The option will be selected.

❄ WHERE CAN I LEARN MORE ABOUT I/O SETTINGS?

Your I/O settings determine the assignments and names of inputs, outputs, inserts, and buses. Don't worry if this doesn't make a lot of sense now; you'll learn more about how to make the most of your I/O settings in Chapter 3, "Getting Started with Audio."

8 You've made some very important choices. The next step is to choose a name and location for your session. **Click** on the **OK button** to proceed. The Save dialog box will appear, and you're ready to move on.

Choosing the Name and Place

Two of the most important skills you can learn as a DAW user are file management and documentation. Although these are fairly simple and straightforward tasks, you shouldn't underestimate their importance. The last thing you want is to misplace a session and waste valuable time trying to find it—or worse, inadvertently delete a session because it was in the wrong place!

1 If you followed the steps in the previous section, you should now be seeing a Save dialog box. The next thing you have to do is to choose the name of your session. **Type** a descriptive **name** in the Save As text box in the Save dialog box.

2 **Navigate** to the desired **drive**. If you have a hard drive devoted to digital audio, choose that drive. In some cases, you might also want to create a new folder in which to put your session folder—for example, when grouping sessions of a similar genre or artist. If you do, create a new folder according to the normal conventions of your operating system. Remember, Pro Tools will automatically create a session folder as well!

3 Once you've set your name and location, **click** on the **Save button**. Your session will be created and loaded into Pro Tools. Good job!

Playing a Session

Let's assume you have Pro Tools running and you've opened a pre-existing session (for example, the Chapter 01 Exercise Session you may have opened earlier). Wondering how to play it? No problem—it's easy!

You'll find a transport section in the top area of the Edit window (which you'll learn more about in the next chapters). It will help you with basic play and record operations. It looks very much like the controls you would find on almost any media player. Let's take a look at the basic functions:

> ✳ **HOW TO GET TO THE EDIT WINDOW AND TRANSPORT CONTROLS**
>
> If you're not seeing any transport-style controls at the top of your Pro Tools window, you've probably opened your session into the other main window (called the Mix window, which looks very much like a mixing console). Getting to the Edit window is very easy: Just open the Window menu at the top of the Pro Tools window and choose Edit.

If you are in the Edit window and you are still not seeing any transport controls, click on the small triangular button in the upper-right corner of the Edit window and choose Transport from the list that appears. (This is a section of the Edit window that I'll go into in greater detail in Chapter 2, "Getting Around in Pro Tools.")

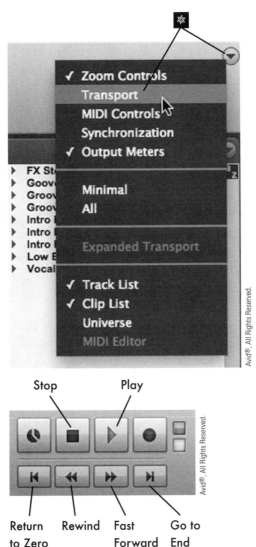

Stop   Play

Return   Rewind   Fast   Go to
to Zero   Forward   End

- ※ The Stop button—you guessed it—stops playback.
- ※ The Play button plays back your session from the current position.
- ※ The Return to Zero button takes you directly to the beginning of your session.
- ※ Rewind quickly moves your playback point earlier in your session.
- ※ Fast Forward quickly moves your playback point later in your session.
- ※ The Go to End button takes you directly to the end of your session.

Saving Your Work

Now that you have the basics down, it's time to think about how to wind things up. This is a crucial stage, and it's important to do the job correctly. There are a number of ways to save your work, each with its own specific advantages.

Save and Save As

Saving a session is about as straightforward as they come:

1. **Click** on **File**. The File menu will appear.

2. **Click** on **Save**. Your work will be saved, and you can continue to work on the saved session.

If you use the Save command, the previous version of the session will be overwritten with the one that you just saved. What if you *don't* want to overwrite the old session? That's where Save As comes into play.

1. **Click** on **File**. The File menu will appear.

2. **Click** on **Save As**. The Save Session As dialog box will open.

3. **Type** a **different name** for your session in the Save As text box to avoid overwriting the original session.

4. **Click** on **Save**. The new version of the session will be saved with the name you specified in step 3. You are all set at this point to continue work on the newly saved session.

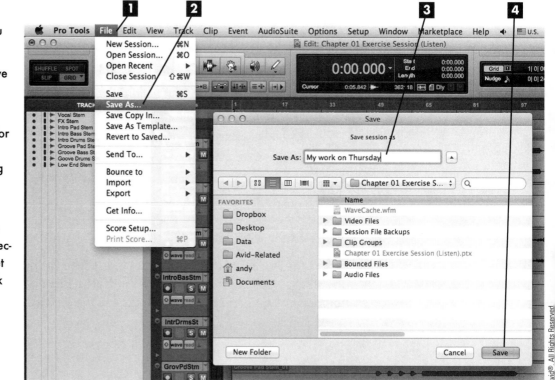

❋ WHERE DO I SAVE THE NEW SESSION FILE?

It's important to note that both the original session file and the new version of the file can reside in the same session folder and can access the same source audio files. You just need to make sure they don't have the same name.

Save Copy In

If you want to save your session with a different name and create a new folder, complete with all the dependent audio files, the *Save Copy In* feature is for you! This is commonly a part of the final archiving process when a project is complete (which you'll learn more about later).

1 **Click** on **File**. The File menu will appear.

2 **Click** on **Save Copy In**. The Save Session Copy dialog box will open. Save Copy In enables you to save elements of your session (audio files, fade files, and so on), which gives you a whole new dimension of flexibility. Here are some things you can specify:

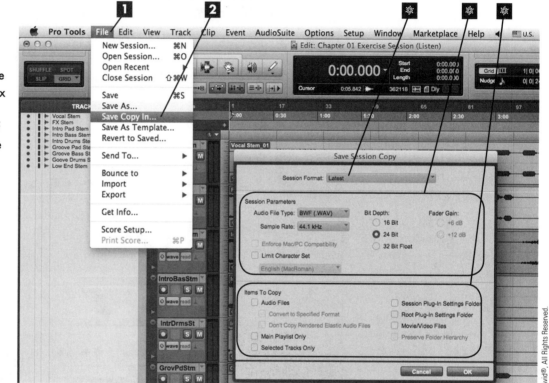

* **Session Format.** This menu contains options for previous versions of Pro Tools. Select one of these formats if you intend to open this session in an older version of Pro Tools.

* **Session Parameters.** These are the same options you saw when you created your session. You can select different file types, sample rates, and/or bit depths for your session. Pro Tools will automatically convert audio files as needed in your new session's Audio Files folder.

* **Items to Copy.** You can choose the elements of your original session that you want to copy over to your new session folder. Click on the appropriate checkboxes to copy aspects of your old session to your new session folder.

❋ THE IMPORTANCE OF BACKING UP YOUR WORK!

Backing up (or archiving) your work is a tremendously important part of production. It might not be terribly exciting, but you'll be glad you established good file-saving habits when something unexpected happens. The Save Copy In feature is particularly suited to archiving because it makes copies of your original session in a separate (and hopefully safe) place. Additionally, this process can intelligently gather all the elements your session needs (assuming you selected them in the Items to Copy section) and save them in one central location. Bottom line: When you're backing up your session, Save Copy In is a very smart way to go!

❋ PRESERVE FOLDER HIERARCHY

Sometimes, particularly in sessions with higher track counts, you'll need to utilize multiple audio hard drives for your session for reliable playback (something I'll discuss in Chapter 4, "Recording Audio," and in Chapter 10, "Moving to the Next Level: Tips and Tricks"). Checking the Preserve Folder Hierarchy checkbox will archive your session with individual audio file folders for each hard drive within your saved copy session folder. This makes it much easier to reconstruct large sessions spanning multiple drives!

3 When you've made the appropriate selections, **click** on the **OK button**. The Save dialog box will appear.

4 In the Save As text box, **type** a descriptive **session name** that is different from the original session name.

5 **Select** a **location** for your session. This section is identical to the related sections in the dialog boxes when you choose Save or Save As. This time, a new folder will be created for your new session, though.

6 **Click** on the **Save** button.

Exporting Selected Tracks as a New Session

What if you want to create a new session, but you want that session to include only some of the tracks in your original session? Don't worry—Pro Tools has you covered! This is a variation on what you just learned about Save Copy In:

1 **Choose** the **tracks** in your session you want to export. The horizontal rows in the Edit window are called tracks (which you'll learn more about in later chapters). You can select the tracks that you want to export by clicking on the track name. To select a range of tracks, hold down the Shift key as you click on the first and then the last track in the range. To select multiple tracks that aren't part of a range, hold down the Command (Mac) or Ctrl (PC) key and click on each track you want to select. In this image, I've chosen the Groove Pad Stem, Groove Bass Stem, and Groove Drums Stem Audio tracks.

2 **Click** on **File**. The File menu will appear.

3 **Click** on **Export**. The Export submenu will appear.

4 **Click** on **Selected Tracks as New Session**.

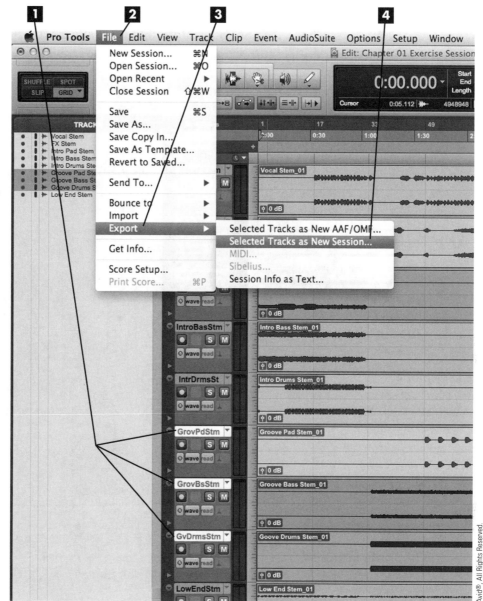

The Save Session Copy dialog box will open, which you already worked with earlier in this chapter. Note that the Selected Tracks Only box is checked (in the lower-left corner). Once you choose your Session Parameters and Items to Copy settings, a session copy will be created, but the copy will include only the tracks that you specified in step 1.

Session Templates

As you saw in the Quick Start dialog box, you already have a list of useful templates that are installed with Pro Tools, but you also have the ability to create templates of your own. It's easy!

1 Click on **File**. The File menu will appear.

2 Click on **Save As Template**. The Save Session Template dialog box will open. You have two options as far as location is concerned:

3a Choose the **Install Template in System option button** to automatically create your template in the default system location. This will enable you to easily access the template from the Quick Start dialog box in the future.

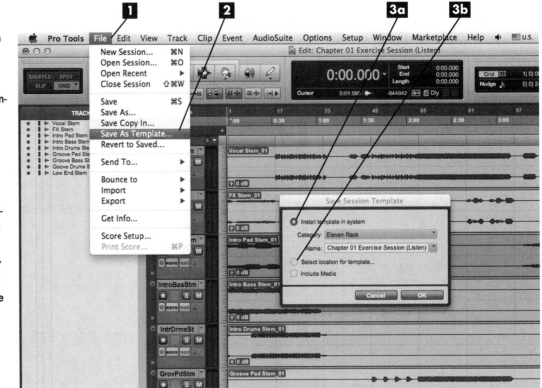

3b Choose the **Select Location for Template option button** to be able to choose any name and location for your template file after you click on the OK button. This is particularly handy for Pro Tools users who work in multiple studios. (An inexpensive USB drive can hold many session templates, and you can carry it with you easily.)

Before clicking the OK button and creating a template, let's assume that you want to create this template on your system, and that you've chosen the Install Template in System option button. Let's take a look at the different options open to you:

1 **Click** on the **Category selector**. A list of category options will appear.

Avid®, All Rights Reserved.

✤ The top section of the list shows you pre-existing categories, into which you can place your template. Just click on the desired category to choose it.

✤ The Add Category menu item enables you to create a new category and add it to the list shown in the top section. Click on this option, and you will be prompted to name your new category.

✤ The Reveal Session Templates Folder menu item will open the template folder using your computer's file browser (Finder or Windows Explorer, depending on your platform). This is useful for managing your template files (renaming, deleting, and so on). It's worth mentioning at this point that Pro Tools template files are not session files themselves, and that they have a .ptt file extension.

2 After you've chosen the appropriate category, **type** a **name** for your template in the Name text box. (Clicking on the arrow button to the right of the field will display a list of all the templates currently in that category.)

3 In most cases, you won't want your template to include any audio or video files. But if you do, **select** the **Include Media checkbox**.

Avid®, All Rights Reserved.

4 When you're finished, **click** on the **OK button** to create your template.

Closing Your Session and Finishing Up

The last basic procedure you have to master is to close down your session.

> ❊ **DO YOU WANT TO SAVE YOUR CHANGES?**
>
> Before your session closes completely, a message box might prompt you to save your changes. This message box appears when you make any changes to your session and then try to quit Pro Tools before saving those changes. You can choose Save or Don't Save and move on.

1 **Click** on **File**. The File menu will appear.

2 **Click** on **Close Session**. Pro Tools will shut down the current session and make itself ready for the next step (either quitting Pro Tools or opening another session).

3 Quitting the Pro Tools application follows the normal conventions of your computer for closing applications.

That's it—good job!

2 } Getting Around in Pro Tools

In Chapter 1, "Welcome to Pro Tools 11," you took some time to properly install and set up your Pro Tools system. You then went the extra mile and learned how Pro Tools "thinks" about sessions and files. You even got to the point of creating, opening, and playing session files. Now let's go to the next level of using Pro Tools and get better acquainted with the layout of the Pro Tools environment.

Think of this chapter as a brief primer in the Pro Tools way of getting the job done. Based on the general architecture discussed in this chapter, you'll be able to efficiently navigate the operations and features I'll go through later.

Some more experienced computer-based producers will immediately see similarities between Pro Tools 11 and other well-designed DAWs. Even if you fall into that category, it will still be a good use of your time to learn the proper names and layouts of these new workspaces. There are a number of windows in Pro Tools, many with specific functions, and trust me: Getting acquainted with the most common ones will really pay off later.

In this chapter, you'll learn how to do the following:

* Recognize the main sections of the Edit window and how to customize them.
* Recognize the basic layout and functions of the Mix window.
* Access other useful windows, such as the Big Counter, System Usage windows, the Playback Engine dialog box, and the Workspace.
* Make the most of your tracks and clips.

The Edit, Mix, and Transport Windows

When you open a session, Pro Tools displays the windows that were visible the last time you saved that session. In most cases, that will include one of Pro Tools' two main windows: the Edit window or the Mix window. It's important to know what these two windows do and how to navigate within them.

There's one more window that's crucial for all kinds of Pro Tools operations: the Transport window. (You used a smaller version of that window when you played a session in Chapter 1.) Let's take a quick look at the general layout of these important windows.

> ❋ **USING THE TUTORIAL SESSION**
>
> To follow along, just open the session named "Chapter 02 Exercise Session," which is included with this book's downloadable materials. This is the same piece you worked with in the first chapter, altered somewhat to better illustrate the concepts you'll go through in this chapter. For information on downloading this book's exercise materials, please refer to the "Setting Up Your Session" section of the introduction.

> ❋ **A QUICK WAY TO CHANGE WINDOWS**
>
> You'll switch between the Edit and Mix windows often, so knowing how to do so as quickly as possible can be very useful. The shortcut to toggle between the Mix and Edit windows is Command+= (Mac) or Ctrl+= (PC).

Working with the Edit Window

If there's a primary window in Pro Tools, it's the Edit window. This environment is packed with useful tools and information about your Pro Tools session—so much so that it can be a little daunting at first! If you break it down into the basics, though, you'll find it easy to understand and use.

The Playlist Area

When you begin a new session from scratch, there will be an empty area in the middle of your Edit window, called the playlist area. Any kind of track you create will appear in this area as a horizontal row. Here, for example, there are already 11 tracks (nine Audio tracks, plus two Instrument tracks, which I'll get into in more detail in the next chapter). As discussed in Chapter 1, the colored blocks are called clips.

❄ For each track, there is a specific track name (located in the upper-left corner of each track strip). You can select a track by clicking on the track name button. Selected tracks are indicated with a highlighted name. (In this image, the FX Stem track is selected.) Each track row shows a lot of information besides clips and track names, which I'll get into in Chapter 3, "Getting Started with Audio."

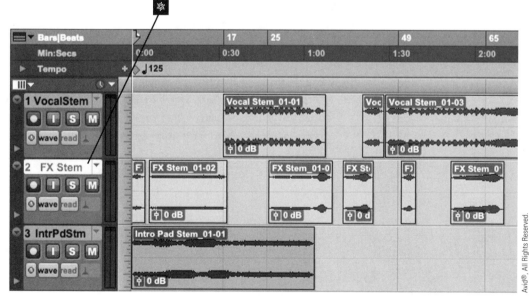

❄ ❄ ❄

The Tracks and Groups Column

Immediately to the left of the tracks, you'll notice a column that includes the Tracks list and the Groups list. Let's take a look at the Tracks list first. All the tracks in your session, whether visible or hidden, appear in the Tracks list. This list gives you important information about your session:

❋ The left column indicates which tracks are shown and which are hidden. Shown tracks are marked with a dark dot, and hidden tracks are indicated with a light-gray dot. (In this example, all the tracks are shown except the Intro Bass Stem track.) This column gives you not only information, but control as well; just click on any track's dot (technically called the Track Show/Hide icon) to change its state.

❋ Moving to the right, the Track Color column shows the coloring for each individual track. I'll talk about track colors and how to use them later in this chapter.

❋ Next, you'll see a column of icons indicating track type. (I'll go into track types in the next chapter.) In this case, the first eight tracks are Audio tracks, followed by two Instrument tracks, and finally another Audio track.

❋ Of course, you'll want to be able to see the track names, and you'll find them in the right-most column.

❋ Not only can you identify the tracks that are shown and hidden in the Tracks column, but you can also see which of your tracks are currently selected. Selected tracks are highlighted, as shown here. (The Groove Bass Stem track is a selected track.)

❋ You'll find the Tracks List button in the upper-right corner of the Tracks list. Think of this as command central for showing and hiding tracks. You have options to show or hide all tracks, only selected tracks, or track types. (For example, with the Show Only submenu, you can show only Audio tracks.) There is another submenu for sorting tracks (shown here), which enables you to arrange your tracks in a variety of ways.

❋ WILL HIDDEN TRACKS BE HEARD?

All active and unmuted tracks, whether they are shown or hidden, will sound during playback. The ability to hide or show tracks is simply to help you manage your editing and mixing desktop. It's a feature for which you'll be extremely grateful when your tracks start adding up!

✳ NEW IN PRO TOOLS 11: RESTORE PREVIOUSLY SHOWN TRACKS

In the Tracks List menu, you'll see a new option: Restore Previously Shown Tracks. This does just what it says: After using one of the show or hide options in the list (Show All Tracks, for example), this option will allow you to revert to the tracks that were previously visible.

Just below the Tracks list is the Groups list, which shows a list of all edit groups in your session. An *edit group* is a selection of tracks that can be edited as one. (You'll learn more about edit groups in Chapter 6, "...And More Editing!") The layout of this list is similar to the Tracks list.

As you create edit groups, they'll show up in the Groups list. (Active groups are highlighted.) Here again, this list is divided into columns:

* The left-most column indicates the tracks that are selected within the group. A circle (shown here) indicates that some members of that group are selected, but not all. A dot will tell you that all the members of that track are selected. A bull's-eye icon signifies that all the members of that group are selected, *plus* other tracks.

* The next column shows the group's color assignment. When a group is active, it is indicated in the Mix window using this color.

* Immediately to the left of the group name is a column that shows the group's letter. Every group you create will have a letter assigned to it. (The All group shown here is a special case, and is indicated by an exclamation mark.)

* Finally, as you create edit groups, they will populate the Groups list on the right-most side of the list.

* You'll find the Groups List pop-up button in the upper-right corner of the Groups list. As with the Tracks List button, you'll see a list of group-related functions when you click on the Groups button.

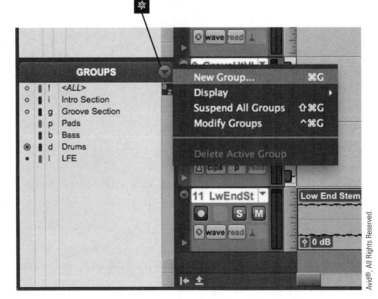

The Clips List

39

To the right of the tracks, you'll find another vertical column. This is the Clips list—a storage area for clips that are (or could be) used in your session.

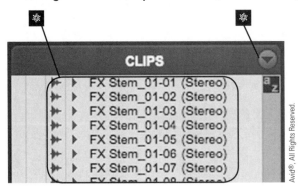

* **Clips list.** This is a complete collection of all the clips (audio and MIDI) available in your session, regardless of whether they're being used actively in a track. From here, you can drag and drop clips onto the appropriate tracks. This list is broken down into columns, which can vary, depending on the options you choose in the Clips List menu. (Click on the Clips List button, open the Show submenu, and you'll see a number of different aspects that you can choose to show or hide.)

* **Clips List pop-up button.** At the top of the Clips list, you'll find the Clips List pop-up button. Clicking on this button displays a drop-down menu of clip-related functions.

❋ WHAT HAPPENED TO THE REGIONS LIST?!?

If you've used previous versions of Pro Tools, you might notice that there's been a change in terminology: What used to be called *regions* are now called *clips*. This is a one of a few terminology changes introduced to standardize the names used between Avid's professional audio and video applications.

❋ WHAT'S MIDI?

You might notice that I've been mentioning a thing called MIDI (short for *Musical Instrument Digital Interface*) from time to time. I'll go into MIDI and how to use it in Pro Tools in Chapter 7, "Using MIDI."

Rulers

The Ruler area enables you to view the passage of time in your session in a number of different ways. Different scales, such as minutes and seconds or bars and beats, can be useful to you, depending on the kind of work you are doing in Pro Tools. Any combination of the following rulers can be shown:

Timeline rulers (Bars|Beats, Min:Secs, Timecode, Timecode 2, Feet+Frames, and Samples). These rulers mark the passage of time in a number of different formats.

Conductor rulers (Tempo, Meter, Key, Chords, and Markers). These rulers enable users to mark important points along the session's timeline, such as section changes, key modulations, and so on.

You can display the timeline in many time scales simultaneously, with each visible ruler's format displayed to the left of the timeline.

Edit Tools

You can display a number of tools in the top row of the Edit window. What tools you see and their placement in this area are up to you to decide (and you'll do just that later in this chapter), but here are some basic tool clusters:

- ❋ Edit modes
- ❋ Zoom tools
- ❋ Basic Edit tools
- ❋ Grid and Nudge settings

In addition to these tool clusters, the location and selection displays give you location information.

- ❋ The Main Counter tells you exactly where you are in your session.
- ❋ The Edit selection area tells you the beginning, end, and duration of your selection. (The format for this section is based on the format you've chosen for the Main Counter.)

❋ ❋ ❋

The Universe View

As you gain experience with Pro Tools, you'll find that one of the most time-consuming parts of production is often simply navigating within your session. The Edit window's Universe view can make that process much quicker and easier. Take a look:

1 **Click** on the **Edit Window button**. A list of display options will appear. Options that are currently shown will be indicated with a checkmark.

2 If it's not already selected, **click** on **Universe**.

3 Alternatively, you can **click** on the **downward pointing arrow** in the upper-right corner of the Rulers area.

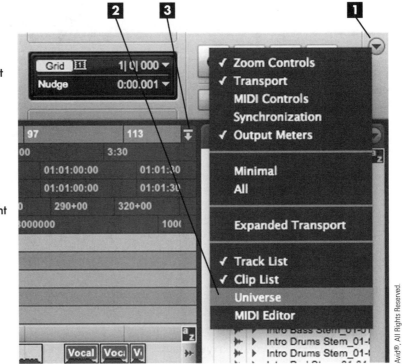

The Universe view will appear just above the ruler(s) and will show your session in its entirety. Let's take a closer look:

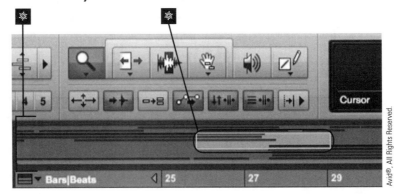

❋ Clips on tracks in your session (audio or MIDI) will be represented as colored horizontal lines. Their color reflects the color of the corresponding clips in your session.

❋ The Universe view is divided into a dark area and a light area, with the light area representing what you're actually seeing in your Edit window. Here's where it really gets interesting: Just click within this light area and drag it to the desired position in your session. You'll immediately see your Edit window update to reflect the movement of this light-colored area.

Customizing the Edit Window

Now that you've identified the overall layout of the Edit window, the following sections will describe a few ways to set up the window to make working easier.

Adjusting List Size

If your session calls for more groups than the Groups list can show at one time, you might want to give a little more space to the Groups list on your desktop. Here's how:

1 Move your **cursor** to the boundary between the Tracks list and the Groups list. Your cursor will change to the double arrow shown here.

2 Click and drag the **boundary** up or down as needed. As you drag, you'll see a light-gray line marking the movement of the boundary.

3 Release the **mouse button**. The boundary will be "dropped," and the lists will be reorganized.

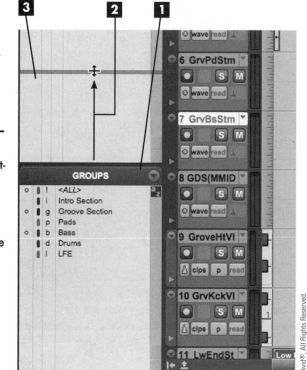

Hiding Lists

In addition to adjusting the sizes of these lists, you can hide them entirely when you're not using them. Follow these steps:

❊ You can similarly adjust any of the horizontal or vertical boundaries for the Tracks list, Groups list, and Clips list. Adjusting the vertical edges of these areas can help you control how much space you have on your screen for tracks.

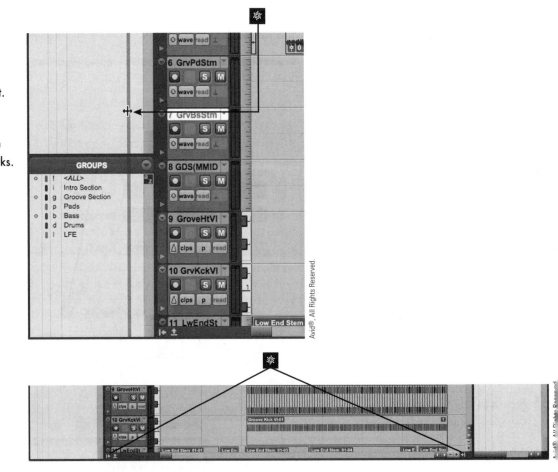

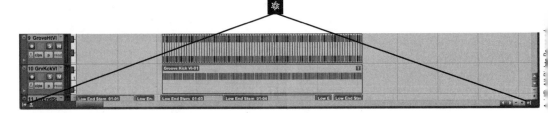

1 **Click** on the **arrow** at the bottom inside corner of either column. Pro Tools immediately hides the corresponding column, making more of your Edit window available for your tracks.

2 Not seeing your lists? That means they're currently hidden. **Click** on the **arrow** in either lower corner of the Edit window. The corresponding column immediately reappears.

❊ WHAT WILL I SEE WHEN I OPEN A SESSION?

Remember, the window arrangements that appear when you open a session will be the same as they were in the session when you last saved it. It might be a bit jarring to open a session and see no Tracks list or Clips list in your Edit window, but don't worry. You can always follow the previously mentioned steps to display the lists.

Displaying Track Columns

At the left of each track is one or more columns that provide track-specific information on such things as inputs, outputs, inserts, sends, comments, and more. I'll go into each of these in due course. For now, here's how to show or hide the columns you want:

1 **Click** on **View**. The View menu will appear.

2 **Click** on **Edit Window Views**. A submenu containing the columns that can be shown will appear. Checked columns are currently displayed.

3 **Click** on any **menu item** to check or uncheck it; the appropriate column will be displayed or hidden.

❋ Here's another way to get to the same list. Click on the Edit Window View Selector icon, which you'll see just above the top track in your session and below the Rulers area. Here again, you'll see a menu of viewable columns, with visible columns indicated with a checkmark.

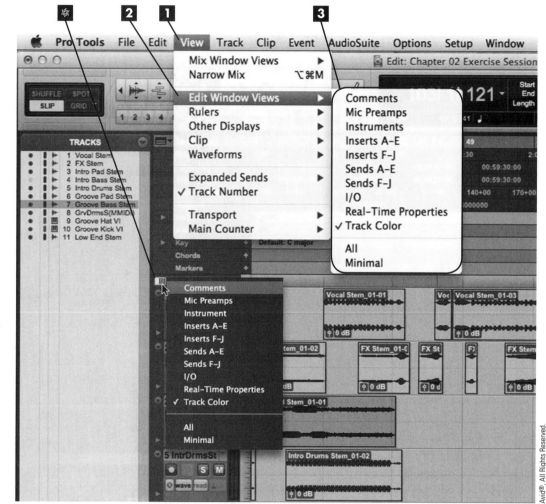

❋ **TOTALLY EXTREME VIEWING, DUDE!**

In addition to selecting columns individually, you can select All or Minimal to show or hide all columns.

Displaying Rulers

You can also choose which rulers are to be shown. Here's how:

1 **Click** on **View**. The View menu will appear.

2 **Click** on **Rulers**. A list of available rulers will appear. (A checkmark by a ruler indicates that the ruler is being shown.)

3 **Click** on any **ruler** to change its state (shown versus hidden).

❄ There's another way to get to the same list. Click on the Ruler View selector to show the Ruler View menu. You'll find this button to the left of the highlighted ruler. (The highlighted ruler is the ruler that corresponds to your Main Counter format.)

Adjusting Track Heights

In Pro Tools, you can change the height of individual tracks. This can come in handy, particularly when you have many tracks in your session and you want to see them all or, conversely, when you really want to do some microsurgery on one track in particular. Here's how:

1 To the right of each track's columns (I/O, Inserts, Sends, Comments, etc.) is a small vertical area (in this case, showing the amplitude scale). **Right-click** in this **area**. The Track Height drop-down menu will appear.

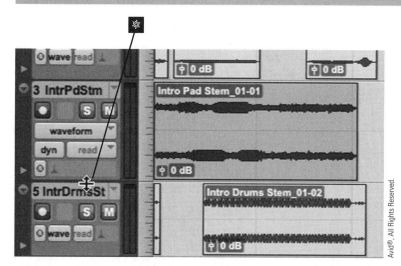

2 **Select** the desired **track height.** The track will immediately change to match your height choice.

❋ **CHANGING THE TRACK HEIGHT FOR DIFFERENT TRACK TYPES**

You can change the height of any Pro Tools track (including MIDI and Aux tracks, which you'll explore in later chapters). However, this thin vertical area for other types of tracks looks a little different from the amplitude scale of an Audio track. MIDI tracks, for example, show a keyboard-like display. In any case, right-clicking in this area will bring up the same Track Height menu.

❋ There's an even easier way to change track heights. Simply move your cursor to the bottom of the track you want to change, in the columns area. When your cursor turns into a double-arrow icon (shown here), click and drag up or down to decrease or increase that track's size.

❋ **MAKING GLOBAL CHANGES**

Here's another useful shortcut: Press the Option key (Mac) or the Alt key (PC) while you change the height of any one track, and the heights of all shown tracks will change at once.

❋ ❋ ❋

Custom Colors

The ability to apply the color of your choice to a track, clip, or group isn't a new feature in Pro Tools 11; it was introduced back in version 6. But like so many other features, it has been greatly improved upon since its introduction. Like other Edit window customizations, this won't change the *sound* of your session, but it can really help you work more efficiently. Users of all levels will find this sort of control a powerful ally in organizing tracks, clips, and more!

Let's take a look at how this feature can be used to mark your tracks. The first step is to make sure that you can view track colors:

1 **Click** on **View**. The View menu will appear.

2 **Move** your **cursor** to the **Edit Window Views menu item**. The Edit Window Views submenu will appear.

3 **Click** on the **Track Color menu item** if there is not already a checkmark by it. Track colors will be visible only if this menu item is checked.

❋ You will now see a colored tab at the left of each track.

That's only the beginning of the power you have over the appearance of your tracks. Let's start off by changing the color of a specific track:

1 **Select** a **track** by clicking on the track name (or select multiple tracks using the modifier keys discussed earlier).

2a **Click** on **Window**. Then **choose Color Palette**. The Color Palette window will appear.

OR

2b **Double-click** on the **Track Color column** (at the left-most edge of the track). The Color Palette window will appear.

3 **Click** on the desired **color box**. The selected track's color column will immediately change its color-coding to match.

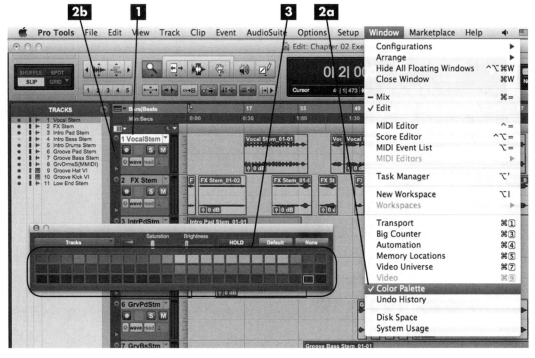

But wait, there's more!

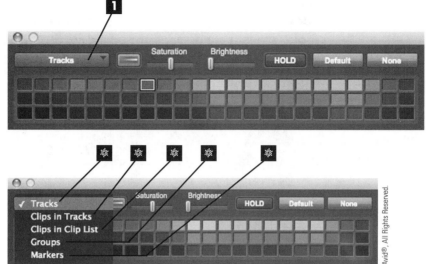

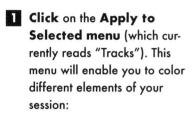 **Click** on the **Apply to Selected menu** (which currently reads "Tracks"). This menu will enable you to color different elements of your session:

❄ **Tracks.** As you just saw, this menu item enables the Color Palette window to change a track's color tab.

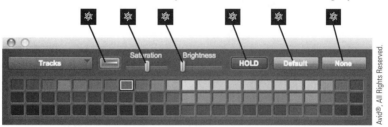

- ❄ **Clips in Tracks.** Choosing this option changes the color of clips selected in the playlist.
- ❄ **Clips in Clip List.** Selecting this menu item enables you to color code clips selected in the Clips list.
- ❄ **Groups.** Choosing this menu item enables you to change the color-coding of selected groups.
- ❄ **Markers.** Markers can also be color coded. (You'll learn about markers in Chapter 6.) If there are no markers in your session, this item will be grayed out.

❄ Click on the Apply to Channel Strip button to the immediate right of the Applied to Selected menu. This will apply your track color to the entire track strip, as opposed to just the track's color tab. The button will be blue when channel-strip coloring is active.

- ❄ If channel strip coloring is enabled, adjust the Saturation slider to change the intensity of the track coloring. As you move the slider from left to right, the channel strip's color becomes less subtle. (Note that this slider is accessible only when the Apply to Channel Strip button is activated.)
- ❄ Adjust the Brightness slider to control the overall brightness of the channel strips. (This control will affect your Mix window whether you have chosen to color your channel strips or not.) Used in combination with the Saturation slider, you'll be able to get a look that suits your tastes.
- ❄ Click on the Hold button to place a focus box around the currently selected color. From that point on, the selected color will not change, even if you change track selections, until the Hold button is turned off.
- ❄ Click on the Default button to reset the track's color to the Pro Tools default colors.
- ❄ Click on the None button to remove all track coloring for the track.

Movable Tools

Not only can you show or hide different tool clusters in the top row of the Edit window (by clicking on the Edit Window button in the upper-right corner), you can also move them to suit your particular work style. Follow these steps:

1 **Hold down the Command key (Mac)** or **Ctrl key (PC)** and move your cursor over the tool cluster that you want to move. (In this case, I want to move the Transport cluster.) The cursor turns into a hand icon to indicate that the cluster is ready to be moved.

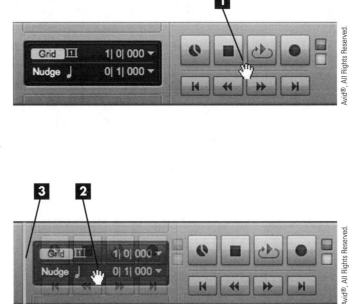

2 **Click and drag** the **cluster** horizontally to the desired location. You will see a semi-transparent representation of the tool cluster as you drag it.

3 A vertical yellow line indicates where the cluster will be inserted. When you get to the desired location, **release** the **mouse button**. The clusters will be rearranged to reflect your changes.

❋ NEW IN PRO TOOLS 11: TOOLBAR OUTPUT METER

Previously in this chapter, you learned how to show and hide various tools in the Edit window, and you just discovered how to reposition those shown tools to suit your tastes. Now in Pro Tools 11, Avid has a new display option for you, and a very useful option it is!

With Pro Tools 11, a number of improvements in terms of metering have been introduced, many of which you'll explore in this book, including the ability to view levels in the top area of the Edit window. You'll find this a convenient way to quickly check your levels as you edit your audio:

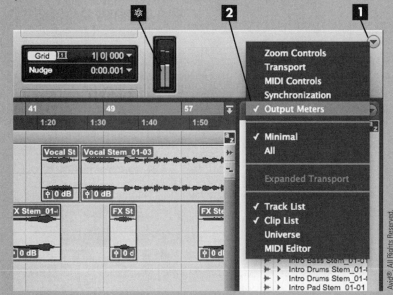

1. **Click** on the **Edit Window pop-up button** (you used this in Chapter 1 to display the transport tool cluster). A menu of display options will appear, with shown options indicated with a checkmark.

2. **Click** on **Output Meters**. A meter will appear among your Edit Window tool clusters. (This is assuming you have enough space on your screen for more tools. If you do not, you might have to hide other tools to make room for the meters.)

   ❋ The meters shown here can display level information in a number of different ways, which you'll explore in Chapter 8, "Basic Mixing."

Waveform Views

The graphic representation of audio within an audio clip is technically referred to as the *waveform overview*. It's worthwhile to note that this overview is stored in the *WaveCache* file (which was discussed briefly in Chapter 1). You can look at your waveforms in a number of different ways:

1 **Click** on **View** and then **Waveforms**. The Waveforms submenu will appear.

The Waveforms submenu allows you to view the waveform in a number of different ways:

* **Peak.** This is the most common way of looking at your waveform. It is a faithful representation of the amplitude of each sample of your audio. This is important because it gives you a sense of how you're using your dynamic range and when you're in danger of clipping (something that is particularly nasty when dealing with digital audio).

* **Power.** Although viewing your waveforms in Peak view is certainly useful, it sometimes doesn't faithfully represent the perceived loudness of a sound. For a waveform view that looks a bit more like it sounds, choose Power from the Waveforms submenu. I find this view especially useful for picking out beats (for music editing) or words (when editing dialogue for audio post-production).

In addition to these two ways of looking at your audio waveforms, you have more view options:

* **Rectified.** Pro Tools has long had the ability to show you waveforms in a rectified manner, and has recently made this feature even more accessible by placing it in this submenu (introduced in Pro Tools 8). (If the term *rectified* doesn't sound familiar, check out the following sidebar.)

* **Outlines.** Particularly when working with a light-colored clip, the difference between the color of the waveform and the background color of the clip can be pretty subtle. This can make the waveform a bit difficult to distinguish. Choosing the Outlines view enables you to view your waveforms with a very thin dark line. I think you'll appreciate how this makes your waveforms easy to read!

* **Overlapped Crossfades.** Later in this book, you'll learn how to create all kinds of fade effects, including crossfades, which enable you to gradually transition and blend one sound into another. As one sound fades out, another one will fade in. Enabling this view option will allow you to see outlines of each element of the crossfade within the fade clip.

❋ RECTIFIED WAVEFORMS

The term *rectified waveform* might be unfamiliar to many readers, but once you see one, it's easy enough to understand. To understand what a rectified waveform shows, though, it's useful to take a second look at the traditional un-rectified view:

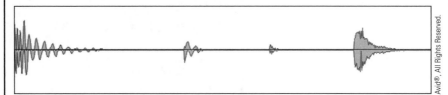

You'll notice that the waveform is centered around a virtual horizontal axis going through the middle of the wave. This axis represents zero volts, or silence. If you zoom into the waveform, you'll find that the wave oscillates above and below this *zero-volt line*, indicating positive and negative voltage.

Now let's take a look at a rectified waveform:

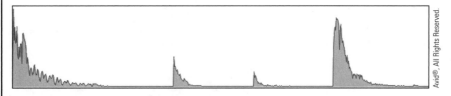

When you look at a rectified waveform, the zero-volt line is at the *bottom* of the waveform display. Whether the voltage is positive or negative, the visual representation ascends with increasing voltage. In many cases, this makes peaks and transients much easier to distinguish, particularly when working with drums or spoken words.

Working with the Mix Window

Along with the Edit window, another production environment you'll use extensively is the *Mix window*. Although there's a good bit of common ground between the Mix and Edit windows, the layout and function of the Mix window is geared toward the mixing and automation phases of your session.

Understanding the Mix Window Layout

Much of the general layout of the Mix window is similar to the Edit window's layout.

* **Tracks list.** This area functions identically in both the Edit and Mix windows. It enables you to select and show/hide specific tracks.

* **Groups list.** As you create mix groups, they will show up in this area, just as edit groups showed up in the Edit window's Groups list.

* **Channel strips.** When you create an Audio, Aux, Master Fader, MIDI, or Instrument track, it will appear here as a vertical strip. (You'll learn more about the elements that make up these channel strips in Chapter 8.)

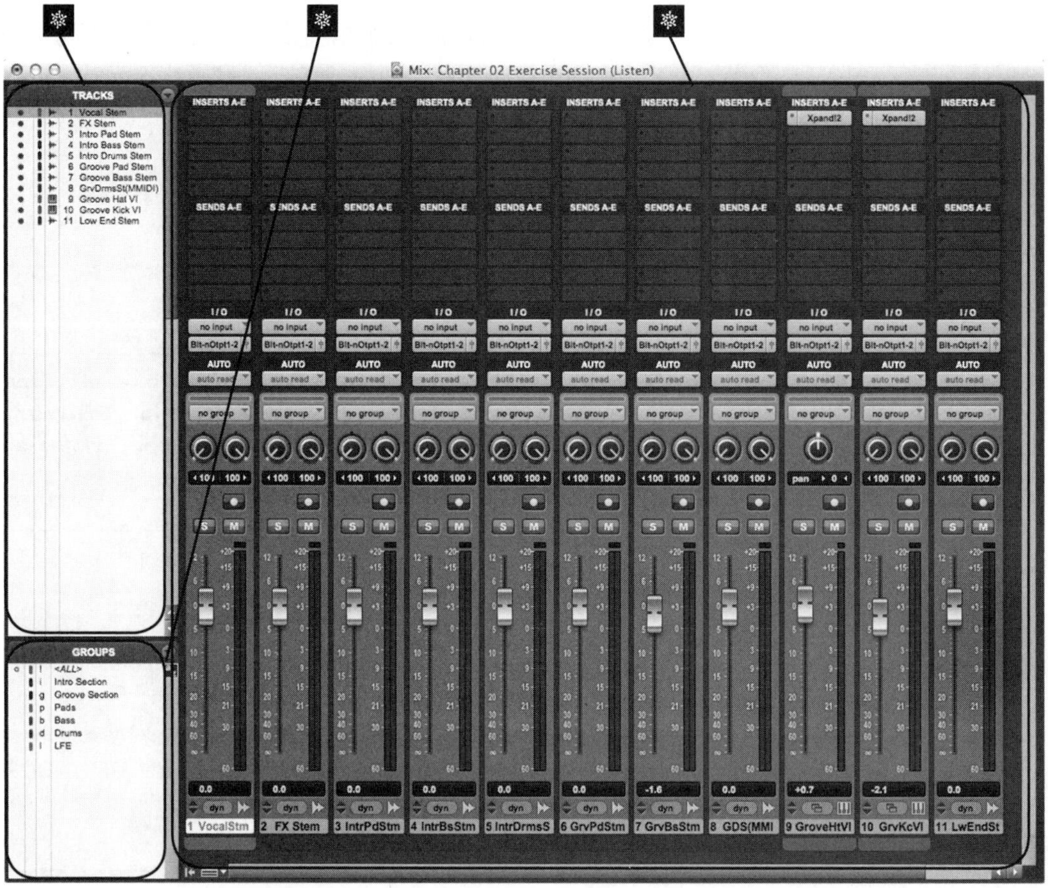

TRACK ORDERS IN THE EDIT AND MIX WINDOWS

Tracks that appear at the top of the Edit window appear on the left side of the Mix window. As tracks descend in the Edit window, they move from left to right in the Mix window.

TRACK SHOW/HIDE IN THE EDIT AND MIX WINDOWS

Tracks that are shown or hidden in the Mix window are likewise shown or hidden in the Edit window (and vice versa). Also, remember that a track being shown or hidden doesn't affect that track's audibility.

Customizing the Mix Window

Tailoring your Mix window for maximum ease of use will make mixing both more efficient and more fun. This section explores some of the most common customizations in the Mix window.

HIDING THE LISTS COLUMN IN THE MIX WINDOW

As in the Edit window, you can click on the arrows in the corner of the Groups list to hide the lists column. This can give you more space on your desktop for channel strips.

Just as with the Edit window, you have the ability to control the aspects of the Mix window that will be shown or hidden.

1a **Click** on the **View menu** and then choose **Mix Window Views**. The Mix Window Views submenu will appear.

OR

1b **Click** on the **Mix Window View Selector icon**. The Mix Window Views menu will appear.

2 **Click** on any **element** (Comments, Inserts, Sends, Track Color, or Instruments) to check or uncheck it. As with the Edit window, checked items will be shown.

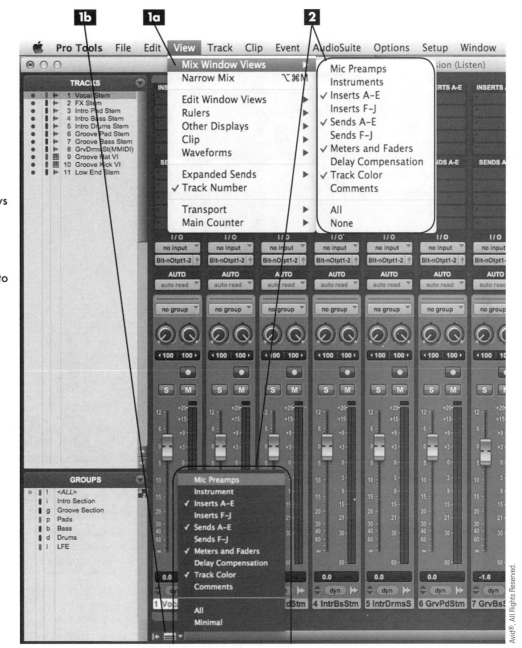

❊ SENDS AND INSERTS

Sends and inserts are essential to the mixing process, and the ability to show and hide them will be helpful as you tweak your mix. You'll learn more about mixing techniques in Chapter 8.

Suppose you have a lot of tracks in your session, and you'd like to see as many of them as possible in the Mix window. Here's how to squeeze more tracks onto a limited desktop:

1 **Click** on **View**. The View menu will appear.

2 **Choose Narrow Mix.** Technically, the Mix window itself doesn't narrow, but the individual channel strips do, enabling you to fit more tracks in a given space.

You might be wondering whether you can use track color-coding in the Mix window, as you did in the Edit window. The answer is a resounding yes. In fact, you'll find that coloring your channel strips will be particularly useful in organizing more complex mixes. You can apply color-coding to the Mix window in a few different ways:

* Double-click on either of the color-code areas of a given track to open the Color Palette window. From there, you can change the color-coding of selected tracks just as you did in the Edit window.

* You can also click on the Window menu and choose Color Palette to access the Color Palette window (again, just as I discussed earlier with the Edit window).

* You explored the Color Palette window earlier in the chapter, and its function is identical whether working in the Edit or Mix window. The ability to color channel strips, and to control the overall saturation and brightness, however, is especially effective in the Mix window.

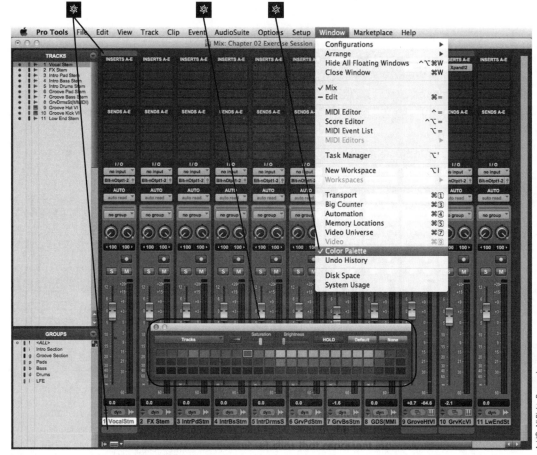

> ✳ **COLOR-CODING AND THE MIX WINDOW**
> Because the Mix window doesn't deal with clips, you will probably want to limit your color-coding to tracks and groups in this window. Color changes made in this window will be applied to the Edit window as well.

The Transport Window

Yet another window, called the Transport window, will be useful in playing your session. The Transport window is especially useful when you're working in the Mix window (the Mix window has no built-in transport controls). The shortcut to access the Transport window is Command+1 (Mac) or Ctrl+1 (PC) on your computer's numeric keypad.

Although using the Transport window is fairly intuitive, this window bears discussion, as does how to customize it.

1 **Click** on **Window**. The Window menu will appear.

2 **Click** on **Transport**. The Transport window will appear. Like the Edit and Mix windows, the Transport window has a number of functions. For now, I'll just focus on basic transport controls:

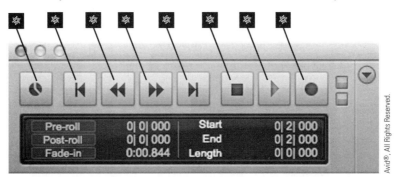

❄ Go to Beginning

❄ Rewind

❄ Fast Forward

❄ Go to End

❄ Stop

❄ Play

❄ Record

3 **Click** on the **Go to Beginning button** to make sure you're at the beginning of your session.

4 **Click** on the **Play button**. Your audio will begin playing. You'll notice that a long vertical line travels from left to right in the Edit window. This is called the *timeline insertion point*. As it intersects with different clips, sound will be produced.

5 **Click** on the **Stop button** when you're finished. The playback will stop.

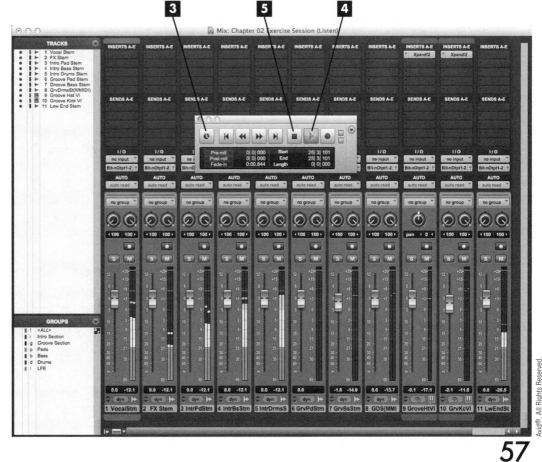

❄❄❄

Customizing the Transport Window

Depending on the type of work you're doing, you may want additional transport-related control. Here's how to show (or hide) specialized Transport window sections:

1a **Click** on the **View menu** and then **choose Transport**. The Transport submenu will appear.

OR

1b **Click** on the **Transport Window pop-up button** (in the upper-right corner of the window, as shown in the following image).

There are a number of different segments you can display:

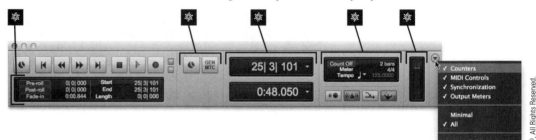

- ❋ **Synchronization.** Choose this option if you are controlling Pro Tools remotely or using Pro Tools to control other devices. You'll learn how to use these features in Chapter 4, "Recording Audio," and Chapter 7, "Using MIDI."

- ❋ **Counters.** This option will add the Main Counter to the Transport window.

- ❋ **MIDI Controls.** This option will add basic MIDI controls to the Transport window. (These controls are discussed in detail in Chapter 7.)

- ❋ **New in Pro Tools 11: Output Meters.** This is imilar to what you saw in the Edit window's toolbar section. With this feature, you now have the ability to show output metering in the Transport window. This will come in handy for keeping track of your main output levels.

- ❋ **Expanded.** This option shows secondary transport controls, including pre-roll and post-roll, the sub-counter, and secondary MIDI controls.

❋ WHAT IS THE SUB COUNTER?

Think of the Sub Counter control as a way to view the passage of time in a different format from the Main Counter. You'll learn how to work with both counters in Chapter 5, "Editing."

New in Pro Tools 11: Transport Fade-In

When jumping around to different sections of your session (something that happens frequently in all phases of production), you might find yourself unpleasantly surprised by starting playback in the middle of a loud section. Invariably, you'll wind up immediately jumping to the volume control to protect your ears (and possibly your speakers)!

Pro Tools 11 introduces a simple but quite handy new feature: the ability to enable a smooth fade-in whenever playback is started. You can adjust the length of this fade-in (up to four seconds) to suit your workflow, allowing you time to adjust your output levels if needed. Typically, music production will use shorter fade-in times, whereas audio post-production will employ longer fade-ins (particularly in cases where multiple devices must be synchronized).

Setting up transport fade-in is simple:

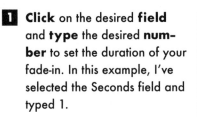

1 Click on the desired **field** and **type** the desired **number** to set the duration of your fade-in. In this example, I've selected the Seconds field and typed 1.

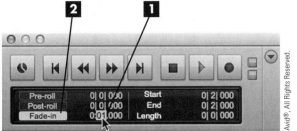

2 Click on the **Fade-in button** to enable the feature. When active, the button will appear green.

Other Useful Windows

Even though you'll spend the majority of your time in Pro Tools working in the Edit and Mix windows, there are a number of other windows that serve more specific purposes. These windows usually operate in conjunction with either the Edit or the Mix window (whichever one you're using). You can access these secondary windows through the Window menu—just click the Window menu and choose the window you want to display.

Let's take a first look at two useful floating windows:

❊ **Big Counter.** The Big Counter window is simply a larger display of your Main Counter, but it really comes in handy when you want to watch your session's progress from across a room! The shortcut for the Big Counter window is Command+3 (Mac) or Ctrl+3 (PC) on your computer's numeric keypad.

❊ **RESIZABLE!**
You'll be very happy to hear that the Big Counter window is resizable. By dragging the lower-right corner of the window, you can adjust it to fill as much of your screen as you like!

✻ **Video.** Pro Tools is an audio application, but that doesn't mean you can't use it to work with video. Importing video files into your session is easy (and is something you'll learn to do in Chapter 10, "Moving to the Next Level: Tips and Tricks"). Moreover, viewing your movie as your session plays is as simple as choosing Video from the Window menu. You can also get to this window quickly by pressing Command+9 (Mac) or Ctrl+9 (PC) on the numeric keypad.

Session Setup

The Session Setup window displays useful information about your session's configuration, including synchronization and timecode settings for more advanced workflows. Here's how to open the Session Setup window:

1 **Click** on **Setup**. The Setup menu will appear.

2 **Choose Session.** The Session Setup window will appear.

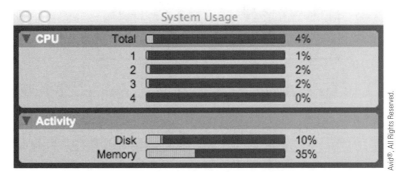

The shortcut for opening the Session Setup window is Command+2 (Mac) or Ctrl+2 (PC) on the numeric keypad.

System Usage and Disk Usage

Last but not least among the traditionally popular windows, the System Usage and Disk Usage windows will give you important information about how your system is doing. There are no shortcut keys for these windows—you'll have to open them from the Window menu—but they're critical nonetheless!

As you learn more about how to efficiently use Pro Tools, you'll want to refer to the System Usage window from time to time to see how your computer is dealing with the tasks associated with Pro Tools. This window gives a simple and efficient view of the workload your session is dealing with, including the activity level of each computer processor, disk throughput, and system RAM usage.

❄ ❄ ❄

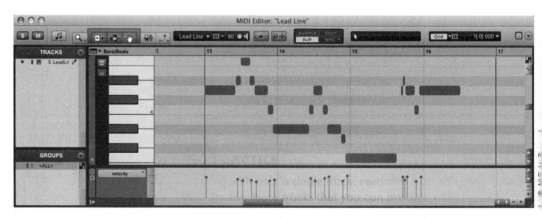

The size of a hard drive in a DAW is kind of like the amount of tape in an analog recording studio—the more you have, the more you can record. The Disk Usage window lets you know how much free space you have on each drive for recording audio and how much time that space represents (at your session's sample rate and bit depth).

> ❊ **DISK SPACE VERSUS DISK ACTIVITY**
>
> You'll notice that there's a disk meter in the System Usage window as well as a standalone Disk Usage window. What's the difference? The System Usage window's disk meter tells you the activity of the hard drives in your system (in terms of data throughput), whereas the Disk Usage window gives you information about storage capacity.

MIDI Editor and Score Editor

Over the last few versions, Pro Tools has made impressive advancements in the world of MIDI. First introduced in Pro Tools 8, the MIDI Editor and Score Editor windows provide powerful new environments for music creation (which I'll talk more about in Chapter 7).

The MIDI Editor window is more than your typical floating window. For many users, it's their primary creative environment. To the left, you'll see the familiar-looking Tracks and Groups lists, and you'll be able to view MIDI data in a number of different ways in the main section of the window. The top row of the MIDI Editor window also shows you the same set of tools you saw in the Edit window.

If you want to print music for musicians (or even if you just prefer creating music in a more traditional environment), the Score Editor window can also serve you well. Here, as with the MIDI Editor, you'll see the familiar Tracks list on the left side and editing tools on the top row. What makes the Score window unique, though, is its ability to add notational aspects—song title, composer, chord symbols, and so on—that musicians need to see in order to play your music.

Window Management

This chapter has covered a lot of important introductory ground, but if you'll indulge me just a bit longer, I'd like to walk you through some features you can use to get the most out of your desktop!

Window Configurations

A powerful (but sometimes underused) feature of Pro Tools is its ability to recall specific window arrangements. With window configurations, you can quickly change which windows are displayed, as well as their sizes and positions. The process is as simple as it is useful:

❊ ❊ ❊

1 **Arrange** your **windows** in any way that suits your workflow. In this case, I've chosen a simple arrangement of both Edit and Mix windows.

2 Capture this arrangement of windows. To do so, **click** on the **Window menu**, **choose Configurations**, and then **choose New Configuration**. The New Window Configuration dialog box will appear.

3 In the New Window Configuration dialog box, **click** on the **Window Layout option button** to capture the entire layout. Alternatively, **click** the **drop-down menu** next to the bottom option button to capture specific aspects of your desktop. In this case, **click** on the **Window Layout option button** and **type** a descriptive **name** in the Name field.

4 **Click** on the **OK button**. The dialog box closes. Now you can recall your screen arrangement at a moment's notice!

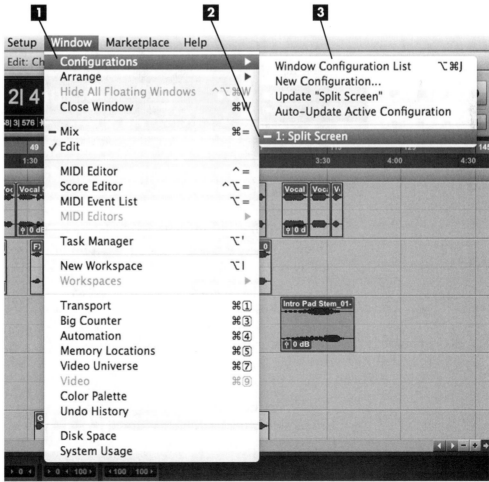

Recalling a window configuration is easy—and, as with most things in Pro Tools, there are a number of ways to do it. Here's one:

1 **Click** on the **Window menu** and **choose Configurations**. The Window Configurations submenu will appear.

2 Any existing window configurations appear at the bottom of the submenu. Just **click** on the **layout** you want to recall.

3 There is also a convenient floating window that shows a list of your window configurations. **Choose Window Configuration List** from the Window Configurations submenu to show the Window Configurations window.

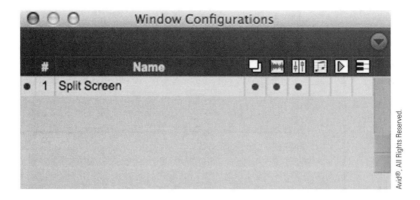

This window will not only show you a list of window configurations, it will also show you the aspects that are recalled with each configuration through the icons that are to the immediate right of the configuration name (Window Layout, Edit Window, Mix Window, Score Editor, Transport Window, and MIDI Editor). Just click on the configuration you want to recall.

✻ WINDOW CONFIGURATIONS SHORTCUT

Here's a shortcut for recalling a window configuration, but be careful—the key order is important. First, press the period key on your numeric keypad. Then press the number of the window configuration that you want to call up (again on your numeric keypad). Finally, press the asterisk key (yet again on your numeric keypad).

✻ UPDATING A WINDOW CONFIGURATION

In the Window Configurations submenu, you'll notice that there is an Update "[Configuration Name]" option. This option enables you to change a given configuration to reflect the current window arrangement. Alternatively, choose Auto-Update Active Configuration to do this automatically.

Hiding Floating Windows

From time to time, your desktop may become a bit cluttered with floating windows, which could prevent you from seeing the Edit or Mix window clearly. There are two ways to quickly hide (and bring back) all floating windows in one fell swoop:

- ✻ Click on the Window menu and choose Hide All Floating Windows. All floating windows will immediately disappear, and the menu item will be checked. To reveal all hidden floating windows, again click on Hide All Floating Windows (when it is checked).

- ✻ Press Command+Option+Control+W (Mac) or Ctrl+Alt+Start+W (PC) to hide or show all floating windows.

You'll find that this feature, though simple, is useful when you're using plug-in effects and virtual instruments, and it enables you to quickly shift your focus.

Window Arrangements

Like many multi-window applications, Pro Tools 11 gives you the ability to quickly arrange your windows in some standard configurations. This last bit is very straightforward, but let's take a look before moving on to the next chapter.

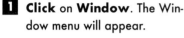

1 **Click** on **Window**. The Window menu will appear.

2 **Click** on **Arrange**. The Arrange submenu will appear.

Setup **Window** Marketplace Help

Configurations	▶
Arrange	▶
Hide All Floating Windows	^⌥⌘W
Close Window	⌘W
— Mix	⌘=
✓ Edit	
MIDI Editor	^=
Score Editor	^⌥=
MIDI Event List	⌥=
MIDI Editors	▶
Task Manager	⌥'
New Workspace	⌥I
Workspaces	▶
Transport	⌘①
Big Counter	⌘③
Automation	⌘④
Memory Locations	⌘⑤
Video Universe	⌘⑦
Video	⌘⑨
✓ Color Palette	
Undo History	
Disk Space	
System Usage	

Arrange submenu:
Tile
Tile Horizontal
Tile Vertical
Cascade

- ❋ **Tile.** Choose this option to arrange all active windows on the desktop in a standard tile pattern.
- ❋ **Tile Horizontal.** Choose this option to arrange windows from top to bottom. Note that this option is not available when too many windows are currently active.
- ❋ **Tile Vertical.** Select this option to arrange windows side by side. Here, too, this option will be grayed out if there are too many active windows in your session.
- ❋ **Cascade.** Select Cascade to lay all active windows on top of each other in a standard cascade pattern, showing the title bar of each window so that you can easily see what windows are currently open.

Congratulations! You now have a fundamental understanding of what Pro Tools is and how it functions, which will help you be a more intelligent user as you delve more deeply into this powerful environment. Now you're ready to begin actively using Pro Tools and start working with audio!

3 } Getting Started with Audio

Now that you have a basic understanding of what Pro Tools is and what it can do, it's time to start making things happen. The first step on the path to Pro Tools proficiency is to set up a session and start using audio. In this chapter, you'll learn how to do the following:

* Configure Pro Tools to make the most of your computer system.
* Set up and customize your inputs, outputs, inserts, and buses.
* Create Audio, Auxiliary Input, and Master Fader tracks.
* Import audio into your session.
* Play your session in a variety of ways to suit different circumstances.

Setup

Before you can get your show on the road, you'll need to call upon knowledge that you gained in the first chapter to create a session upon which you can work.

1 **Launch Pro Tools**.

  ❋ At this point, you could click on the Create Blank Session option button in the Quick Start dialog box. If you do that, be sure the session parameters are visible and jump down to step 5.

  ❋ Alternatively, you can choose to exit from the Quick Start dialog box by clicking on the Cancel button and move on to step 2.

2 **Click** on the **File menu**.

3 **Click** on **New Session**. The New Session dialog box will appear, as you saw back in Chapter 1, "Welcome to Pro Tools 11."

4 In the New Session dialog box, **choose** the **Create Blank Session option button**.

5 **Select BWF (.WAV)** from the Audio File Type menu.

6 **Select 44.1 kHz** from the Sample Rate menu.

7 **Select** the **24 Bit option button** in the Bit Depth area.

8 **Select Stereo Mix** from the I/O Settings menu.

9 **Click** on the **OK button**. The Save dialog box will appear.

10 In the Save dialog box, **type** a descriptive **name** for your session in the Save As field.

11 **Choose** an appropriate **place** for your session.

12 **Click** on the **Save button**. Pro Tools creates your session, and you're off and running!

The Playback Engine Dialog Box

Every DAW application has a certain amount of code devoted to the tasks of digital audio recording and playback. This bit of programming is so important that it has its own name: the *audio engine*. Let's start this chapter by taking a look at the Playback Engine dialog box, where you can choose settings for Pro Tools' audio engine and make the most of your overall system.

1 **Click** on **Setup**. The Setup menu will appear.

2 **Click** on **Playback Engine**. The Playback Engine dialog box will appear.

You saw this dialog box before—back in Chapter 1, when you chose an audio engine (from the menu at the top of the Playback Engine dialog box). Let's take a deeper look:

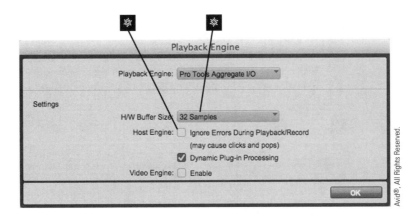

❈ **New in Pro Tools 11: Input Buffer Control.** H/W Buffer Size (hardware buffer size) has changed its function somewhat in Pro Tools 11. In previous versions of Pro Tools, this setting affected all host-based real-time processes used in your session. This required users to be cognizant of what they were doing and the best settings in a number of different circumstances. Now, in Pro Tools 11, H/W Buffer Size has been split into two "domains"— a low-latency domain and a "normal" domain.

The setting you can choose in the Playback Engine is the low-latency domain, which any track that is receiving live input will use. (You'll learn more about what a live input is during discussions of recording and mixing later in this book.) Other tracks—for example, Audio tracks that have audio on them and that aren't in record arm mode—use a buffer set at 1,024 samples. This allows you to record with low latency by setting the level at a lower sample level (such as 32 Samples, as shown here), while still maintaining playback of processor-intensive sessions.

❈ WHAT'S A BUFFER?

You've probably heard the term *buffer* tossed around in discussions about computers, but you might be a bit foggy on what exactly a buffer is and what it does. A buffer is a certain amount of computer memory that is used for short-term data storage during operations. Although buffers are used in different ways for different kinds of applications, as a general rule, buffers will enable a processor to work with large amounts of data more efficiently.

❈ **Ignore Errors During Playback/Record.** One thing I like about Pro Tools' audio engine is that it's a stickler for quality. If there are any errors in the recording or playing back of your audio, the audio engine will stop everything and tell you about the problem. I do find, however, that these messages (which stop playback or recording) can get a bit bothersome when I'm working in a noncritical situation—for example, when I'm launching plug-ins during playback, just to see which effect suits my needs. In these situations, where a few clicks or pops are tolerable, check the Ignore Errors During Playback/Record checkbox.

> ❄ **WHEN NOT TO IGNORE THE ERRORS!**
>
> As a general rule, you should check the Ignore Errors During Playback/Record checkbox only when you run into problems in noncritical situations (such as editing). When you're in the important recording or final mixdown stages of your project, remember to uncheck the Ignore Errors During Playback/Record checkbox. You certainly don't want to hear clicks and pops then!

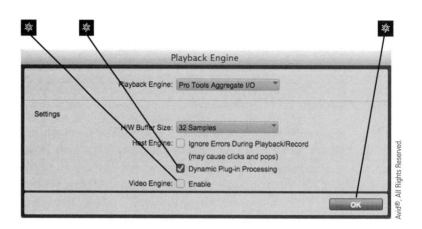

❄ **New in Pro Tools 11: Dynamic Plug-In Processing.** This is a serious improvement in Pro Tools—one that will allow you to create much more complex mixes than has been possible with previous versions! In previous versions of Pro Tools, plug-in effects always required CPU processing, whether there was signal passing through them or not. With the Dynamic Plug-in Processing option selected, processing power is dynamically allocated to plug-ins on an as-needed basis. That means if there's no signal passing through that plug-in, it doesn't draw upon CPU resources.

> ❄ **WHEN NOT TO USE DYNAMIC PLUG-IN PROCESSING!**
>
> Many users will simply leave this feature enabled nearly all the time but occasionally might need to know whether their session is in danger of overloading CPU processing during playback. Disabling this feature and playing the session will quickly give you a sense as to whether your plug-in usage will cause playback problems, even in dense sections.

❄ **New in Pro Tools 11: Video Engine.** Pro Tools 11 now supports the Avid video engine, which is used in Avid's video-production platform, Media Composer. (You'll learn more about using video in Pro Tools in Chapter 10, "Moving to the Next Level: Tips and Tricks.") Enabling this feature will enable you to use Avid video interfaces.

❄ If you change any settings in the Playback Engine dialog box, you can click on the OK button (in the bottom-right corner of the dialog box) to make your changes take effect.

Customizing Your Session: I/O Setup

An understanding of Pro Tools' signal flow is critical to using this powerful DAW. At the heart of signal flow is the I/O (input/output) Setup dialog box.

Setting Up Inputs

When you created this session, you chose Stereo Mix as your I/O setting. This I/O setting is Pro Tools' generic setup for stereo work. Although it often works fine as is, you can customize it to match your own studio's setup and boost your productivity right from the start! Let's begin by taking a closer look at the input setup for your studio—in other words, the connections going *into* your audio interface and from there to the Pro Tools software environment.

1 **Click** on **Setup**.

2 **Click** on **I/O**. The I/O Setup dialog box will open.

❋ A WORD ABOUT THE SCREENSHOTS

The examples in this section show the windows you'll see if you have an Mbox Pro system. If you have any other kind of interface, the window will look a little different (although the functions will be the same). If your audio interface doesn't support the same number of I/O channels as an Mbox Pro, you may not be able to create the same number of paths as described in the steps in this section.

Customizing Your Inputs

The grid area and the labels to the left represent input paths, which enable you to match the virtual inputs in the Pro Tools software to the physical inputs of your audio hardware. If you're following the steps so far, the dialog box displays a default setup.

Let's go through the process of creating a custom input setup from the ground up. To make sure you're creating everything from scratch, let's start by deleting any existing paths.

1 **Click** on the **Input tab**. The tab will move to the front.

2 **Click** on the **top path name**.

3 **Press and hold** the **Shift key** and **click** on the **last path name**. All the paths will be highlighted

4 **Click** on the **Delete Path button**. All the input paths will disappear.

5 Now let's create some new input paths. **Click** on the **New Path button**. The New Paths dialog box will appear.

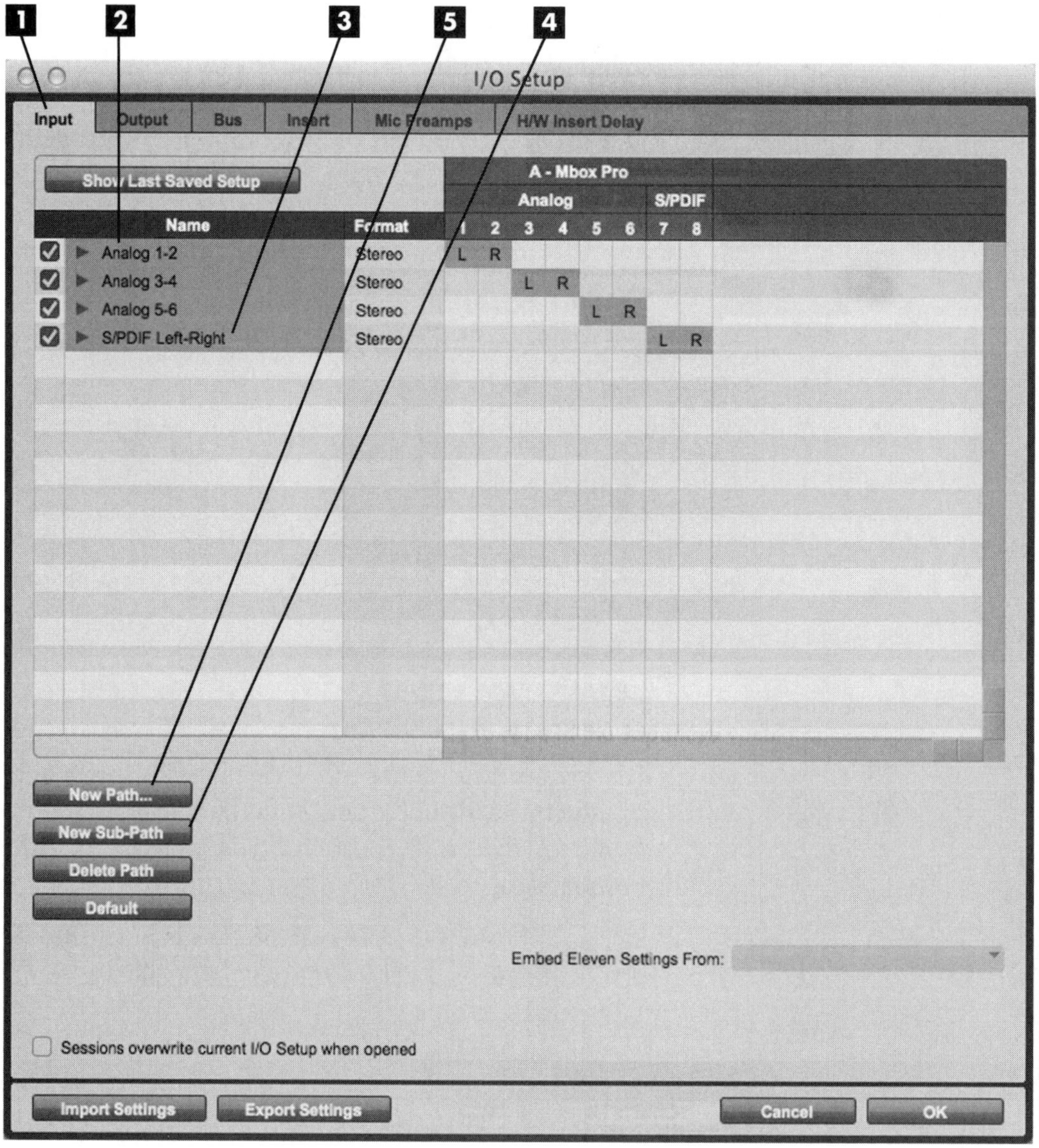

Now that you've cleared the Input tab of the I/O Setup window, you're set to start creating new paths of your own:

1 In the Create field, **type** the **number of input paths** you want to create. In this case, just leave this field at the default (1).

2 In the New menu, you can choose the format of your input path. For this example, **click** on the **New menu** and **choose Stereo**.

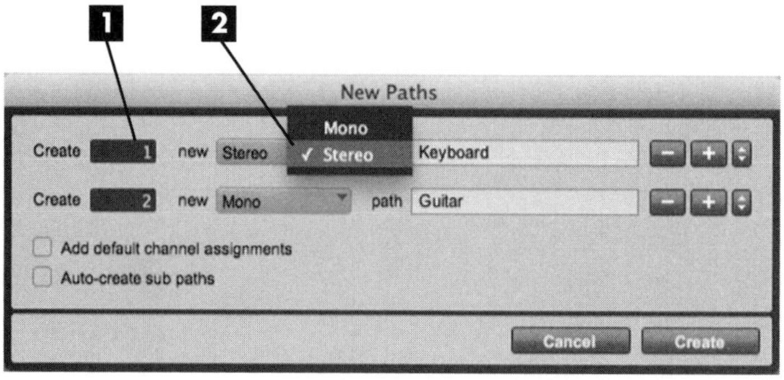

3 **Type** a **descriptive name** for your input path. (In this example, I'll be using the path for recording a keyboard.)

4 At this point, you're poised to create a single stereo input path. You could easily click the Create button and create this path. Before you close that window, however, let's create a few more paths. **Click** on the **Add Row button**. A new row of input paths appears.

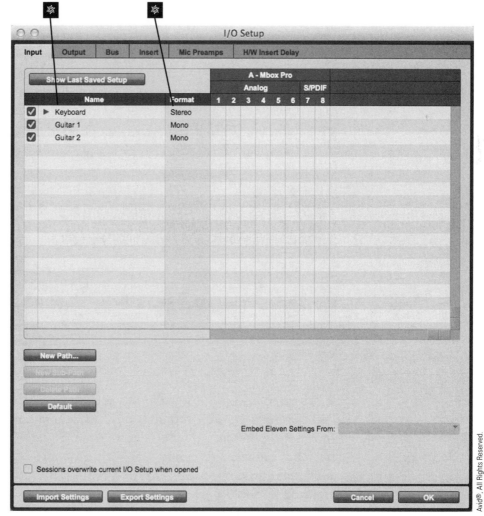

5 In the second row, you'll be creating two paths, so **type 2** in the Create field.

6 For this example, you'll create mono paths, so you can leave the New menu alone.

7 For this I/O setup, these paths will be used for recording guitars, so **type Guitar** in the Path field.

8 **Click** on the **Create button**. Pro Tools will create the paths.

You'll see a single stereo path and two mono paths in the I/O Setup dialog box.

❄ If you decide you want to change the name of a path, double-click on the path name, type a new name, and press Return (Mac) or Enter (PC).

❄ To change a path's format after its creation, click the appropriate setting in the Format column and choose the format you want (i.e., Mono, Stereo, etc.) from the menu that opens.

❄ ❄ ❄

HOW SHOULD I NAME MY INPUTS?

A good rule of thumb is to name your inputs for the devices that are connected to your system.

※ **HOW I'VE ARRANGED MY INPUTS**

In my system, I've set up my I/O Setup dialog box to reflect the devices that I've attached to the Mbox Pro in my home studio. The first path is reserved for a synthesizer (stereo), followed by two guitars (both mono inputs).

Assigning Your Path

Now it's time to assign each path to specific inputs of your audio interface. Let's start with the Keyboard path:

1 Move your cursor to the grid area in the top row. Your cursor will change from an arrow to a pencil.

	Name	Format	1	2	3	4	5	6	7	8
☑ ▶	Keyboard	Stereo								
☑	Guitar 1	Mono								
☑	Guitar 2	Mono								

Avid®, All Rights Reserved.

2 Click on the square that matches the input you desire—in this case, the square in the Analog 1 column. Because this happens to be a stereo path, two blocks will appear, marked L and R (for left and right). Don't worry if you click on the wrong box; you can click and drag each block to the appropriate cell.

3 Repeat steps 1 and 2, assigning the Guitar 1 path to analog input 3 and the Guitar 2 path to analog input 4. For each of these, a single block will appear, labeled M (for mono).

※ **ASSIGNING A STEREO PATH**

When setting up a stereo path, click on the square that is assigned to the left channel. An L and an R block will be created automatically.

	Name	Format	1	2	3	4	5	6	7	8
☑ ▶	Keyboard	Stereo	L	R						
☑	Guitar 1	Mono			M					
☑	Guitar 2	Mono				M				

Avid®, All Rights Reserved.

If you've followed the steps in this section (and assuming that your audio interface supports enough channels of I/O), you might see something like the image shown here. In this example, I have a stereo path dedicated to my keyboard (which is attached to inputs 1 and 2), a bass (using the Guitar 1 path, which is assigned to analog input 3), and a guitar (using the Guitar 2 path, which is mapped to analog input 4).

❊ ADD DEFAULT CHANNEL ASSIGNMENTS

In the lower-left part of the New Paths dialog box, you might have noticed an Add Default Channel Assignments checkbox. Checking this box will automatically assign each track in turn to the first available input channel(s). If you had checked this box when you created your paths, it would have done your assignment work for you, but what fun would *that* be?

Setting Up Outputs

Good job! You've set up your system to deal with incoming audio. The next step is to customize how audio exits your audio interface, which is a little more complex. For the examples shown in this section, we'll once again create a basic setup that works in my studio and that you can adapt to reflect your own needs and I/O capabilities.

The good news is that the Output tab of the I/O Setup dialog box is laid out very similarly to the Input tab, so this should go a lot more quickly!

1 **Click** on the **Output tab** in the I/O Setup dialog box. The tab will move to the front.

2 Just as you did in the previous section, select all existing paths and **click** on the **Delete Path button**. (Technically, this isn't necessary, but for the sake of this example it'll make things clearer.)

3 **Click** on the **New Path button**.

4 Following the same steps you took when creating input paths, create one stereo path and a number of mono paths (here, I'm creating four mono paths). In this case, let's go with the default path names. In this case, I'll also **check** the **Add Default Channel Assignments checkbox** to make things easier.

5 **Click** the **Create button** in the New Paths dialog box.

When you're finished, your Output tab might look something like this:

	Name	Format	1	2	3	4	5	6	7	8
	Show Last Saved Setup					A - Mbox Pro				
						Mixed				
✓	Output	Stereo	L	R						
✓	Output 1	Mono			M					
✓	Output 2	Mono				M				
✓	Output 3	Mono					M			
✓	Output 4	Mono						M		

For reasons that will become more obvious in the next section, let's name these paths—not for their function, but as a description of the actual physical connection on your interface. Remember, you can rename your paths by double-clicking the path name. By way of example, here's what I've wound up with in my Mbox Pro scenario:

	Name	Format	1	2	3	4	5	6	7	8
	Show Last Saved Setup					A - Mbox Pro				
						Mixed				
✓	Mbox Pro Output 1-2	Stereo	L	R						
✓	Mbox Pro Output 3	Mono			M					
✓	Mbox Pro Output 4	Mono				M				
✓	Mbox Pro Output 5	Mono					M			
✓	Mbox Pro Output 6	Mono						M		

Setting Up Buses

It's probably easiest to think of buses as virtual audio cables that you can use within the Pro Tools mixing environment. You use them for all sorts of internal routing, such as sending dry audio from an Audio track to a reverb on an Aux track. (Don't worry if this all sounds like Greek—you'll learn all about this starting in Chapter 8, "Basic Mixing.") You'll also use buses as a bridge between your Pro Tools software and the output paths you set up earlier in this chapter.

Although the Bus tab in the I/O Setup dialog box has made subtle alterations automatically to reflect the output paths you just created, perhaps the best way to illustrate the role of buses is to create a bus from scratch:

1 Click on the **Bus tab**. The tab will move to the front.

2 Because you're building the bus from scratch for the sake of illustration, select all existing paths and **click** on the **Delete Path button**, just as you did in the previous sections.

The basic idea behind buses is that they can be either assigned (or mapped) to a physical output path (in which case they're called *output buses*) or unmapped to a physical output path (in which case they're called *internal buses*). Let's start out by creating some buses:

1 Click on the **New Path button** in the Bus tab.

2 Following the same steps you performed in the previous sections, **create** a **single stereo path** (which I've named "Main Mix") and **four mono paths** (which I've called "Cue Mix"). You might notice that these are the same numbers and types of paths as when you created your outputs—it's no coincidence! You'll be mapping these paths to physical output paths next.

3 **Create five new stereo buses.** In this case, don't worry about naming them. You'll do that individually later.

4 Click the **Create** button, and your paths will be created.

5 Click on the **Mapping to Output checkbox** for the first bus. If you've been following the steps so far in the chapter, this bus is a stereo bus. Because you've created only one stereo path, it'll automatically map to that stereo output path (named "Main Mix").

6 Click on the **Mapping to Output checkboxes** for each of the Cue Mix buses. In these cases, the default map will be the first available mono path.

7 You'll want to assign each individual Cue Mix bus to individual output paths. To do that, **click** the **current mapping assignment** for a bus and **choose** a **new output path** from a list. In this example, you'll want to assign each Cue Mix bus to its own mono output path.

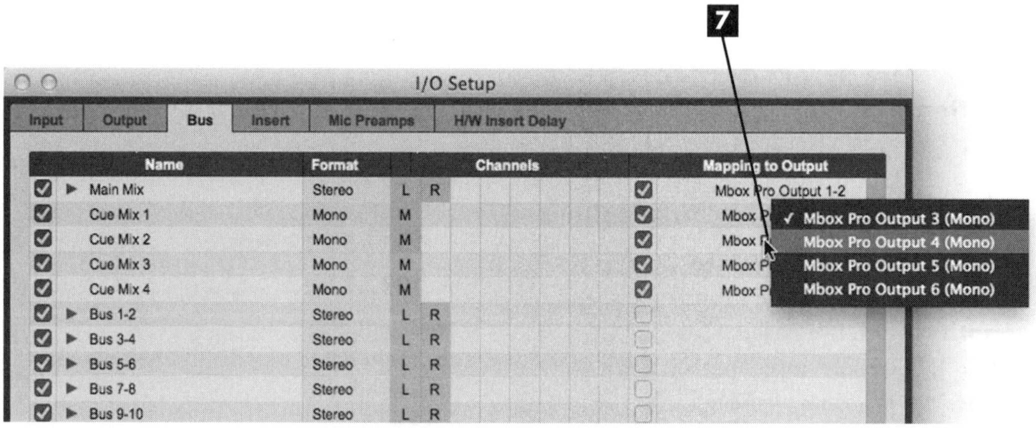

In addition to these output (mapped) buses, you also have five internal (non-mapped) buses. You'll use these buses for various recording and mixing tasks that I'll go into later in the book.

Next, let's name the five internal buses:

1 Individually naming paths is easy: Just **double-click** on the **path name** and **type** the **name** that you want to use. For the purposes of this exercise, let's use the following names for the buses you created:

- Drum Submix
- GTR Submix
- Key Submix
- Vox Submix
- Reverb Bus

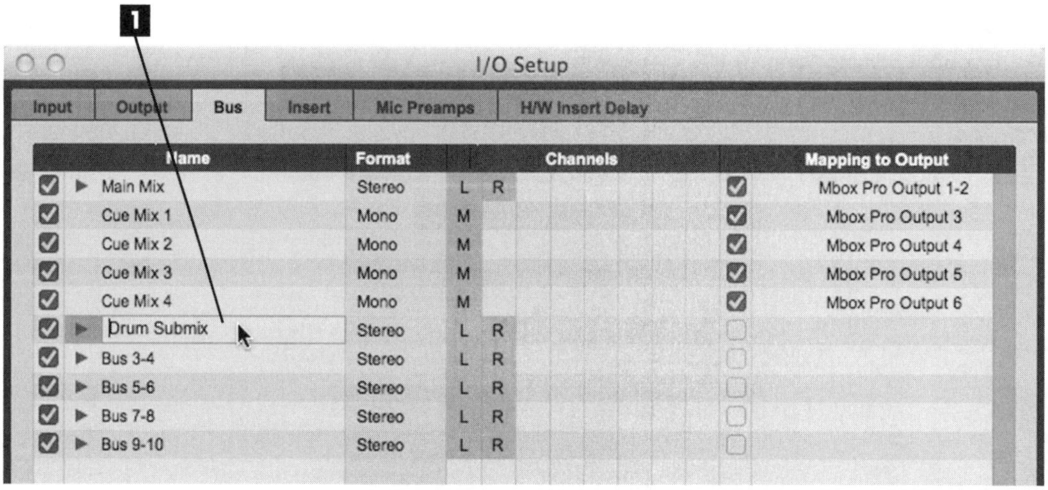

2 **Press** the **Return key** (Mac) or **Enter key** (PC). Here's what you should see:

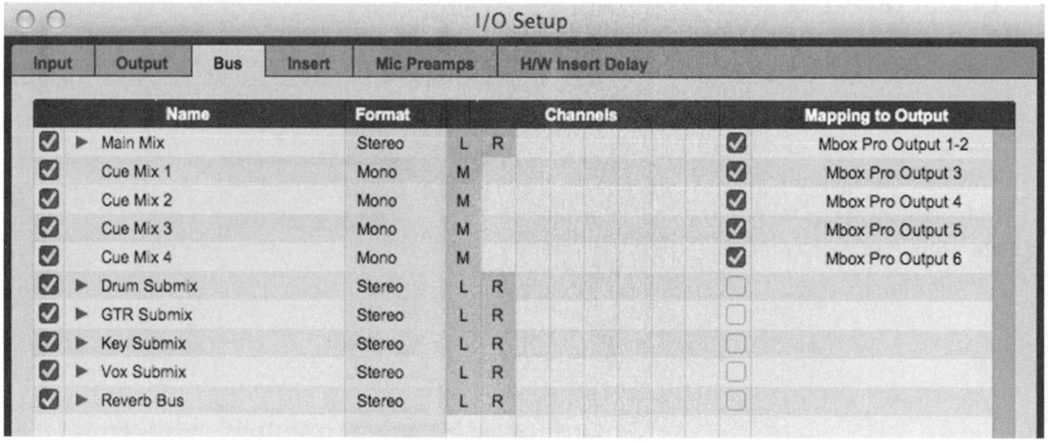

Here's where the work you've done will pay off:

Say you want to play your Guitar submix through your main speakers to hear how the parts blend. With buses, it's no problem—just assign the desired bus to the desired output path. (In this case, you'd be assigning the GTR Submix bus to the Main Out output path.) Basically, what you're doing is changing that bus from an internal bus to an output bus. Incidentally, in this case, you'd want to unmap the Main Mix bus, as shown here:

This is not only a great way to take a look at a particular part of your session, but this structure also makes moving sessions from one studio to another an easy and straightforward matter. For example, I moved my session from a studio with an Mbox Pro to one that is using a laptop computer's built-in output. Just reassign your buses to the available output paths, and you're all set to go!

❋ MORE BUSES, MORE FUN!

The Bus tab that you set up here is pretty typical, but you'll almost certainly need more buses as your session grows. Don't fret—you can create up to 256 internal buses in your session.

❋ GET YOURSELF SORTED

You can arrange your buses in a number of ways. One of the easiest ways is to sort them by name, format, or mapping to output. Just click on the appropriate column heading button to sort your buses. (Clicking on the heading button a second time will invert the sorting.) If none of those automated sorting modes suits your needs, you can also manually drag your paths to the order you desire by clicking on the path's name and dragging it up or down.

Setting Up Sub-Paths

You've set up your paths. Now it's time to think about sub-paths. *Sub-paths* are individual assignments within a path. For example, take a look at the Main Mix bus (a stereo path). If you will only ever have a stereo signal going into that pair of outputs, you're all set. However, if you want to also be able to use each output separately—for example, to send a signal to only the right or left speaker— you might consider setting up a couple of sub-paths within that stereo path.

1 **Click** on the desired **stereo path name**. The name will be highlighted.

2 **Click twice** on the **New Sub-Path button**. Two sub-paths will be created below the path, with default names (Path 1 and Path 2).

3 **Double-click** on each **sub-path** and **name it**, just as you did with the paths.

4 As you did with paths, you need to assign a channel to each sub-path. **Click** on the desired **grid square**. A block with an M (for mono) will appear.

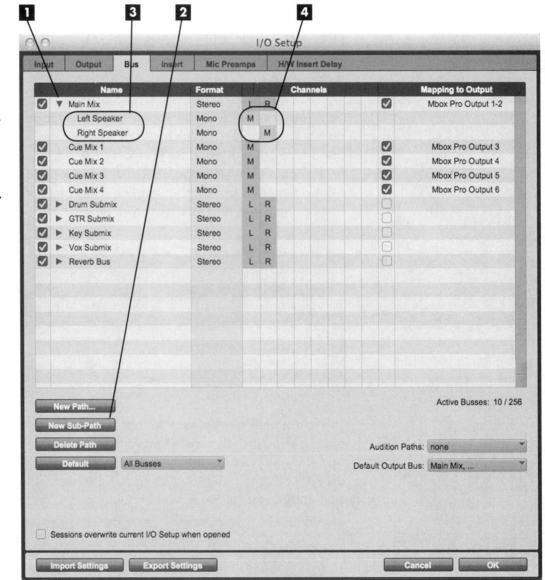

❄ AUTO-CREATE SUB-PATHS

In the lower-left part of the New Paths dialog box, you might have noticed an Auto-Create Sub-Paths checkbox. Checking this box will automatically create the appropriate sub-paths for multichannel buses or inputs. (Output paths don't have sub-paths.)

❄ ❄ ❄

Audition Paths and Default Outputs

From time to time, you'll want to *audition* audio files before you bring them into your session. (This is something I'll talk about later in this chapter.) You can choose to have this auditioned signal come out of any active output path you want. Here's how to set it up:

1 In either the Output or Bus tab of the I/O Setup dialog box, **click** on the **Audition Paths down arrow**. A list of available paths will appear, based on your current output paths.

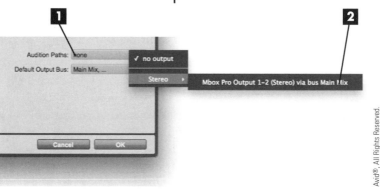

Avid®, All Rights Reserved.

2 **Choose** the **path** you want to use for auditioning files. (Because I have only one stereo output path, you're seeing only one option in this example.)

Do you have a favorite output path—one you usually use when creating new tracks? You can configure Pro Tools so that new tracks are automatically set up with any output you desire!

1 **Click** on the **Default Output Bus down arrow**. A list of available paths will appear, based on your current output paths.

2 **Choose** the **path** that you want to be your default output path for newly created tracks.

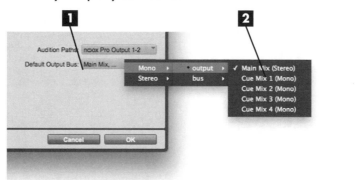

Avid®, All Rights Reserved.

More I/O Tabs

Before you move on from this very important dialog box, let's take a quick look at the remaining tabs.

❄❄❄

Setting Up Inserts

In the world of DAWs, you can use a wide variety of software effects (reverbs, delays, and so on) called *plug-ins*. Does that mean you won't be able to use any of the rackmount effects you've got in your studio? Not at all. You can bring them into the Pro Tools environment through a configuration of your inputs and outputs called *hardware inserts* or *I/O inserts*. You'll learn more about inserts and how to use them in Chapter 8. Right now, our job is to set things up correctly.

One thing you need to know about hardware inserts is how to connect your gear. The rule is simple: Use input numbers that correspond to the ones you used for the outputs. For example, if you have a rackmount stereo reverb unit that you want to use with Pro Tools, and you use outputs 3–4 to send signal to the reverb unit, you have to use inputs 3–4 to get audio from the reverb back into Pro Tools.

In this example, I'll set up my system to use a digital reverb, with signal going to the unit from my S/PDIF outputs and taking the processed signal back in through the S/PDIF inputs.

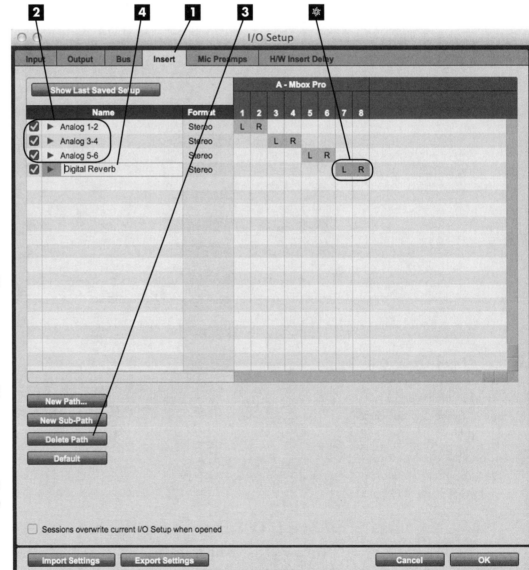

1 **Click** on the **Insert tab** in the I/O Setup dialog box. The tab will move to the front.

2 Because you're only going to be using the S/PDIF path for the reverb unit, let's delete all the paths that you won't need. **Hold down** the **Command key** (Mac) or **Ctrl key** (PC) and **click** on every **path name** that you *don't* plan to use for routing signal to and from your external gear.

3 **Click** on the **Delete Path button**. The paths you clicked on will disappear.

4 **Double-click** on the remaining path's name and **type** a **descriptive name** for your Hardware Insert path. (Technically, this is an optional step, but doing this will make working with your external gear easier and more straightforward.)

❄ Similar to the Input and Output tabs, if you need to change the channel assignments, you can easily do so by clicking and dragging the channel icons to the desired position.

❄ ❄ ❄

The H/W Insert Delay Tab

On the topic of external effects units, it's important to mention that *all* devices exhibit some amount of delay (also caused *latency*). Although it might be overstating things a bit to say that this delay can wreak havoc on your mixes, even small amounts of latency can affect the phase alignment of audio within your system, which *will* affect the sound of your mix. Not to worry—the H/W Insert Delay tab enables you to enter values that will compensate for the latency of your external devices. The details on how to enter the correct value is part of a larger discussion on Automatic Delay Compensation (ADC), which is covered in Chapter 10.

The Mic Preamps Tab

Certain external microphone preamp units—including the Avid PRE—can be controlled remotely directly from within Pro Tools. This is a real convenience, particularly in situations where the microphone preamp is some distance from the Pro Tools user. You can set up your preamp in the Mic Preamps tab of the I/O Setup dialog box. This sort of setup is beyond the scope of an introductory book and is covered with your preamp documentation.

Managing Your I/O Settings

Now that you've created a tailor-made I/O setup, you might want to save your settings so you can use them in other sessions.

Saving Your I/O Settings

To save your I/O settings to an I/O settings file, follow these steps:

1 **Click** on the **Export Settings button** in the I/O Setup dialog box. The Save I/O Settings As dialog box will open.

2 **Type** a **name** for these settings in the Save As text box.

3 **Click** on the **Save button**. Your settings will be saved to Pro Tools' default I/O location.

THE IMPORTANCE OF NAMING

Choose a descriptive name for your settings so you can recall them easily when you want to use them in another session.

I/O SETTINGS AND NEW SESSIONS

There's another benefit to exporting your tweaked I/O settings: If you save the I/O settings to the default location (which you just did if you were following the steps outlined here), your new setup will be an option in the I/O Settings drop-down menu when you next create a new session.

Recalling Your Settings

After you've customized and exported your I/O settings, you can easily recall them. That means the time you spend now tweaking your I/O settings to work in a variety of situations is time that will be saved later when you import them into a session.

1 To load previously saved I/O settings, **click** on the **Import Settings button** in the I/O Setup dialog box. The Select I/O Settings to Import dialog box will open.

2 **Select** the desired **I/O settings file**.

3 **Click** on the **Open button**. The I/O settings you selected will be loaded.

4 **Click** on the **OK button**. The I/O Setup dialog box will close. You're finished!

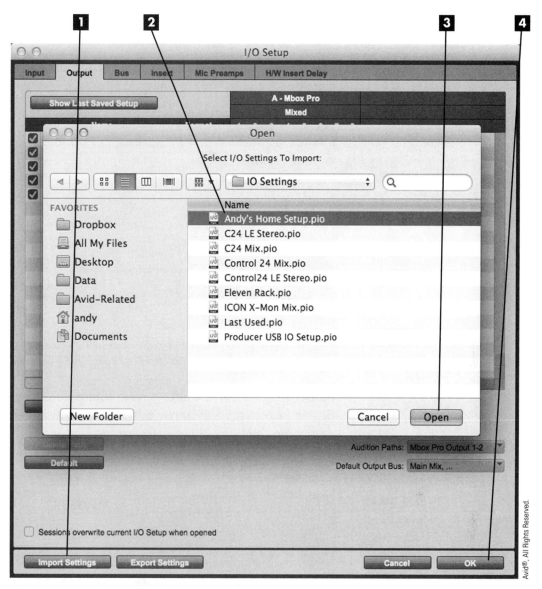

❆ SELECTIVE IMPORTING

The active tab of the I/O Setup dialog box (the tab you're looking at when you import settings) will be the only one affected by the import. For example, if you are looking at the Input tab and you import an I/O settings file, only the Input tab will be changed by the operation. That being said, because of the special relationship between the Output tab and the Bus tab, sometimes importing into the Output tab will have some effect on the Bus tab.

❆ SESSIONS OVERWRITE CURRENT I/O SETUP WHEN OPENED

In older versions of Pro Tools, when a session was opened, the session's own I/O settings would overwrite any previously active I/O settings. While this worked well in some cases, it did pose some difficulties in other types of workflows—particularly in situations where sessions were moved from one studio to another. Selecting the Sessions Overwrite Current I/O Setup When Opened checkbox (in the lower-left corner of the I/O Setup dialog box) will enable you to choose the older behavior if that suits your workflow best.

☑ Sessions overwrite current I/O Setup when opened

Import Settings Export Settings   Cancel   OK

❆❆❆

Tracks

Now that you've finished with the I/O Setup dialog box (and if you haven't closed that dialog box by now, do so by clicking on the OK button), let's start making things happen within Pro Tools' main windows. Whether you're looking at the Edit window or the Mix window, you'll notice that your new session opened up without any tracks in it. It's up to *you* to create the tracks you'll need in your session.

Making Tracks

No matter what kind of track you want to create, you'll start with the following steps:

1 **Click** on **Track**. The Track menu will appear.

2 **Click** on **New**. The New Tracks dialog box will open.

> ❖ **NEW TRACK SHORTCUT**
>
> Because you'll be making many tracks as you work more and more in Pro Tools, you might want to learn the shortcut for launching the New Tracks dialog box: Command+Shift+N (Mac) or Ctrl+Shift+N (PC).

By default, the New Tracks dialog box is set up to create one mono Audio track. (If you just finished the previous section, you'll see a great similarity between this dialog box and the New Paths dialog box, accessible from the I/O Setup dialog box.) For this example, let's create five stereo tracks instead.

1 **Click** in the **Create field** to highlight it (if it isn't already highlighted) and then **type the number of tracks** you want to create (in this case, **type 5**).

2 Click the **Track Format button** to reveal a list of available track formats. In this case, you can choose to create mono or stereo files. For the purposes of this example, **choose Stereo**.

3 The next menu will allow you to choose what kind of track you'll be creating. Since this is something we'll go into later, you can stick with the default setting of **Audio Track**.

4 **Click** on the **Create button**. The New Tracks dialog box will close, and the tracks will be created in your session.

❊ TRACK COUNT

A Pro Tools 11 system allows you to create a maximum of 128 Audio tracks. That's a *lot* of tracks. However, it's worth noting that there are also limits as to how many *active* Audio tracks you can use at one time. (You'll learn more about active versus inactive tracks in Chapter 10.) The maximum number of active Audio tracks varies according to your session's sample rate:

❊ If your session is at a sample rate of 44.1 or 48 kHz, you'll be able to use up to 96 active Audio tracks.

❊ If your session is at a sample rate of 88.2 or 96 kHz, you'll be able to use up to 48 active Audio tracks.

❊ If your session is at a sample rate of 176.4 or 192 kHz, you'll be able to have up to 24 active Audio tracks.

Creating an Aux Track

An Auxiliary Input track (also commonly called an *Aux Input* or simply an *Aux* track) is identical to an Audio track except that it doesn't contain any audio clips. Its main function is to serve as a means of routing audio from a source to a destination or as a means to process one or more audio signals with plug-in effects.

You'll learn how to use Aux tracks in Chapter 7, "Using MIDI," and Chapter 8, "Basic Mixing," and you'll find them very handy indeed—particularly when you get down to the business of mixing. In this chapter, though, let's start with the process of creating a couple of stereo Aux tracks, a process almost identical to creating Audio tracks.

1 **Open** the **New Tracks** dialog box as you did in the previous sections.

2 **Type 2** in the Create field to create two tracks.

3 **Click** on **Stereo** in the Track Format selector to make these Aux tracks *stereo* Aux tracks. The option will be selected.

4 **Click** on the **Track Type selector**. A list of all the different track types available in Pro Tools will appear.

5 **Click** on **Aux Input**. The option will be selected.

6 **Click** on the **Create button**. Two stereo Aux tracks will be created, just as you specified.

Master Faders, MIDI, and Instrument Tracks

As you probably noticed, there are three other kinds of tracks listed in the Track Type drop-down menu: Master Fader, MIDI, and Instrument tracks. Although you might not use these kinds of tracks in every session you create, they'll come in very useful when you need them.

If you've ever worked with a traditional mixing board, you know what a Master Fader does. These are the faders that control the overall volume of your entire mix after you have blended all the individual tracks. A Master Fader track in Pro Tools does pretty much the same thing. Simply put, it's a fader that controls the overall volume of a given output path or bus. It will also enable you to add plug-in effects to the entire mix at once. You'll learn about Master Fader tracks in Chapter 9, "Finishing Touches."

When it comes to MIDI tracks, there's one thing to keep in mind: MIDI is *not* audio. Instead, it is a digital language that allows different musical devices to communicate—something like a network. You can record (and then edit) MIDI data on a MIDI track in Pro Tools. When combined with Pro Tools' powerful virtual instruments, this can open all sorts of creative doors!

There's another MIDI-related track, called an *Instrument track*, which can enable you to use MIDI and virtual instruments together in one convenient track. You'll learn about MIDI and Instrument tracks in Chapter 7.

The method of creating a Master Fader, MIDI, or Instrument track is almost identical to creating any other kind of track. The only difference is that you'll choose your type of track accordingly. Just for practice, try creating one new stereo Master Fader track using the steps outlined earlier. (Refer to the preceding image for your reference.)

Managing Your Tracks

This section contains a few techniques you can use to make the creation of tracks even easier and to set tracks up for efficient use after they've been created.

Creating Multiple Tracks

If you completed the previous sections on the I/O Setup dialog box, you'll notice more than a passing resemblance between the New Tracks dialog box and the New Paths dialog box, accessible from the I/O Setup dialog box. Just as you can in the I/O Setup dialog box, you can create multiple types of tracks in a single pass. Here's how:

1 If you've opened up the New Tracks dialog box, and you want to create more than one type of track, simply **click** on the **plus (+) sign** on the right side of the dialog box. A second row of track parameters will appear.

✤ You can continue creating different kinds of tracks by repeatedly clicking on the plus sign, as shown here.

✤ Did you go one step too far? Do you want to remove one of the rows? It's easy—just click on the minus (−) sign to the right of the row you want to delete.

✤ The tracks will be created in your session from top to bottom, as shown in this dialog box. If you want to reorder the tracks, just click and hold the double-arrow icon at the far right of the row you want to move. A blue box will appear around that row (the Master Fader, in this case), indicating that it's ready to be moved. Still holding down your mouse button, drag the row up or down. A line will appear, displaying where the track will be deposited when the mouse is released.

✳ **MORE SHORTCUTS!**

There's also a shortcut to create or delete rows in the New Tracks dialog box. If you're a Windows user, you can press the Ctrl+Plus/Minus(+/−) keys on the numeric keypad or the Ctrl+Shift+Up/Down Arrow keys. If you're a Mac user, you can use the Command+Plus/Minus(+/−) keys on the numeric keypad or the Command+Shift+Up/Down Arrow keys.

Naming Your Tracks

One of the most important aspects of working in a DAW is documentation. (It may be *the* most important, depending on whom you talk to.) Keeping track of your sessions, files, tracks, patches, and so on is absolutely critical, especially as your sessions become more complex.

When Pro Tools creates a new track, it assigns a generic name (such as "Audio 1") as a default. Descriptively naming your tracks is a big part of session documentation—and the good news is, it's easy.

1 **Double-click** on the **track name** of the track you want to rename. A dialog box will open.

2 **Type** a **name** for the track in the Name the Track field.

3 If you want to continue naming tracks, **click** on the **Next button** to name the track below the current track or **click** on the **Previous button** to name the track above the current track.

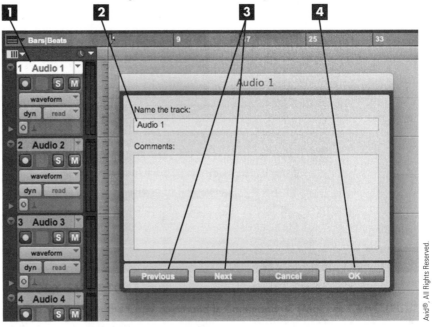

4 When you're finished naming tracks, **click** on the **OK button**. The dialog box will close.

✳ **NAMING YOUR TRACKS FOR THE TUTORIAL SESSION**

If you've been following along with this chapter's examples, you should have five stereo Audio tracks, two stereo Aux tracks, and one stereo Master Fader track. To keep the ball rolling, name each of the tracks as follows: Pad, Blorp, Bass, Snare, Kick, Pad Reverb Aux, Drum Reverb Aux, and Master Volume.

Moving Tracks

After you've assigned names to all your tracks, you might want to reorganize them so that related tracks are near each other. Although moving tracks around in the Edit or Mix window won't change how they play back, a logical arrangement of tracks can make the entire production process much easier. There aren't any hard and fast organizational rules—each session is unique, and you'll have to decide how to arrange your tracks so they make sense to you. (When you prepare your session to be used by somebody else, there are some conventions to adhere to, which I'll go into in Chapter 10.)

In this example, I want to move my Pad Reverb track to just below my Pad track:

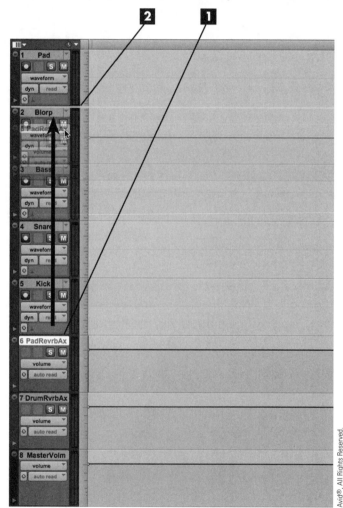

1 **Click and hold** on a **track name**. The track will be selected.

2 **Drag** the **track** up or down to the desired location. As you move the track, a gold line will appear, indicating the position the track would assume if you were to release the mouse button.

3 **Release** the **mouse button** when you have the gold line at the desired position. The tracks in your session will be reorganized.

In the Mix window, as in the Edit window, you can click and drag any track to a new location. Of course, instead of dragging up or down, you drag left or right.

1 **Click and hold** on a **track name**. The track will be selected.

2 **Drag** the **track** left or right to the desired location. As you drag the track, a gold line will appear, indicating the position the track will assume when it is dropped in its new location.

3 **Release** the **mouse button** when you have the gold line at the desired location. The tracks in your session will be reorganized.

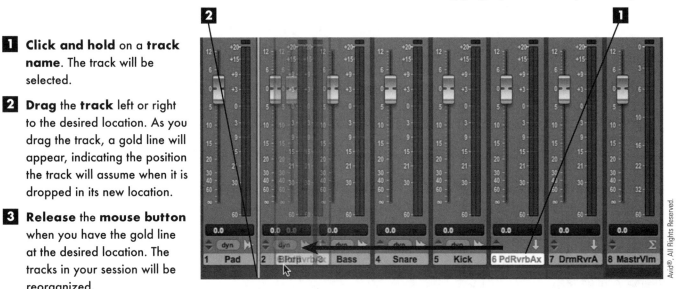

❄ ANOTHER WAY TO MOVE TRACKS

Here's another way to move tracks: Click and hold the track name in the Track Show/Hide list, and then drag the track up or down to the desired position. A thin line will indicate where the track will be moved; when you release the mouse button, your tracks will be reordered.

Duplicating Tracks

From time to time, you might want to do a little more than simply create a new blank track. In some cases, you might want to clone an existing track, making an exact copy (including any clips that are on the track). Here's how it's done:

1 **Select** the **track(s)** you want to duplicate by clicking on the track name(s).

2 **Click** on **Track**. The Track menu will appear.

3 **Click** on **Duplicate**. The Duplicate Tracks dialog box will open.

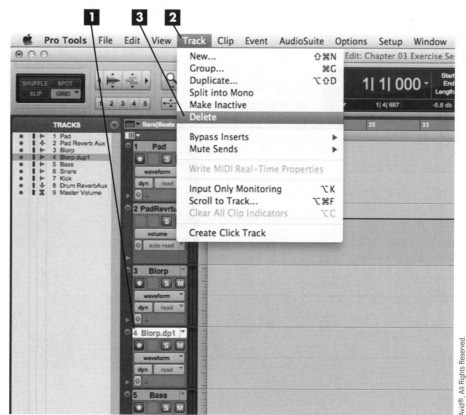

4 In the Number of Duplicates field, **type** the **number of duplicates** you want to make.

5 In the Data to Duplicate section, **choose** the **aspects** of the track that you want to copy. (If these terms have little meaning to you, don't fret; we'll explore their meanings in later chapters.) To make a complete duplicate of the selected track(s), select all the checkboxes in the Data to Duplicate section.

6 **Check** the **Insert After Last Selected Track checkbox** if you want to create your duplicate tracks directly adjacent to your selected tracks. If you leave this box unchecked, your new tracks will be created at the bottom of your Tracks list.

7 When you're finished, **click** on the **OK button**. The duplicate track(s) will be created.

Deleting Tracks

Suppose you've created a duplicate track (as you have just done), and then you decide it was a bad idea. No worries—deleting tracks is nearly as easy as creating them.

1 **Select** the **track(s)** you want to delete by clicking on the track name(s).

2 **Click** on **Track**. The Track menu will appear.

3 **Click** on **Delete**. The track(s) will be deleted.

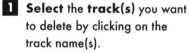

❄❄❄

Note that there's no shortcut for deleting tracks as there is for creating them. This is deliberate, so that you don't accidentally delete tracks.

❋ RIGHT-CLICK POWER

If you have a mouse that supports right-clicking, I have some great news for you: Pro Tools has incorporated many common operations into right-click commands. This makes already-easy jobs even easier.

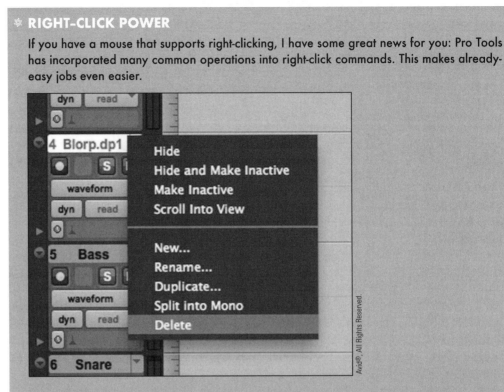

Track functions are a great example of right-click functionality. Simply right-click on the desired track's name, and you'll see the list shown here. This list of common track-related operations includes many of the operations I just covered, plus some that I'll cover in chapters to come.

New in Pro Tools 11: Add New Track Enhancements

In this section, you've learned a number of different ways to make new tracks. While these methods will serve you well, Pro Tools 11 adds even more (and in many cases, easier) ways to add new tracks!

This new feature is not so much a matter of shortcut keys or menus but of *where* you click:

❋ No matter how many tracks you have in your session, you'll always be able to scroll to an empty area at the bottom of the Edit window.

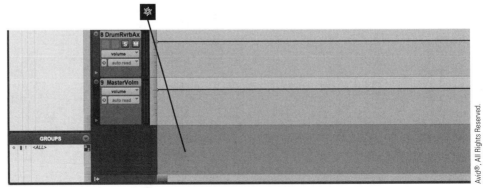

✻ You'll see a similar space on the right side of the Mix window…

✻ …and finally, you've got empty space in the Tracks list in either the Mix or Edit window.

Double-clicking in any of these empty spaces will create a new track of the same type and format as the last new track you created. So for example, if the last new track you created was a stereo Master Fader (and it probably would be, if you've been following the exercise session), double-clicking would create another stereo Master Fader track.

But what if you don't want to create a second Master Fader? No problem—this great new feature includes modifier keys that you can use to create different kinds of tracks:

✻ Command+double-click (Mac) or Control+double-click (Windows) to create an Audio track of the same number of channels as the last new track you created.

✻ Control+double-click (Mac) or Start+double-click (Windows) to create an Aux track of the same number of channels as the last new track you created.

✻ Shift+double-click to create a Master Fader track of the same number of channels as the last new track you created.

✻ Option+double-click (Mac) or Alt+double-click (Windows) to create an Instrument track of the same number of channels as the last new track you created.

✻✻✻

It gets better! If you want to create multiple tracks at the same time, just hold down multiple modifier keys. For example, if you want to create a new Audio track and also a new Aux track, Command+Control+double-click (Mac) or Control+Start+double-click (Windows)

Importing Audio

Although you can certainly record live audio into Pro Tools (it wouldn't be much of an audio workstation if you couldn't!), that's not the only way to get sounds into your session. Indeed, one of the big advantages of a computer-based DAW is that you can import digital audio files into your session, bypassing the recording process entirely.

Importing files into Pro Tools is a quick and easy way to get started. As with many Pro Tools operations, there are a number of ways to get the job done. In this section, you'll explore the two basic methods: using the File menu and using the Workspace Browser.

❋ **USING YOUR TUTORIAL SESSIONS**

The examples shown in this section use the Chapter 03 import materials. You'll find these files included in this book's downloadable materials, in the Chapter 03 Import Audio folder. (For information on downloading this book's exercise materials, please refer to the "Setting Up Your Session" section of the introduction.) You should leave the current session open so that you have a session to import into!

Importing from the File Menu

Importing audio using the File menu is a tried-and-true way to get the files you want into your session. The first thing you need to do is locate the file you want to import into Pro Tools.

❋ **GETTING STARTED**

Although you can use the File menu while viewing either the Mix window or the Edit window, it's typically done while working in the Edit window. For the purposes of this demonstration, if you're currently looking at the Mix window in Pro Tools, switch to the Edit window. (Open the Window menu and choose Edit.)

1 **Click** on **File**. The File menu will appear.

2 **Choose Import.** The Import submenu will appear.

3 **Choose Audio.** The Import Audio dialog box will open.

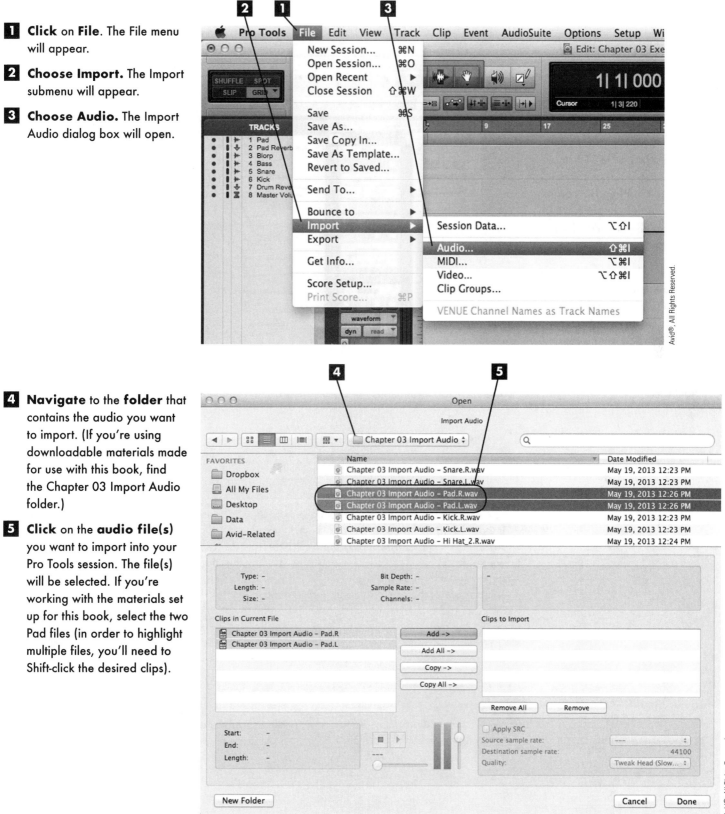

4 **Navigate** to the **folder** that contains the audio you want to import. (If you're using downloadable materials made for use with this book, find the Chapter 03 Import Audio folder.)

5 **Click** on the **audio file(s)** you want to import into your Pro Tools session. The file(s) will be selected. If you're working with the materials set up for this book, select the two Pad files (in order to highlight multiple files, you'll need to Shift-click the desired clips).

Before you proceed, let's take a look at a couple of things:

6 The box in the lower left shows clips in the audio files you've selected, but those clips haven't actually been incorporated into your session yet. To audition any single clip before importing, **select** the desired **audio clip** (in the Clips in Current File area) and then **click** on the **Play button** to preview it. (Note that multiple clips can't be previewed simultaneously.)

7 Next, you'll need to add those clips to the box on the right (called Clips to Import). Select the clip(s) you want to import, and then **click** on the **Add button** or the **Copy button**. The clips will be added to the right box.

ADDING FILES VERSUS COPYING/CONVERTING FILES

You'll notice that there are Add buttons and Copy buttons in the bottom-center section of the Import Audio dialog box. Clicking on the Add button will simply add clips to your Pro Tools session, and Pro Tools will play the audio file from its original location on your hard drive, wherever that may be. Clicking on Copy, on the other hand, will actually make copies of those files and place the copies in your session's own Audio Files folder. In cases where the sample rate of the audio to be imported does not match the session's, the Copy button will instead read *Convert* and will change the audio file(s) to match the session's sample rate as it copies the files.

WHAT IF I CAN'T HEAR ANYTHING WHEN I TRY TO PREVIEW A FILE?

If you don't hear your selected audio, you might want to check the Audition Paths setting in the I/O Setup dialog box. Review the "Audition Paths and Default Outputs" section earlier in this chapter for more information.

You'll notice that one file has an .R listed before the file extension (in this case, it's a WAV file), and the other file has an .L in the filename. This indicates to Pro Tools that these files are two halves of a stereo clip. (The L is for left, and the R is for right.) When these files are imported, they'll be listed in your Clips list as a single stereo audio clip.

Clips to Import

Chapter 03 Import Audio – Pad.R	Add
Chapter 03 Import Audio – Pad.L	Add

[Remove All]   [Remove]

☐ Apply SRC

Source sample rate:	---
Destination sample rate:	44100
Quality:	Tweak Head (Slow...

[Cancel]   [Done]

❋ Checking the Apply SRC checkbox will enable you to manually specify the source file's sample rate, even if it's different from the reported sample rate shown in the middle-left area. You can also specify a conversion quality setting, which will override the Pro Tools default setting. Manual sample-rate conversions like this are most commonly necessary when converting between NTSC, PAL, and film video sessions.

8 **Click** on the **Done button** when you're finished. If you chose to add audio to your session, the imported audio will immediately be added. (You can choose whether to add this to a new track or to the Clips list.) If you chose to copy the audio into your session or were required to convert it, you'll have to choose a destination folder for your copied files—read on!

Choosing Where to Import To

If you clicked on the Copy button (as opposed to the Add button), you'll need to specify a location for your new files. By default, Pro Tools will choose to copy the audio files to your session's own Audio Files subfolder. You can, however, choose to place them anywhere on your hard drive. If you want to change the location of the copies, follow these steps:

1 **Navigate** to the desired **location**.

* If you want to create a new subfolder for your audio, click on the New Folder button. You'll be prompted to name your new folder, and the folder will be opened. Once you've reached your desired location, click on the Choose button, and you're finished.

2 **Click** on the **Open button**. The audio files will be copied to the folder and imported into your session.

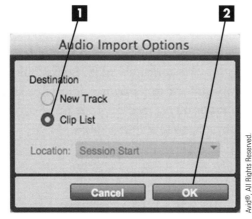

Importing to the Clips List

Regardless of whether you chose to copy audio files or simply add clips to your session, the next window will enable you to add clips to the Clips list or create a brand-new Audio track. For starters, let's run through the steps involved in importing to the Clips list only.

1 In the Audio Import Options dialog box, **click** on the **Clip List option button**.

2 **Click** on the **OK button**. The clip(s) will be created in your session.

You'll notice that although the audio clip is added to the Clips list, it hasn't been added to any of the Audio tracks you've created. Don't worry—that's the way this method of importing is supposed to function. Later, you'll drag this audio file onto an Audio track and use it as an element of your session.

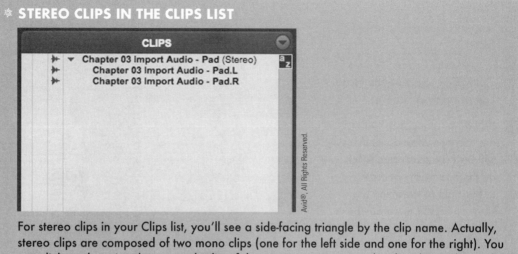

❋ STEREO CLIPS IN THE CLIPS LIST

For stereo clips in your Clips list, you'll see a side-facing triangle by the clip name. Actually, stereo clips are composed of two mono clips (one for the left side and one for the right). You can click on that triangle to reveal a list of the component mono audio clips that make up that stereo audio clip, as shown here.

Importing Audio to a Track

Sometimes, instead of importing an audio clip to the Clips list and using it later, you'll want to import the clip onto a new track directly. Just for practice, let's import the Hi Hat_1 audio into a brand-new track. The steps for importing audio to a track are, for the most part, the same as importing to the Clips list.

1 **Click** on **File**. The File menu will appear.

2 **Choose Import.** The Import submenu will appear.

3 **Choose Audio.** The Import Audio dialog box will open, just as you've seen before.

4 **Select** the **audio file(s)** to import into your session. In this example, choose Chapter 03 Import Audio–Hi Hat_1.L and Chapter 03 Import Audio–Hi Hat_1.R. These files are located in the same folder you used previously.

5 For the purposes of this example, you can choose to either add or copy/convert your audio. To do so, **click** on the **Add button** or the **Copy (or Convert) button.**

6 **Click** on the **Done button** when you're finished making your choices. If you choose to copy files, you will see the Choose a Destination Folder dialog box. Otherwise (or thereafter), the Audio Import Options dialog box will open.

7 In the Audio Import Options dialog box, **choose** the **New Track option button**.

8 When you select this button, the Location drop-down menu will become available. **Click** on the **Location arrow** to the right of the menu (as shown here) to see a number of placement options.

❊ **Session Start.** This will place the audio clip at the very beginning of the new track.

❊ **Song Start.** You can set your song to start at a place other than the beginning of your session (something you'll explore in Chapter 6, "...And More Editing!"). If your song start is anywhere other than the beginning of your session, the option to place your audio at the song start will become available.

❊ **Selection.** Choosing this option will place your audio at the beginning of any selected area. (You'll learn more about making selections in your session later in this chapter.)

❊ **Spot.** The term *spot* (usually used in a video context) describes the placement of audio at a specific point in time. Choosing this option will open the Spot dialog box, where you can type a specific time location for your audio. You'll learn more about using the Spot dialog box in Chapter 5, "Editing."

9 For the purposes of this exercise, **choose** the **Session Start option**.

10 **Click** on the **OK button**. The dialog box will close, and your track will be created.

You'll notice that Pro Tools has done a couple of significant things with the click of a single button:

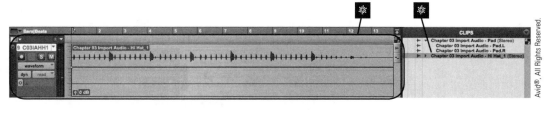

❊ Pro Tools has imported the desired clip (in this case, Chapter 03 Import Audio–Hi Hat_1) into the Clips list. That means you can use this clip in your session.

❊ Pro Tools has created a brand-new track, Chapter 03 Import Audio–Hi Hat_1 (named for the audio file being imported), and automatically placed the imported clip at the beginning of that track. Because the imported clips had an L and an R after them, Pro Tools recognized them as left and right channels and incorporated them into a single stereo Audio track. Pretty cool, don't you think?

The Workspace Browser

A powerful window called the Workspace was added to Pro Tools in version 6, and it has become even more streamlined and easy to use in Pro Tools 11. Think of the Workspace Browser as being similar to the Mac Finder or Windows Explorer, but with added features specifically for Pro Tools. In this section, you'll see how the Workspace provides you with yet another way to import audio into your session and more!

1 Click on **Window**. The Window menu will appear.

2 Click on **New Workspace**. The Workspace Browser will appear.

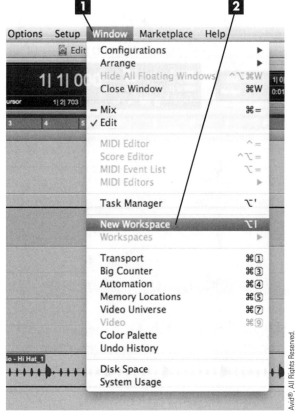

Searching for Audio Using the Workspace Browser

Finding the file you want is easy, and it's one of the Workspace Browser's special advantages.

❊ ❊ ❊

1 **Click** on the **magnifying glass (search) button.**

2 In the Locations pane, you have the ability to search all volumes (attached drives), your open session, your catalogs (which you'll learn about later in this chapter), or a Mac's User folder. For the most global search, **choose Volumes.**

3 **Type** the **name** of the file (or keyword) you want to search in the text box. The search will begin immediately, and the main Workspace pane will be populated with items that match your search.

You might find that the list that is generated includes a lot of what you're *not* looking for. Here are ways to refine your search:

❄ Click the checkbox at the top of the Locations pane. You will be presented with checkboxes for each item in the pane, allowing for more specific searches.

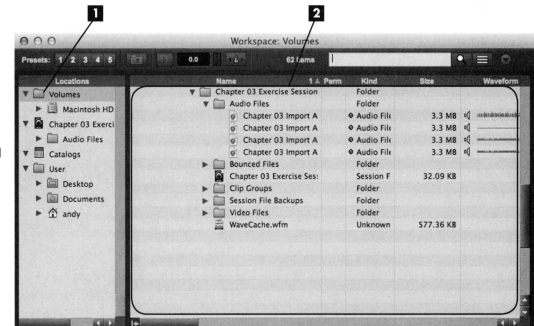

❄ Click the Advanced Search button to reveal a row directly below the search field. You can refine your search via logical functions. In this example, I searched by name (must include "drum") and kind (must be an audio file). As a result, only audio files including the word "drum" are being shown. By clicking the plus and minus buttons to the right of each row, you can add and remove search criteria.

❄ To stop the search, click the Search button again (now represented by an "×"). Clicking the button again will exit search mode.

You can also navigate in a more traditional way, if you know where to look for a specific file.

1 In the Locations pane, select the domain in which you want to navigate. Here again, **choose Volumes** for the most comprehensive navigation.

2 Similar to searching in general on your computer, **navigate** through the **folders** and **subfolders** until you locate the file you want.

❄ ❄ ❄

The Workspace Browser has a few more nifty features as well:

* Similar to the lists in the Mix and Edit windows, you can hide or reveal the Locations pane by clicking the small side-pointing arrow in the lower-left corner of the Workspace main pane.

* There's a lot of data you can choose to see, and it's likely that you won't be able to see it all at once in the Workspace Browser. You can easily scroll through the different columns by using the scrollbar at the bottom of the browser.

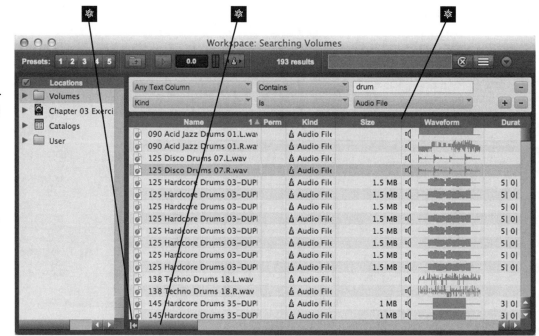

* You can show or hide specific columns by right-clicking in the column heading area. A list of available columns will be shown, with displayed columns indicated with a checkmark. Just click on the desired menu item to change its state.

* You can audition an audio file by clicking on the speaker icon to the left of the waveform overview or clicking the Preview button. The waveform will give an indication of the file's characteristics. To stop playback, simply click on the speaker icon or Preview button again.

❋ AUDITIONING LONG FILES

If you're auditioning a particularly lengthy audio file, you can click at any point within the blue audio waveform to begin playback from that point.

If you click on the Workspace menu button (in the upper-right corner), you'll find a list of useful options. I'll talk about many of these in due course, but let's start off with a look at some that are specifically relevant to auditioning audio:

Loop Preview. If you select this option, the file will automatically repeat when you preview it. This is especially useful when you are previewing drum beats and other kinds of files that are typically repeated in a mix.

❋ **Auto-Preview.** Choosing the Auto-Preview option will set up the Workspace Browser to automatically play an audio file as soon as it has been selected. This means you won't have to click on the speaker icon to hear it. It also means, however, that files will always start playing as soon as you select them, which can be distracting to some users.

❋ **Spacebar Toggles File Preview.** In the normal Pro Tools environment, pressing the spacebar will start or stop playback in your session. It's one of Pro Tools' most fundamental shortcuts (and one I'll cover later in this chapter). If you enable this option, the spacebar will have a similar behavior in the Workspace Browser. Just select a file and press the spacebar to start or stop playback of the audio.

❋ You can also access these three preview options by right-clicking on the Preview button.

In earlier versions of Pro Tools, previewed files would play at their full volume. This was often a shock to the ears and could potentially even damage speakers! Thankfully, those days are over.

❋ ❋ ❋

❄ **Preview volume control.** Simply click and hold on the volume field (indicated here), and a volume slider will be revealed. Then drag the slider up or down to increase or decrease the volume of the previewed audio.

❄ PREVIEW AND PLAYBACK

Another nice feature of using the Workspace Browser is the ability to preview audio while your session is playing. Doing this in conjunction with adjusting the preview volume control can give you a great sense of how the audio works with your session before you commit to importing it. The process is easy—just start playback of your session, open the Workspace Browser, and preview to your heart's content!

❄ SHOWING AND HIDING A WORKSPACE BROWSER WINDOW

During the normal course of production, you might open a Workspace and then click on the Edit window to do some work. As soon as you click the Edit window (or Mix window), the Workspace window will dutifully move behind the window so that it's not in the way. Getting the Workspace back, though, can be a bit of a pain!

One way to manage the Workspaces you create is to go to the Window menu and from there move your cursor to Workspaces to reveal a number of options. You can also easily show or hide Workspace windows via shortcuts. Pressing Option+J (Mac) or Alt+J (Windows) will bring the Workspace Browser to the front, and pressing Shift+Option+J (Mac) or Shift+Alt+J (Windows) will move the Workspace to the rear.

Importing Audio Using the Workspace Browser

❄ CHAPTER 03 AUDIO FOR IMPORT

For the purposes of this chapter, use the Workspace Browser to navigate to the Exercise 03 Import Audio folder for this section.

Once you've located the audio you want to use in your session, the Workspace Browser will give you a few options for importing.

1 **Click and drag** the **file(s)** you want to import into your session. Note that where you drag it will affect *how* it will be imported:

❄ If you drop the file into the session's Clips list, a new clip will appear in the Clips list. When you move your mouse into the Clips list, the list will be outlined in gray, indicating that you can release the mouse button.

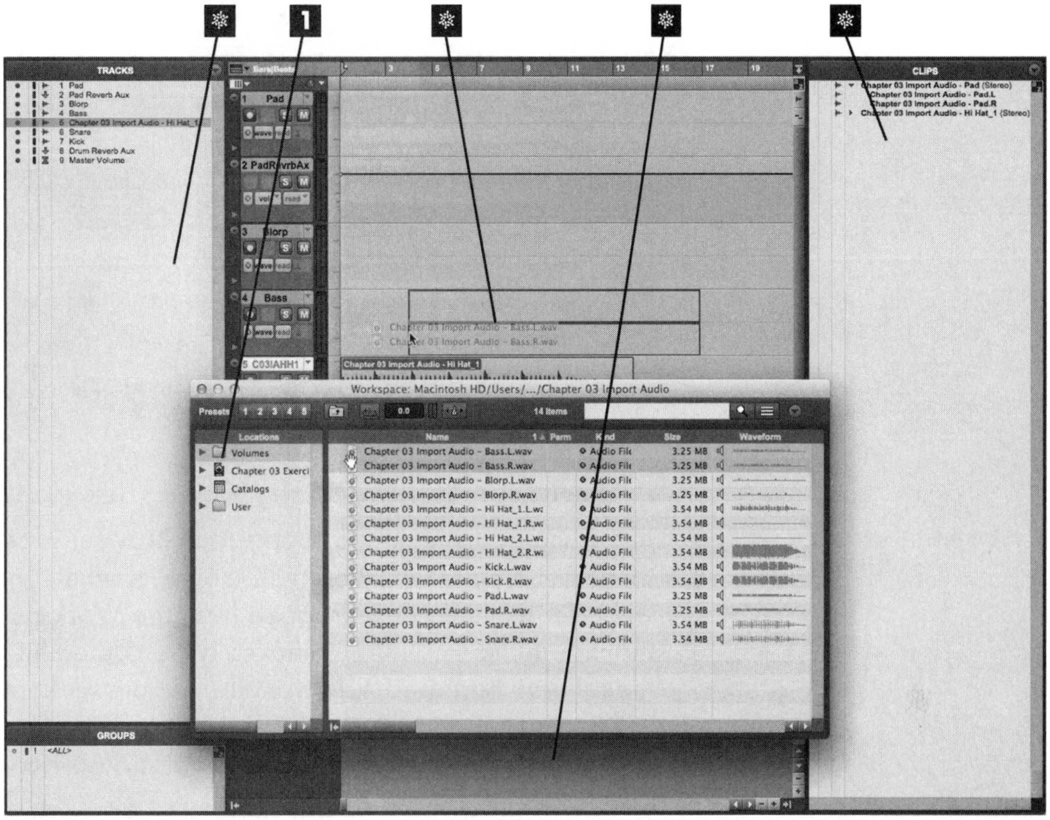

❄ If you drop the file onto an existing track, a new clip will appear on that track. As shown here, a rectangle will indicate where the clip will be placed when your mouse is released. The clip will also appear in the Clips list.

❄ If you drop the file into an area with no track, a new track will be created, and a clip will be placed on that new track. The clip will also appear in the Clips list.

❄ If you drop the file into the Tracks list, a new track will be created, and a clip will be placed at the beginning of that track (regardless of the edit mode you're using). The clip will also appear in the Clips list.

❄ IMPORTING AND EDIT MODES

When you drag a file onto either an existing track or a blank area where there is no track, the placement of the clip will depend on the edit mode you're using. You'll learn more about the edit modes in Chapter 5.

2 **Release** the **mouse button** to complete the importing process—easy!

❄ ❄ ❄

> ❋ **IF YOU'RE USING THE EXERCISE MATERIALS**
>
> If you're following the chapter step by step, let's import some audio to the Clips list and the Tracks list. In addition to the audio you've already imported in this chapter, please import the following files to the Clips list:
>
> ❋ Chapter 03 Import Audio–Bass.L and Chapter 03 Import Audio–Bass.R
>
> ❋ Chapter 03 Import Audio–Blorp.L and Chapter 03 Import Audio–Blorp.R
>
> ❋ Chapter 03 Import Audio–Kick.L and Chapter 03 Import Audio–Kick.R
>
> ❋ Chapter 03 Import Audio–Snare.L and Chapter 03 Import Audio–Snare.R
>
> Then drag the following files to the Tracks list to create a new track with the clip on it:
>
> Chapter 03 Import Audio–Bass.L and Chapter 03 Import Audio–Bass.R

Preference: Automatically Copy Files on Import

Importing audio from the Workspace Browser is certainly very convenient, but there's one thing you should be aware of when you do it. By default, Pro Tools will *refer* to audio files dragged from the Workspace Browser, which means that the audio will *not* automatically be copied into your Audio Files folder (as though you had used Add from the Import Audio dialog box). Instead, Pro Tools will access the audio from its original location. Sometimes, especially for new Pro Tools users, this can lead to confusion about where your audio files actually are!

This leads us to a very important dialog box in Pro Tools—the Preferences dialog box—which enables you to decide how Pro Tools will behave in a wide range of situations. Let's take a quick first look at this window and a preference that will enable you to *always* copy files when you import them.

1 **Click** on **Setup**. The Setup menu will appear.

2 **Choose Preferences.** The Pro Tools Preferences dialog box will open.

3 **Click** on the **Processing tab**. The processing preferences will be revealed.

4 **Click** on the **Automatically Copy Files on Import checkbox** to select it. It's that simple! Now your dragged-and-dropped files will always be copied to your Audio Files folder.

4   **3**

Pro Tools Preferences

| Display | Operation | Editing | Mixing | Metering | Processing | MIDI | Synchronization |

AudioSuite

Default Handle Length:
- ○ Whole File
- ● Length: 2.00 Seconds

Import

- ☐ Convert Imported ".wav" Files to AES31/Broadcast Wave
- ☑ Automatically Copy Files on Import
- ☑ Convert Copied Files to Session Format
- ☐ Don't convert Sample Rate on Import
- ☐ Import REX Files as Clip Groups
- ☐ Automatically Create Fades

Drag and Drop from Desktop Conforms to Session Tempo:
- ○ No Files
- ● REX and ACID Files Only
- ○ All Files

Sample Rate Conversion Quality: TweakHead (Slowest)

TC/E

TC/E Plug-in: Time Shift

Default Settings: <factory default>

Elastic Audio

Default Plug-in: Polyphonic

Default Input Gain: 0.0 dB

☐ Enable Elastic Audio on New Tracks

Cancel   OK

Using Catalogs

A *catalog* is a user-definable collection of audio, sessions, effects—basically anything you find yourself using frequently. A catalog doesn't include the files *per se*, but actually is a collection of file aliases, or shortcuts.

Using catalogs is very straightforward. Let's take a quick look at the basics:

1 In the Locations pane, **click Catalogs** to view your catalogs in the main pane. If you're just starting out, the main pane will be empty, as shown here.

2 **Click** the **Workspace Browser menu button** in the upper-right corner of the Workspace Browser and **choose New Catalog**.

3 **Type** a descriptive **name** for your catalog.

4 **Click** on the **OK button**. The catalog will be created.

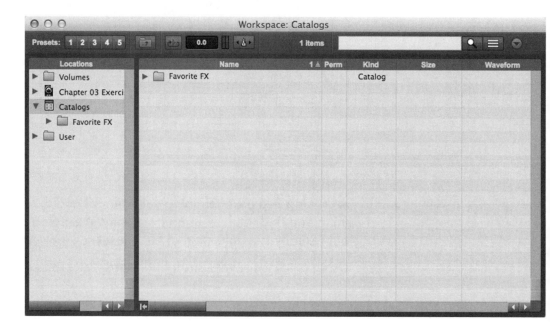

You'll see that a subfolder has been created in the Catalogs view. Here are a couple ways to get files into your catalogs:

❄ Drag and drop selected files into the desired catalog folder. Clicking the triangular button to the left of the Catalogs section in the Locations pane will reveal all of your Catalog folders and make it easy to drag audio from the main pane after tracking down audio that you want to add.

❄ Alternatively, if you want to quickly create a new catalog and add selected files to that catalog, you can do that as well. Select the files you want to put into a catalog and then choose Create Catalog from Selection from the Workspace Browser menu.

Once you've created a catalog and populated it with your favorites, you can easily search and import files from that catalog, just as if it were a folder on your computer. You'll find this especially useful with often-used files, such as sound-library audio and commonly used effects.

Importing Tracks

Importing audio to a track is certainly an easy way to get started, but there is a limitation: The clip that you import will simply be placed at some point on your track's timeline, with no specific editing or mixing. But what if you want to import a fully tweaked-out track that you created in *another* session? No problem—Pro Tools can import tracks from other sessions, including all edits, volume, panning, and so on, for you to use in your current session!

❄ **CHAPTER 03 IMPORT SESSION**

Included in the downloadable materials, you'll see a folder named Chapter 03 Import Session, and within that folder a session of the same name. It is from this session that you'll be importing three tracks.

❄ ❄ ❄

1 **Click** on **File**. The File menu will appear.

2 **Choose Import.** The Import submenu will appear.

3 **Choose Session Data.** The Open dialog box will open.

4 **Select** the **session file** from which you want to import. Remember, you're not importing just audio anymore, but rather entire tracks. Those tracks exist in the session file, which is why you're selecting a session file, not an audio file.

5 **Click** on the **Open button**. The Import Session Data dialog box will open.

❋ The Source Properties section of the Import Session Data dialog box provides a wealth of information about the session from which you'll be importing.

6 The bottom of the dialog box contains a list of all tracks in this session, and that's where you'll select your tracks. **Click** on the **selector** in the Destination column of the Control Tower (Mono Audio) track. The Destination menu will appear.

7 The Destination menu gives you the option to import to a new track in your session or to any pre-existing compatible track. In this example, the open session doesn't have any mono Audio tracks, so **choose New Track** to create a new track in your session.

8 It's possible to import more than one track at a time. **Click** on the **Synth Pad 1 and Synth Pad 2 (Mono Audio) menus** in the Destination column and **select New Track**.

❋ IMPORTING TO EXISTING TRACKS

If you're following along with the steps in this chapter, you'll see that in addition to the option for creating a new track, there's an option to import the track into any existing track of the same type (mono, stereo, etc.). If you choose any of these pre-existing tracks, the track in the session will be replaced by the track being imported. You can go one step further, however: By clicking on the Match Tracks button (just below the Tracks list on the right side), imported tracks will automatically be mapped to tracks of the same name and type.

9 You can choose whether to simply add the tracks' audio clips to your session or copy their audio files to your Audio Files folder (similar to what you did in the Import Audio dialog box earlier in this chapter). **Click** on the **Audio Media Options selector**. A drop-down menu will appear.

* **Link to Source Media (Where Possible).** Linking to source media will not make a copy of any audio files, but rather will direct the session to refer to the audio files in their original location.

* **Copy from Source Media.** Copying from source media will copy any audio files used in the imported tracks into the session's Audio Files folder.

* **Consolidate from Source Media.** Consolidating from the source media is another type of copying, but in this case, instead of copying entire files associated with tracks, only the portion of those files actually being used in a track will be imported. In many cases, this can be a more efficient copying option and can save space on your hard drive.

* **Force to Target Session Format.** This option takes a hybrid approach to importing audio. In cases where the imported audio matches the session's audio file format, the audio will be linked. In cases where the audio doesn't match, the audio files will be converted and copied.

10 The Link to Source Media (Where Possible) and Copy from Source Media options are the most commonly used. For the purposes of this example, choose **Copy from Source Media**.

11 Let's take a look at the Timecode Mapping Options and Track Offset Options sections. You'll find these in the top-right corner of the window. These are mostly used in situations involving SMPTE timecode. **Click** on the **Timecode Mapping Options menu**. You'll see various options:

* **Maintain Absolute Timecode Values.** This will ensure that the timecode location of clips on your imported tracks will remain unchanged. For example, a clip that has a SMPTE time of 01:01:15:06 will keep that value. In cases where the two sessions have different SMPTE start times, this will result in the clips having different positions on the Pro Tools timeline.

* **Maintain Relative Timecode Values.** This will keep clips in the same position on your Pro Tools timeline. In other words, a clip that is at the beginning of a session will continue to be at the beginning of the timeline once it's imported. In cases where the two sessions have different SMPTE start times, this will result in the clips having different SMPTE times.

❄ **Map Start Timecode To.** This setting enables you to specify a timecode time for your imported tracks to begin. You can enter the timecode in the field below the Timecode Mapping Options menu.

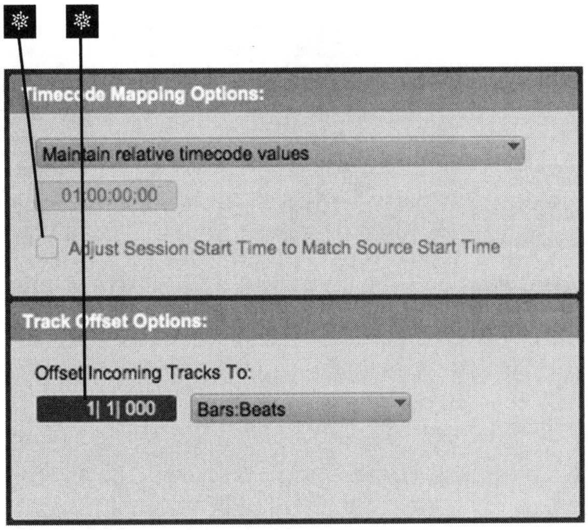

Avid®, All Rights Reserved.

❄ Clicking on the Adjust Session Start Time to Match Source Start Time checkbox will adjust your session's start time to match the start time of the session you're importing from. If the two sessions already share the same start time, the option will be grayed out (as shown here).

❄ You can choose to offset incoming tracks to any time you choose. This offset time can be in a number of time scales (including SMPTE timecode).

You also have a number of options in terms of what *kinds* of session data to import:

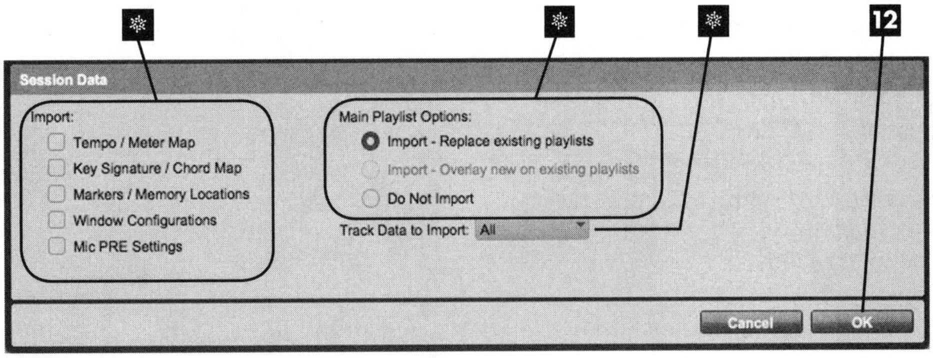

❄ In the Track Data to Import menu, you'll see a list of the aspects of the tracks that you want to import (clips, plug-ins, automation, and so on). From this list, you can specify precisely what parts of your tracks to import.

Avid®, All Rights Reserved.

❄ Some aspects of a session are global. That is, they apply to the entire session. These include such things as tempo, key signatures, and so on. In this section, you can choose to import these session aspects.

❄ You can choose how to address your edit playlists in this section. I'll talk about edit playlists in Chapter 5.

12 When you're finished, **click** on the **OK button**.

Again, you'll see that Pro Tools performs a number of operations with one user command, including the following:

❄ ❄ ❄

❋ New tracks will be created in your session. The interesting thing about these tracks is that you've imported a number of audio clips, and they are already arranged at specific times in your session.

❋ Each separate clip in each of the tracks is listed individually in the Clips list to the right.

Working with Tracks

This section will put some things discussed in the first chapter into more practical use.

Selecting and Moving Tracks

Let's start by moving your newly created tracks to the top of the Edit window.

1 To select a range of tracks, **hold down** the **Shift key** and **click** on the **track names** of the tracks you want to select. You can make this selection either on the tracks themselves or in the Tracks list. In this case, I've selected the Control Tower, Synth Pad 1, and Synth Pad 2 tracks.

2 Just as you did when you moved a single track, **click and drag** the **group of tracks** to the desired location in your Edit window.

Deleting Tracks

If you've been following the steps throughout this chapter, you'll notice that you have two Aux tracks (named Pad Reverb Aux and Drum Reverb Aux). You don't really need either of them, so let's delete them.

> ❄ **SELECTING NONADJACENT TRACKS**
>
> The Shift key is handy for selecting a range of tracks, but what if the tracks you want to select aren't next to each other? No problem. Just hold down the Command key (Mac) or the Ctrl key (PC) and click on the individual track names that you want to select.

1 **Click** on the **track name** of the track(s) that you want to delete (in this case, the Pad Reverb Aux and Drum Reverb Aux tracks).

2 **Click** on **Track**. The Track menu will appear.

3 **Click** on **Delete**. The track(s) will be removed permanently.

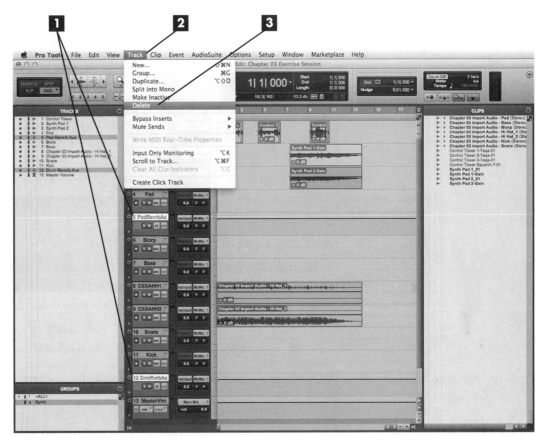

If you have a mouse with a right-click button, you can easily delete any track from that track's individual menu. (If you don't have a right-click button on a Mac mouse, you can reveal the menu by Control-clicking on the track name.)

1 **Right-click** on the **track name** of the track you want to delete in either the track itself or the Tracks list. A menu will appear.

2 **Click** on **Delete**. The track will be removed permanently.

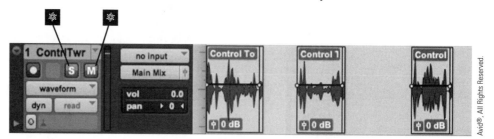

Muting and Soloing Tracks

Mute and solo are two of the most traditional functions in audio production. They are used in a variety of situations, some of which you'll explore as this book progresses. Many readers already know what these terms mean, but here are some definitions for those who don't know what exactly *mute* and *solo* mean.

* **Mute.** Tracks that are muted will be inaudible.

* **Solo.** Tracks that are soloed will be heard, and any non-soloed tracks will be inaudible.

❋ **MUTE AND SOLO ON MULTIPLE TRACKS**

Clicking on the M (mute) or S (solo) button on multiple tracks will enable you to mute or solo more than one track at a time.

❋ **MUTE AND SOLO SHORTCUTS**

Pressing Shift+M will mute and pressing Shift+S will solo any tracks that contain an edit cursor (the vertical play line, which indicates your current location).

❋❋❋

❄ Pro Tools 11 includes two indicators in the selection area of your Edit window to show you whether any tracks in your session are soloed or muted. If so, the Solo (S) or Mute (M) indicator will appear bright yellow or orange, respectively. When no tracks are soloed or muted, the indicators appear dark green.

Making Selections and Playing Audio

Being able to play your session in different ways (in addition to being able to play it from the beginning) will enable you to be flexible in your work. In this section, you'll take a look at the two primary variations: playing a selection and loop playback.

Playing a Selection

Playing a selection just may be the easiest process I'll discuss in this chapter, but being able to do it correctly is an absolutely essential skill. First, let's start with a basic playback scenario.

1 Click on the **Selector Tool** button.

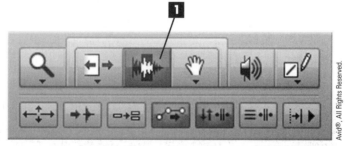

2 In this case, you just want to operate in a basic playback mode, so let's make sure that Loop Playback (which I'll talk about in just a bit) is disabled. To do so, click on **Options** and choose **Loop Playback** to uncheck it if it is selected.

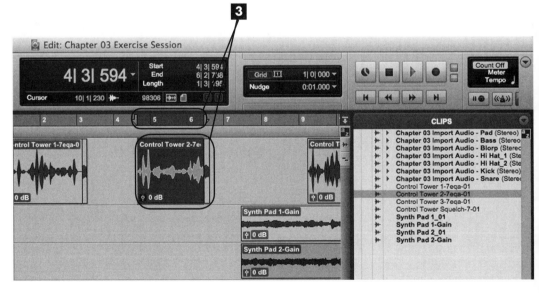

| AudioSuite | Options | Setup | Window | Marketplace | Help |

Destructive Record
Loop Record   ⌥L
QuickPunch   ⇧⌘P

Transport Online   ⌘J
Video Track Online   ⇧⌘J
Pre/Post-Roll   ⌘K
Loop Playback   ⇧⌘L
Dynamic Transport   ⌃⌘P
Edit Window Scrolling   ▶

✓ Link Timeline and Edit Selection   ⇧/
Link Track and Edit Selection
Mirror MIDI Editing
✓ Automation Follows Edit

Click
✓ MIDI Thru

Auto-Spot Clips   ⌥⌘P
✓ Pre-Fader Metering
Solo Mode   ▶

Edit/Tool Mode Keyboard Lock   ⌃⇧T
Delay Compensation

3 With the Selector tool chosen, **click and drag** over any **section** in your session. (This can be done in a track or in a ruler.) Alternatively, to select an entire clip (as shown here), **double-click** on the desired **clip**. The area you select will appear dark.

❄ **EDIT AND TIMELINE SELECTIONS**

Note that any selection you make in the playlist (this is called your *edit selection*) is mirrored in your rulers (this is called your *timeline selection*), and vice versa. This is a default setting for Pro Tools, and it is useful in the vast majority of cases. If you find that this is *not* the case in your session, see the section in Chapter 10 called "Timeline Versus Edit Selection."

4 Click on the **Play button**. The selected area will play back one time and then stop.

❄ **WHERE'S MY PLAY BUTTON? (ANOTHER USEFUL SHORTCUT)**

The transport section at the top of your Edit window can be moved, as you saw in Chapter 2, "Getting Around in Pro Tools," or even hidden completely! No worries—you can press the spacebar instead of clicking on the Play button to play the selection.

Loop Playback

Loop playback does just what it says: It loops, or repeats, any selected area of your session until you stop playback.

1 Click on **Options**. The Options menu will appear.

2 Choose **Loop Playback**. The option will be checked, and a curving arrow will be shown on the Play button of your transport controls.

3 Click on the **Play button** or **press** the **spacebar** to begin loop playback of your selec-tion. The selection will repeat until you click on the Stop button (or until you press the spacebar again).

❈ ANOTHER QUICK WAY TO ACTIVATE LOOP PLAYBACK

In the transport control section of the Edit window (or in the Transport window), right-click on the Play button and choose Loop from the list shown.

❈ RESTORE LAST SELECTION

During the course of playback, you will often jump from one section to another and then back again. Restore Last Selection does just what it says: It re-selects the previous selection you made. You can find this useful little option in the Edit menu. The shortcut is Option+Command+Z (Mac) or Ctrl+Alt+Z (PC).

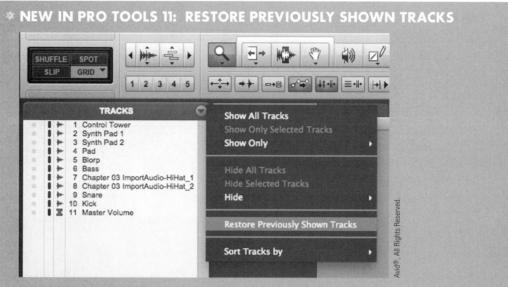

❈ NEW IN PRO TOOLS 11: RESTORE PREVIOUSLY SHOWN TRACKS

Before I close out this chapter, here's one more useful feature for you, and one that is new in Pro Tools: Restore Previously Shown Tracks. This feature, which you'll find in the Tracks list pop-up menu, will restore previously shown tracks after showing or hiding tracks using any of the other of the Tracks List pop-up menu items (for example, Show All Tracks).

❈ FINISHED CHAPTER 03 SESSION

Just so you can check your work, I've included a "finished" version of the Chapter 03 Exercise session with the book's downloadable materials, as an example of what you should end up with if you've followed the steps outlined in this chapter.

Good work! Next up...recording!

❈ ❈ ❈

4 } Recording Audio

The things you've learned in previous chapters are some of the most important parts of becoming a strong Pro Tools user. Sooner or later, though, you'll want to move beyond simply importing audio and actually *record* an audio performance. The ability to record quickly and easily is a key area where Pro Tools really shines, and the flexibility this software offers has helped it earn its place as a leader in the field. In this chapter, you'll learn how to do the following:

- ❋ Set up a click track.
- ❋ Make your first recording.
- ❋ Use punch-in/punch-out recording and other recording options.
- ❋ Make the most of your monitoring options.

Getting Started: Signal Flow 101

You took a good first look at the Edit window in the first few chapters. Now it's time to dig deeper.

Setting Things Up

To start off, you'll need to create a new blank session. (Refer to Chapter 1, "Welcome to Pro Tools 11," for a complete rundown of this process.)

If you don't have any musicians on hand to record, don't worry—I've got you covered. The downloadable materials included with this book include a number of vocal and instrumental audio files for you to practice with. The files are in "Red Book" format (44.1 kHz sample rate, 16-bit stereo interleaved files) and should play easily from any music player.

You can easily record these tracks by connecting the line outputs of your music player to the line inputs of your audio interface. It's imperfect, but it'll simulate a live musician well enough to suit our purposes. Here's a typical setup to use in connecting your music player to your system:

1 **Connect** the **left output** of your CD player to the **first available input** of your audio interface (for example, input 1).

2 **Connect** the **right output** of your CD player to the **next available input** (for example, input 2).

3 In the I/O Setup dialog box, **create** a **stereo input path** that corresponds to the two physical inputs (this is the path you'll use for stereo recording).

❋ A NOTE ON THE CHAPTER 04 RECORDING MATERIALS

This book's downloadable materials include a number of tracks for you to practice with, found in a folder named Chapter 04 Audio for Recording. (For information on downloading this book's exercise materials, please refer to the "Setting Up Your Session" section of the introduction.) These tracks are a recording of an American traditional song named "Shady Grove" played in a bluegrass style. I hope you enjoy it.

These tracks were played by an American ensemble called Under the Radar, hailing from the state of Florida. It consists of Paul McCaskill (vocals and guitar), Jason Thomas (fiddle), Lamont Goff (mandolin), and Jessica Goff (bass). I was privileged to work with this group as a Pro Tools editor and mixer. They are all fantastic players, and if you agree, I hope you'll check them out on their forthcoming recording project.

Then do the following:

1 **Create** a **new session**. For a refresher on how to do this, refer to Chapter 1, in the section "Creating a New Session."

2 Because you're going to be recording audio, you need to create a few Audio tracks upon which to record. To do so, **click Track**, then **choose New**. The New Tracks dialog box will open.

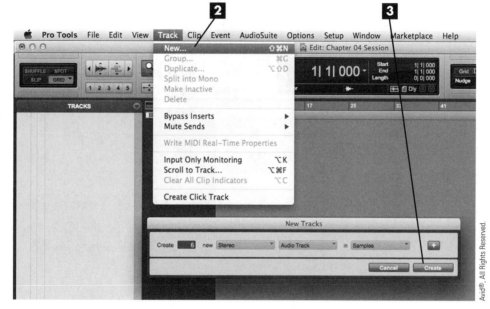

3 In the New Tracks dialog box, **create six stereo Audio tracks**.

4 It's a good practice to **name** your **tracks** before recording (the name of your clips and audio files derives from the track names). If you're working with this book's exercise materials, name your tracks the following:

- ❋ Lead Vocal
- ❋ Backing Vocals
- ❋ Fiddle
- ❋ Mandolin
- ❋ Guitar
- ❋ Bass

❋ STEREO VS. MONO TRACKS

In this exercise, you'll be recording onto stereo tracks exclusively. This is being done for simplicity's sake and for ease of use with a music-playing device as a recording source. In actual practice, you'll record to both stereo and mono tracks, based upon the number of input channels.

5 If you're not seeing the I/O column in your Edit window, you'll need to for the next section. (You learned how to do this in Chapter 3, "Getting Started with Audio," in the section "Customizing the Edit Window.") An easy way to do this is to **click** the **Edit Window View selector** and **choose I/O** from the list.

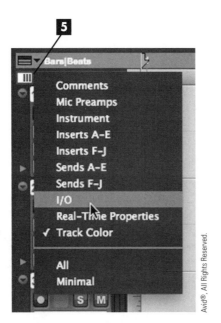

How I/O Settings Affect Your Session

It's time for the work you put into your I/O settings to start paying off. Your configuration of the I/O setup will determine how your tracks receive and output audio.

Setting Up the Output

There is an Output Path selector button (which, from here on out, I'll call the *Output button* for the sake of simplicity) in the I/O column of each track. By default, each track will be assigned to the default output as specified in the I/O Setup dialog box. In a typical studio setup, this output might be connected to your studio monitors. In any case, setting the output is easy—just follow these steps:

1 **Click** on the **Output button** for the track you want to change. An Output drop-down menu will appear.

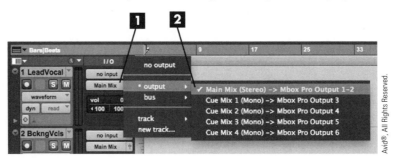

2 **Move your cursor** to **Output**. A submenu will appear, from which you can select any output path or sub-path that you created earlier in your I/O setup. In the case of recording sessions, you can change the output of any given track to be routed to your musicians' individual, or cue, mixes. (You'll learn more about setting up cue mixes in Chapter 10, "Moving to the Next Level: Tips and Tricks.") If you're using the tutorial materials, you should choose your main output path.

Setting Up the Input

The top button in the I/O column of each track shows the current input (or lack thereof) of that track. To record, you'll need to select the input that matches your recording source.

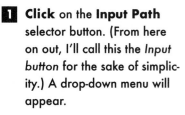

1 **Click** on the **Input Path** selector button. (From here on out, I'll call this the *Input button* for the sake of simplicity.) A drop-down menu will appear.

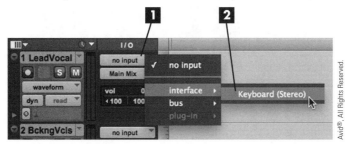

2 **Click** on the **physical input or bus** from which your audio will be coming (as specified in your I/O settings). As you did when setting up outputs, move your mouse to the appropriate type of input (interface or bus) and from there choose the specific path you want to use. The input will be selected. If you're following the tutorial, the path should be where your music player is connected. If you're recording a live musician, the input you choose for a track in a typical recording session should match the physical input on your audio interface to which his or her instrument or microphone is connected.

✳ INPUT OPTIONS

Your input options will reflect the track type. Because the track in this example is a stereo track, only stereo input paths will be displayed.

✳ INPUT VERSUS OUTPUT PATH NAMES

If you take a close look at the names of your inputs and outputs, you'll notice that the inputs are named for the paths you created in the Input tab of the I/O Setup dialog box. In contrast, the output paths are named for the paths you created in the Bus tab, followed by the output path to which the bus is assigned.

✳ RECORDING WITH BUSES

So far, you've only dealt with physical inputs as sources for audio recordings. But what about buses? Actually, using a bus as an input is done all the time, especially when working with virtual instrument plug-ins. (You'll explore that scenario in Chapter 7, "Using MIDI.") Don't worry if you're not a MIDI whiz; the section "Recording Virtual Instruments to Audio Tracks" shows a classic bus-recording scenario.

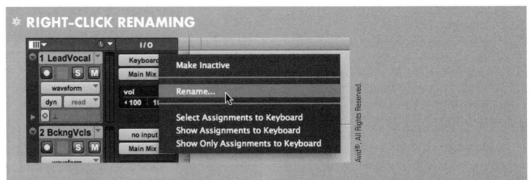

Here's a handy feature: the ability to rename inputs, outputs, and buses *without* having to go into the I/O Setup dialog box. Simply right-click on either the Input or the Output button (depending on which one you want to rename), and you'll see the drop-down menu shown here. Choose Rename from the menu to open the Rename I/O dialog box, type a new name, and click the OK button. The changes you make there will be reflected in the I/O Setup dialog box.

Setting the Output Volume

Right below the Output button, you'll see a display showing the output volume of the track. You can easily adjust the volume by clicking in the Volume field.

1 **Click and hold** in the **Volume field**. A volume fader will appear.

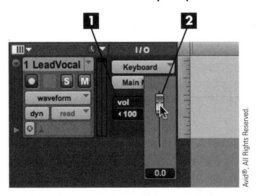

2 Still holding down your mouse button, **drag** the **fader** to the volume level you desire, and then **release** the **mouse button**. The volume will be changed.

Setting the Output Pan

Just below the Volume field, you'll find a display showing you the pan value (the placement of the audio between the left and right speakers) for the track. On mono Audio tracks, you'll see a single pan control, while on a stereo track, you'll see two pan controls (one for the left channel and one for the right channel). You can adjust a pan setting by clicking in the Pan field.

1 **Click and hold** in the Pan field. A horizontal slider will appear.

2 Still holding down your mouse button, **drag** the **slider bar** to the pan you desire and then **release** the **mouse button**. The output pan will be set.

> ❈ **IMPORTANT: RECORDING LEVELS VERSUS TRACK OUTPUT LEVELS**
>
> The changes you make to the output volume and output pan controls will affect the track's output only, not its input level. That means if you're recording an especially loud signal that is clipping (distorting) your input, you'll need to bring down the level of your sound source (instrument, microphone, and so on) rather than the volume fader on the track.

Using an Output Window

There's another way to view and manipulate essential track-related data. A track's Output window (sometimes called a *tear-away strip*) enables you to adjust many of your track's parameters through a single mixer-like interface. You can launch the Output window from either the Mix window or the Edit window. The Output window is particularly useful when adjusting mix settings in the Edit window.

1 **Click** on the **Output Window button** to the right of the Output button. (The icon looks like a tiny fader.) The track's Output window will appear. Notice that much of the track-related data you set up earlier in this chapter is shown here as well. The Output window contains the following controls:

* Track selector
* Output View selector (which enables you to quickly switch over to one of that track's sends—something I'll discuss in Chapter 8, "Basic Mixing")

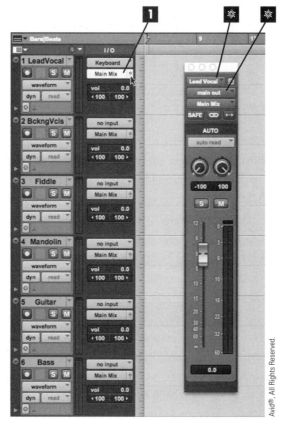

135

❈ ❈ ❈

* Output Path selector
* Pan controls
* Solo button
* Mute button
* Volume fader, with a volume meter to its right

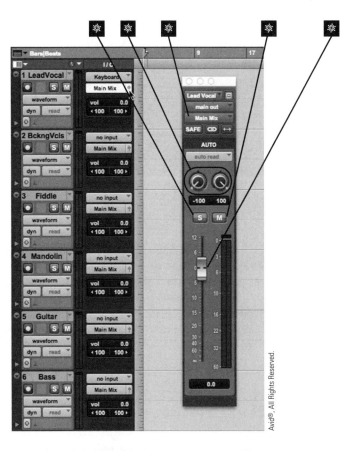

※ QUICK RESET SHORTCUT

You can quickly reset your volume to unity (0.0) or your pan to center (0) by holding the Option key (Mac) or Alt key (PC) while you click on the volume or pan controls in either the track's display fields or the Output window.

Synchronization

In many recording scenarios, you'll have to make sure that the timing of your musicians—and sometimes even the timing of other machines—lines up with the timing of your Pro Tools session. This is an essential skill for all sorts of work and is generally referred to as *synchronization*. In this section, you'll examine a number of ways to get everything in sync.

Setting Up a Click Track

You might be wondering just what a click track is. Fair question. Even though it's a common term within recording circles, it's surprising how many musicians don't know what a click track is or what it's used for. The answer is pretty straightforward: A *click track* is an audible track that indicates the tempo of a song through a series of short tones (usually click sounds, hence the name). This is similar to what a metronome does when it helps a musician keep tempo in the practice room, and the two terms are often used interchangeably.

This feature is not specific to Pro Tools. Click tracks have been used for decades, dating back to early analog recording studios, when multiple musicians would all listen to the same click track in their headphones as they played in order to stay in time with each other. Although you certainly won't need a click track every time you work with Pro Tools, you'll find that using one is a convenient way to keep everything in sync, and the ability to work with one is considered an essential skill.

Creating a click track is very simple:

1 **Click** on **Track**. The Track menu will be displayed.

2 **Choose Create Click Track**. A click track will be created.

❊ ANATOMY OF A CLICK TRACK

In case you're curious, here's what you've created: a mono Aux Input track. On this track, you'll see a small box in the Inserts column. This is a very simple virtual instrument plug-in called Click II. This primitive instrument has one simple job: to make clicks that follow the session's tempo. (You'll learn more about setting your session's tempo later in this chapter.) Despite its simplicity, you do have a few options at your disposal.

❊ NEW IN PRO TOOLS 11: CLICK II PLUG-IN

A click track is an important tool for recording musicians, and Pro Tools 11 sees an upgrade of its click plug-in. The Click II plug-in features more flexibility in terms of volume control, tonal variety, and even click resolution.

❊ IF YOU'RE FOLLOWING THE EXERCISE...

For the next section, you'll be taking a closer look at the Click II plug-in. To access the plug-in, show the Inserts A-E column in your Edit window (using the same steps you used to show the I/O column at the beginning of this chapter).

3 **Click** on the Click II plug-in's **Insert button**. (On this track, it is the small box with the C on it, for Click.) The Click II plug-in window will open.

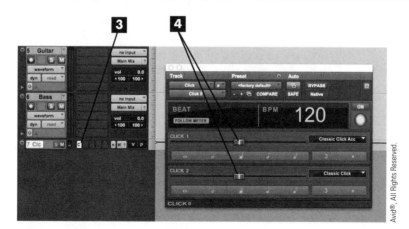

Avid®, All Rights Reserved.

4 **Adjust** the **Click 1 slider** (for each measure's Beat 1) and **Click 2 slider** (for the other beats) to get the best overall volume.

❊ ❊ ❊

5 If you want different sounds for your metronome, **click** on the **field** to the right of either click volume slider (which shows the current sound assigned to the click). A drop-down menu will appear, from which you can choose the best tone for your click. Note that you can set the Click 1 and Click 2 sounds independently.

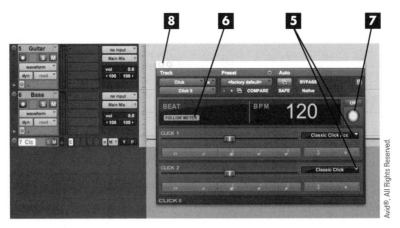

6 By default, the Click plug-in will follow the session's meter, but you do have the option of selecting any click resolution that you desire for either Click 1 or Click 2. Just **click Follow Meter** to disable the function and choose the desired click resolutions from the buttons below each volume slider.

7 Finally, a nice little new feature: a visual indicator! If you have difficulty hearing your click in a mix, you can open the plug-in window and watch the click as a flashing light. To turn off the feature, **click** the **ON button** above the visual indicator.

8 When you're finished, **click** on the **Close button**. The Click plug-in window will close.

The next thing you'll need to do is set up how your click track will behave.

1 **Click** on the **Setup** menu.

2 **Choose Click/Countoff.** The Click/Countoff Options dialog box will open.

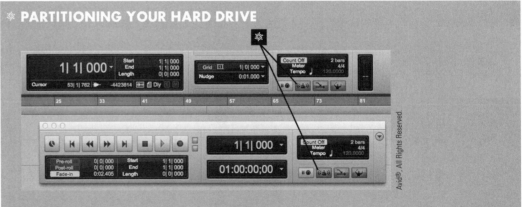

❋ **PARTITIONING YOUR HARD DRIVE**

Another way to access the Click/Countoff Options dialog box is to double-click on the Metronome icon in the MIDI controls section of either the Edit window or the Transport window.

The top three option buttons enable you to control the fundamental behavior of your click. The most common way to use a click is to hear the click when you're *recording* audio, but not when you're playing back your session. To set up your click in this manner, select the Only During Record option button.

Click/Countoff Options

Click
- During play and record
- ● Only during record
- Only during countoff

	Note	Velocity	Duration
Accented	G1	127	100 ms
Unaccented	G#1	80	100 ms

Output none

Countoff
☑ Only during record   2 Bars

Cancel   OK

Avid®, All Rights Reserved.

❆ You have the option to send click information to a MIDI synthesizer (something I'll discuss in greater depth in Chapter 7). In the case of using a MIDI synth for a click, you can enter specific notes, velocities, and durations for the accented and unaccented click sounds, according to the layout of your specific MIDI device.

❆ If you're using a MIDI synthesizer for your click source, you'll need to click on the Output button and select a MIDI output port from the menu that appears for your click information.

❆ **CLICK PLUG-IN CONVENIENCE!**

If you're using the Click plug-in (which is probably the most common way of working these days), you don't need to worry about assigning specific MIDI notes, velocities, durations, or MIDI output ports, because the Click plug-in is not a MIDI synthesizer in the traditional sense. If you followed the steps earlier in this section and created a click track from the Track menu, settings in the Accented, Unaccented, and Output rows of the Click/Countoff Options dialog box won't affect your click track one way or the other.

3 In the Countoff section, **select the Only During Record checkbox** to ensure that your countoff will be heard only before recording. During regular playback, you won't be bothered with the countoff. Of course, if you *do* want to hear a countoff when you're playing your session, just uncheck the box.

4 **Type** the **number of bars** you want for your countoff in the Bars field. The default of two measures is a common setting.

5 **Click** on the **OK button**. The Click/Countoff Options dialog box will close.

Now that the parameters of the click have been set up, the last step is to make sure that the click is actually *enabled*. The Options menu is a good place to check on the status of your click (and many other features in Pro Tools as well).

1 **Click** on **Options**. The Options menu will appear.

2 If your click is enabled, you'll see a checkmark next to the Click menu item. If there's no checkmark shown, just **click** the **menu item** to turn it on.

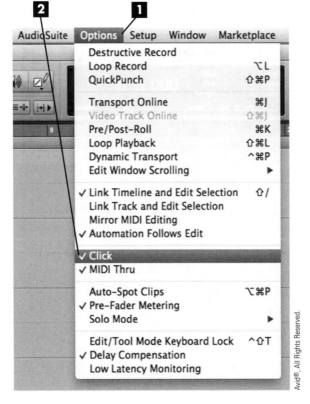

If you've followed the steps in this chapter so far, you're all set—but as with many things in Pro Tools, there's more than one way to get the job done. You can also enable the click (and the countoff) from the MIDI controls section of either the Edit or Transport window.

1 Click on the **Metronome icon** in the MIDI controls section to activate the click. When active, the button will have a blue color.

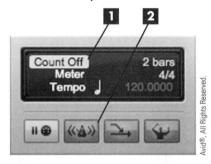

2 To activate or deactivate your countoff, **click** on the **Count Off indicator** in the MIDI controls section. An active countoff (shown here) will be displayed in black text with a green background, and an inactive countoff will be indicated by green text with a black background.

Tempo and Meter

Now that you have your click track set up, you'll need to choose the tempo and meter of your song—the two main factors controlling your session's metronome.

Basic Tempo Setup

A Pro Tools session's tempo can operate one of two ways: Either the session will follow a single tempo value (giving you a static tempo) or it will follow the Tempo ruler (which will allow you to have your song speed up and/or slow down as it plays). In this chapter, let's choose to use a static tempo. (You'll learn how to use the Tempo ruler in Chapter 7.)

1 If it is active (highlighted in blue), **click** the **Conductor Track button** to deactivate the Conductor. With the Conductor inactive, a numeric tempo display will be shown in green just above it. (You'll learn more about the Conductor in Chapter 7.)

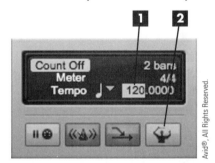

2 Click the **Tempo value area**, which will highlight the tempo number. At this point, you have a number of options as to how to set your session's tempo.

3a Type a **tempo** in the numeric Tempo value field, and then **press Return** (Mac) or **Enter** (PC).

OR

3b Click and drag your **mouse** up or down to increase or decrease the tempo value.

OR

3c Press the **T key** on your computer keyboard in tempo, and **press Return** (Mac) or **Enter** (PC) when you are finished. The numeric display will change to reflect the tempo of your taps.

Basic Meter Setup

As with tempo, you can have a constant meter (time signature) throughout your session, or you can make metric changes during the course of your song—something I'll discuss in Chapter 7. For now, though, let's set a single meter for the session. There are two ways to get the ball rolling:

1a

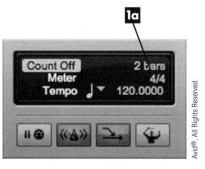

1a In the MIDI controls section of either the Edit window or the Transport window, **double-click** on the **Meter display**. The Meter Change dialog box will open.

OR

1b **Click Event, choose Time Operations**, and then **select Change Meter**. The Time Operations dialog box will appear.

2

2 Although the Meter Change and Time Operations dialog boxes appear to be quite different, they do the pretty much the same thing. Regardless of which dialog box you're looking at in your session, setting your meter is a straightforward process. **Type** a **location value** to indicate where the meter change should take place. In the Meter Change dialog box, the value is displayed in bars|beats|ticks. For this example, you want your meter to start at the beginning of the song, so **enter** a value of **1|1|000** in the Meter Change dialog box. Alternatively, simply **type 1** in the Time Operations dialog box.

❋ SNAP TO BAR

When dealing with meter changes, it's *very* unusual to have a metric change at any point other than the beginning (beat 1) of a bar. In the Meter Change dialog box, checking the Snap to Bar checkbox will place the meter change at the beginning of the bar indicated in the Location field.

3 **Type** a **value** in the New Meter field to select the meter you want to use.

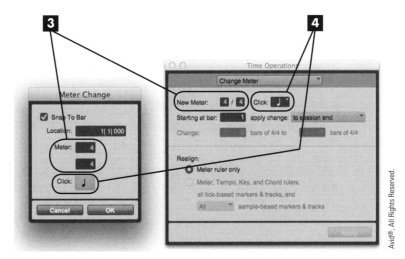

Avid®, All Rights Reserved.

4 Although a quarter note is most commonly used in click tracks, you can choose any note value for your click. **Click** on the **Click button** (or in the **Click field**, if you're working in the Time Operations dialog box). The click resolution menu will appear:

Avid®, All Rights Reserved.

5 **Click** on the **note value** that matches the desired value of your click.

6 **Click** on the **dot** if you want to use a dotted-note value for your click.

7 When you're satisfied with your settings, **Click** on the **OK button** in the Meter Change dialog box or **click** on the **Apply button** in the Time Operations dialog box. Your meter changes will be applied.

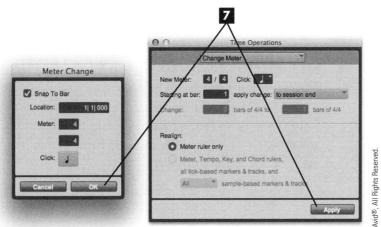

Avid®, All Rights Reserved.

❄ ❄ ❄

Online Mode

In some complex recording scenarios, Pro Tools must operate in concert with other hardware systems. Commonly, this means that Pro Tools must be set up to work with tape-based devices (video or audio) in such a way that all devices start, stop, and play together. For this sort of arrangement to work, they must be *synchronized*—in other words, when a master device starts and stops, the slave devices will follow.

Although the complexity of such setups is beyond the scope of this book, enabling Pro Tools to operate as a synchronization slave device is an easy matter— it's called *Online mode*.

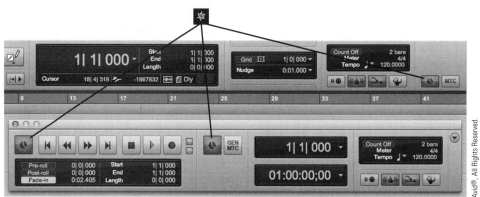

※ You'll find the Online button in your Transport window or in the Synchronization tool cluster of the Edit window. When active, the button will appear blue. With this option enabled, Pro Tools will follow the master device (which you can determine by opening the Setup menu, choosing Peripherals, and selecting Machine Control).

Once Pro Tools is put online, all transport operations will be carried out remotely. You won't need to touch the transport controls.

Generating MIDI Time Code (MTC)

Pro Tools can operate as a synchronization master device. One of the most common ways for Pro Tools to control a complex setup is through the use of *MIDI Time Code*, also known as MTC. For those technical readers, MTC is a digital form of SMPTE timecode and is transmitted to slave devices via MIDI (which you'll learn more about in Chapter 7).

❄ You'll find the Generate MTC button in the Synchronization tool cluster of the Edit or Transport window. When active, the button will appear blue. When Pro Tools is acting as an MTC master device, all devices configured to follow MIDI Time Code will follow your Pro Tools session.

❄ FOLLOWING MTC

Setting up an external device to follow MIDI Time Code is a very straightforward process, and one you'll go through in Chapter 7.

❄ WHAT ABOUT MIDI BEAT CLOCK?

Pro Tools can use two kinds of MIDI synchronization: MIDI Time Code, which I've just touched on, and MIDI Beat Clock. MIDI Beat Clock is used to keep different MIDI musical devices working at the same tempo. This is a bit different from MTC, which deals with synchronization in terms of hours, minutes, seconds, and divisions of seconds called *frames*. You'll learn more about MIDI Beat Clock and how to use it in Chapter 7.

Basic Recording

You're all set—let's go! Now you're ready to record some audio from the outside world into the Pro Tools environment.

❄ TRACKS FOR RECORDING PRACTICE

Here's where the included disc's audio CD tracks can help. If you don't have a live musician on hand, just play the audio CD. In this chapter, you'll be recording a number of tracks in series, and it's recommended that you mute each track after it's been recorded so you can listen to the track you're recording without distraction.

❄ ❄ ❄

✳ RECORDING AND TRANSPORT FADE-IN

In the Chapter 2, "Getting Around in Pro Tools," you learned about Pro Tools 11's new Transport Fade-in feature. While it's a very convenient feature to have, it's a good practice to get into to turn this feature off before recording. Having the fade-in on or off in this particular scenario won't affect the recording, but other recording scenarios (such as recording one track to another within the Pro Tools environment) will be recorded with the fade-in if it's not turned off prior to recording.

1 **Click** on the **Track Record Enable button** to "arm" the desired track for recording. Bear in mind that as soon as the track is armed, its input will be active, so take care to avoid situations that can cause feedback.

2 **Click** on the **Record button** in the Transport window or in the Edit window's transport controls. The Record button will begin to flash.

3 **Click** on the **Play button** (again, either in the Transport window or in the Edit Window's transport controls). Recording will begin. If you're following the tutorial, begin the playback of your music player after recording has started.

✳ RECORDING SHORTCUT

The shortcut for record/play is Command+spacebar (Mac) or Ctrl+spacebar (PC).

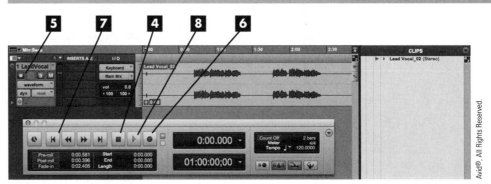

4 **Click** on the **Stop button** when you want to stop recording. A new clip will be shown in the track and will also be listed in the Clips list.

5 Before you listen to your track, **click** on the **Track Record Enable button** (to disarm the track). Otherwise, you will hear signal being inputted to the track, not the clip you've just recorded.

6 **Make sure** the **Record button** is not highlighted.

7 To make sure you're starting playback from the beginning, **click** on the **Return to Zero** button.

8 **Click** on the **Play button** or **press** the **spacebar**. You will hear your newly created track. Whoo hoo!

Other Recording Options

Congratulations! You've taken another important step down the Pro Tools road. Now let's explore some different ways to record audio that can come in useful in specific situations.

Punching In and Punching Out

Suppose you recorded a perfect take, except for just one problem section. It's something that happens in recording sessions again and again. Don't worry—with Pro Tools, you can specify a section of your track and redo it, a technique commonly called *punching in*. Remember, too, that Pro Tools generally operates *non-destructively*, so you don't have to worry about losing any of your original take!

> ❊ **IF YOU'RE USING THE EXERCISE MATERIALS...**
>
> If you're using the tutorial materials, you probably don't have any means by which to punch in another performance. In this case, recording silence is just fine for learning the process of punch-in recording.

1 **Click** on the **Selector tool**. The tool will be highlighted in blue.

2 **Mark** the **area** of **audio** that you want to re-record by clicking and dragging with your mouse.

Avid®, All Rights Reserved.

> ❊ **ANOTHER WAY TO MAKE A SELECTION**
>
> You can also make a selection during playback. Just press the Down Arrow key to begin your selection and the Up Arrow key to end your selection.

3 If your track isn't record armed already, **click** on the **Track Record Enable button** on the track you want to redo. The track will be armed for recording. The selected area, which is usually bordered by blue selection markers in the ruler area, is now bordered by red markers. These indicate that there is a track in your session that is record armed.

4 If your performer wants to hear a little bit of the original track before you start recording (that is, before you punch in), you'll want to set up pre-roll. **Click** on the **Pre-Roll button**. When active, it will be black text against a green background.

5 If you want to hear a little bit of your original track *after* your recorded section is finished (that is, after you punch out), you'll want to set up some *post*-roll. **Click** on the **Post–Roll button**. When active, it is black text against a green background.

6 **Click** inside the **numeric displays** to the right of the Pre-Roll and Post-Roll buttons, **type** the respective **lengths** of each (which can vary based on the situation and who you're recording), and **press Enter** to confirm each entry. Bear in mind that the scale of these values follows the Main Counter display.

❋ Two small gold flags will appear in the ruler area. The one to the left of your selected area represent your pre-roll, while the one to the right of the selected area is your post-roll.

❋ MAKING CHANGES

You can click and drag the arrows and flags in the ruler area to change your selection, pre-roll time, or post-roll time. You can also hold down the Option (Mac) or Alt (PC) key and, using the Selector tool, click in a track before or after a selection to instantly move your pre- or post-roll to that location.

7 **Click** on the **Record button**.

8 **Click** on the **Play button**. If you've selected a pre-roll value, your session will begin playback from the pre-roll position. If no pre-roll is selected, recording will begin immediately at the selected area.

Pro Tools will automatically start recording when the timeline insertion reaches the selected area. Pro Tools will continue recording until the end of the selection and then switch back to normal playback and continue playing for the post-roll duration (if any). When the timeline insertion reaches the end of the post-roll duration, playback will stop.

Here's what you'll end up with:

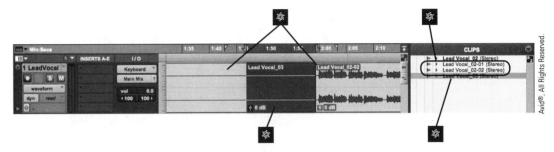

❈ Two new clips will be created, representing the "good" parts of the original take.

- ❈ Both of these new clips will appear in the Clips list. However, these clips are not shown in bold text because they are only incomplete parts of a whole file. Notice that the original take is still in the Clips list as well and is displayed in bold type (because it represents a whole file—see the sidebar "Whole-File Clips Versus Subset Clips").

- ❈ Your punch has been recorded as a new clip. In this example, I've recorded silence for visual effect.

- ❈ Your punched clip appears in bold text in the Clips list because it is a whole-file clip, which means that it represents an entire file in your Audio Files folder.

❈ WHOLE-FILE CLIPS VERSUS SUBSET CLIPS

When using Pro Tools, audio files fall into one of two categories: whole-file clips and subset clips. This is a simple but important distinction:

- ❈ Whole-file clips are clips that represent entire audio files. In other words, the clip begins at the very beginning of an audio file and ends at the very end of that file. Whole-file clips are most commonly created during the recording process and are displayed in bold text in your Clips list.

- ❈ Any clip that represents anything *other* than an entire audio file is a subset clip. Subset clips are commonly created during the editing process, when unwanted sections are trimmed from a clip. Subset clips are also automatically created when punching in and out, as shown in the preceding example.

❈ IF YOU'RE USING THE EXERCISE MATERIALS...

If you're following along with the exercise materials provided for this chapter, please undo your punch-in so that you have a complete Lead Vocal track. You can undo your punch-in by going to the Edit menu and choosing Undo Record.

QuickPunch Recording

The main limitation of the basic punch-in, punch-out workflow is that it's a one-time thing. You punch in, you punch out, and you're done. So what if you want to punch in and out more than once in a single pass? Rejoice! QuickPunch mode is for you!

1 **Click** on **Options**. The Options menu will appear.

2 **Click** on **QuickPunch**. QuickPunch record mode will be enabled, indicated by a letter P displayed inside the Record button.

❋ QUICKPUNCH SHORTCUT

Here's another way to access QuickPunch mode: Right-click on the Record button to reveal a menu of the various recording modes and select QuickPunch.

---

3 If your track isn't record armed already, **click** the **Track Record Enable button** on the track you want to redo. The track will be armed for recording.

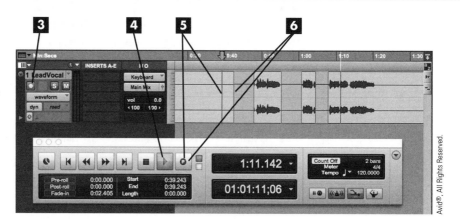

4 **Click** on the **Play button** at any point prior to when you want to record new audio. In this case, I'll start from the beginning of the session. The session will play as normal.

5 When you want to punch in, or begin recording, **click** on the **Record button** (either in the Transport window or at the top of the Edit Window). Recording will start.

6 **Click** on the **Record button** again when you want to punch out, or *stop* recording. Recording will stop, and playback will continue. When you wish to resume recording, you simply click the Record button again.

❋ ANOTHER QUICKPUNCH SHORTCUT

Here are a few ways to punch in and out in QuickPunch mode: During playback, press Command+spacebar (Mac) or Ctrl+spacebar (PC), press the 3 key on the numeric keypad, or press the F12 key.

New clips will be created in your track to reflect each time you engaged and disengaged recording. As before, new clips are also created that represent the good parts of the original take. As you might expect, new clips will also be added to the Clips list. The clips created in the track are not whole-file clips, although a whole-file clip is also created in your Clips list. This additional whole-file clip is significant in that it means that from the time you started playing back

❋ ❋ ❋

in QuickPunch mode to the time you stopped playback, you were creating a new file. That's great news for the editing phase, as you can adjust the boundaries of the clips on your track if needed.

Loop Recording

Suppose you want to record several passes of a certain section (a guitar solo, for example) and then pick the best one. In cases like this, you'll want to use Pro Tools' Loop Record function. Loop recording essentially records a selected area over and over, enabling the artist to create as many takes as desired without stopping. When you're finished, you can choose the best take or even combine takes (a process called *comping* a track, which I'll discuss in Chapter 5, "Editing").

Although loop recording has existed in Pro Tools for quite some time, how you work with loop-recorded tracks—especially in the editing phase of a project—has changed massively. I'll go through these new features and workflows in depth in Chapter 5. For now, let's lay the foundation for those workflows by setting a few preferences *before* you start loop recording.

1 **Click** on **Setup**.

2 **Choose Preferences**. The Pro Tools Preferences dialog box opens.

3 **Click** on the **Operation tab**.

4 In the upper-right area of the Pro Tools Preferences dialog box, **click** the **Automatically Create New Playlists When Loop Recording checkbox** to select it. You'll learn more about the effect of this preference in Chapter 5.

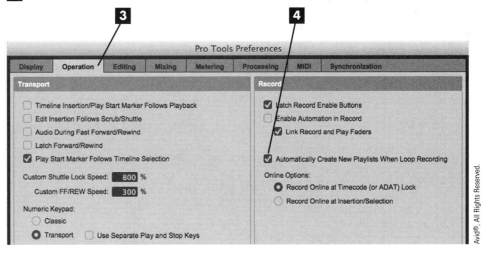

5 **Click** on the **OK button** to apply your changes and return to the session.

Now that you've laid the groundwork for more effective editing later on, you're all set to go through the normal process of loop recording.

1 **Click** on the **Options** menu.

2 **Click** on **Loop Record**. The Loop Record feature will be enabled, indicated with a check-mark next to the Loop Record option in the Options menu and a looped arrow around the Record button icon.

❋ LOOP RECORDING SHORTCUT

Alternatively, you can right-click the Record button and choose Loop from the menu that appears.

---

3 Using the Selector tool, **click and drag** over the **section** you want to loop.

4 If your track isn't record armed already, **click** on the **Track Record Enable button** on the track on which you want to loop record. The track will be armed for recording.

5 **Click** on the **Record button**.

6 **Click** on the **Play button**. Playback will begin at the pre-roll position (if pre-roll is enabled). When the selected area is reached, Pro Tools will begin recording. At the end of the selection, recording will immediately begin again from the beginning of the selection (even if pre-roll is enabled).

7 When you have enough takes, **click** on the **Stop button**. The last take will appear in the selected area.

❋ WHOLE-FILE CLIPS AND LOOP RECORDING

When you're finished with a loop-recording pass, you'll notice that there are new clips in the Clips list representing each time you looped—plus one. In the list, note that there is a whole-file clip (in bold text) in addition to the subset clips that represent individual takes. Although it's not specifically used in the track, it represents the parent file in which all the individual takes reside in sequence. Below the whole-file clip are individual takes numbered sequentially in the order in which they were recorded.

Once you're done, you can check your takes to see whether you captured a good one:

8 **Choose** the **Selector tool**.

9 **Command-click** (Mac) or **Ctrl-click** (PC) on the **loop-recorded clip**. A menu of alternate takes will appear.

10 **Click** on the **take** you want to use. The take will be selected, and the clip will be replaced. This is a great way to audition different takes to find just the right one.

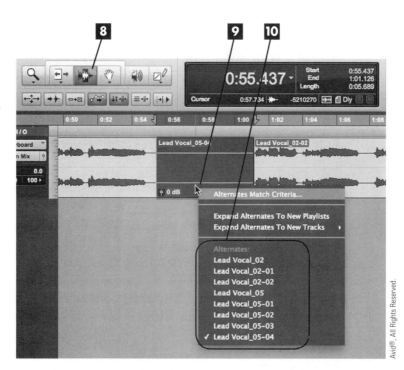

❋ RIGHT-CLICK RENAMING

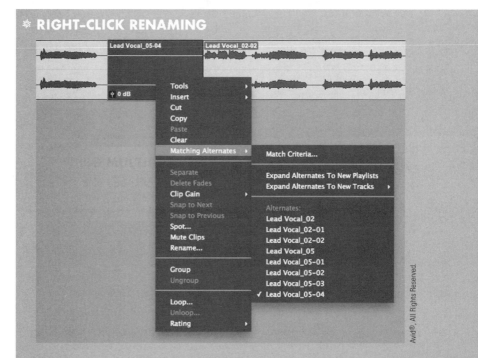

Just when you thought there couldn't *possibly* be more uses for that right mouse button, here's another one: If you right-click on your loop-recorded clip, you'll see a menu of common clip-related functions (many of which I'll get into later in this book). If you choose Matching Alternates, as shown here, you will see a submenu of matching takes, and you can choose your favorite take from the list. This method has the advantage of not requiring a modifier key, and it works with any edit tool, not just the Selector.

For the Brave: Destructive Recording

Thus far, you've seen only nondestructive recording modes—meaning that you never actually erase any audio in the process of punching in, punching out, or looping, and you can always recover your original recording pass with no loss. This is a huge advantage over working with tape, and it was one of the initial advantages of DAWs in general. With Destructive Record mode, however, you can record directly—and permanently—onto a pre-existing audio file. In some workflows—for example, final mixdown for movies and other long projects—this can be a real timesaver. Be careful, though; there's no way to undo what you've done if you make a mistake!

1 **Click** on **Options**.

2 **Click** on **Destructive Record**. Destructive Record mode will be enabled (indicated by a checkmark by the menu item and a letter D inside the Record button).

3 Using the Selector tool, **select** the **section** of the Audio track that you want to overwrite.

4 If your track isn't record armed already, **click** on the **Track Record Enable button** on the track on which you want to record. The track will be armed for recording.

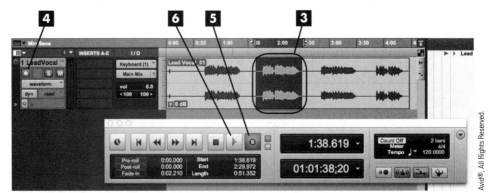

5 **Click** on the **Record button**.

6 **Click** on the **Play button**.

At this point, the process works much the same as basic punch-in and punch-out recording. Just as you saw when you did basic punch-in/punch-out, your session will begin playing at the pre-roll position (if you've enabled pre-roll), and then it will automatically begin recording at your selected area. It will stop recording at the end of your selection and play for the post-roll amount (if post-roll has been enabled).

The important distinction between Destructive Record mode and the other modes becomes apparent when the recording pass has finished.

❋❋❋

❄ Unlike the other record modes in Pro Tools, with Destructive Record mode, *no new clips* have been created—in the track itself or in the Clips list. What you've done is permanently changed the file you originally recorded!

> ### ❄ RECORD-ARMING SHORTCUT
>
> If you read the previous chapter, you know that Pro Tools includes shortcuts for mute and solo—Shift+M and Shift+S, respectively—for any tracks that contain a timeline insertion (the vertical "play" line that indicates your current location). Well, you can add another shortcut to that list: Shift+R will record-arm any tracks that contain an edit cursor.

Tips, Tricks, and Troubleshooting

Fantastic! You're on your way to running a great recording session! Before I close this chapter, here are a few tidbits to call on when you need them.

Naming Clips and Files

When it comes to good file-management practices, remember this: The names of clips and files that you create during recording will follow the names of the tracks upon which they're being recorded. For example, a track named Drums will yield recording passes named Drums_01, Drums_02, and so on. Bottom line: The best work habit is to name your tracks *before* you start recording. However, if you ever forget to do this, or if you ever want to change the name of a clip after that clip has been created, it's easy to do.

1 **Double-click** on the **clip** you want to rename (either in the Clips list or in a track with the Grabber tool selected). The Name dialog box will open.

2 **Type** a new **name** for the clip in the Name the Clip text box.

2

Name

Name the clip:

Lead Vocal_01

○ name clip only

● name clip and disk file

Cancel   OK

3a To rename the clip only and leave the audio file's name unchanged, **click** on the **Name Clip Only option button**.

OR

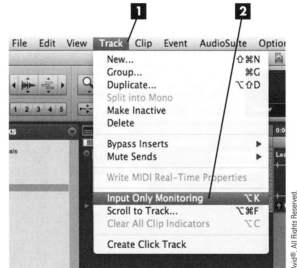

3a **3b**

4

Name

Name the clip:

Lead Vocal_01

○ name clip only

● name clip and disk file

Cancel   OK

Avid®, All Rights Reserved.

3b To rename the clip in the session *and* the audio file's name, **click** on the **Name Clip and Disk File option button**. Note that this option will be available only if the clip you are renaming is a whole-file clip.

4 **Click** on the **OK button**. The Name dialog box will close, and the clip will be renamed.

Understanding the Monitor Modes

In addition to all the different record modes you've learned about, there are two monitor modes that affect how you hear your audio during the recording process. The two modes, Auto Input Monitoring and Input Only Monitoring, will be useful in different situations.

1

2

1 **Click** on **Track**. The Track menu will appear. The monitor mode that you're *not* in will be shown as an option in this menu. In the case of the image shown here, the menu item reads Input Only Monitoring, which indicates that the current monitoring mode is Auto Input Monitoring.

File Edit View **Track** Clip Event AudioSuite Optio...

New...   ⇧⌘N
Group...   ⌘G
Duplicate...   ⌥⇧D
Split into Mono
Make Inactive
Delete

Bypass Inserts   ▶
Mute Sends   ▶

Write MIDI Real-Time Properties

Input Only Monitoring   ⌥K
Scroll to Track...   ⌥⌘F
Clear All Clip Indicators   ⌥C

Create Click Track

Avid®, All Rights Reserved.

2 **Choose** a **monitor mode**.

❋ Choose Auto Input Monitoring mode if you want to hear what was previously recorded right up to your punch-in point. Pro Tools will behave as if it is in playback mode during any pre-roll and post-roll and will automatically switch over to monitoring your live input in the selected area only. Although both monitoring modes are useful, many users employ Auto Input Monitoring mode more frequently.

❋ Choose Input Only Monitoring mode if *you don't* want to hear what you've already recorded during a punch-in/punch-out situation. Pro Tools will still only record during the selected area, but for the pre-roll and post-roll durations, you'll hear live input rather than the previously recorded track.

To the right of the transport controls (in the Edit window or the Transport window), the Input Status indicator will tell you which mode you're in. If you're in Auto Input Monitoring mode, the indicator will be off (the box will be gray), and if you're in Input Only Monitoring mode, the indicator will be green.

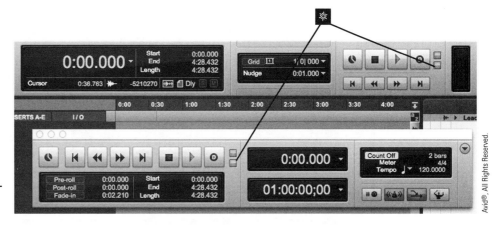

Low-Latency Monitoring

When you're recording, you might sometimes notice a bit of delay between when a note is played and when it is heard through your monitor speakers or headphones. This is called *latency*, and it's an unavoidable part of host-based DAWs in general. In Chapter 3, you learned that reducing your hardware buffer during recording can help minimize latency. There's another option available however: low-latency monitoring. This monitoring mode minimizes the process of running audio through the host computer's CPU, reducing the delay you hear.

1 **Click** on the **Options** menu.

2 **Click** on **Low Latency Monitoring** (when the option is enabled, the menu item will be indicated with a checkmark). That's it!

The good news is that your latency situation just got a lot better, but there's a small price to pay for low-latency monitoring: All inserts on any record-enabled tracks will be bypassed. For example, if you need to have an EQ plug-in on the track's insert while you're recording, low-latency monitoring isn't for you. Fortunately, having inserts on your recorded tracks is fairly rare in normal situations.

✳ LATENCY AND HD

Recording latency is an issue that must be dealt with in all host-based systems. Regardless of whether you reduce the hardware buffer or use Low Latency mode, you must make concessions in terms of the quantity and quality of the low-latency recording experience. One of the advantages of hardware-based Pro Tools|HD systems is that the business of recording isn't managed by your computer's CPU, but rather by dedicated processors that reside on cards that are added to the host computer. The result is that latency is typically not an issue when recording audio, with no need for low hardware buffer settings or low-latency modes.

❋ LOW LATENCY FOR CORE AND ASIO HARDWARE

In previous versions of Pro Tools, low-latency monitoring was an option that was possible with only a select few hardware interfaces (the Avid Mbox Pro, for example). With Pro Tools 10, that restriction was greatly reduced. Pro Tools now supports low-latency recording for devices that support Core Audio or ASIO and have built-in mixers. That said, there are a few rules to bear in mind:

* If your Core Audio or ASIO hardware doesn't have a built-in mixer, you will not have access to low-latency monitoring.
* Only outputs 1 and 2 can be used for low-latency monitoring.

❋ MBOX MINI NO LATENCY OPERATION

If you're working with an Mbox Mini audio interface, you've got yet another option for combating recording latency: the Mbox Mini's Mix knob, which is on the front panel of your Mbox Mini interface. When the knob is all the way to the input side (fully counterclockwise), you'll be monitoring signals coming directly into the interface only, and you won't hear the Pro Tools software play back at all. When the Mix knob is set all the way to playback (fully clockwise), you'll only hear audio coming from the Pro Tools software. Here's how to eliminate the latency problem using the Mbox Mini's Mix knob:

1 Set the Mix knob to 12 o'clock as a starting point, giving you an even balance between input and playback.

2 Record-arm the Audio track upon which you wish to record. If you play now, you should hear a doubled signal. The earlier signal is from the input side of the Mix knob; the latent (delayed) signal is coming from the Pro Tools software, routed through the playback side of the Mix knob.

3 Mute the track upon which you wish to record. You can still record onto the track, but you won't hear that annoying delayed signal.

4 Adjust the Mix knob to get the desired balance between your live input and the Pro Tools software playback.

5 Record as normal.

6 When you're finished recording, you can change your mix fully to playback (clockwise) so you won't be distracted by any audio going into your Mbox or Mbox 2.

❋ A SETUP FOR RECORDING PRACTICE

In this chapter, you've been working with only a single track, recorded from this book's companion exercise materials. There are five more tracks that you can practice with. If you want to check your work, you'll find a Chapter 04 Session–Finished session amongst the download materials to give you an idea of what your recording session might look like when you're finished.

I have two recommendations for working though this exercise. First, when you're finished recording each track, mute that track before moving onto the next one. That way, you'll be able to focus on the track you're currently working on. Second, when you're finished, you'll notice that the timing of the tracks will not be lined up properly. Don't fret—in Chapter 10, you'll learn a very powerful technique that'll make lining up these tracks a breeze!

Next step: editing!

5 } Editing

Audio production can be broken down into a number of phases: recording (or *tracking*), editing, mixing, and mastering, to name but a few. Like many DAWs, Pro Tools perhaps shines brightest in the editing phase. In its nonlinear environment, you can accomplish in seconds what used to take minutes or hours with tape-based systems. And of course, there is always the Undo function if you make a mistake. Even among DAWs, Pro Tools has led the pack in the world of audio editing.

In this chapter, you'll learn how to do the following:

- ❋ Take advantage of the Pro Tools Edit window.
- ❋ Use the edit modes, and know the best one to choose in any given situation.
- ❋ Work with Pro Tools' basic editing features.
- ❋ Use processes such as Cut, Copy, and Paste to create your own arrangements.
- ❋ Use Pro Tools' Playlist lanes to work with loop-recorded tracks.

> ## ❋ TUTORIAL NOTE
>
> For the purposes of this chapter, I'll be reconstructing the song from Chapter 1, "Welcome to Pro Tools 11," and Chapter 2, "Getting Around in Pro Tools," from rough elements. If you want to follow the screenshots, launch the Chapter 05 Exercise Session file included with this book's downloadable materials. For information on downloading this book's exercise materials, please refer to the "Setting Up Your Session" section of the introduction.

Understanding the Edit Window

You took a good first look at the Edit window in Chapter 2. Now it's time for a closer examination of this powerful editing environment.

Using the Tools of the Trade

Some of Pro Tools' most useful tools are located in the top row of the Edit window. Let's start with the tool clusters included with the minimal tool set.

The four edit modes—Shuffle, Spot, Slip, and Grid—are at the heart of the editing process. The mode you choose will determine how clips can be moved in time within your session. You'll learn more about these modes in the section "Moving Clips on the Timeline: The Edit Modes," later in this chapter.

The Edit tools cluster includes the most popular editing tools in the Pro Tools arsenal. From left to right on the top row, the tools are as follows:

* Zoomer
* Trim
* Selector
* Grabber
* Scrubber
* Pencil

These tools can operate directly on specific clips within your session.

The bottom row of the Edit tools cluster includes different features that you can enable or disable. These are as follows:

* Zoom Toggle
* Tab to Transients
* Mirrored MIDI Editing
* Automation Follows Edit
* Link Timeline and Edit Selection
* Link Track and Edit Selection
* Insertion Follows Playback

You'll learn more about these in the section "Basic Tool Functions" later in this chapter.

Avid®, All Rights Reserved.

The counters and edit-selection indicators give you a variety of information about both your session and where you are within it. On the left side, you'll see your session's Main Counter display, which shows you exactly where you are in your session. To the right are the Start, End, and Length displays, which show you the beginning, end, and duration of any selected area. Other displays in this cluster are related to session status.

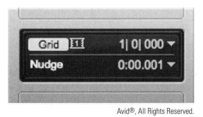

Avid®, All Rights Reserved.

I've already mentioned the Grid edit mode. Here's where you can choose the size of the grid (a topic I'll cover later in this chapter). There's also a feature that enables you to move clips by very small amounts, called *nudging*, and you can choose your nudge amount right below the grid amount. I'll talk about nudging clips in Chapter 6, "...And More Editing."

Avid®, All Rights Reserved.

Although they're not part of the minimal tool set, you'll find the Zoom controls cluster particularly useful. The Zoom controls cluster enables you to quickly zero in on a very brief section of your session (useful for fine editing) or zoom out to view longer sections in your project. The numbered buttons on the bottom of the Zoom controls cluster enable you to save your favorite zoom settings as zoom presets.

You can also zoom in or out using other methods, which will enable you to view your clips in different ways. I'll discuss these later in this chapter.

Navigating Your Session

Before you can do anything else, you need to know the basics of how to get around. You'll find that the Selector tool is well suited to this task. Along with this tool, you'll want to use the location displays to their best advantage.

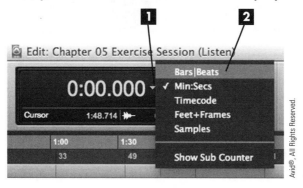

1 Right now, the Main Counter display shows time in terms of minutes and seconds. You can view time in a number of other ways, however. **Click** on the **arrow** to the right of the Main Counter display. A drop-down menu will appear.

2 **Choose** the desired **scale** for your session. For this example, **choose Bars|Beats**. The time scale of the Main Counter display will change to reflect your selection.

In many cases, you might want to see the passage of time in two ways simultaneously. In the case of a music project, for example, you might be working in terms of bars and beats, but you might also want to see where you are in the real-time scale of minutes and seconds. That's where the Sub Counter can help.

1 **Click** on the **arrow** to the right of the Main Counter display. A drop-down menu will appear.

2 **Choose Show Sub Counter.** The Sub Counter display will appear.

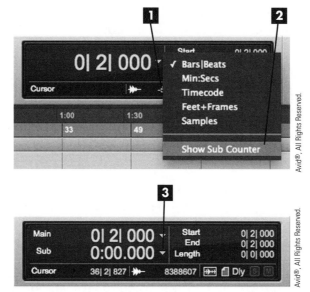

3 **Choose** the desired **scale** for your Sub Counter display. In this case, I'll **choose Min:Secs**, or minutes and seconds, so that I can view my position in terms of not only bars and beats (in the Main Counter display), but in real time as well.

Now that you have your counters set up, you're all set to roam your session!

1 Click on the **Selector tool**.

2 Click anywhere in the session's edit area. A small line (called the *timeline insertion*) will appear where you clicked. Your timeline insertion's location is precisely noted in the Main Counter and Sub Counter displays.

> ✻ The Start display will also show the timeline insertion location. Because you've selected only a single location, the End value is identical to the Start value, and the Length value is zero.

✻ SELECTION DISPLAY SCALE

The scale of the edit-selection indicators (to the right of the Main Counter display) will change to match the Main Counter's scale. For example, if you change the Main Counter's scale to Bars|Beats, any selections you make will also be shown in bars and beats in the edit-selection display area.

Now, try to make a different kind of selection:

1 Still using the Selector tool, click and **drag** (to the left or right) in a track to make a selection with a length greater than zero. The selection you make in the track is mirrored in the ruler. A blue down arrow in the ruler indicates the beginning of the selection, and an up arrow indicates the end.

> ✻ The Main Counter and Sub Counter displays show the start of your selection.
> ✻ The edit-selection indicators show the start, end, and length of your selection.

Navigating with the Tab Key

The Selector tool is one way to get around your session, but it's not the only way. For example, the Universe section of the Edit window (which you explored back in Chapter 2) is a way to navigate as well. There's also the Tab key (on your computer's keyboard), which can really be useful in a number of different ways. Let's take a look.

The Tab key can be set up to operate in one of two different modes. You'll look at the most basic mode first, so you need to make sure that the Tab to Transients mode is *disabled*.

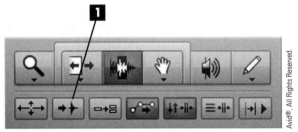

Avid®, All Rights Reserved.

1 Immediately below the Trim tool in the Edit tools cluster, you'll find the Tab to Transients button. When enabled, this button is colored blue. Because you want this mode to be disabled for the time being, **make sure** the **Tab to Transients button is toggled off** and is shown in a basic gray color.

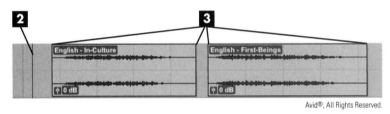

Avid®, All Rights Reserved.

2 Using the Selector tool, **click** on a **track** with a number of clips, before a given clip. (If you're working with the tutorial session, try working with the English track.) The timeline insertion will appear wherever you click.

3 **Press** the **Tab key**. The timeline insertion will move to the next clip boundary (in this case, the start of a clip). Each additional time you press the Tab key, the timeline insertion will move to the next clip boundary (moving from left to right).

❋ **MODIFYING THE TAB KEY BEHAVIOR**

Here's a twist on using the Tab key: Hold the Ctrl key (PC) or the Option key (Mac) while you press the Tab key to move the timeline insertion to the *previous* clip boundary (moving right to left).

With Tab to Transients enabled, the Tab key will continue to jump to clip boundaries, but it will also stop at each transient.

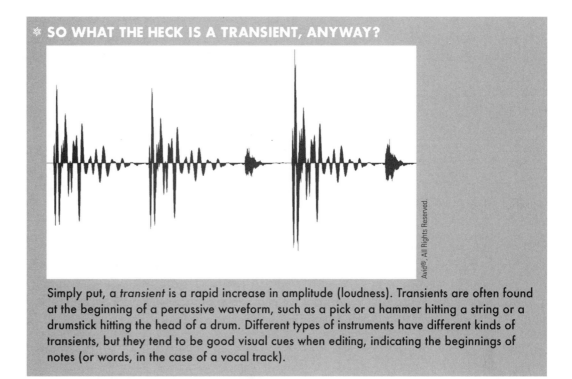

❋ SO WHAT THE HECK IS A TRANSIENT, ANYWAY?

Simply put, a *transient* is a rapid increase in amplitude (loudness). Transients are often found at the beginning of a percussive waveform, such as a pick or a hammer hitting a string or a drumstick hitting the head of a drum. Different types of instruments have different kinds of transients, but they tend to be good visual cues when editing, indicating the beginnings of notes (or words, in the case of a vocal track).

The first step in the process is to turn Tab to Transients mode on:

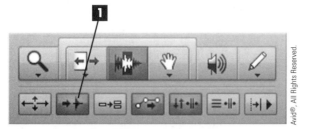

1 The Tab to Transients button will let you know if it's enabled or disabled. When enabled, this button will be colored blue. If the button is disabled (the color will be a basic gray), just **click** on the **Tab to Transients button** to turn Tab to Transients mode on.

2 Using the Selector tool, **click** on a **track** with at least one clip, before a clip, as shown here. (If you're using the tutorial session, the Intro Drum track shows this feature well.)

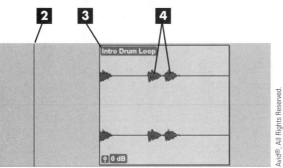

3 **Press** the **Tab key**. The timeline insertion will immediately jump to the start of the clip. Regardless of whether Tab to Transients is enabled or disabled, the Tab key can always be used to quickly move to clip boundaries (start or end).

4 **Press** the **Tab key** again. This time, instead of moving directly to the next clip boundary, the timeline insertion will jump from transient to transient. This is a fantastic way to locate drum hits and other transient-based audio.

❋❋❋

Again, the Ctrl key (PC) or the Option key (Mac) will move the timeline insertion backward in time, this time to the *previous* transient peak.

✳ MAKING SELECTIONS WHILE TABBING

If you want to make a selection while you're moving with the Tab key, just hold down the Shift key as you tab. This is particularly useful in combination with Tab to Transients and is a quick and effective way to select transient-heavy phrases (such as drum beats, for example).

Zooming

Sometimes, when you're editing a specific section, you'll want to get a close look at your audio. Then, once you're finished, you might want to take a step back and get an overview of your entire session. To do either of these things, you'll need to know how to use the zoom tools.

If your Zoom controls cluster isn't showing, follow these steps to display them:

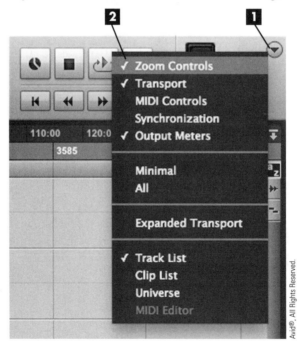

1 **Click** on the **Edit Window Toolbar Menu button** (in the upper-right corner of the Edit window). The Edit Window Toolbar menu will appear.

2 **Choose Zoom Controls.** The tools currently displayed in your Edit window will be indicated by a checkmark.

With the Zoom controls cluster visible, zoom in and out as follows:

1 **Click** on the **left zoom arrow button** to zoom out. Each time you click on this button, the Edit window will show you a greater span of time.

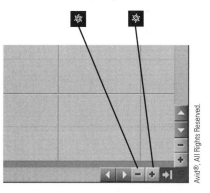

2 **Click** on the **right zoom arrow button** to zoom in. Each time you click on this button, you will gain a finer view of your session's timeline.

❉ ZOOMING BEHAVIOR

Notice that your zooming centers on your timeline insertion's location.

Even if you don't have the Zoom controls cluster shown at the top of the Edit window, you still have access to zoom buttons. You'll find them in the lower-right corner of the playlist area in the Edit window.

❉ Click on the minus (−) button to zoom out.

❉ Click on the plus (+) button to zoom in.

❉ CONTINUOUS ZOOMING

Clicking any of these zoom buttons (either at the top or the bottom of the Edit window) will incrementally zoom you in or out, but you can also smoothly zoom by clicking and holding on any horizontal zoom button and dragging your mouse to the left or right.

❉ ZOOMING SHORTCUTS

You might use these shortcuts more than any others covered in this book. On a PC, you press Ctrl+] (right bracket) to zoom in and Ctrl+[(left bracket) to zoom out. On a Mac, pressing Command+] will zoom in, and Command+[will zoom out. You can also press Command+T (Mac) or Ctrl+T (PC) to zoom in and Command+R (Mac) or Ctrl+R (PC) to zoom out.

❉ ❉ ❉

Here's another way to zoom in on a specific section.

1 **Click** on the **Zoom tool**.

2 **Click and drag** horizontally on a **track** to select an area.

3 **Release** the **mouse button**. The view will zoom in on the selected area.

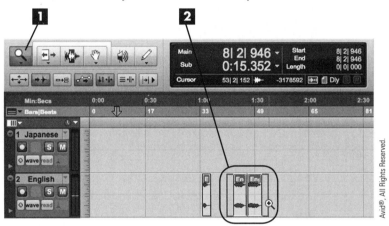

Moving Clips on the Timeline: The Edit Modes

Pro Tools has four basic edit modes that determine how clips can be moved in your session. Each mode is unique, and as you gain experience with each of them, you'll get a feeling for which mode is best suited to any given task. In the examples shown, you'll use different edit modes to bring audio clips from the Clips list onto tracks, but you can also use these edit modes to move existing clips on a track.

Using Shuffle Mode

Shuffle mode is a very simple and straightforward edit mode, so it's a good place to start. When you see how this mode works, you'll see how it can be useful for stitching together verses, choruses, and so on into a seamless final product!

If you're using the Chapter 05 Exercise session, you'll see that the top track (named "Japanese") is empty. In this section, you'll use Shuffle mode to reconstruct that track.

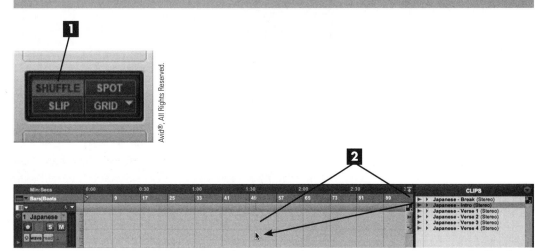

1 **Click** on the **Shuffle button**. The mode will be selected.

2 Let's start off by dragging a clip onto an empty track. If you're using the exercise session, **drag** the **Japanese–Intro clip** onto the blank Japanese track. You can drop the clip anywhere on the timeline.

❋ Note that, regardless of where you dropped the clip, the clip is deposited at the beginning of the track.

3 Now let's try dragging additional clips onto the track. If you're using the exercise material, add the clips to the track in the following order:

- ❋ Japanese–Verse 4
- ❋ Japanese–Verse 2
- ❋ Japanese–Verse 3
- ❋ Japanese–Verse 1
- ❋ Japanese–Break

Notice that when you drop the clips into an empty section of the track, they snap end to end with the previous clip, starting with the first clip, which automatically snaps to the beginning of your track.

❋ ❋ ❋

4 These clips are out of order. Let's shuffle them a bit. **Click** on the **Grabber tool** if it's not already selected.

5 **Click and hold** on a **clip** that you want to move. For the purposes of this example, use the Japanese-Verse 1 clip.

6 **Drag** the **clip** over another clip on the track. A gold-colored line will appear at the clip boundaries, indicating where the clip would be repositioned if the mouse button were released. If you're using the exercise materials, move the track so that it is deposited after the Japanese-Intro clip.

7 **Release** the **mouse button** when the clip is at the desired location. The clips will be reorganized.

> ❋ **IF YOU'RE USING THE EXERCISE MATERIALS...**
>
> In this section, you're using Shuffle mode to rebuild the Japanese vocal track. Here's the correct order of the clips:
>
> Japanese-Intro
>
> Japanese-Verse 1
>
> Japanese-Break
>
> Japanese-Verse 2
>
> Japanese-Verse 3
>
> Japanese-Verse 4

Note that all clips are still adjacent to each other, despite the fact that their order has been changed. Of course, you can move more than one clip at a time. In fact, you can shuffle clips forward and backward at will and create new arrangements of these clips, while keeping all the clips snugly end to end.

Using Slip Mode

When you need flexibility, Slip mode gives you the most freedom of clip movement.

❋ **IF YOU'RE USING THE EXERCISE MATERIALS...**

If you're using the downloadable Chapter 05 Exercise session, you'll be placing a reverse guitar sound effect after the first verse of "Listen."

1 **Click** on the **Slip button**. The mode will be selected (indicated by the word "Slip" shown in black text against a green background).

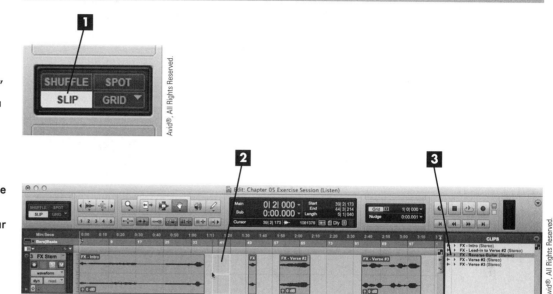

2 **Click and hold** a **clip** in the Clips list. (In this case, I've chosen the FX–Reverse Guitar clip.)

3 **Drag** the **clip** onto the desired track. (If you're using the exercise session, you'll want to deposit the clip on the FX Stem track.) You will see an outline of the clip, indicating where it will be placed when you release the mouse button.

❋ **IF YOU'RE USING THE EXERCISE MATERIALS...**

If you're using the downloadable Chapter 05 Exercise session, deposit the FX–Reverse Guitar clip on the FX Stem track at approximately 39|2|000.

❋ **SOME RULES ON ADDING CLIPS TO TRACKS**

It's important to remember that when you're working with mono clips, you can drop them only onto mono tracks. However, when you drag stereo clips onto the timeline, they can occupy a single stereo track or two mono tracks.

❋ **HEY, WHERE AM I?**

It might seem unusual, but your Main Counter display will not be much help while you're moving clips. It will continue to show the current position of your timeline insertion. However, the edit-selection indicators (to the right of the Main Counter display) will reflect the beginning, end, and duration of the dragged clip as you move it, helping you get it to the desired position.

Using Grid Mode

Sometimes it's convenient to have your clips snap to a grid of user-definable increments. This can be particularly useful when you're working on a music-based project, when it's often helpful to have your clips align themselves to bars and beats. Pro Tools actually gives you two ways of doing this sort of grid-based work, which I'll cover here.

> ❋ **TAKING A BREAK FROM THE CHAPTER 05 EXERCISE SESSION**
>
> The demonstration of Grid mode that follows isn't based upon the Chapter 05 session that you've been working with up to now. If you'd like to follow along with the steps here, save and close the Chapter 05 Session file and open the Chapter 05–Grid Mode Session file, which is included with the book's downloadable materials.

Absolute Grid Mode

First, let's take a look at Grid mode in a typical music context.

> ❋ **IF YOU'RE USING THE EXERCISE MATERIALS...**
>
> If you're looking at the Chapter 05–Grid Mode Session file, you'll see that the Kick track is empty. You'll use Absolute Grid mode to create a kickin' Kick track. (Sorry, couldn't resist!)

1 Make sure that your Main Counter display is showing you the kind of information you need. In this example, you'll want to view your location in terms of bars and beats. If that's not what you're seeing in your Main Counter display, **click** on the **Main Counter display's down arrow** and **choose Bars|Beats**. The scale will be shown in Bars|Beats|Ticks. Notice that the edit-selection indicators also change scale.

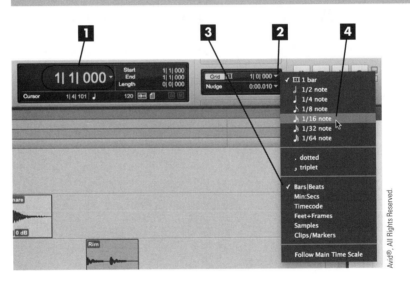

2 Check your grid value to make sure it's what you want, and make the appropriate changes if needed. **Click** on the **Grid Value arrow**. The Grid Value menu will appear.

3 **Select** the desired **scale** for your grid. Because you're working with music in this case, Bars|Beats is a good fit. The scale will be selected, indicated by a checkmark.

4 **Choose** the desired **resolution** for your grid. For the purposes of this example, let's **choose 1/16 note**.

❋ FOLLOW MAIN TIME SCALE

At the very bottom of the Grid Value menu, you'll find a Follow Main Time Scale option. When you choose this (indicated by a checkmark), the grid scale will automatically change whenever you change the Main Counter display's scale. For many users, it's a very convenient way to work.

❋ BARS|BEATS GRID INCREMENTS

Because this scale is musical, you will see grid resolutions such as bars, half notes, quarter notes, and so on. At the bottom of the resolution section of the menu, you'll also see options for dotted-note and triplet-based grids.

❋ HEY, WHERE ARE MY GRID LINES?!?

Normally, you'll see a series of vertical lines to indicate your grid positions. When grid lines are being shown, the word "Grid" will appear in black text against a green background. If you're not seeing them, just click the word "Grid" in the Grid Value display. On the other hand, if you ever want to hide your grid lines for any reason, you can click the word "Grid" to toggle the lines off. (When the grid lines are hidden, the word "Grid" appears in green text against a black background.)

5 In the Edit Modes tool cluster, **click** on the **Grid button**. When Absolute Grid mode is active, the word "Grid" will appear in black text against a blue background.

6 Just as you did before, **drag** a **clip** from the Clips list onto the track area. In Absolute Grid mode, the clip will snap to the nearest bar as you drag it. If you're using the exercise session, drag the Kick 1 clip onto the Kick track, and move it to the beginning of the track.

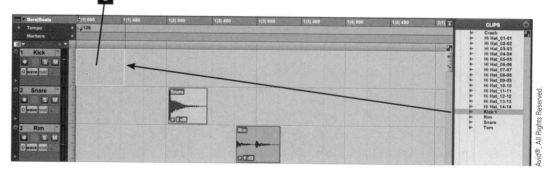

The essence of Absolute Grid mode is simple: Clips will strictly align themselves with the grid values. In this case, with our grid value being a 1/16 note, your clips will always snap to the nearest 1/16 note increment.

You can experiment to your heart's content when it comes to creating your Kick track. If you're at a loss as to where to put the Kick 1 clip, just drag it to these three locations:

❋ 1|1|000

❋ 1|3|000

❋ 1|3|720

With these locations used, the final Kick track should look like this:

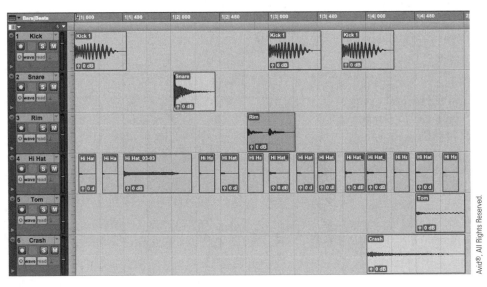

The format of these locations is Bars|Beats|Ticks. So, for example, the first clip is positioned at the first beat of the first bar, with no ticks. The second clip is positioned at the third beat of the first bar, with no ticks. Finally, the last clip is positioned 720 ticks after the third beat of the first bar. Don't worry if this sounds like gobbledygook—I'll discuss this in more detail in the next chapter.

Relative Grid Mode

There's a second Grid mode available to you, called *Relative Grid mode*. This mode won't move clips to the nearest grid line, but rather will move clips by the grid value that you set. Here's a hypothetical situation that shows the operation of Relative Grid mode.

This Chapter 05–Grid Mode Session example has a number of drum tracks. On the Snare track, you have a single snare drum hit. Using Slip mode, I've dragged this clip a little to the right of the beat 2 grid line. (If you're working with the tutorial session, you'll see that the clip has been placed at 1|2|027.) This is to "lay back" and give the beat a bit of a groove.

Suppose you want to move that snare clip to the fourth beat, but you don't want to lose that laid-back feel. Relative Grid mode will enable you to do just that: Move the clip and maintain a consistent distance from the grid line.

1 Click and hold the **Grid button**. The Grid Mode menu will appear.

2 Choose **Relative Grid** from the menu. The Grid button will now appear in purple and will read "Rel Grid."

3 If it's not already selected, **choose** the **Grabber tool** from the Edit tools cluster at the top of the window.

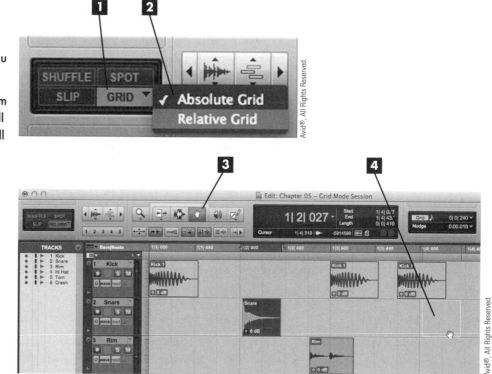

4 With Relative Grid mode selected, **click and drag** the **clip** to its new position. (In this case, I've dragged it to just after the fourth beat.) You'll see that as you drag your clip, it moves by the 1/16-note grid value, maintaining its offset from the grid lines.

❋ COPYING WHILE DRAGGING: A NEW KEY COMMAND

I'll talk more about editing in the next chapter, but there's one thing you might like to try with this example. Hold down the Option (Mac) or Alt (PC) key as you drag a clip with the Grabber tool to make a copy of the clip as you drag it.

❋ A FINISHED EXAMPLE

In addition to the Chapter 05–Grid Mode session, you'll also see another session file named Chapter 05–Grid Mode–Finished. This session is what you'll see if you followed the steps in this section.

❋ BACK TO THE TUTORIAL

If you're following the steps outlined here, you should move back to the Chapter 05 Exercise Session file that you saved before working with Grid mode.

❋ ❋ ❋

Using Spot Mode

Spot mode is very popular in audio post-production situations, where users commonly want to assign a clip to a specific place in time. For example, if you want a specific sound effect to occur at a specific point, with Spot mode, you can just type in the location for your clip.

> ❋ **IF YOU'RE USING THE EXERCISE MATERIALS...**
>
> If you're following along with the "Listen" exercise session, you might notice that there is no spoken word at the end of the piece, as there was in the original version. That's where you come in. Your job is to move the missing clips from the Clips list to the English track, and to use Spot mode to place them in exactly the right place.

1 **Click** on the **Spot button**.

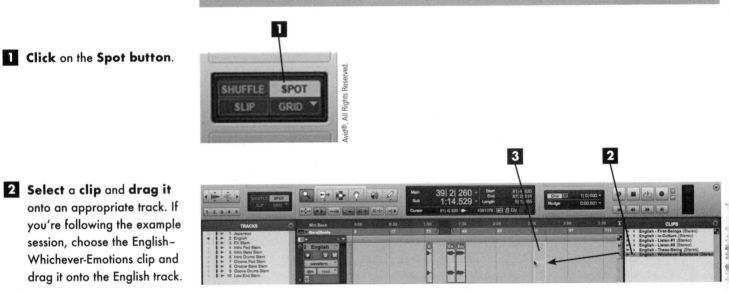

2 **Select** a **clip** and **drag it** onto an appropriate track. If you're following the example session, choose the English–Whichever-Emotions clip and drag it onto the English track.

3 **Release** the **mouse button** to drop the clip on the track. Similar to when you used Shuffle mode, it doesn't matter where in the timeline you drop the clip. The Spot dialog box will open.

4 **Click** on the **Time Scale menu** and **select** the **time scale** you want to use to position your clip. (You can choose Bars|Beats, Min:Secs, Timecode, Feet+Frames, or Samples.) For the purposes of this example, **choose Min:Secs**.

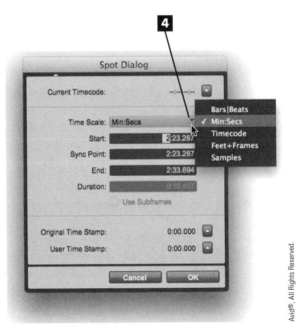

5 You can choose to place your clip's start, end, and sync point at a position that you type into the appropriate field. (I'll talk about sync points in Chapter 10, "Moving to the Next Level: Tips and Tricks.") Very often, users are most concerned about the placement of the start of the clip, so let's try moving the clip's beginning to a specific point in time. **Type** exactly **where you want your clip to begin** in the Start field. If you're using the exercise session materials, **type 3:17.991**.

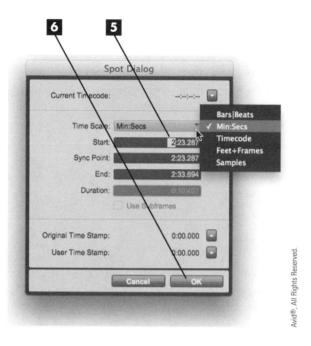

Avid®, All Rights Reserved.

6 **Click** on the **OK button**. The clip will be placed on the track at the specified location.

❋ **IF YOU'RE USING THE EXERCISE MATERIALS...**

If you're working with the exercise session, there are three clips to move to the English track. Using Spot mode, you can place them just where they need to go:

* ❋ English–Whichever-Emotions: 3:17.991
* ❋ English–These-Being: 3:29.366
* ❋ English–Listen #2: 3:38.302

❋ **MULTIPLE EDIT MODES**

Avid®, All Rights Reserved.

The idea of having more than one edit mode active at a time might seem a bit strange to long-time Pro Tools users, but it's a recent feature that is actually quite useful and straightforward. With this feature, you can combine either Shuffle, Slip, or Spot mode with Grid mode. Setting this up is easy: Simply select your primary mode (Shuffle, Slip, or Spot), and then hold the Shift key as you click the Grid button.

Once you've set up your two modes, how will your tools behave? It's actually pretty simple: The Selector and Trim tools will operate in Grid mode, and your Grabber tool will work according to the rules of the other mode. For example, if you choose both Shuffle and Grid mode, you can select an area of a large clip according to a grid and then separate the clip (something you'll learn more about later in this chapter) and move the clip in Shuffle mode.

Basic Tool Functions

The three main edit tools you'll use are the Trim, Selector, and Grabber tools. I've touched on some of their functions already, but let's go just a bit deeper so you can make the most of them.

Understanding the Trim Tool

The first tool you'll look at is the Trim tool. Its basic function is to change the left or right boundary of a clip.

> ### ❈ IF YOU'RE USING THE EXERCISE MATERIALS...
>
> If you're going through the steps with the exercise session provided, you'll see that the Intro Bass Stem track has audible material at the beginning of the song, but a stretch of silence after about measure 34. Removing the unneeded part of that clip will help with your session's performance, and the Trim tool will help you do just that!

> ### ❈ MAKING THINGS GO A BIT MORE SMOOTHLY
>
> This tool can get a little tricky when you're working in Spot mode. For simplicity's sake, change your edit mode to Slip mode.

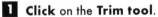

1 Click on the Trim tool.

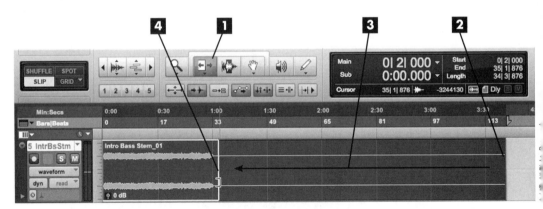

2 Position your cursor near the beginning or end of a clip that you wish to change. The cursor will take on the appearance of a bracket, indicating that the Trim tool is ready to be used. The direction the cursor is facing depends on your cursor's position within a clip.

3 Click and drag the clip boundary horizontally. You will see a graphic representation of how your clip will be altered as you drag.

4 When you have reached the desired position, release the mouse button. The clip will be changed accordingly.

There are a few things to keep in mind when you're using the Trim tool:

❄ Trimming a clip is nondestructive. It only changes the part of the audio file you are choosing to hear in your session.

❄ When you use the Trim tool on a whole-file clip, a new clip will be created in the Clips list.

❄ When you're in Grid mode, your trimming will snap to the current grid values. This is particularly useful when you're editing drum beats and other musical material.

Understanding the Selector Tool

You've already used the Selector tool to choose a section of your session to play. You can do other things with the Selector tool as well. For example, let's try removing a portion of a clip.

❄ **IF YOU'RE USING THE EXERCISE MATERIALS...**

Just like the intro Bass Stem track, the Intro Pad Stem track has a long stretch of silence. Because the silence is in the middle of the clip, though, the Trim tool won't do you much good. Let's use the Selector tool to choose the unwanted portion and delete it from the timeline.

1 Click on the **Selector tool**.

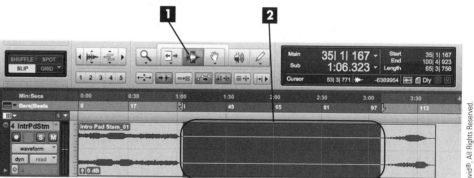

Avid®, All Rights Reserved.

2 Starting in one corner, **click and drag** a **square area** that includes the elements you wish to remove from your session. A dark box will indicate what you've selected.

3 Press the **Delete key**. The clips (or portions of clips) will be removed from your tracks.

❄ **THE POWER OF A NONDESTRUCTIVE ENVIRONMENT**

Remember that Pro Tools is (for the most part) a nondestructive DAW. The clips you clear from your tracks won't be removed from the Clips list or your hard drive. Nondestructive also means that you can easily undo what you've done (by choosing Undo from the Edit menu), which you should do right now, to set up the next section.

If you want to select an area that spans a number of tracks, it's easy to do. Just click and hold in one corner of the area that you want to select, and drag your cursor diagonally until you've highlighted the material that you want.

Link Track and Edit Selection

There's another way to easily make selections over a number of tracks or to move a selected area from one track to another. It's a feature called Link Track and Edit Selection, which enables you to assign edit selections based upon track selections and vice versa. In a nutshell, here's how it works:

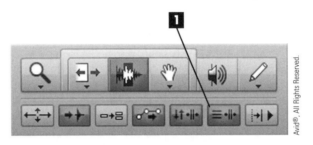

Avid®, All Rights Reserved.

1 The first thing to do is to enable this feature. The Link Track and Edit Selection button is just below the Scrub tool. Just **click** the **Link Track and Edit Selection button** to enable or disable the feature. (When enabled, the button will appear blue.)

✻ Note that any track that has a selected area is also selected.

1 To move the selected area to another track, simply **click** the target track's **name**. The selection will migrate immediately to the newly selected track.

If you want to select a consecutive block of tracks (and hence have a selected area that spans those tracks), just hold down the Shift key when you click the tracks' names. If you want to add or remove track selections individually, just hold down the Ctrl (PC) or Command (Mac) key while you click the desired track name(s).

Understanding the Grabber Tool

Last but not least, you have the Grabber tool. You've used it before, but this section will show you how to move more than one clip at a time.

1 Click on the **Grabber tool**.

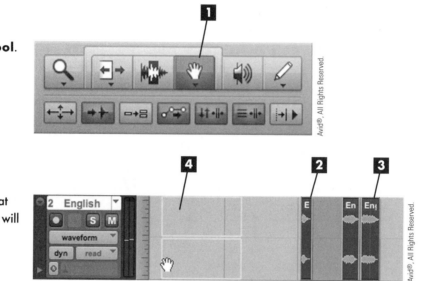

2 Click on a **single clip** that you wish to move. The clip will be highlighted.

3 **Press and hold** the **Shift key** and **click** on any **additional clips** that you might want to move. The clips will be highlighted.

❄ GRABBING A BLOCK OF TIME

As you grab additional clips using the Grabber tool, a shaded area will appear. This area will include not only all the clips you have selected, but also all clips that fall within that shaded area. This is the normal operation of the basic Grabber tool, which is more accurately known at the Time Grabber. There are variations of the Grabber tool (the Object Grabber and the Separation Grabber), which you'll explore in Chapter 6.

---

4 **Drag and drop** the **clips** you selected. As you drag, a box shows you where your clips will be deposited.

❄ SETTING THINGS UP FOR THE NEXT SECTION

Please undo any changes you've made with the Grabber tool before progressing to the next section.

Assembling a Track

Now you're going to combine a number of tools you've already worked with, plus a few editing tricks, to re-create the missing bits of "Listen." In addition to tools from this chapter, you'll be drawing on some knowledge you picked up in earlier chapters as well. When you're finished, you'll have a good idea of how you can assemble tracks of your own!

Creating Clips

You've already created clips through the process of importing and recording audio, but that's only the beginning of the story. In this section, you'll create new clips for your track based upon pre-existing clips.

Here's a scenario: You've got a track in your Chapter 05 Exercise session called "Groove Bass Stem." While there are some good bits in there, there are also a lot of silent spaces that need to be filled. Here are a couple methods you can use to separate the useful bits from the rest, so that you can use those clips later.

Capturing a Selection

> ❄ **SETTING THINGS UP FOR THIS SECTION**
>
> If you're following with the Chapter 05 Exercise session, Grid mode will suit you well in this case. For a grid resolution, choose 1 Bar. Finally, make sure that you've chosen the Selector tool, and you're all set to proceed.

1 **Select** the **material** on a track that you want to use. If you're using the exercise material, **select between 35|1|00 and 37|1|000** on the Groove Bass Stem track.

2 **Click** on **Clip**. The Clip menu will appear.

3 **Click** on **Capture**. The Name dialog box will open.

4 **Type** a descriptive **name** for your new clip in the Name the Clip text box. If you're using the tutorial session, **name** this clip **Bass Loop–Capture**.

5 **Click** on the **OK button**. The Name dialog box will close, and the new clip—a copy (or capture) of the area you selected—will be created. You can see your newly created clip in the Clips list.

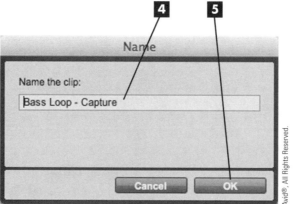

Separating a Clip

Here's another way to create a clip from a selected area. This time, instead of capturing a selection, you're simply going to start chopping up your big clip into smaller, more manageable bits. Visually, these two methods might appear quite similar, but by separating a clip, you'll be creating a new clip in the Clips list *and* in your track simultaneously. (Capturing will only create a new clip in the Clips list.)

1 Using the Selector tool, **select** the **material** on a track that you want to use. If you're using the exercise material, **select between 35|1|00 and 37|1|000** on the Groove Bass Stem track.

2 **Click** on **Edit**. The Edit menu will appear.

3 **Move your cursor** to **Separate Clip**. A submenu will appear.

4 **Choose At Selection.** A new clip will be created.

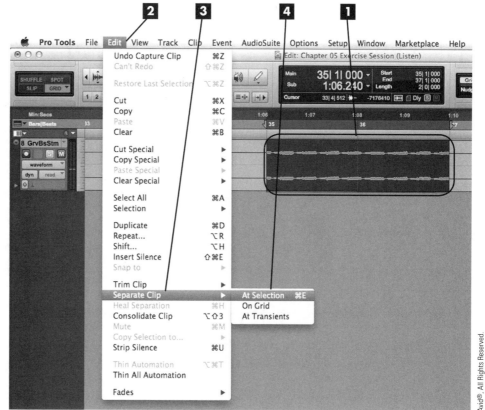

Your original clip has been separated into three smaller clips. The clip that matches your selection will be in the middle.

Renaming a Clip

At any time in the editing process, you might want to manually rename a clip in your session. Here's how to do it:

1 Click on the **Grabber tool**.

2 **Double-click** on the **clip** you want to rename. The Name dialog box will open.

3 **Type** the **name** you want for the clip in the Name the Clip text box.

4 Click on the **OK button**. The Name dialog box will close, and the clip will be renamed.

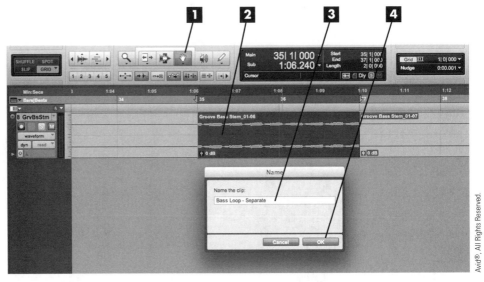

❖ **IF YOU'RE USING THE EXERCISE MATERIALS...**

If you're working with the tutorial session included with this book, rename the clip you just created using Separate Clip as "Bass Loop–Separate."

Cropping a Clip

To finish this section, you'll be trimming a clip—but in a new way. In the Chapter 05 Exercise Session file, there's a clip on the Groove Drum Stem track that begins with silence, then a drum beat, and then more silence. What you'll need to do is select the drum beat that you want to keep and remove the rest. You know by now that there are a number of ways you could create this clip: capturing, separating, or trimming with the Trim tool. In this section, you'll trim the clip, but in a different way.

1 Using the Selector tool, **select** the **area** of the audio clip that you want to retain. (In this case, **select between 35|1|000 and 43|1|000**.)

2 **Click** on **Edit**. The Edit menu will appear.

3 **Move your cursor** to **Trim Clip**. A submenu will appear.

4 **Choose To Selection.** The clip will be trimmed to your selection on the track, and a new clip will be created in your Clips list.

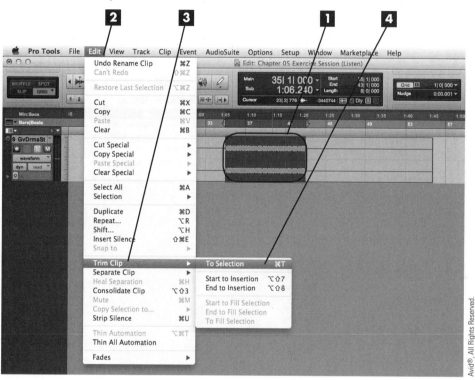

> ❉ **IF YOU'RE USING THE EXERCISE MATERIALS...**
>
> If you're working with the tutorial session included with this book, rename the clip you just created using Trim Clip as "Drum Loop."

Arranging Clips

Now that you've created the clips we need, the next step in the process is to organize them on the track. In this part of the process, what you've already learned about the edit modes will serve you well, and a couple additional tricks will make the process even easier!

Duplicating Clips

Of course, you *could* just drag the same clip onto a track over and over to create a looping phrase, but that can get really boring very quickly. Here's another way to make a copy of a clip or selection and place it immediately after the original:

1. **Select** the **clip** you want to duplicate (either by single-clicking with the Grabber tool or by double-clicking with the Selector tool). If you're using the exercise materials, **select** the **Intro Drum Loop clip**, at 9|1|000 on the Intro Drum Stem track.

2. **Click** on **Edit**. The Edit menu will appear.

3. **Click** on **Duplicate**. A duplicate of the selected clip will appear immediately after the selection.

※ **DUPLICATE SHORTCUT**

The shortcut for the Duplicate function is Command+D (Mac) or Ctrl+D (PC).

※ **IF YOU'RE USING THE EXERCISE MATERIALS...**

If you're using the tutorial session upon which this chapter is based, duplicate the Intro Drum Loop clip 23 times, for a total of 24 loops. That's quite a few duplications, but using the shortcut will make quick work of it!

Repeating Clips

Repeating clips is similar to duplicating clips, but with a twist. Instead of repeating the process for each additional loop, you can create multiple loops in one quick process.

※ **IF YOU'RE USING THE EXERCISE MATERIALS...**

For this section, you'll focus on the Groove Bass Stem and Groove Drum Stem tracks, starting with the Groove Bass Stem track.

1 **Select** the **clip** you want to repeat (either by single-clicking with the Grabber tool or by double-clicking with the Selector tool). If you're using the exercise materials, **select the Bass Loop–Separate clip**, at 35|1|000 on the Groove Bass Stem track.

2 **Click** on **Edit**. The Edit menu will appear.

3 **Click** on **Repeat**. The Repeat dialog box will open.

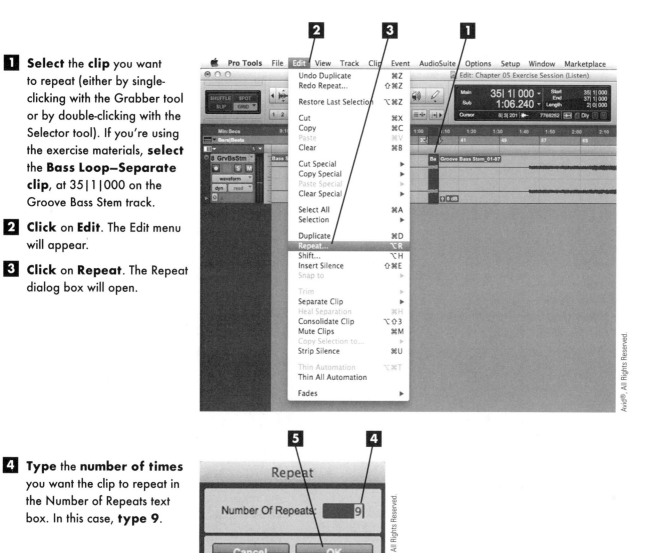

4 **Type** the **number of times** you want the clip to repeat in the Number of Repeats text box. In this case, **type 9**.

5 **Click** on the **OK button**. The selected clip will be repeated the specified number of times, just as if you had used the Duplicate command multiple times.

❋ **IF YOU'RE USING THE EXERCISE MATERIALS...**
Now that you have the Groove Bass Stem track finished, you'll need to do one more repeat. On the Groove Drum Stem track, select the Drum Loop clip (which also starts at 35|1|000), and repeat it seven times.

Cutting, Copying, and Pasting

Cutting, copying, and pasting are tried-and-true staples of many kinds of software, and Pro Tools is no exception. These processes are very straightforward and easy to use.

Copying a Clip

To copy a clip, follow these steps:

1 **Select** the **clip** you want to copy (either by single-clicking with the Grabber tool or by double-clicking with the Selector tool). If you're using the exercise materials, **select** the **Verse 2 Synth Stab clip**, at 51|1|000 on the Groove Pad Stem track.

2 **Click** on **Edit**. The Edit menu will appear.

3 **Click** on **Copy**. The clip will be copied to the Pro Tools clipboard, ready to be pasted.

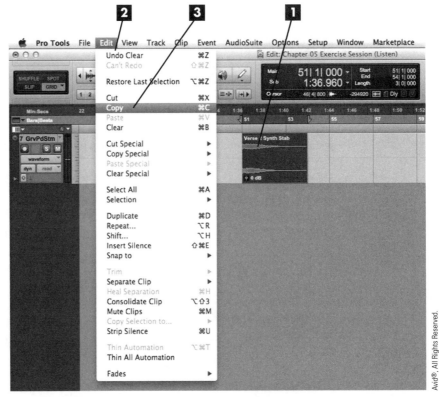

✲ **COPY SHORTCUT**

The shortcut for the Copy command is Command+C (Mac) or Ctrl+C (PC).

Pasting a Clip

A copied clip means nothing until it's pasted to a new location. Here's how to do it:

1 **Click** on the **Selector tool** if it's not already selected.

2 **Click** in a **track** at the location where you want the pasted clip to begin. If you're using the exercise materials, **choose 55|1|000** on the Synth Pad Stem Track. (Tip: Using Grid mode makes placing the cursor at the beginning of the bar very easy!)

3 **Click** on **Edit**. The Edit menu will appear.

4 **Click** on **Paste**. The clip will be pasted at the location you selected.

❈ PASTE SHORTCUT

The shortcut for the Paste command is Command+V (Mac) or Ctrl+V (PC).

❈ IF YOU'RE USING THE EXERCISE MATERIALS...

If you're following the steps, you just pasted the copied clip at 55|1|000. Paste it once more, at 59|1|000.

Cutting a Clip

If you've got a clip that doesn't sound quite right, and you want to remove it, it's easy to do so:

1 **Select** the **clip** you want to cut. If you're using the exercise session, **select** the Verse 2 **Synth Stab clip**, which starts at 55|1|000.

2 **Click** on **Edit**. The Edit menu will appear.

3 **Click** on **Cut**. The clip will be cut and placed on the Pro Tools clipboard (for pasting, if desired).

❋ CUT SHORTCUT

The shortcut for the Cut command is Command+X (Mac) or Ctrl+X (PC).

❋ NOW'S A GOOD TIME TO SAVE YOUR WORK

If your session sounds good (and it shouldn't sound too bad if you've been following the steps in this chapter), you should save your work before moving on.

❋ CHECK YOUR WORK

The steps covered so far in this chapter have been saved to a session named "Chapter 05 Exercise Session (Listen)–Finished," which is included with this book's downloadable materials.

Working with Overlapping Clips

From time to time, you'll want to move one clip so that it partially overlaps another clip. This is absolutely not a problem—it happens all the time—but there are some things you should be aware of. First, you will only ever hear the clip that's "in front," meaning that you won't hear both audio clips play together. Second, this sort of action is nondestructive, meaning that when you overlap clips, no audio is being removed from your audio files.

❄ CHAPTER 05–OVERLAPPING CLIPS

The best way to show this feature is to show it simply. A very simple session has been included with the book's downloadable materials, named "Chapter 05–Overlapping Clips." This session has a single Audio track with two clips: one pink (with silence) and one green (with a 1 kHz sine wave).

First, let's take a look at the normal behavior of overlapped clips:

❄ Drag a clip over another clip using the Grabber tool (in this case, the second clip on the Chapter 05–Overlapping Clips track is dragged over the first). You'll notice that when you play back the track, only the clip (or portions of a clip) that is immediately visible will be heard.

❄ OVERLAPPING CLIPS' BEHAVIOR

Move the clip that was "on top" out of the way, and you'll see that the clip that was partially blocked hasn't changed at all! If only one clip boundary overlaps another clip, the overlapping clip can be moved out of the way with no change upon the clip beneath.

If, however, a smaller clip is dragged completely over a larger clip and dropped (in other words, both clip boundaries are overlapping), a hole will be left when that smaller clip is moved away again. Last but not least, if a larger clip completely covers a smaller clip, that clip will be removed from the track (although it will still be in the Clips list).

Sometimes it's hard to visually determine when clips are overlapping versus when they are simply next to each other. It would sure be easier if there were some sort of visual cue to show an overlapped arrangement. No sooner said than done!

1 **Click** on **View**. The View menu will appear.

2 **Move your cursor** to **Clip**. The Clip submenu will appear. This submenu is a checklist of clip-related attributes that can be shown or not shown.

3 **Click** on **Overlap**. (It will appear checked when activated.)

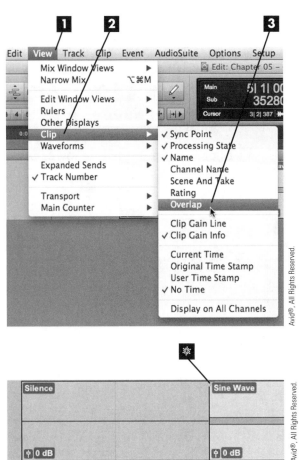

❋ Note that now you'll see a small bevel in the overlapping upper corner of a clip that is covering another clip.

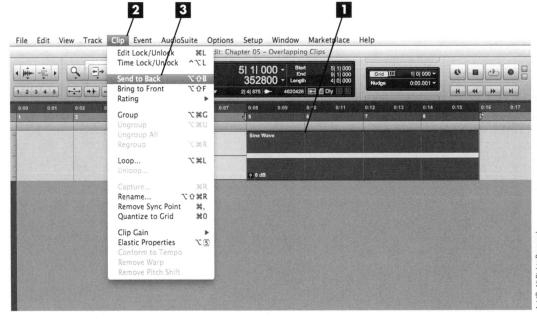

But wait, there's more! What if you want to reverse the way the clips are overlapped *without* moving either of the clips?

1 **Select** the **clip** in front.

2 **Click** on **Clip**. The Clip menu will appear.

3 **Click** on **Send to Back**. The selected clip will be moved behind the first clip and will now be partially covered by it. Here again, there will be a beveled upper corner to indicate the overlap (although it is now in the first clip, indicating that it is covering another clip).

❋❋❋

You can similarly choose a clip that is in back and choose Bring to Front from the same menu. Again, the relationship between these two overlapping clips has been reversed, while leaving their timing untouched.

Edit Playlists

An *edit playlist* is perhaps best defined as a sequence of clips on a track. For example, any given stereo Audio track may have clips that sound like anything (music, dialogue, sound effects, etc.). The track is the same; only the edit playlist is different. Although edit playlists are among the most unsung of Pro Tools' features, they're easy to use. Better still, there's no limit to the number of edit playlists you can have, so if you know how to use playlists, you have a whole new dimension of editing flexibility to work with.

> ❋ **CHAPTER 05–PLAYLISTS AND TRACK COMPING**
>
> For this remainder of this chapter, you'll be using a session specifically designed to illustrate the power of edit playlists. You'll find it with your downloadable materials, as a session named "Chapter 05–Playlists and Track Comping."

Here's a simple scenario: You've got two stereo Audio tracks, one with a guitar and one with a keyboard solo. What if you wanted to hear something other than a guitar on that accompanying track?

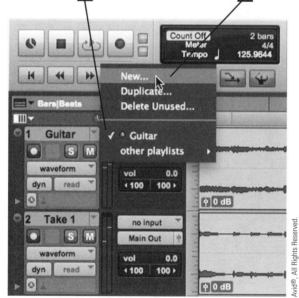

1 **Click** the **Playlist selector**. In this case, I've clicked the Guitar track's Playlist selector. A menu will appear.

2 To start off, create a blank playlist—one with no clips on it—so you can do something completely different. **Click** on **New** to do this. A dialog box in which you can name your new playlist will open.

3 **Type** a descriptive **name** for your new playlist. (In this case, I typed Piano.)

4 **Click** on the **OK button**. The dialog box will close, and your new playlist will be created.

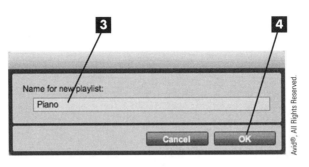

You still have your stereo Audio track, but now you have one with a brand-new edit playlist—a blank track ready for you to work with. You can add new audio clips to this track in any manner—recording, dragging from the Clips list, you name it.

> ❄ **IF YOU'RE USING THE EXERCISE MATERIALS...**
>
> If you're using the exercise session, I've made it easy for you to create a number of additional playlists. There is a clip named "Piano" in the Clips list—drag this onto the new Piano playlist, so that the clip starts at the beginning of the timeline. (Tip: Shuffle mode makes this easy.)
>
> Once that's done, create two more new playlists, named "Organ" and "Pretty Pad," and drag the respective clips onto their timelines similarly. Once you're done, the top Audio track will have four edit playlists on it: Guitar, Piano, Organ, and Pretty Pad.

Here's the coolest part: You can change between playlists anytime and compare the two different edits!

❄ Now, if you click the Playlist selector, you'll see a list of the edit playlists that you've created, and you can choose the desired one at any time—even during playback! Edit playlists are a great way to explore different creative directions nondestructively.

Here's another way in which edit playlists can be useful. Let's say, for the sake of argument, that you want to try some edits on an existing playlist, but want to keep the original as well. No problem—edit playlists are good for that as well!

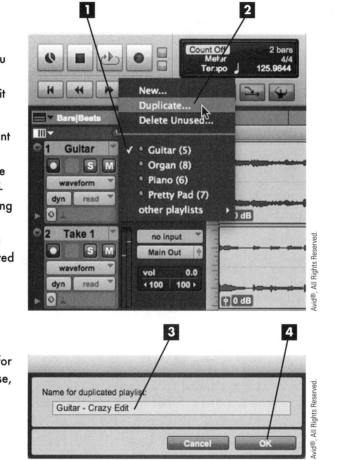

Avid®, All Rights Reserved.

1 Making sure that you're viewing the playlists that you want to alter, **click** on the **Playlist selector**. The Edit Playlist menu will appear.

2 Because in this case you want to make a change on an existing playlist, **choose** the **Duplicate menu item**. Effectively, what you'll be doing is copying this sequence of clips. A dialog box in which you can name your duplicated playlist will appear.

3 **Type** a descriptive **name** for your new playlist. In this case, I've named this variation of the Guitar playlist "Guitar–Crazy Edit."

Name for duplicated playlist:

Guitar - Crazy Edit

Cancel   OK

Avid®, All Rights Reserved.

4 **Click** on the **OK button**. The dialog box will close, and your new playlist will be created.

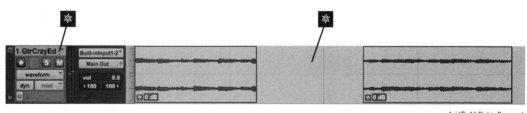

Avid®, All Rights Reserved.

❄ Notice that your track name (which you now know is actually the edit playlist name) has changed to match your new edit playlist.

❄ Now you're free to make whatever changes you like to your clips. (In this case, I'll go into Slip mode, select a large portion out of the middle, and delete it.)

Here as well, you can go back into your list of playlists and switch between playlists any time you want—even during playback. This is a great way to try out different edits of a track to see which one works the best in context.

❄ ❄ ❄

Track-Comping Tools

Let's say you've just finished multiple takes of a section (either by recording a number of times or though loop recording). In most cases, the next step is to compile a final track that includes the best parts of each take. This process is called *comping* a track, and it is one of the cornerstones of professional editing. As with many other processes in Pro Tools, there are a number of ways to comp a track, with different methods appropriate for different situations.

The most advanced workflows for track comping center around a solid understanding of edit playlists, which you now have. Essentially, what you'll be doing is putting the best parts of the different takes, each of which will reside on individual edit playlists, onto a blank track (which you now know is simply an edit playlist with no clips on it). How you record your individual takes is important; it will enable you to utilize these new track-comping tools during the editing phase of your process. So let's start there.

> ❋ **COMPING PRACTICE**
>
> If you don't have any material of your own for track-comping practice, don't worry—the bottom track of the exercise session has four separate takes for you to practice on.

If you're recording multiple takes *without* loop recording:

1 **Record** the **first take** normally.

2 Before recording the second take, **create** a **new edit playlist**, as discussed in the previous section. The track will now be empty, because the first take's clip resides on a different edit playlist.

3 **Record** the **second take** normally.

4 For each additional take, **create** a **new edit playlist** before recording. This will ensure that each recording pass will be represented individually on its own edit playlist.

If you are recording multiple takes *with* loop recording:

1. In the Preferences dialog box (which you access from the Setup menu), **click** the **Operation tab** and **check** the **Automatically Create New Playlists When Loop Recording checkbox**.

2. **Click** on the **OK button** to close the Preferences dialog box.

3. **Loop record** normally.

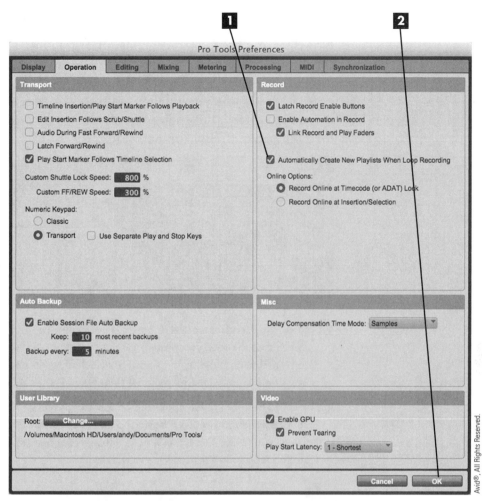

In either case, you can access each individual take by clicking the Playlist selector (again, as discussed in the previous section) and choosing the desired take from the list of edit playlists.

Viewing Playlists in the Edit Window

Now that you have all your takes separated into individual playlists, you can get down to some serious comping. In this example, you have a single stereo Audio track, upon which was recorded four different takes of a keyboard solo. In this case, it doesn't matter whether the solo was recorded using Loop Record or by manually creating new edit playlists; your job is to pull out the best parts of each take and make a final comped track.

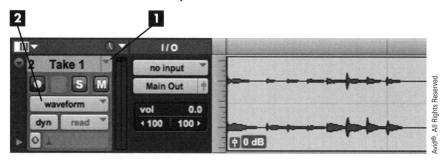

Avid®, All Rights Reserved.

1 **Click** the **Playlist selector** to reveal a menu of edit playlists. As you've done before, you can choose the take you want to view. Once you see a take you like, you can select an area, copy it, change playlists, and paste the section to the new playlist. Although that's an effective way of editing, it's not the most efficient way of working.

2 It would be great if you could see *all* the edit playlists for a given track at one time and create your comped track without having to switch playlists all the time. That's exactly what Pro Tools allows you to do. **Click** the **Track View selector** (which reads "waveform" in this example) on the desired track. A menu will appear.

3 **Click** the **Playlists menu item**.

✳ In Playlists view, you'll see all the edit playlists associated with a given track, displayed as different lanes.

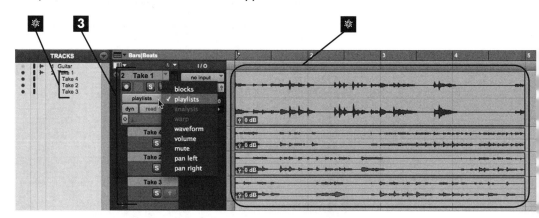

✳ Working in Playlists view—especially when you're using this view with multiple tracks simultaneously—can result in a pretty complicated-looking Edit window. To let you know which lanes are associated with which tracks, alternate Playlist lanes are indented (both in the playlist area and in the Tracks list).

Basic Track Comping

Now the fun starts. The first thing to do is to create a new playlist, giving you a blank track to comp to. Playlists view makes this easy!

1 Using the Grabber tool, **drag** the top **clip(s)** to the empty lane at the bottom of the track. When the clip has been dragged to the proper place, you'll see an empty box, as shown here. **Release** the **mouse button**, and the clip will be moved to a new playlist, leaving a blank area at the top for comping.

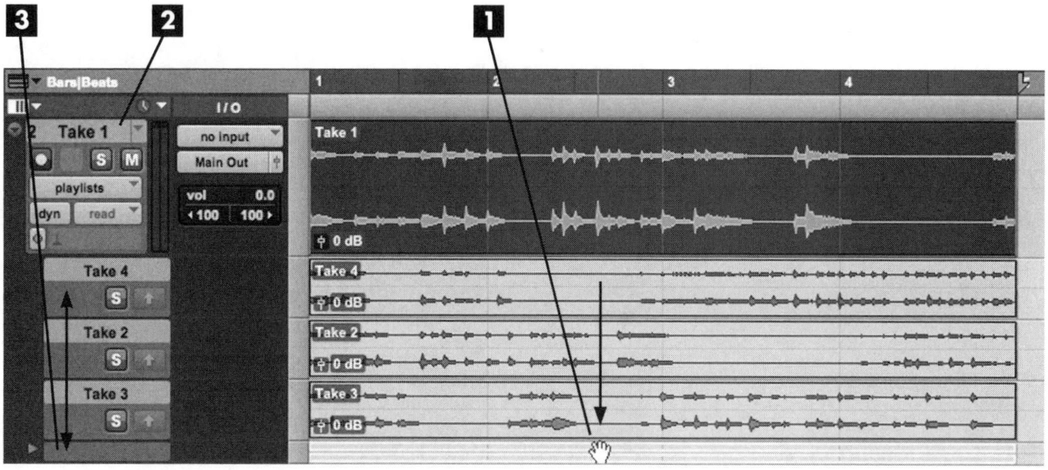

2 You can **double-click** on the track's **name** to rename the main playlist if you wish. Similarly, you can **click** on the **alternate playlists' names** to name individual takes.

3 You can **rearrange** the **alternate playlists** by clicking the playlist name and dragging it up or down, just as if you were rearranging tracks. If you're working with the tutorial session, you might want to rearrange your takes sequentially.

4 To preview alternate playlists, **click** on the **Solo button** for the desired Playlist lane. The soloed playlist will be heard instead of the active edit playlist.

5 If you **click** on the track's main **Solo button**, all the other non-soloed tracks in your session will be muted.

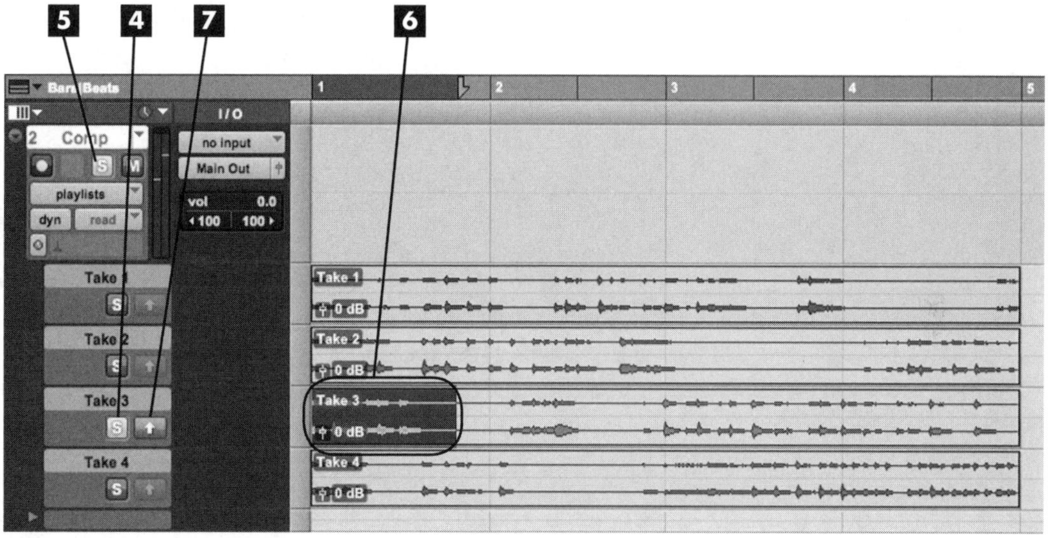

6 With the Selector tool, **mark** an **area** that you wish to use in your comped track.

7 **Click** the **Copy Selection to Main Playlist button**.

As you can see here, the selected area has been copied from the original play-list and automatically pasted to the main playlist. At this point, you can audition other sections, pick your favorites, and send them from the alternate playlist to the comped track playlist as well, creating a new track that represents the best parts of each take. Because this is all nondestructive, you can still adjust boundaries with the Trim tool or move segments around with the Grabber tool. If a particular transition from one clip to another is abrupt, you can use crossfades to smooth things out. (You'll learn more about crossfades in the next chapter.)

> ❄ **COMPING SHORTCUT**
>
> Instead of clicking the Copy Selection to Main Playlist button, you can press Control+Option+V (Mac) or Start+Alt+V (PC) after selecting an area on a Playlist lane to paste the selected area in the main edit playlist.

Beyond the Basics

As if this radical improvement in the editing process wasn't enough, Pro Tools has more ways to organize and view your takes!

Clip Ratings

In the preceding example, you had four takes. In a normal comping situation, you might have dozens! It might be hard to believe, but the mere act of separating the good takes and sections from the bad is often an important and time-saving step. Pro Tools has some important features to help with this as well, in the form of clip ratings.

The first thing to do is make sure you can see the ratings of clips.

1 **Click** on **View**. The View menu will appear.

2 **Move your cursor** to **Clip**. The Clip submenu will appear, showing different display options for clips.

3 As with other menus you've seen so far, aspects that are shown are indicated with a checkmark. Because you want to see clips' ratings, **click** the **Rating menu item** to check it (assuming that it's not already checked).

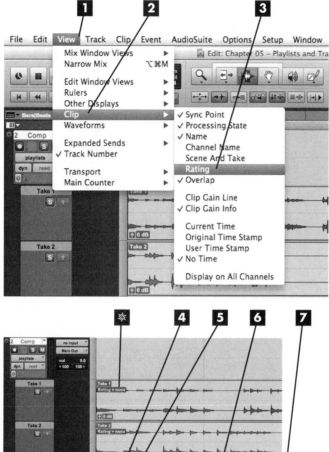

❋ You'll see that all the clips on your track show an initial rating of none.

4 When you find a section of a clip that you want to rate, simply **separate** the **section**, creating a new clip (you can also rate a complete take, of course). This new clip also has an initial rating of none.

5 **Right-click** the **clip** you want to rate. A menu will appear.

6 **Choose** the **Rating menu item**. The Rating submenu will appear.

7 **Choose** the desired **rating** for the clip. It's up to you whether 5 or 1 is the best rating, but it's important to be consistent with your method.

Filtering Lanes

When you've picked out the best takes, you can show only the lanes containing good takes and hide the lanes that you don't want to include in the comping process.

1 While still in Playlists view, **right-click** the **name** of any playlist (either active or alternate). A menu will appear.

2 **Choose** the **Filter Lanes menu item**. The Filter Lanes submenu will appear.

3 In this menu, you can **show** or **hide** all **lanes** or show/hide lanes based on their rating. Here's where your rating system will make a difference:

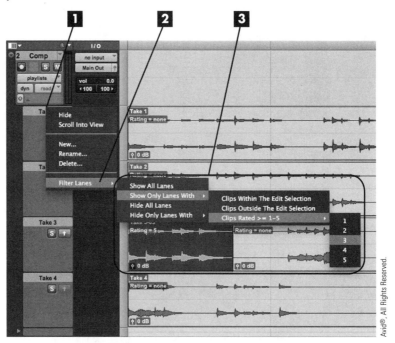

Avid®, All Rights Reserved.

＊ If your rating system is set up so that your best takes are rated higher (the best being rated a 5), you'll want to choose Show Only Lanes With and then choose Clips Rated >= 1–5, as shown here. For example, if you choose 3, only lanes with clips rated 3, 4, or 5 will be shown.

＊ If your rating system is set up so that your best takes are rated lower (the best being rated a 1), you'll want to choose Hide Only Lanes With and then choose Clips Rated >= 1–5. In this case, For example, if you choose 3, only lanes with clips rated 3, 2, or 1 will be shown.

That's it for beginning editing! Now on to some of the more "tweaky" features!

6 ...And More Editing

Although the editing power of a DAW like Pro Tools is impressive indeed, the editing process in and of itself is rarely glamorous. A good editor knows that editing essentially boils down to a few simple functions done many, many times. In the editor's world, patience is a virtue, and attention to detail is put to the test when you cut and paste, drag and drop, and switch editing tools time and time again. Indeed, it's not uncommon for a professional editing session to involve thousands of individual editing operations!

The good news is that you already learned the basics of editing in Chapter 5, "Editing." The next step is to expand upon the basic editing tools you've already begun to use and learn more flexible and efficient ways to work. The idea behind these techniques is that the seconds you'll save with each editing function will accumulate, saving you a sizable amount of time by the end of the day. Better yet, you'll not only save time, but you'll also become a better and more creative editor in the process! In this chapter, you'll learn how to:

* Navigate your session with greater ease.
* Use alternate methods of zooming and customized zoom settings to boost efficiency.
* Use variations of the Trim and Grabber tools.
* Boost your editing power by using the Smart tool.
* Put clip-based features (clip looping, clip groups) to use in your session.
* Protect your clips from accidental change by locking them.

More Organization: Memory Locations

As your session gets more complex, organizing and navigating the maze of clips and tracks can become a real issue. This is true not only of the editing phase, but in the mixing stage as well, when you're mainly working in the Mix window and you don't have the convenience of clicking on a specific time on a track (although you will still have the Transport window when you want it). The good news is that you can make navigation significantly easier by setting up a few memory locations.

Memory locations are user-defined presets that enable you to recall a variety of settings with a single click of a button. Not only will you be able to instantly jump to important places in time, but you can also change zoom settings, track visibility, track height, and more!

> ❋ **USING THE TUTORIAL SESSION**
>
> For this section, you can use the session named "Chapter 06 Exercise Session (Listen)," included with this book's downloadable materials. Alternatively, you can use the finished version of Chapter 05 Exercise session. For information on downloading this book's exercise materials, please refer to the "Setting Up Your Session" section of the introduction.

Creating a Memory Location

Before you can use memory locations, you have to create them! Typically, the first step is to set up the Edit window in a way that you would like to be able to recall. In this case (and this is something I commonly do), let's set up the window in a sort of default state, which we'll call "HOME." Here's what to do:

1 Move the **timeline insertion cursor** to the beginning of the session.

2 Show all the **tracks** in the session.

3 **Zoom out horizontally** to see the entire length of the session.

4 Set the **track heights** to see all the tracks in the session.

Once you have your Edit window set up in a way that you'd like to save to a memory location, you're ready to begin the process of creating the memory location itself.

1 Click on the **Window menu**.

2 Click on **Memory Locations**. The Memory Locations window will appear.

3 **Click** on the **Memory Locations Menu button** in the upper-right corner of the Memory Locations window. A menu will appear.

4 **Click** on **New Memory Location**. The New Memory Location dialog box will open.

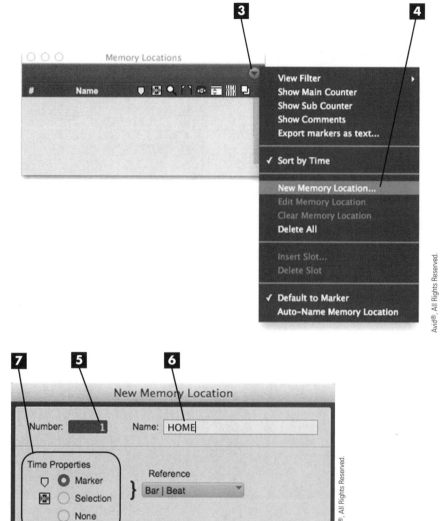

5 Although Pro Tools will automatically assign a memory location number when you create a new memory location, you can **type** a different **number** in the Number field. This number will determine the ranking of the new memory location and the shortcut you will use to recall it (which I'll cover later in this section).

6 **Type** a descriptive **name** for your new memory location in the Name text box. In this case, I'm calling the memory location "HOME," because it recalls some basic settings for my session.

7 **Select** the **time property** that you want this memory location to recall. The choices are as follows:

❊ **Marker.** The timeline insertion cursor will jump to a specific location when the memory location is chosen. (In this case, it will go to the beginning of your session.) This is the kind of memory location you want for this example.

❊ **Selection.** A selected area will be recalled when the memory location is chosen.

❊ **None.** The timeline insertion/selection will not change when the memory location is chosen.

* Clicking the Reference menu button will reveal two basic modes for your time properties:

* **Bar|Beat.** If you choose Bar|Beat, your memory location's position on the timeline will be anchored to a specific bar and beat position and will move on the timeline if the tempo is changed. This is most useful in musical situations.

* **Absolute.** If you choose Absolute, your memory location will be anchored to a sample-based location and will not move if your session's tempo changes. This is most commonly used when working with video soundtracks (since video typically doesn't deal with musical tempo).

8 **Check** the **General Properties checkboxes** that match the settings you want to recall with this memory location. In this example, when the HOME memory location is chosen, the current zoom settings, track show/hide, and track heights will be restored. Other characteristics, such as pre-/post-roll, group enables, and window configuration will not change when you recall this memory location (since these boxes are not checked).

9 **Type** a descriptive **comment** in the Comments field to describe the memory location. This is an optional step, but can save you when things get complex!

10 **Click** on the **OK button**. Your memory location will be saved, and the New Memory Location dialog box will close.

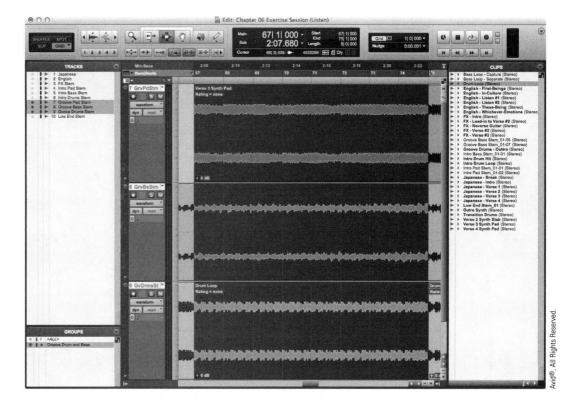

Now let's try setting up a different memory location. Select a different area (in this image, I selected from bar 67 to bar 75) and different zoom settings, track heights, and track show/hides. (In this image, I am showing only the Groove Pad Stem, Groove Bass Stem, and Groove Drums Stem tracks.) This time, enable a group. (I've enabled the Groove Drum and Bass group by clicking Groove Drum and Bass in the lower-left area of the Edit window.)

1 **Create** a new **memory location** by repeating steps 3 and 4 in the preceding numbered list. If you're following this example, name the new memory location "Groove Loop" and choose the following settings in the New Memory Location dialog box:

❋ Choose the Selection option in the Time Properties section. When this memory location is recalled, the selection will be as well.

❋ Check the Zoom Settings checkbox.

❋ Check the Track Show/Hide checkbox.

❋ Check the Track Heights checkbox.

❋ Check the Group Enables checkbox. This will activate the currently active groups (in this case, the Groove Drum and Bass group) when this memory location is recalled.

2 **Click** on the **OK button**.

2

New Memory Location

Number: 2   Name: Groove Loop

Time Properties
○ Marker
◉ Selection   Reference
○ None   Bar | Beat

General Properties
🔍 ☑ Zoom Settings
⌐¬ ☐ Pre/Post Roll Times
👁 ☑ Track Show/Hide
☰ ☑ Track Heights
║║║ ☑ Group Enables
🗔 ☐ Window Configuration (none)

Comments
First half of Verse 3

Cancel   OK

If you're following along with the steps so far in this chapter, your session will now have two different memory locations, and you can begin to get a sense of their usefulness.

❋ By clicking on the desired memory location name, you will instantly recall all the aspects associated with that memory location.

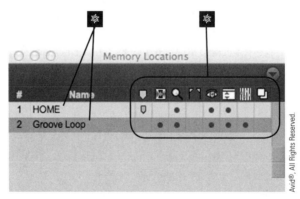

❋ If you're ever unclear as to what parameters are stored in a specific memory location, you can find out just by noting the icons shown to the right of the memory location name. From left to right, the icons are Marker, Selection, Zoom, Pre-/Post-Roll, Track Show/Hide, Track Heights, Group Enables, and Window Configurations (something I'll talk about in just a few pages).

❊ **MEMORY LOCATION SHORTCUT**

You can easily recall a memory location from your keyboard. Just press the period (.) key on your keyboard's numeric keypad, then the number of the memory location you want to recall (again, on your computer's numeric keypad), and then the period key again. This works identically for both Mac and PC systems.

❊ **ANOTHER WAY TO CREATE MEMORY LOCATIONS**

You can also create memory locations by pressing the Enter key on your computer keyboard's numeric keypad. You can even do this on the fly as your session is playing. After creating the memory locations, you can then go back and edit them by right-clicking the desired memory location or double-clicking the memory location that you want to change.

Using Memory Locations

There's no big mystery to creating and using memory locations, but before you delve into the next section, let's take a quick look at some of the various options available to you.

1 **Click** on the **Memory Locations Menu button.** A number of options will be presented to you:

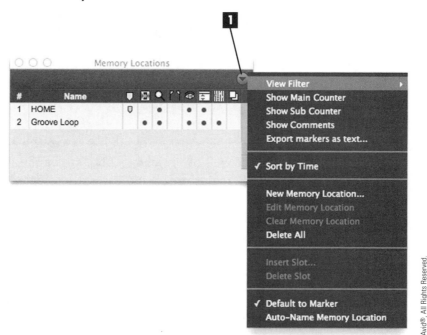

- ❊ Selecting the View Filter item will open a second menu, from which you can choose to show or hide different kinds of memory locations. For example, if you wanted to only see marker memory locations that include zoom settings, this menu would allow you to filter your list.
- ❊ When you select the Show Main Counter option, the location of each memory location in relation to the main time scale will be shown in a column in the Memory Locations window.
- ❊ When you select the Show Sub Counter option, the location of each memory location in relation to the sub time scale will be displayed.

❊ ❊ ❊

✳ When you select the Show Comments option, any comments you've entered for your memory locations will be shown.

✳ Clicking the Export Markers as Text item will open the Export Session Text dialog box. This dialog box will enable you to choose various aspects of your session to be logged into a text file. This is commonly done as a backup measure so that if your session is damaged or deleted, you have a record of specific details (such as the names and locations of your markers).

✳ When you select the Sort by Time option, your memory locations will be sorted according to how early or late they are in your session rather than by the order in which they were created or their numeric ranking.

✳ When you select the Default to Marker option, the New Memory Location dialog box will open with the Marker option chosen by default. This is particularly useful when you're creating memory locations while your session is playing. (See the earlier note "Another Way to Create Memory Locations.")

✳ The Auto-Name Memory Location option is also very handy when you're creating memory locations on the fly. It will remove the need for you to type in a name for your memory location. In fact, the New Memory Location dialog box will not even open, making the creation of a memory location a one-click (or one-keystroke) operation.

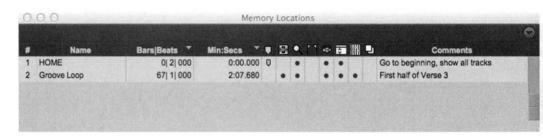

Here's what the window will look like when the Main Counter and Sub Counter are shown, as well as the comments. Notice the two new columns created and that their time scales reflect the currently selected main and sub time scales. Either (or both) of these columns can come in mighty handy, particularly when you're working in the Mix window, where it's harder to visualize your time position in your session.

Inserting a Memory Location Slot

Those of you who have been using memory locations for some time already will appreciate a relatively new bit of functionality in the Memory Locations window. The Insert Slot feature will enable you to create a new memory location between two existing memory locations. Here's how it's done:

1 Select the **memory location** that you want to be *after* the new memory location. In this image, I've selected memory location 2, because I want to create a *new* slot 2 and shift the selected slot to position 3.

2 After you set up your desired memory-location settings (selections, zoom settings, track show/hide, and so on), **click on the Memory Locations Menu button**. The menu will appear.

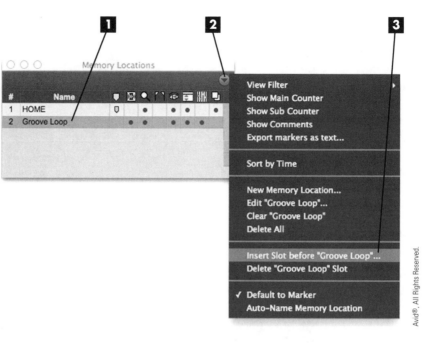

3 Select Insert Slot Before "[memory location name]." The New Memory Location dialog box will open, and you'll be able to create the new memory location as usual. When you're finished, this new memory location will be inserted in the desired slot, and the appropriate existing memory locations will be moved to later slots.

Window Configurations

In the discussion of memory locations, you may have noticed a setting called Window Configurations and wondered what the heck a window configuration was. Well, a window configuration is just what it sounds like: a recallable arrangement of windows that you can create to make your editing work go even more smoothly.

Creating a Window Configuration

Creating a recallable window configuration is even easier than creating memory locations. For the purposes of illustration, let's start with the Edit window. Here are the steps:

1 **Arrange** your **windows** as desired, including any columns, rulers, and lists that you want shown in the Edit and Mix windows. For this example, let's set up a basic Edit window layout. (If you're using the tutorial session, the Edit window is already set up this way.)

2 **Click** on the **Window menu**.

3 **Move the cursor** to **Configurations**. The Configurations submenu will appear.

4 Because you want to create a *new* window configuration, **click** on **New Configuration**. The New Window Configuration dialog box will open.

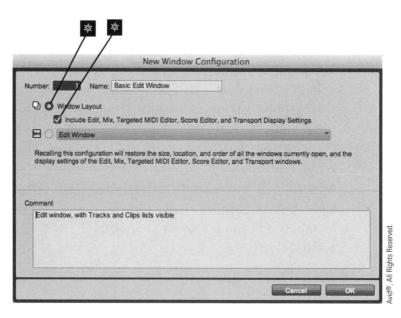

5 **Choose** what **aspects** of your layout you want to be able to recall. The two option buttons will enable you to choose what aspects of your desktop will be incorporated into the window configuration (similar to the General Properties section of the New Memory Location dialog box). The choices are pretty simple:

❋ Clicking the Window Layout option button will set up your window configuration to recall all the windows you see on your desktop, sized and positioned as they are right now. In this example, since I want to recall the entire desktop, I'll choose this option.

❋ If you check the Include Edit, Mix, Targeted MIDI Editor, Score Editor, and Transport Display Settings checkbox, the view settings that you've chosen for these windows (things such as column show/hide settings) will also be recalled.

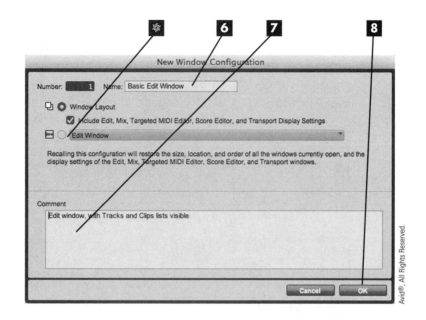

❄ The second main option button allows for finer control. It will enable you to recall settings for *only* the Edit, Mix, Score Editor, Targeted MIDI Editor, or Transport window. For example, if you *only* want to recall your ruler settings for the Edit window, you would click this option button and then select Edit Window Display Settings from the drop-down menu. The Edit window would be changed, but any other active windows would be unaffected.

6 **Type** a **name** for your window configuration in the Name text box.

7 This is an optional step, but a useful one: **Type** a **description** for your window configuration in the Comment section.

8 **Click** on the **OK button**.

❄ ❄ ❄

Now that you've created a basic Edit window configuration, let's set up a basic Mix window view (you can use the one shown here for reference) and create a second window configuration by repeating the previous steps. Name the new window configuration Basic Mix Window. For a refresher on how to customize the Mix window, you can refer to Chapter 2, "Getting Around in Pro Tools."

Window configurations aren't limited to single-window views only. In fact, the ability to arrange multiple windows as you please and save that arrangement is where window configurations really shine. Try this: Create a layout that has the Edit window across the top of your monitor and a minimal Mix window along the bottom. (This is a personal favorite desktop arrangement of mine.) Once that's done, create another new window configuration and call it Edit/Mix Split.

Recalling Window Configurations

Now that you've created a few window configurations, you can recall them easily, much as you did with memory locations. There are three main ways that you can do it. Here's one way:

1 **Click** on the **Window menu**.

2 **Move the cursor** to **Configurations**. The Configurations submenu will appear.

3 At the bottom of the submenu, you'll see a list of all the session's window locations. (The currently targeted one will be indicated with a diamond to the left of the name.) Just **click** the **window configuration** that you want to recall, and your desktop will be instantly rearranged.

Here's another way:

1 **Click** the **Window menu**.

2 **Move the cursor** to **Configurations**. The Configurations submenu will appear.

3 **Choose Window Configuration List.** The Window Configurations window will appear.

❄ ❄ ❄

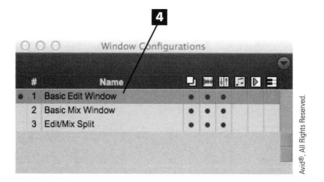

4 The Window Configurations window not only looks like the Memory Locations window, it acts like it as well. Just **click** the **window configuration** you want to recall. The dots to the right of the window configuration's name will let you know what settings have been stored in it (window layout, Edit window settings, Mix window settings, Score Editor settings, Transport window settings, and targeted MIDI Editor settings).

In addition to these two methods, you can also recall a window configuration as a property of a memory location. Basically, this means you can associate a window configuration with a memory location and change not only your desktop's layout, but any memory-location property as well, all in one click! Here's how:

1 In the Edit Memory Location dialog box, in the General Properties area, **click** the **Window Configuration checkbox**. This will configure the memory location to recall a window configuration along with any other properties that you've chosen to associate with that memory location.

2 **Choose** which **window configuration** will be recalled with that memory location. Just select the desired window configuration from the Window Configuration drop-down list. (Click on the menu button to reveal a list of all the window configurations that you have created in the session.)

3 **Click** on the **OK button**.

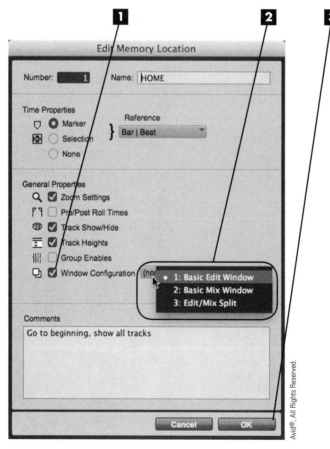

Zoom

Zooming is not only one of the most basic of operations; it's also one of the most frequent things you'll do in any editing session. In Chapter 5, you learned the basics of zooming. The following sections discuss other ways to zoom and how to use them.

❄ **TIME TO CHANGE TUTORIAL SESSIONS!**

For the next section of this chapter, you'll take advantage of what you just learned about memory locations. Please download the Chapter 06 Exercise Session–Part 2 folder to your audio hard drive and launch the session. Once it's launched, go to memory location 1, named "Zooming." For a refresher on recalling memory locations, take a look at the "More Organization: Memory Locations" section earlier in this chapter.

More Zoom Tools

Let's start from what you already know and work from there.

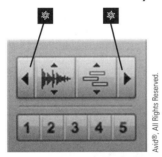

Avid®. All Rights Reserved.

❄ Click on the Zoom Out button of the Zoom controls cluster. As you've seen before, your view of your session's timeline will expand, and a longer duration will be shown in your Edit window. Note that this horizontal zooming affects all tracks in your session.

❄ Click on the Zoom In button. Again, you'll see that Audio and MIDI tracks are zoomed at the same rate. The Zoom In and Zoom Out buttons will enable you to zoom in on the time scale, and although they won't affect the speed at which your session will play back, they will enable you to view your clips and data differently to suit different kinds of editing.

Remember that even if your Zoom controls cluster isn't displayed in the top row of the Edit window, you still have access to zoom controls in the lower-right corner of the Edit window:

✳ Click the minus sign (−) on the bottom of the Edit window to zoom out.

✳ Click the plus sign (+) on the bottom of the Edit window to zoom in.

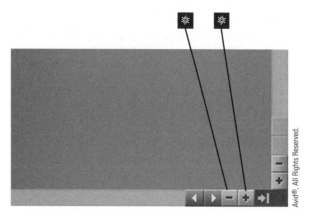

Avid®, All Rights Reserved.

In addition to these basic horizontal zoom controls, you have the ability to zoom in and out *vertically* as well.

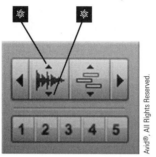

Avid®, All Rights Reserved.

✳ Click on the top half of the Audio Zoom button. With each click, your audio data will zoom up vertically, allowing you to more clearly see low-level signals.

✳ Click on the bottom half of the Audio Zoom button. The height of your audio waveforms will be reduced with each click of this button.

✳ The Zoom controls cluster's Audio Zoom button is duplicated in miniature in the upper-right corner of your Edit window's playlist area. Click on the top or bottom half of this button to zoom up or down on your audio clips.

Avid®, All Rights Reserved.

✳ **VERTICAL ZOOM (AUDIO) SHORTCUT**

Although vertical zooming is not quite as common as horizontal zooming, the shortcut keys are still useful to know. On a Mac, the shortcut is Command+Option+] (right bracket) to zoom up and Command+Option+[(left bracket) to zoom down. On a PC, it's Ctrl+Alt+] (right bracket) to zoom up and Ctrl+Alt+[(left bracket) to zoom down.

✳✳✳

❋ Click on the top half of the MIDI Zoom button. With each click, your MIDI data will zoom up vertically, allowing you to more clearly see individual notes. Note that all your MIDI clips have zoomed up at the same time, but audio clips are left unchanged.

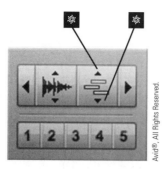

❋ Click on the bottom half of the MIDI Zoom button. Your MIDI data will zoom down, allowing you to see a greater range of notes at one time in the Edit window.

❋ You'll also find a MIDI Zoom button in the upper-right corner of your Edit window's playlist area, just below the small Audio Zoom button. Click on the top or bottom half of this button to zoom up or down on your MIDI clips.

As you zoom up or down, you will see less or more of the keyboard graphic on the left edge of each MIDI track. You can use this display as a reference point to see how broad (or narrow) of a tonal range you're viewing. Low pitches are displayed toward the bottom of each MIDI track, and high notes are toward the top.

❋ You can scroll up and down the MIDI note range by clicking on the up and down arrows at each end of the keyboard graphic.

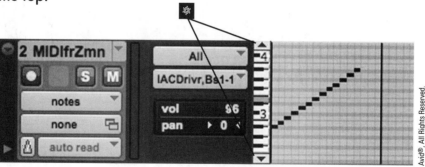

❋ VERTICAL ZOOM (MIDI) SHORTCUT

Here are the shortcuts for vertical zooming for MIDI data. On a Mac, the shortcut is Command+Shift+] (right bracket) to zoom up and Command+Shift+[(left bracket) to zoom down. On a PC, it's Ctrl+Shift+] (right bracket) to zoom up and Ctrl+Shift+[(left bracket) to zoom down.

❋ ❋ ❋

Zoom Presets

If you're a music lover, you probably use your car radio quite a bit. On most car radios, there are a number of buttons (usually below the main display) that you can use to quickly get to the stations you listen to most often. Once you set up these presets, you can simply press a button and immediately jump to your favorite station.

Many Pro Tools users find that, although they use all the zoom tools a *lot*, they tend to use certain zoom settings more frequently than others. Like on a car radio, you can set up your most common zoom presets and recall them with the click of a button. In fact, setting these zoom presets is pretty similar to setting the presets on your car radio!

1 Using the horizontal zoom tools, **adjust** your **zoom level** until you arrive at a setting that you want to be able to recall.

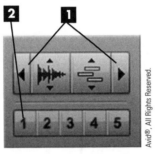

Avid®, All Rights Reserved.

2 **Hold down** the **Command key (Mac)** or **Ctrl key (PC)** and **click** on the **Zoom Preset button** that you want to assign to the current zoom level. The button will flash briefly to let you know that the preset has been stored.

From this point on, it's easy. Simply set the five presets for the five zoom settings you use the most. To recall any preset, you can click on the desired Zoom Preset button. It's worth noting that these settings are session specific, so you can customize a session's presets without changing the zoom presets in other sessions.

❋ SETTINGS?

The Zoom Preset buttons will recall only the horizontal (time) zoom amount, not the vertical zoom levels for Audio and MIDI tracks.

❋ ZOOM PRESET SHORTCUTS

The shortcuts to switch between your presets are pretty straightforward. While pressing Control (Mac) or Start (PC), press 1, 2, 3, 4, or 5 on your computer's keyboard (above the alphabet section) to access the corresponding zoom preset.

❄ ZOOM PRESETS IN THE WORKSPACE

Back in Chapter 3, "Getting Started with Audio," you learned how to search for audio and import it using the Workspace Browser. You also learned how to show, hide, and arrange the different informational columns in that window.

This window also has view presets, located in the upper-left corner. They can be customized just as you did with zoom presets. The only difference in this case is that the presets will recall your column show/hide status, column widths, and pane sizes. Unlike the Edit window's zoom presets, these presets are not session specific, and the presets that you set up here will be accessible regardless of any session that is currently open.

Zoom Toggle

Zoom toggle does just what its name would suggest: It enables you to quickly take a close-up look at a section and then get back out to the previous zoom level. Although it's been a Pro Tools feature for some time (it was introduced in version 7), it's often underutilized, so in this section, you'll learn how to make the most of it.

Actually, using zoom toggle is very easy when you use the Zoom Toggle button.

❄ FOLLOWING ALONG

Using the Chapter 06 Exercise Session–Part 2 tutorial session, go to Memory Location #2–Getting Specific.

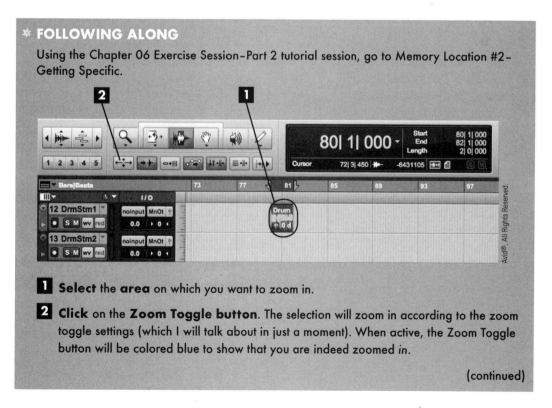

1 **Select** the **area** on which you want to zoom in.

2 **Click** on the **Zoom Toggle button**. The selection will zoom in according to the zoom toggle settings (which I will talk about in just a moment). When active, the Zoom Toggle button will be colored blue to show that you are indeed zoomed *in*.

(continued)

❄ ❄ ❄

❊ FOLLOWING ALONG (continued)

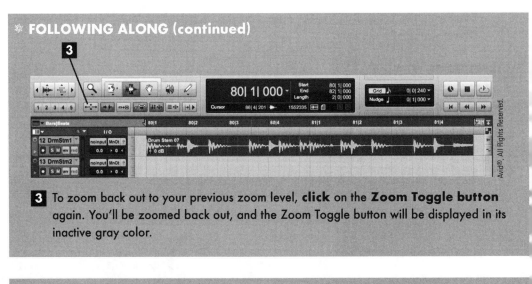

3 To zoom back out to your previous zoom level, **click** on the **Zoom Toggle button** again. You'll be zoomed back out, and the Zoom Toggle button will be displayed in its inactive gray color.

❊ ZOOM TOGGLE SHORTCUT

There is a shortcut for zoom toggling: Just press Control+E (Mac) or Start+E (PC).

What makes the zoom toggle function particularly useful is the customization you can get through the setting of preferences. The settings you establish will determine how the zoom toggle feature will behave when you engage it. Here's how to set these preferences:

1 **Click** the **Setup menu**.

2 **Choose Preferences.** The Preferences dialog box will appear.

3 If your Preferences dialog box isn't already showing the Editing tab, **click** the **Editing tab** at the top of the Preferences dialog box.

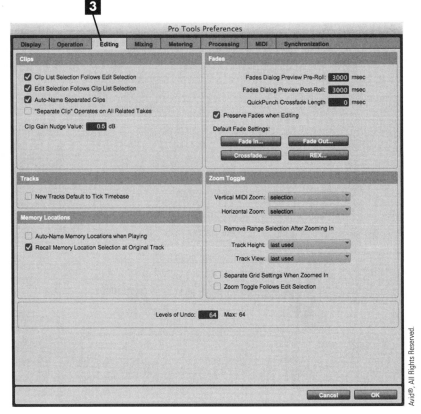

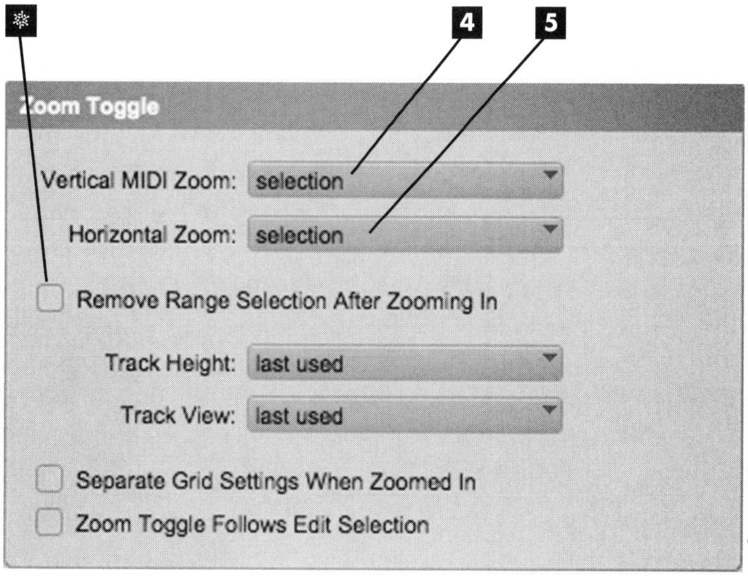

Avid®, All Rights Reserved.

4 The Zoom Toggle section is in the lower-right corner of the Preferences dialog box's Editing tab. The first set of choices you need to make covers just how much you want to zoom in. To control zoom toggle behavior when MIDI data is selected, **click** on the **Vertical MIDI Zoom** drop-down menu. (MIDI is a topic you'll tackle later (in Chapter 7, "Using MIDI." For now, it's sufficient to know that you can view MIDI data in fundamentally different ways than you view audio.) You have two options in this menu:

 ❋ **Selection.** This option configures zoom toggle to zoom into only the note range that is currently selected in the Edit window.

 ❋ **Last Used.** This option will recall the MIDI vertical zoom level that you used last time zoom toggle was engaged.

5 To control how the Zoom Toggle tool deals with zooming in on the time axis, **click** on the **Horizontal Zoom drop-down menu**. Again, there are two options.

 ❋ **Selection.** With this option, the selected area will be zoomed in so that it spans from the left edge to the right edge of the tracks area.

 ❋ **Last Used.** This option will recall the horizontal zoom level that was used when zoom toggle was last engaged.

 ❋ When the Remove Range Selection After Zooming In checkbox is checked, as soon as you engage zoom toggle, your selected area will be deselected so that you can quickly make a different selection.

6 But wait—there's more! To choose the track height that will be recalled when zoom toggle is engaged, **click** on the **Track Height drop-down menu** and **choose** a **track height**. Tip: The Fit to Window setting is a favorite of mine for this sort of work. When you zoom toggle, you'll maximize your viewable space.

7 To change your track view to a desired view when zoom toggle is engaged, **click** on the **Track View drop-down menu** and **choose** a **track view**. Here are your options:

※ **Waveform/Notes.** This is Waveform view for Audio tracks and Notes view for MIDI tracks.

※ **Warp/Notes.** This is Warp view for Audio tracks and Notes view for MIDI tracks.

※ **Last Used.** This will recall the format view you used when you last used zoom toggle on that track.

※ **No Change.** This will make no view format change when you zoom toggle.

❋ Checking the Separate Grid Settings When Zoomed In checkbox will enable you to choose two different zoom resolutions—one you see when you're toggled in and one you see when you're in your normal mode. To set the zoom toggle zoom resolution, activate zoom toggle and then select the grid resolution that you want to use. It's really that easy! When you zoom back out, you'll see the grid resolution change back.

Zoom Toggle

Vertical MIDI Zoom: selection

Horizontal Zoom: selection

☐ Remove Range Selection After Zooming In

Track Height: fit to window

Track View: last used

☐ Separate Grid Settings When Zoomed In
☐ Zoom Toggle Follows Edit Selection

❋ The last checkbox, Zoom Toggle Follows Edit Selection, is an option that requires a bit of explanation. With this option selected, aspects such as track height and horizontal zoom settings will continually follow any tracks or clips that you have selected. For example, suppose you select a clip on the top track in your session and then turn on zoom toggle. Your chosen zoom toggle settings will be recalled. Now, suppose you click a clip on *another* track while zoom toggle is still engaged. With Zoom Toggle Follows Edit Selection checked, *that* track will immediately change its track height to the zoom toggle level. (Admittedly, this can be a little distracting from time to time!)

8 Once you've made your desired selections, just **click** on the **OK button** in the lower-right corner of the Preferences window, and you're ready to rock!

> ❋ **USING LAST USED**
>
> The Last Used option found in many of the zoom toggle menus might be a bit puzzling at first, but it's actually pretty straightforward. Practically speaking, this means that if you zoom toggle in, change your settings (zoom level, track view format, etc.), and then toggle out, the next time you engage zoom toggle, you will recall those last-used settings.

More Ways to Work with Selections

Now that you're comfortable with these more flexible ways of zooming, let's take a look at some different ways of making selections.

> ❋ **SETTING THINGS UP**
>
> For this section, go to Memory Location #3–Selections.

Making Selections Using the Arrow Keys

In Chapter 3, you learned that the boundaries of a selected area are represented in the ruler area (above the tracks) by two halves of a downward-pointing arrow, representing selection start and end points. Using the arrow keys on your computer's keyboard is an easy way to make a selection as your session plays.

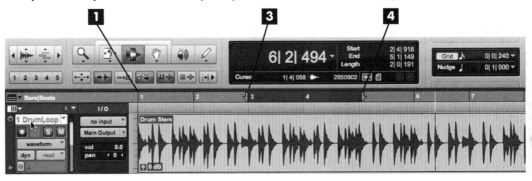

1 **Choose** a **starting point** for playback, making sure that it is *before* the spot where you want your selection to start.

2 **Start playback.** (Remember, you can click on the Start button on the transport controls or you can press the spacebar.)

3 As your session continues playing, **press** the **Down Arrow key** on your keyboard at the point where you want to begin your selected area.

4 With your session still playing, **press** the **Up Arrow key** on your keyboard when you want your selection to end.

✳ TWEAKING YOUR SELECTION

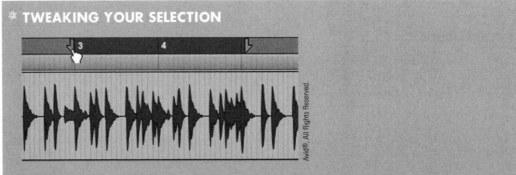

If your timing is a little off on a selection start or end, don't worry. You can adjust your selection by clicking and dragging either half of the downward-pointing arrow in your ruler.

✳ HEY—I JUST STOPPED PLAYBACK, AND MY SELECTION DISAPPEARED!

If you find that you lose your selection when you stop playback, don't worry—it's not a malfunction of Pro Tools. Here's a quick fix: Deactivate the Insertion Follows Playback button (which I'll talk more about later in this chapter).

❄ You'll find the Insertion Follows Playback button immediately below the Pencil tool button in the Edit tools cluster. When inactive, the button will be colored gray.

Making Selections Using the Return or Enter Key

You've already learned that pressing the Return key (on a Mac) or the Enter key (on a PC) will send the timeline insertion back to the beginning of the session. Here's a useful variation that will enable you to make a selection from the beginning of your session to a specified point:

1 Choose the **Selector tool**.

2 **Click** on the **point** on a track (or ruler) at which you want your selection to end. A flashing timeline insertion will appear where you clicked. (If you click on a ruler, a flashing timeline insertion will appear on all the shown tracks in your session.)

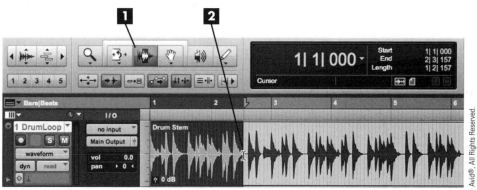

3 **Press and hold** the **Shift key** and then press the **Return key** (Mac) or **Enter key** (PC). A selection will be made from the timeline insertion back to the beginning of your session (as shown here).

Here's a variation of the same technique that will enable you to make a selection from a specified point to the *end* of your session.

1 **Click** on the **Selector tool** if it is not already selected.

2 **Click** on the **point** on a track at which you want your selection to start.

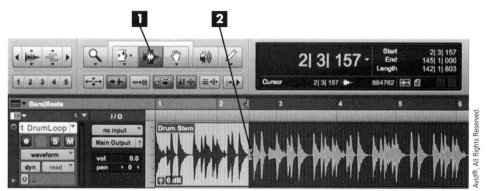

3 Press and hold Option+Shift (Mac) or Control+Shift (PC), and **press** the **Return key (Mac) or Enter key (PC)**. A selection will be made from the timeline insertion the end of your session.

❄ ❄ ❄

Making Selections Using Tab to Transients

The Tab to Transients feature is a great way to make selections with transient-based audio, particularly for those of us who enjoy chopping up beats into loop-able segments.

1 Click on the **Tab to Transients tool**. When active, it will be colored blue.

2 Use the **Selector tool** to set a timeline insertion a little before the transient with which you want to start your selection.

3 Press the **Tab key** once. The timeline insertion will jump to the next transient (where you want to begin your selection).

4 Press and hold the **Shift key** and press the **Tab key**. As you've seen before, the timeline insertion will jump from transient to transient each time you press the Tab key, but the addition of the Shift key will cause a selection to be made in the process.

5 When you reach the end of your desired selection, **stop pressing** the **Tab key**. You've now made a selection based on Pro Tools' analysis of the transients, which can help you find the right start and end points quickly and accurately!

Timeline Insertion Follows Playback

Consider this scenario: You've selected a nice, loopable selection. You wisely put yourself into Loop Playback mode to hear your selection in the proper context. Sounds great, doesn't it? Then you click on the Stop button, and the selection goes away! Is this a bug within Pro Tools? Nope—it's the effect of a mode of operation called Timeline Insertion Follows Playback, which you can set in the software in a number of ways. You want to enable or disable this mode to fit your circumstance, but it's important to understand how it works so you'll know when to use it and when not to!

One of the ways to enable or disable this mode of operation is from the Preferences dialog box. You've opened the Preferences dialog box before, so let's take a look at that method first.

1 **Click** on the **Setup menu**.

2 **Click** on **Preferences**. The Pro Tools Preferences dialog box will open.

3 **Click** on the **Operation tab**.

Avid®, All Rights Reserved.

4 You'll find the preference you're looking for in the Transport section, located in the upper-left corner of the Operation tab. **Select** or **deselect** the **Timeline Insertion/Play Start Marker Follows Playback checkbox**. Here's what the options mean:

❄ **Checked (enabled).** Playback will begin wherever the timeline insertion is set. When playback is stopped, the timeline insertion will jump to the point where playback ended. When you start again, playback will pick up where you left off. If you have a selected area in your timeline, that selection will be lost when you click on the Stop button.

❄ **Unchecked (disabled).** Playback will begin wherever the timeline insertion is set. When playback stops in this mode, the timeline insertion will stay where it was originally set. When you start playback again, it will start from this original position. If you have a selected area in your timeline, that selection will be maintained when you click on the Stop button, making this the ideal mode for editing loopable selections.

Prior to Pro Tools 8, there was no way to visually check to see whether the Timeline Insertion/Play Start Marker Follows Playback setting was enabled or disabled—until you stopped playback and observed Pro Tools' behavior. Now, you not only have a visual cue as to what mode you're working in, but you have a quick and easy way to enable or disable this feature.

❄ You'll find the Insertion Follows Playback button immediately below the Pencil tool. When the mode is active, the button will be colored blue. You can toggle the mode on and off simply by clicking the button.

Avid®, All Rights Reserved.

Separate Clips Options

Once you've made a selection within a clip, you can separate your clips based on that selection, as you've done already in Chapter 5. Let's take a quick look at two more ways to use your selected area to separate your clip.

For the purposes of this example, select the entire Drum Stem clip shown in Memory Location #3–Selections. You can easily do this by double-clicking with the Selector tool or single-clicking with the Grabber tool.

Separate Clip on Grid

As the name might suggest, Separate Clip on Grid will chop up any selected clip on every grid point. In the case of the tutorial session, our grid value is 1/16 notes, so this will create new clips in 1/16-note increments.

1 Click on the **Edit menu**.

2 Click on **Separate Clip**. The Separate Clip submenu will appear.

3 Click on the **On Grid menu item**. The Pre-Separate Amount dialog box will open.

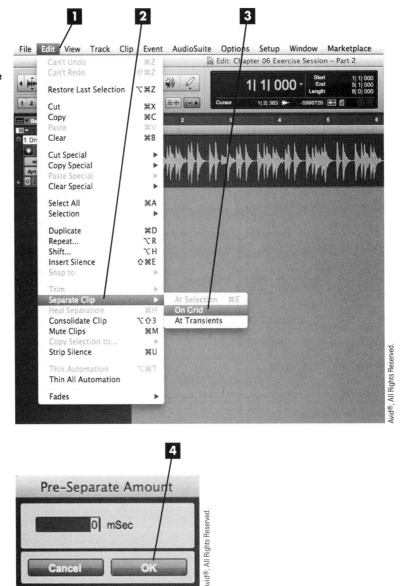

Avid®, All Rights Reserved.

4 Setting any value above zero in the Pre-Separate Amount dialog box will add a bit of "padding" to the start of the clips to be created. The greater the value, the farther ahead of the grid the separations will be. To separate clips exactly on the grid lines, **choose 0**. When you're finished, **click** on the **OK button**.

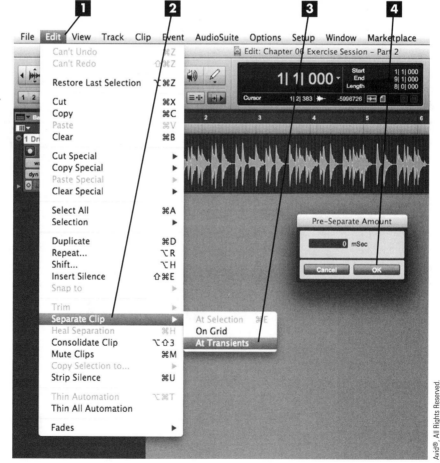

The result is immediate: Your clip will be separated regularly according to the grid value you have and any pre-separate amount you've entered. If you look at your Clips list, you'll see that you've created new clips as well (in the case of the tutorial session, *lots* of them).

Separate Clip at Transients

A variation on a theme, this is a handy little feature that creates a new clip boundary at each detected transient. Take a look.

❄ SETTING THINGS UP

If you're going through this chapter and have just separated the Drum Stem clip on the grid, undo that separation before proceeding. Again, select the entire Drum Stem clip.

1 **Click** on the **Edit menu**.

2 **Move the cursor** to **Separate Clip**. The Separate Clip submenu will appear.

3 **Choose At Transients.** The Pre-Separate Amount dialog box will open.

4 Here again, setting any value above zero in the Pre-Separate Amount dialog box will add padding to the clips you are about to create. The greater the value, the farther ahead of each transient the separations will be. To separate clips exactly at the beginning of each transient, **choose 0**. When you're finished, **click** on the **OK button**.

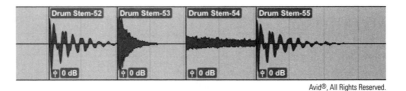

Again, you'll see your clip immediately separated into a number of clips. Each new clip will be represented in the Clips list, but the placement of the clip boundaries will be a little different from when you separated at each grid line. This time, you'll see that your clip has been separated at each transient (just ahead of the transient, if you entered a Pre-Separate amount).

Navigating and Auditioning a Selection

Usually, when making a selection, the most important parts to get right are the beginning and the end. You'll listen to the boundaries of your selections many times, just to make sure you have everything you want and nothing you don't.

> ❋ **SETTING THINGS UP**
> For this section, go to Memory Location #4–Navigating a Selection.

There are various shortcuts you can use to navigate a selection:

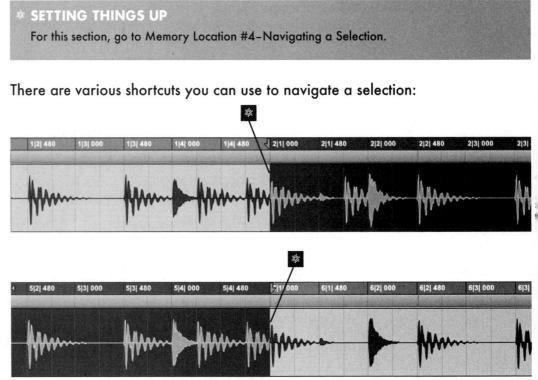

❋ Press the Left Arrow key. The Edit window's focus will move to the beginning of the selection, as shown in this image.

❋ Press the Right Arrow key. The Edit window's focus will move to the end of the selection and center that boundary in your Edit window.

The next shortcuts depend on the value entered for your pre-roll and post-roll.

❄ As you learned in Chapter 3, you can set the values for both of these by typing the desired number in the appropriate fields in the lower-left corner of the Transport window. You don't have to enable pre-roll or post-roll—just set a value.

Now it's time to audition the boundaries of your selection:

❄ Press and hold the Option key (Mac) or the Alt key (PC) and press the Left Arrow key. Your audio will play up to the beginning of your selection by the pre-roll amount. If, for example, the pre-roll amount is set as one measure, playback will start one measure before the beginning of the selection and stop when the selection begins.

❄ Press and hold the Option key (Mac) or the Alt key (PC) and press the Right Arrow key. Your audio will play up to the end of your selection by the pre-roll amount.

❄ Press and hold the Command key (Mac) or the Ctrl key (PC) and press the Left Arrow key. Your audio will play from the beginning of your selection by the post-roll amount.

❄ Press and hold the Command key (Mac) or the Ctrl key (PC) and press the Right Arrow key. Your audio will play from the end of your selection by the post-roll amount.

❄ These shortcut keys also work in combination: Hold down Option+Command (Mac) or Alt+Ctrl (PC) to play up to a selection boundary (start or end) by the pre-roll amount and past it by the post-roll amount.

Beyond the Basics

You've already worked with the basic editing tools, and things such as trimming, selecting, and grabbing are starting to become familiar by now. Some of these tools have secondary layers to them, giving them added functionality. And then there's the Smart tool....

The TCE Trim Tool

First on the list is the Time Compress/Expand (TCE) Trim tool. This useful variation of the standard Trim tool enables you to stretch or compress the duration of an audio clip without changing the pitch!

❄ **SETTING THINGS UP**

To follow with this demonstration, go to Memory Location #5–TCE Trim Tool.

1 **Click and hold** the **Trim tool button** until the Trim tool pop-up menu appears. The currently selected version of the Trim tool will be indicated by a checkmark.

2 **Choose TCE.** The TCE Trim tool becomes the active tool. The icon for the Trim tool will change to reflect the currently active version of the tool.

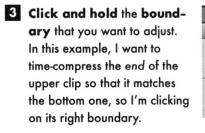

✳ TRIM TOOL TIP

The TCE Trim tool is really useful in Grid mode. Suppose you've imported a drum loop that doesn't match the tempo of the rest of your session (as is the case in the exercise session). Just make sure your grids are a musical unit and use the TCE Trim tool. The edges of the clip will snap to the nearest grid point when released, and you'll be right in tempo!

3 **Click and hold** the **boundary** that you want to adjust. In this example, I want to time-compress the *end* of the upper clip so that it matches the bottom one, so I'm clicking on its right boundary.

4 **Drag** the **boundary** left or right, just as if you were using the standard Trim tool. When you release the mouse button, a new audio clip will be created with a different duration from the original clip, but with its pitch unchanged.

The Object Grabber Tool

Up to this point, you've used the Grabber tool to move a block of time (and all the clips that are contained within that block)—hence the tool's proper name, Time Grabber. But what if you want to select more than one clip without selecting all the clips between them? That's where the Object Grabber tool comes into play!

✳ SETTING THINGS UP

For this section, go to Memory Location #6—Grabbers.

✳✳✳

1 **Click and hold** the **Grabber tool button** until the Grabber tool pop-up menu appears. The currently selected version of the Grabber tool will be indicated by a checkmark.

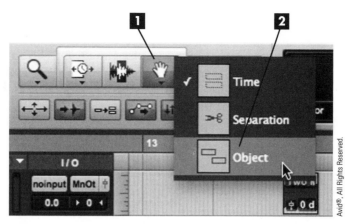

2 **Choose Object.** The Object Grabber tool becomes the active tool. The icon for the Grabber tool will change to reflect the currently active version of the tool.

3 **Click** the first **clip** that you want to move. You'll note that when you're using the Object Grabber, the clip isn't highlighted. Instead, a gold border is displayed around the edge of the clip.

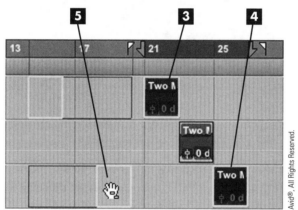

4 **Hold down** the **Shift key** and **click** additional **clips** that you want to move. Note that only the clips (objects) you click are selected, and not a rectangular block of time between them (as would be the case if you were using the Time Grabber tool).

5 **Drag and drop** the selected **clips** to the desired location. As you drag, you'll see an outline indicating where the clips would be placed if you were to release your mouse button.

The Separation Grabber Tool

Either the Time Grabber or the Object Grabber tool will enable you to move clips around in your session, albeit in different ways. The Separation Grabber tool goes a step further, enabling you to take a selection from within a single clip and move just that selected area. This is a cool trick (and a real timesaver as well), but there are a few steps in using this tool most effectively.

1 **Click** on the **Selector tool.** (Have faith—we're going somewhere with this.)

2 **Select** the **section** of a clip that you want to separate and move.

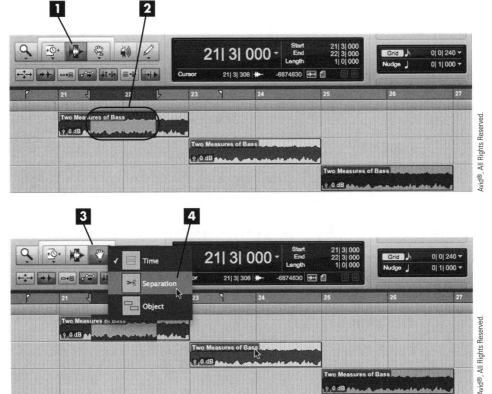

3 **Click and hold** the **Grabber tool button** until the Grabber tool pop-up menu appears. The currently selected version of the Grabber tool will be indicated with a checkmark.

4 **Choose Separation** to change to the Separation Grabber tool. The icon for the Grabber tool will change to reflect the currently active version of the tool.

5 With the Separation Grabber tool selected, **click and hold anywhere** in the selected area.

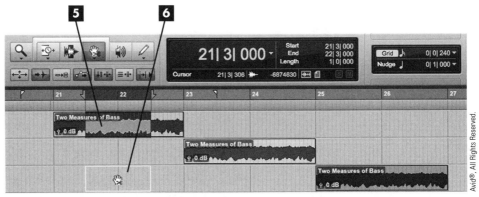

6 **Drag and drop** the **selection** to the desired destination. As with other variations of the Grabber tool, you'll see an outline indicating where the selected area will be placed when you release the mouse button.

The selection will be removed from the original clip and will become its own clip, represented on the track and in the Clips list.

❄ A TWIST ON THE SEPARATION GRABBER

If you want to drag out a selection of a clip but leave your source clip unchanged, hold down the Option key (Mac) or the Alt key (PC) as you drag.

The Smart Tool

The Smart tool is a real timesaver, combining the editing power of the Trim, Selector, and Grabber tools and adding some extra functionality for good measure. It might take you a while to get used to using the Smart tool, but once you have it under your belt, you'll be able to work more efficiently.

❄ SETTING THINGS UP

For this section, go to Memory Location #7–Smart Tool.

---

1 **Click** on the **Smart Tool bracket**, which arches over the Trim, Selector, and Grabber tool buttons. The bracket will be highlighted (blue) when the Smart tool is active, as will the three tools below it.

The concept behind using the Smart tool is simple: Your cursor will take on different tool behaviors based on its location within a track.

❄ When your cursor is in the *upper* half of a track, it will take on the function of the Selector tool.

❋ When you move your cursor to the *lower* half of a track, the cursor will take on the behavior of the currently active version of the Grabber tool (in this image, the Time Grabber).

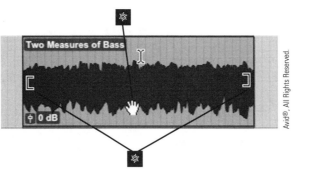

❋ When you move your cursor to either end of a clip, the cursor will change its function to that of the currently active version of the Trim tool (in this image, the standard Trim tool).

❋ THE SMART TOOL AND THE SEPARATION GRABBER

The Smart tool works particularly well when you have the Separation Grabber tool selected. Just move your cursor to the top half of a track to make your selection, and then move your cursor to the bottom half of the track to drag the selection to its new location. Easy!

❋ MORE SMART TOOL FEATURES

You might have discovered that if you move your cursor to the corner of a clip, it takes on a different function, beyond that of the Trim, Selector, or Grabber tool. Be patient—I'll get to that in a couple of pages!

❋ THE SMART TOOL AND TRACK HEIGHTS

Because the position of the cursor within a track is so critical when you're using the Smart tool, shorter track heights can be a little tricky to work with at first. As you get used to using the Smart tool, medium track height (or greater) is a good way to practice.

Edit Groups

Hopefully, you've found the edit tools you've explored to be powerful and easy to use. Now let's boost your effectiveness by enabling you to edit a number of tracks at the same time. To do this, you'll create an edit group.

❋ SETTING THINGS UP

For a simple run-through of how to use an edit group, go to Memory Location #8–Edit Groups.

❋ GROUPS AND MIXING

You'll notice that there are some features I'll pass over in this section. Not to worry—these are features more relevant to the process of mixing, so I'll cover them in Chapter 8, "Basic Mixing."

1 **Click** the **Groups List menu button** (located in the upper-right corner of the Groups list in your Edit window). A menu will appear.

2 **Choose** the **New Group menu item**. The Create Group dialog box will open.

3 **Type** a descriptive **name** for your group in the Name text box.

4 You can choose to have your selected tracks available as an edit group (active only in the Edit window), as a mix group (active only in the Mix window), or as an edit and mix group (active in both windows). In this case, you'll only be using these tracks as an editing exercise, so **choose Edit** in the Type section.

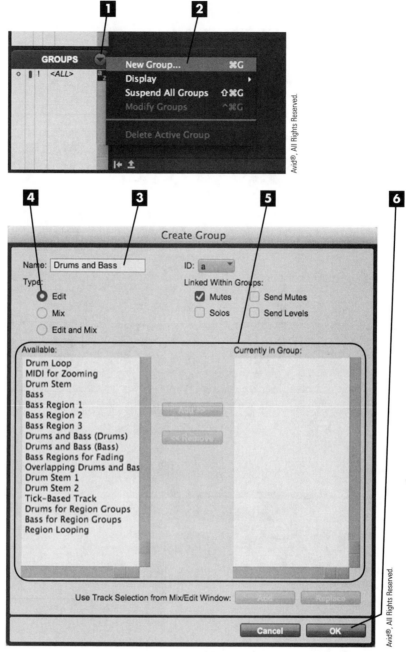

5 Initially, any currently selected tracks will be placed in the Currently in Group area, but that doesn't mean you have to select the tracks you want to group before creating the group. If you want to add more tracks to your group, **select** the desired **tracks** in the Available area and then **click** on the **Add button**. Conversely, if you want to remove a track from the group, **select** the **track** in the Currently in Group area and then **click** on the **Remove button**.

6 **Click** on the **OK button**. The dialog box will close.

❈ FOLLOWING ALONG?

If you're following the steps with the book's tutorial session, make sure the Drums and Bass (Drums) and Drums and Bass (Bass) tracks are the only tracks shown in the Currently in Group area.

❈ A TRADITIONAL TECHNIQUE

In some previous versions of Pro Tools, group membership was determined solely by the tracks that were selected *prior* to creating a new group. Once the Create Group dialog box was open, group membership couldn't be changed. Even now, the Currently in Group area defaults to containing the currently selected tracks. As a result, many long-time users of Pro Tools make it a point to select the tracks they want to use in their group *before* creating the group, saving themselves a few steps in the process.

❈ USE TRACK SELECTION

Just below the track-selection area of the Create Group dialog box, you'll see two Use Track Selection from Mix/Edit Window buttons. Clicking the Add button will add the currently selected tracks to any tracks already in the Currently in Group area. Clicking the Replace button will clear the Currently in Group area and populate it with the currently selected tracks only. These two buttons can come in handy not only when you're creating a new group, but also when you're modifying a group that you've previously created. To modify an existing group, just open the Groups List menu or right-click the group you want to change and choose Modify Groups.

❈ Your new edit group has been added to the Groups list. By default, a newly created group is immediately made active, indicated by a gray highlight around the group name. To make the group inactive, just click the group name to un-highlight it.

When you apply any edit tool to a member of an active edit group, you'll see that the effect of the tool is mirrored on all members of that group. This is particularly handy when you are assembling or tweaking tracks together (for example, drum kits, string or horn sections, or layered sound effects tracks). Shown here, I've made a selection on one of the tracks in a group, and that selection is mirrored on all members of this active edit group (named "Drums and Bass").

Creating and Customizing Fades

Fade-ins and fade-outs are used to gradually transition into or out of a clip. Additionally, you can create *crossfades* between clips to make a smooth transition from one clip into another. Of course, this is nothing new in the world of DAWs, but Pro Tools makes fades easy to create and tweak. You can even use the Smart tool to create them!

> ✳ **SETTING THINGS UP**
> For this discussion of fades, go to Memory Location #9–Fades.

Creating a Fade-In

Everybody has heard fade-ins used on a mix, such as when a song starts from a silent beginning and gradually gets louder until it reaches its running volume. In Pro Tools, you can create a fade-in for an individual clip *within* a mix as well. Here's how:

1 Using the Selector tool (or the Selector mode of the Smart tool), **select** the **area** of a clip that you want to turn into a fade-in.

✳✳✳

ABOUT YOUR SELECTION

It's important to make sure your selection starts at or *before* the clip begins and that it ends where you want the fade-in to end.

2 **Click** on the **Edit menu**.

3 **Move the cursor** to **Fades**. The Fades submenu will appear.

4 **Choose Create.** The Fades dialog box will open.

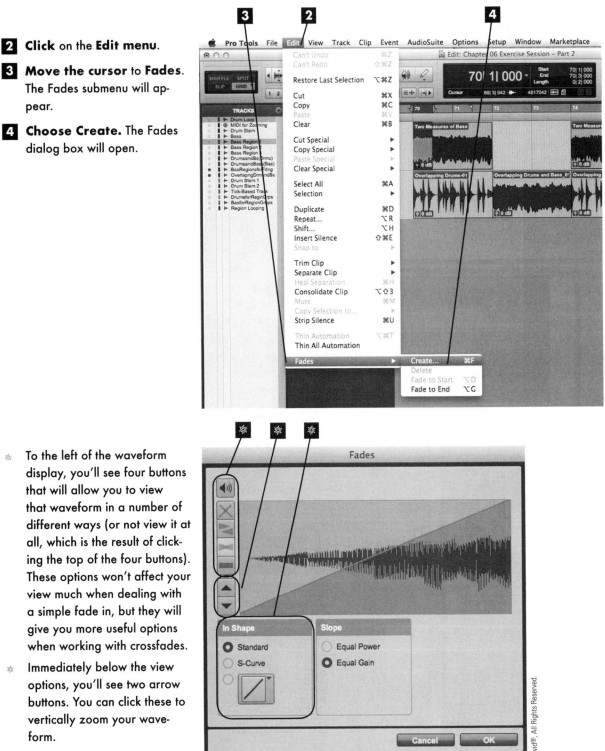

* To the left of the waveform display, you'll see four buttons that will allow you to view that waveform in a number of different ways (or not view it at all, which is the result of clicking the top of the four buttons). These options won't affect your view much when dealing with a simple fade in, but they will give you more useful options when working with crossfades.

* Immediately below the view options, you'll see two arrow buttons. You can click these to vertically zoom your waveform.

* The In Shape section of the Fades dialog box enables you to control the contour of your fade. Here you have three main options:

❋ Click on the Standard option button in the In Shape section to select a basic linear fade or logarithmic curve for the new fade. (This will depend on what you choose in the Slope section, which you'll delve into during the discussion on crossfades.)

❋ Click on the S-Curve option button in the In Shape section to select an S curve for the new fade.

❋ Click on the Preset Curve option button to use a standard fade curve chosen from a menu.

If you've chosen the Preset Curve Option button, you'll have a number of preset curves to choose from:

❋ Click on the Preset Curve Selection down arrow. A menu of fade-in curve presets will appear.

❋ Click on the desired fade-in curve preset from the menu.

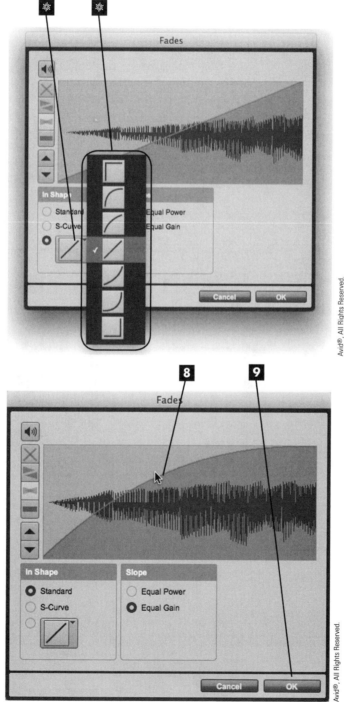

8 Once you've chosen the basic shape of your curve, you can further adjust it by **clicking and dragging** on the fade curve line. The line will change in response to your movements, and the waveform view will adjust accordingly.

9 Once you have the fade curve you want, **click** on the **OK button**. The Fades dialog box will close.

❋❋❋

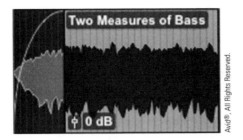

At the beginning of the clip, you'll now see a new fade clip. This clip is shown with an ascending line, indicating that it is a fade-in, as well as indicating the curve of the fade-in.

❈ PREVIEWING A FADE

Often, when creating a fade, it's useful to preview the sound of the fade *before* you've created it. In the Fades dialog box, you'll see a small button in the upper-left corner (shown here) that will do just that. Click the button to hear the effect of the fade curve on the audio clip. You won't hear any other tracks in your session—just the fade that you're creating.

Creating a Fade-Out

After you've created a fade-in, creating a fade-out will be easy. As you might expect, it's essentially a mirror image of the fade-in process.

1 Select the **area** of a clip that you want to become a fade-out. Make sure your selection starts at the point that you want your fade-out to begin and ends *at* or *after* the clip boundary. The next steps are identical to the ones you took in creating a fade-in.

2 Click on the **Edit menu**.

3 Move the cursor to **Fades.** The Fades submenu will appear.

4 Choose Create. The Fades dialog box will open.

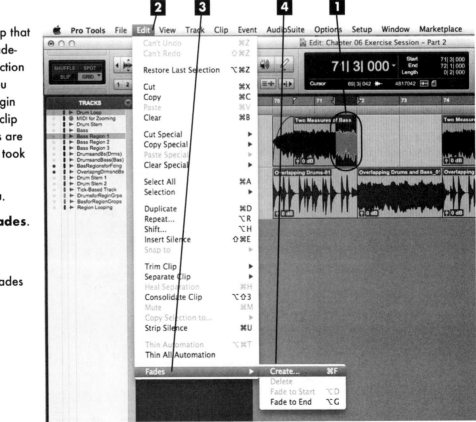

5 **Use** the Fades dialog box's **shaping options** to customize your fade-out curve, just as you did when you created your fade-in. The tools operate in the same way, just in the opposite direction!

6 **Click** on the **OK button**. The Fades dialog box will close.

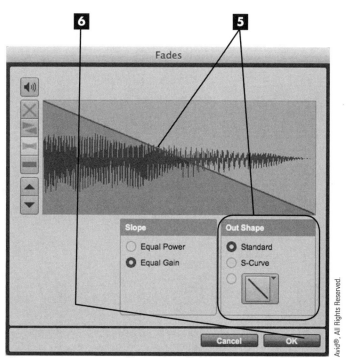

✵ **FADE IN OR FADE OUT?**

Here's something to be careful about when creating fades: If you don't select to the end (or beginning) of a clip, Pro Tools will get confused about what you want to do. Even if you go to the Edit menu and select Fades, the Create option will be grayed out and unavailable.

Crossfades

For readers who are unfamiliar with the term *crossfade*, it's a simultaneous fading out of one sound while another sound fades in, creating a smooth transition from one sound to the other. Here's how to create a crossfade between two overlapping clips:

1 **Select** an **area** of two overlapping clips that you want to become a crossfade. (If you're following the tutorial session, I've created a track of alternating bass and drum clips so that you can easily hear the transition from one clip to another.)

2 **Click** on the **Edit menu**.

3 **Move the cursor** to **Fades**. The Fades submenu will appear.

4 **Choose Create.** The Fades dialog box will open.

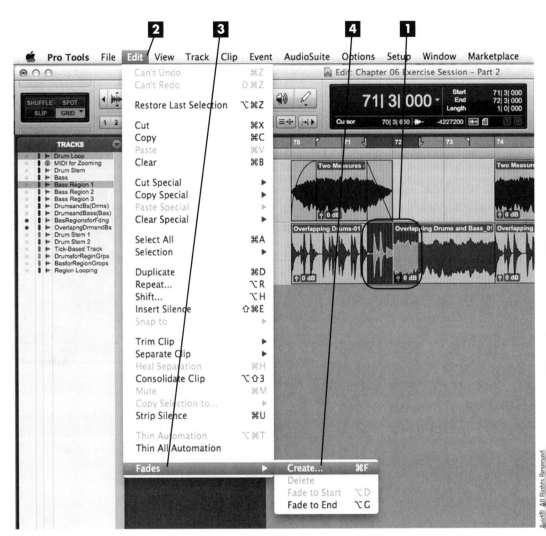

* As you saw when working with fade-ins, the display buttons to the left of the waveform display will allow you to choose the view that works best. When working with crossfades, the differences between these views are more evident than when working with fade-ins or fade-outs. (Tip: The second and third waveform display buttons are commonly used for this sort of work.)

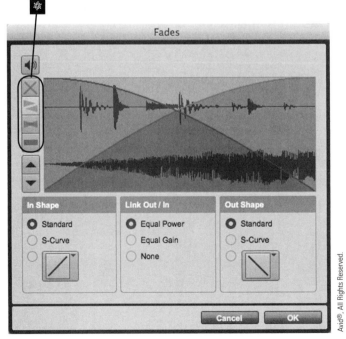

5 **Set up** the **fade-in portion** of your crossfade the same way you would a standalone fade-in.

6 **Set up** the **fade-out portion** of the crossfade the same way you would a stand-alone fade-out.

7 **Drag** the **crossing point** of your crossfade earlier or later, depending on your preference for this particular crossfade.

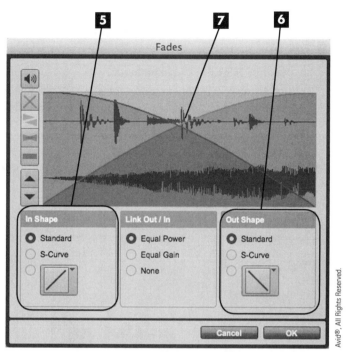

You'll notice that the fade-in and fade-out curves are linked. Changes made to either curve will affect the other. Let's take a look at the different fade-linking options. (Let your ears be your guide as to which is the best in any given situation.)

❄ The Link Out/In section (which is called the "Slope" section when creating a fade-in or fade-out only) allows you to change the way in which gain is treated as your clips crossfade. Here, you have three options:

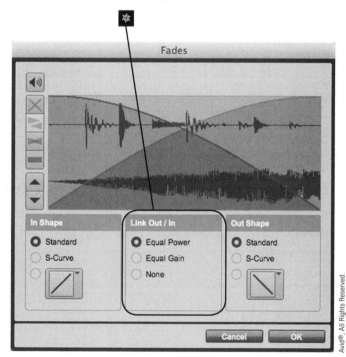

❄ **Equal Power.** This linking option will compensate for the volume drop that can sometimes occur when significantly different waveforms are combined by boosting the midpoint of the fade curves. It is usually heard as a smooth transition between dissimilar clips.

- **Equal Gain.** When you select this as a linking option, the midpoint of the fade curves will not be boosted in any way. When you are crossfading identical or very similar audio, this linking will often give you the desired smooth transition from clip to clip.
- **None.** This option (available only when crossfading) will enable you to change one half of a crossfade without changing the other half. Although it's the least commonly used of all the linking options, it will give you a degree of flexibility that the other linking options don't provide.

Let's take a look at how to use the None linking option:

- With linking set to None, you have the ability to adjust the shape, beginning, and end of either curve independently. Just click on the small black handle at the beginning or end of a fade curve and drag it to the desired position. These handles are small and can be a little difficult to click on with your mouse, but once you do get them, you'll be able to drag and drop them anywhere you want, with all other aspects of the crossfade remaining unchanged.

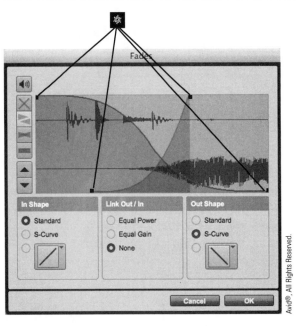

❋ THE ADVANTAGE OF NONE LINKING

Although the None link mode might not be the most commonly used mode of crossfading, it is often the mode of choice if you need a specific nonlinear transition.

Creating Fades Using the Smart Tool

In addition to the triple benefit of the Trim, Select, and Grabber tools that you get with the Smart tool, you can also quickly create fade-ins, fade-outs, and even crossfades!

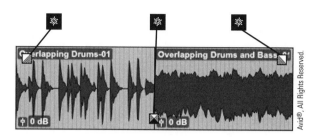

- ❄ **Fade-in.** If you move your cursor to the upper-left corner of an audio clip, the cursor will change to a small square with an ascending diagonal line through it (looking something like a fade-in line). Just click and drag your cursor to the right to quickly create a fade-in clip. Release the mouse button at the point where you want your fade-in to end, and the clip will be created.

- ❄ **Fade-out.** If you move your cursor to the upper-right corner of a clip, the cursor will change to a small square with a descending diagonal line through it (looking like a fade-out line). Just click and drag your cursor to the left to quickly create a fade-out clip. Release the mouse button at the point where you want your fade-out to begin.

- ❄ **Crossfade.** If you move your cursor to the bottom corners of two adjacent or overlapping clips, the cursor will change to a small square with two diagonal lines through it (looking like a crossfade). Just click and drag your cursor to the left or right to quickly create a crossfade clip. Release the mouse button at the point where you want your crossfade to begin or end. Your crossfade will be created and centered on the clips' boundaries.

You'll notice that when you create a fade or crossfade using the Smart tool, the Fades dialog box does not appear. The shape of the fade is automatically determined by the default fade setting. Customizing this default is easy to do and will make the Smart tool even more useful. Once more, the Pro Tools Preferences dialog box comes to the rescue!

1 **Click** on the **Setup menu**.

2 **Click** on **Preferences**. The Pro Tools Preferences dialog box will open.

3 **Click** on the **Editing tab** at the top of the Preferences dialog box, if it's not already selected. The editing preferences will be displayed. The Fades section is located in the upper-right corner of the Editing tab. In this section, you can set up your default fade settings (the ones the Smart tool will apply when creating a fade or crossfade).

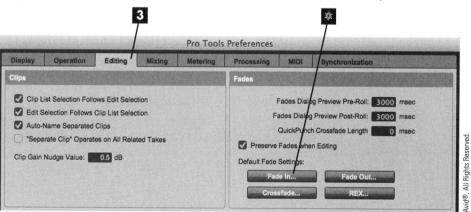

- ❄ Click on the Fade In button to open the (by now familiar) Fades dialog box. From here, you can configure your default fade-in curve in the same way you create a regular fade. Click on the OK button to close the Fades dialog box.

* Click on the Fade Out button in the Preferences dialog box to again open the Fades dialog box, and choose your default fade-out curve. Click on the OK button to close the Fades dialog box.

* Click on the Crossfade button in the Preferences dialog box to again open the Fades dialog box and set up your default crossfade settings. Once more, click on the OK button to close the Fades dialog box.

4 **Click** on the **OK button** in the lower-right corner of the Preferences dialog box. Your settings will be saved, and the dialog box will close.

❄ TWEAKING FADE CLIPS

If you create a fade in your session and later decide that you want to change its contour, just double-click on the fade clip with the Grabber tool. The Fades dialog box will open again so you can adjust the individual fade. Note that any changes you make in this dialog box will not affect the defaults you've set in the Preferences dialog box. Deleting a fade is even easier; just select the fade clip you want to remove (either single-click with the Grabber tool or double-click with the Selector tool) and press the Delete key.

Getting Specific: Nudging Clips

Using the Nudge function, you can move clips (or clip boundaries) by incremental amounts, enabling you to get very specific with your timing. First, though, you'll have to choose a nudge value. Setting up your nudge value is nearly identical to setting up your grid resolution (which you learned back in Chapter 5):

1 Click on the **down arrow** to the right of the nudge value. The Nudge menu will appear.

2 Select the **scale** with which you want to nudge your clip. The currently chosen scale will be indicated by a checkmark. (In this image, Bars|Beats is chosen, which is well suited for music sessions.) Based on the scale you choose, the options at the top of the list will change.

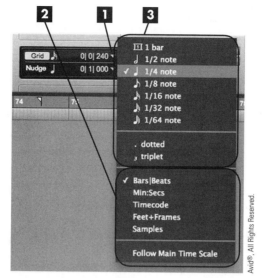

3 Select the **increment** by which you want to nudge your clip. The currently chosen increment will be indicated by a checkmark.

Once you have the nudge value you want, using the feature is very straightforward.

1 Select the **clip(s)** you want to move.

2a Press the **plus (+) key** on your keyboard's numeric keypad to move your selected clip(s) *later* in time (to the right) by the nudge amount.

OR

2b Press the **minus (−) key** on your keyboard's numeric keypad to move your selected clip(s) *earlier* in time (to the left) by the nudge amount.

> ❋ **NUDGING SHORTCUTS**
>
> Holding down the Option key (Mac) or Alt key (PC) while pressing the plus or minus key will nudge only the left boundary of a clip. Holding down the Command key (Mac) or Ctrl key (PC) while pressing the plus or minus key will nudge only the right boundary. Holding down the Shift key while pressing the plus or minus key will move only the selected area and will leave the selected clip in its original position. (If you want to get really creative, you can add the previous modifiers to the Shift key and nudge just the beginning or end of the selected area.)

Cool Editing Tools

Before you move on, let's take a look at four features that can kick your editing up a notch!

Tick-Based Audio Tracks

In many cases, you'll want your audio clips securely anchored to an absolute time location, right down to the sample. In this kind of scenario (which is the default for Audio tracks), audio clips' timing will not change if you change your session's tempo. MIDI notes and clips (which I'll talk about in the next chapter), on the other hand, typically *do* change along with tempo, their position being locked to your session's bars, beats, and ticks. With Pro Tools, you have the option of breaking away from an Audio track's default behavior, setting clips to be aligned to a tick-based location rather than their normal sample-based behavior. In this sort of tick-based Audio track, when you change your tempo, your clips will move accordingly.

❄ SETTING THINGS UP

If you go to Memory Location #10–Tick-Based Audio, you'll see a familiar-sounding drum part, separated at each transient.

1 Click on the **Timebase Selector button**. A menu will appear.

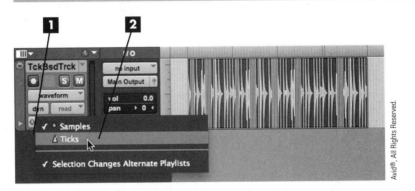

2 In this menu, you choose between having a sample-based or a tick-based timebase for your track. The currently selected timebase is marked with a checkmark. In this image, the Audio track shown is set to Samples, meaning that the placement of clips on the track is based on a real-time location and won't move if the tempo (which is tick based) is changed. To change the track to be tick based, **click** on the **Ticks menu item**.

❄ Now that you have a tick-based Audio track, all the clips on this track are locked to Bar|Beat|Tick-based locations, which means if you change the tempo in your session, each individual clip (in this case, each individual transient) will move accordingly. In this example, I've reduced the tempo from 150 beats per minute down to 75 beats per minute. The clips have moved, and the drum beat now plays at half tempo. (As you change tempo, you may find that the clips move off-screen, so you might have to scroll your view to find them!)

❋ FIXING THE CLICKS (AND THE ZERO-CROSSING RULE)

If you're following the steps using the tutorial session, you might be hearing clicks and pops when you change the tempo (especially if you slow the tempo down, as I have here). This is not uncommon in this sort of situation. The cause of the problem is that some clips have been separated at a point *other* than the zero crossing. Let me explain.

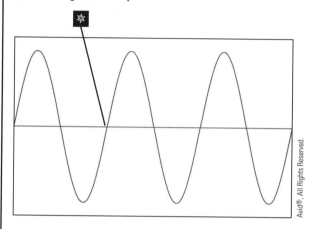

❋   As your audio waveform oscillates, it intersects the line in the center of the Waveform view. This line, commonly called the *zero line*, represents no voltage being sent to a speaker—a speaker at rest.

When a clip begins and ends with the waveform at the zero line, there will be no unwanted clicks and pops. If, however, the waveform has been cut at a point *other* than the zero line, clicks and pops may be heard (as a result of the speaker suddenly receiving a radical change in voltage). Cutting clips at the zero line, with the waveform ascending, has become the general convention when editing.

You can use the Trim tool to change a clip's boundary so that it begins and ends on the zero line, but this is sometimes prohibitively time consuming. Not to worry—you can also treat the problem by creating short fade-ins or fade-outs for the clips, which will create a zero crossing at the beginning or end of the clip.

Clip Groups

Clip groups are a way to link clips together so they move and behave as a single unit, even though they may span multiple tracks. Similar to edit groups, clip groups give you the power to have a single edit applied to multiple tracks, but with even more individual control.

❋ SETTING THINGS UP

For this section, go to Memory Location #11–Clip Groups.

1 **Select** the **clips** that you want to assign to your clip group. It's worth mentioning that any type of clip (audio, MIDI, and even video) can be part of a clip group. If you're following the tutorial session, your clips have been selected for you.

2 **Click** on the **Clip menu**.

3 **Choose Group**.

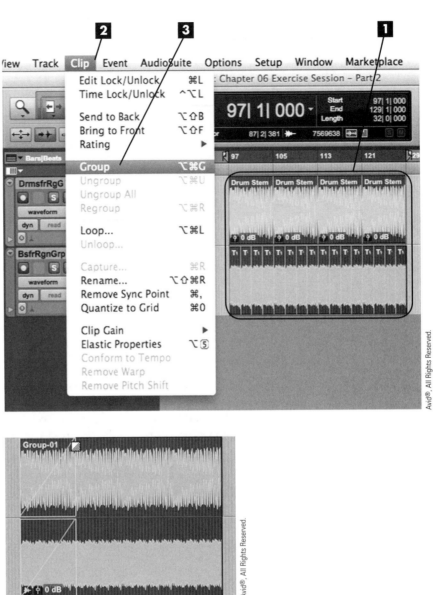

The clip group is a single object that contains all the clips you've selected. It will have its own name and will appear in the Clips list at the right edge of your Edit window. Even though it may span many clips and tracks, you can edit the clip group as a single object, such as moving, trimming, or creating a long fade, as shown here.

Clip Looping

The ability to loop clips is very useful when you're working with repetitious material, such as drum beats. Here's how it works.

❈ **SETTING THINGS UP**

For this section of the chapter, recall Memory Location #12–Clip Looping.

1 **Select** the **clip** you want to loop. If you're following the tutorial session, your clip has been selected for you.

2 **Click** on the **Clip menu**.

3 **Choose Loop.** The Clip Looping dialog box will open. You have a number of choices when it comes to how you want your clip to loop. You can:

❈ Choose the number of repetitions you want your clip to have. This number includes the original instance of the clip.

❈ Specify a length of time (based on the main time scale) that you want to fill with these loops.

❈ Loop until the end of the session or until the next clip (whichever comes first).

❈ Check the Enable Crossfade checkbox to create crossfades between each loop iteration. When this checkbox is checked, you can adjust the crossfade curve by clicking on the Settings button. (This will open the same kind of Crossfades dialog box that you worked with earlier in this chapter.)

4 Once you've chosen how you want your clip to loop, just **click** on the **OK button**. The dialog box will close, and your clip will be looped.

In this example, I've chosen to repeat this clip eight times, and here's the result. This looped clip object, like clip groups, functions in many ways like a single unit and can be moved and edited with great flexibility.

❈ ❈ ❈

The Loop Trim Tool

As if clip looping wasn't easy enough already, the Loop Trim tool will give you even more functionality. For example, you can use the Loop Trim tool to quickly create just the right amount of looping.

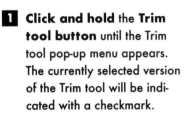

1 Click and hold the **Trim tool button** until the Trim tool pop-up menu appears. The currently selected version of the Trim tool will be indicated with a checkmark.

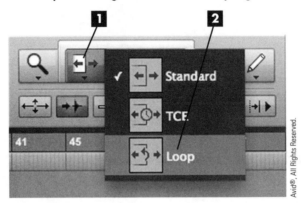

2 Choose Loop to change to the Loop Trim tool. The icon for the Trim tool will change to reflect the currently active version of the tool.

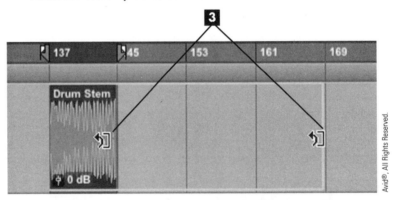

3 The rest is pretty simple, but cursor placement is important to make the Loop Trim tool work. **Position** your **cursor** near a clip boundary until you see the Trim tool with the curved arrow icon (as shown in this image), then **click and drag** the desired **clip boundary**. (You can drag either the left or the right boundary to loop forward or backward.) When you've got the duration you want, all you have to do is **release** the **mouse**, and you'll have your new looped clip.

There's another side of clip looping that's particularly interesting: Using the Trim tool with a looped clip object, you can change the length of the member clips without changing the total length of the looped clip object. Sound confusing? Take a look, and I think it'll become clear.

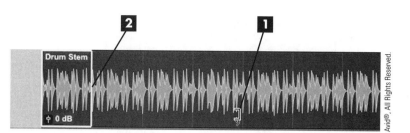

1 With the Trim tool selected (actually, any version of the Trim tool will do the trick), **move** your **cursor** to a lower corner of any member clip of your clip loop object. The Trim tool will be displayed as a basic Trim tool, as shown here.

2 **Click and drag** your **mouse** horizontally to adjust the boundary of the member clip, just as if you were trimming a normal clip.

The difference becomes apparent when you release the mouse button. You'll notice that the overall length of the looped clip object is the same, but the length of member clips within it has changed! This technique can be particularly useful when you are dealing with drum beats, and it can often yield interesting results.

Clip Locking

When you're finished editing a section of a project, you might want to make sure that you don't inadvertently move or change your clips. Clip locking will do just that. It's been a fixture in Pro Tools for quite some time and has benefited from some improvements in recent versions. Whether you're a new user or an experienced editor, it's worth taking a look at the different ways you can protect your work!

Edit Lock

The first kind of clip locking to look at is edit lock. It will prevent your locked clips from being moved or edited accidentally.

1 **Select** the **clip(s)** you want to lock.

2 **Click** on the **Clip menu**.

3 **Choose Edit Lock/Unlock.** The clip will be locked.

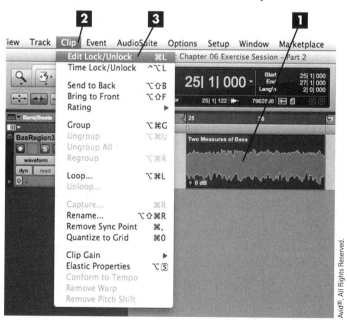

257

An edit-locked clip will be indicated by a small lock icon in the bottom-left corner of the clip.

If you attempt to change the clip in any way (including moving the clip to another location), you will see a dialog box that will enable you to apply the change or leave the locked clip unchanged.

Time Lock

When a clip is time locked, it can be freely edited in all ways *other* than moving the clip to a different location.

1 **Select** the **clip(s)** you want to lock.

2 **Click** on the **Clip menu**.

3 **Choose Time Lock/ Unlock.** The clip will be locked.

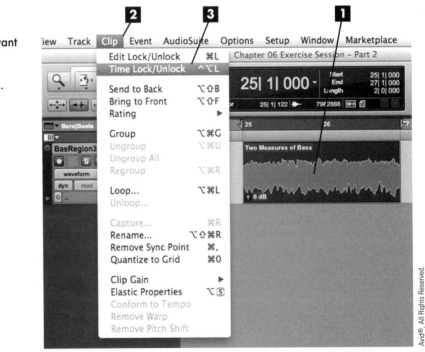

A time-locked clip will be indicated by a small lock icon in the bottom-left corner of the clip. Notice that the edit-lock icon is solid colored, whereas the time-lock icon is an outline of a lock.

When a clip is time locked, all editing processes can be applied normally *except* dragging the clip. This new variation of clip locking is particularly useful, allowing a clip to be tweaked and faded but maintaining the position of the audio within the clip.

Clips List Reveal

I talked about the relationship between clips and files way back in Chapter 1, "Welcome to Pro Tools 11," and you understand that clips—while not being audio files in and of themselves—refer or point to audio files on your hard drive. When you record audio into Pro Tools, files are created in the Audio Files subfolder by default, but in fact audio used by Pro Tools can reside anywhere in your hard disk. The question comes up from time to time: Where is the file that this clip is pointing to?

Pro Tools includes some very simple yet powerful ways to locate audio files to which clips are referring (often called parent files). Here's how it's done:

1 **Right-click** the **clip** that you want to investigate. A menu of clip-related options will appear. The bottom section of the menu will give you three useful options:

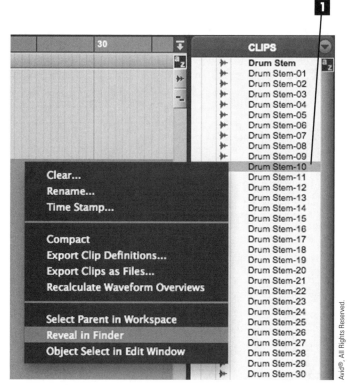

259

* **Select Parent in Workspace.** Choosing this option will open the Workspace Browser window with the clip's parent file selected.

* **Reveal in Finder (Mac)/ Reveal in Explorer (PC).** Choosing this option will open a Finder (Mac) or Explorer (PC) window with the clip's parent file selected.

* **Object Select in Edit Window.** Choosing this option will select the clip in your Edit window's tracks. (The clip must actually be used in a track and the track shown for this option to be effective.)

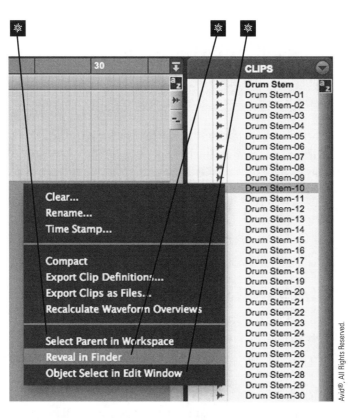

❋ FINISHED SESSION FILES

If you have been working with the tutorial sessions throughout this chapter, you might want to check your work. In each session folder, you'll find one named "Chapter 06–Part 2–Finished," which will show many techniques discussed in this chapter in completion.

That's all for now. Next...MIDI!

7 } Using MIDI

MIDI, short for Musical Instrument Digital Interface, is a language that enables keyboards, synthesizers, and other musical devices to interact with each other. Since its inception in the early 1980s, MIDI has proved to be an invaluable creative tool to musicians of all kinds, and it has changed the face of the music industry.

In the early days of music technology, software worked with *either* audio or MIDI, but usually not both. Thankfully, those days are over. Now, numerous DAW products, including Pro Tools, incorporate the creative power of MIDI and the advantages of digital audio. Pro Tools in particular has made impressive gains in its MIDI power functionality, while remaining a solid audio workstation. In this chapter, you'll learn how to:

* Set up your MIDI studio.

* Route MIDI and audio signals so you can work with synthesizers in Pro Tools.

* Record and edit MIDI data.

* Work with your MIDI data intelligently, including importing to and exporting from Pro Tools.

❋ MIDI RESOURCES

A mastery of MIDI is a study in and of itself, upon which volumes of information have been written. For the purposes of this chapter, a fundamental understanding of MIDI will necessarily be assumed. Here, we'll focus on how to use MIDI in the Pro Tools environment rather than on the underlying principles of MIDI itself. For a good book on the subject of MIDI, check out *MIDI Power! Second Edition: The Comprehensive Guide* (Thomson Course Technology PTR, 2005).

This chapter is devoted to the types of MIDI skills that any engineer might call upon when working with a MIDI musician in a studio environment. For more detail on advanced MIDI features (like the dedicated MIDI and Score Editor windows), see Appendix A, "More MIDI Power," which is included as a PDF file along with this book's downloadable materials.

> **✸ VIRTUAL INSTRUMENTS**
>
> For the purposes of this chapter, you'll be dealing with *virtual* instruments—in other words, instruments that are software based rather than physical devices. The list of free instruments included with Pro Tools is impressive:
>
> ✸ **Boom.** Vintage drum-machine emulation
>
> ✸ **DB-33.** Tonewheel organ emulation
>
> ✸ **Mini Grand.** Acoustic piano emulation, featuring a number of piano models and ambient effects
>
> ✸ **Vacuum.** Vintage monophonic tube synthesizer emulation
>
> ✸ **Xpand2!.** Workstation synthesizer, featuring a wide variety of useful sounds
>
> ✸ **Structure Free.** Sample playback instrument
>
> Again, these instruments are included with your Pro Tools 11 installation files. If you haven't installed them already, now would be an excellent time to do so!

When you were working with audio, one of your first steps was to configure inputs and outputs (in the I/O Setup dialog box). You'll want to do this with MIDI as well, using the MIDI Studio (Mac) or Media Studio Setup (PC) window, identifying your MIDI devices before proceeding. Don't worry; it's easy!

Setting Up Your MIDI Studio

Before you can record any MIDI data, you'll need to physically attach your external MIDI device(s) to your system's MIDI interface. (Refer to the documentation that came with your MIDI gear for more information.) Let's assume you've physically connected your MIDI gear in a traditional configuration—in other words, you've connected the output of your MIDI interface to the MIDI input of your device and then connected the MIDI output (*not* the Thru) of your device into an input on your MIDI interface. Once that's done, you'll need to set up Pro Tools to recognize that connection.

1. **Click** on the **Setup menu**.

2. **Move the cursor** to **MIDI**. The MIDI submenu will be displayed.

3. **Choose MIDI Studio.** The MIDI Studio (Mac) or MIDI Studio Setup (PC) window will appear.

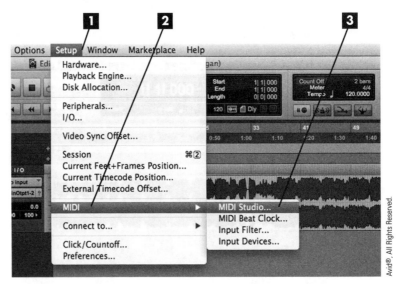

MIDI Studio Setup on a Mac

The MIDI Studio window will give you an overview of the devices attached to your system. Initially, it might show you only your MIDI interface (the device to which you'll attach any external MIDI devices). The next step is to add a device to your system.

1 **Click** on the **Add Device button**. A New External Device icon will appear.

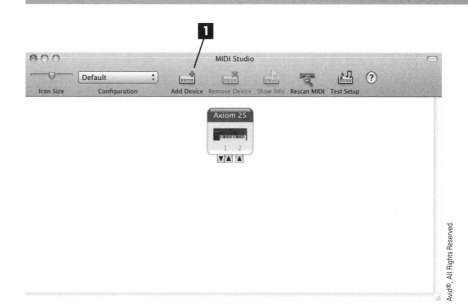

2 **Click and hold** on the **MIDI OUT port** of the MIDI interface that is connected to your external device.

3 **Drag** with your mouse to the **MIDI IN port** of your external device. You'll see a line connecting the MIDI interface icon and the New External Device icon.

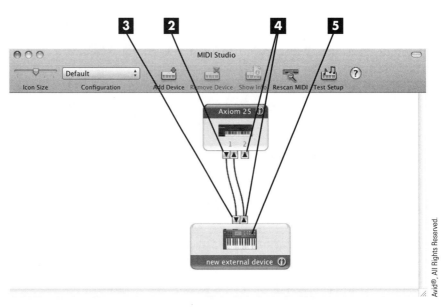

4 **Repeat steps 2 and 3** for the connection from the MIDI OUT port of your external device to the MIDI IN port of your interface, if applicable.

5 **Double-click** the **New External Device icon**. The New External Device Properties dialog box will appear, enabling you to customize the connection.

❄ The top section enables you to type a descriptive name for your device and choose the manufacturer and model that match your gear. If you can't find your manufacturer or model on those lists, don't worry—just leave the fields blank.

6 **Click** on the **transmit channels** that you want to make available to your device. (Enabled channels will be colored blue.) You can also choose to enable the device to transmit MIDI Beat Clock and/ or MIDI Time Code. (Enabled options will be indicated with a checkmark.)

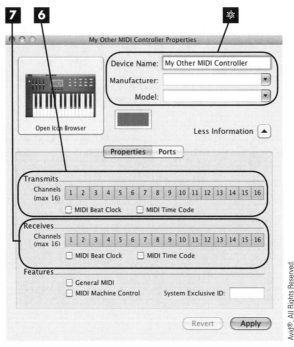

7 **Click** on the **receive channels** that you want to make available to your device. (Enabled channels will be colored blue.) You can also choose to enable the device to receive MIDI Beat Clock and/or MIDI Time Code. (Enabled options will be indicated with a checkmark.)

> **✻ ADVICE ON TRANSMIT AND RECEIVE CHANNELS**
>
> Bearing in mind that MIDI setups come in all shapes and sizes, it's a good general rule to start off by enabling all of your transmit and receive channels. This will give you maximum flexibility when recording and playing back MIDI (which you'll learn about later in this chapter). You can always adjust the device's settings later if you want to change things to better suit your individual studio layout.

✻ You can enable your device to operate as a General MIDI device or a MIDI Machine Control device (to control transport of Pro Tools), or you can assign a System Exclusive ID number (if you have multiple devices of the same model).

8 When you've set up your device, **click** on the **Apply** button. The dialog box will close. When you've created and configured all your external gear, just **close** the **MIDI Studio window**.

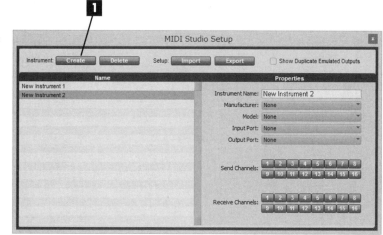

Avid®, All Rights Reserved.

MIDI Studio Setup on a PC

Like the MIDI Studio window on a Mac, the MIDI Studio Setup window on a PC enables you to set up your MIDI device. The steps vary a bit, however:

1 **Click** on the **Create button**. A new device, initially named New Instrument 1, will be created.

Avid®, All Rights Reserved.

❉ The top section of the window's Properties pane will enable you to type a descriptive name for your device, plus choose the manufacturer and model that match your gear. If you don't see your manufacturer or model, don't worry—just leave the fields blank.

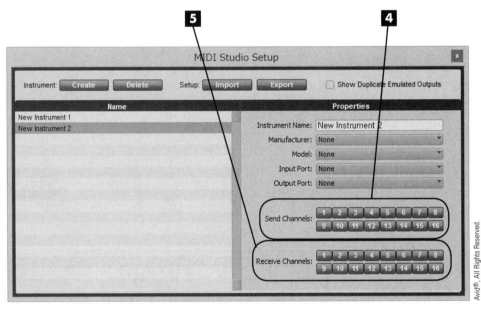

Avid®, All Rights Reserved.

2 **Click** the **Input Port down arrow**. A menu will appear. **Choose** the appropriate **MIDI IN port** on your MIDI interface (the MIDI IN port that is connected to your external device).

3 Now it's time to choose how your system will *send* MIDI information to the device. **Click** the **Output Port down arrow**. A menu will appear. **Choose** the appropriate **MIDI OUT port** on your MIDI interface (the MIDI OUT port that is connected to your external device).

4 **Click** the **send channels** that you want to make available to your device. (Enabled channels will be colored blue.)

5 **Click** the **receive channels** that you want to make available to your device. (Enabled channels will be colored blue.)

You can repeat this process for each of the external MIDI devices in your system. Before you leave this window, though, let's take a look at some of its other features:

Avid®, All Rights Reserved.

❄ The Import button will enable you to open any MIDI setup file (stored with a .dms file extension) that has been previously created. Be careful, though—this will overwrite your current settings.

❄ Want to store the setup you have now for future use or to transplant to another system? Just click the Export button. You will be prompted to save your settings as a DMS file.

6 When you're finished, **close** the **window**, and your settings will be applied to your system.

Signal Flow 201: MIDI Versus Audio

If there's one important thing to remember about MIDI, it's this: MIDI is *not* audio. MIDI isn't even audible—it's a digital language that enables musical devices to communicate with each other on a fundamental level. It's a common (and dangerous) misconception that MIDI and audio are somehow related, and this probably stems from the fact that the use of MIDI enables musical gear to make sound.

Given that MIDI and digital audio are fundamentally different, it should come as no surprise that MIDI has its own rules for signal flow. The good news is that if you know the rules, setting up your instruments is easy, and you can manage MIDI signal paths and audio signal paths simultaneously in a single Pro Tools session.

Managing the MIDI Signal Path

You've already gone over the process of basic audio signal routing. You'll find that managing your MIDI tracks has a familiar look and feel.

1 Create a **MIDI track** and **assign** it a descriptive **name**. (Refer to Chapter 3, "Getting Started with Audio," if you need a refresher on how to do this.) You'll notice that the overall layout of a MIDI track is consistent with other tracks you've seen so far:

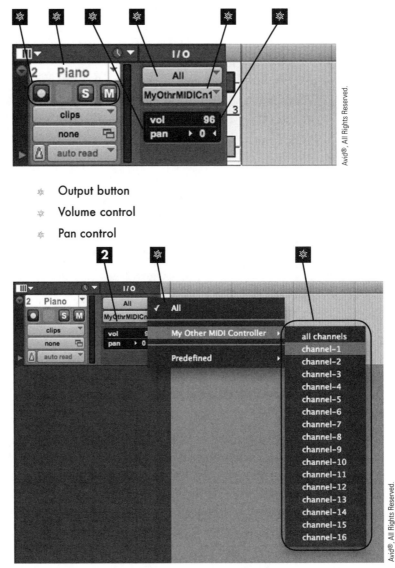

* Track name
* Record, Solo, and Mute buttons
* Input button

* Output button
* Volume control
* Pan control

2 **Click** on the **Input button**. The Input menu will appear, including the following options:

* By default, a new MIDI track will have All set as the input and will enable the track to accept MIDI data from any port on any channel. This is a convenient way to work if you're a single user in a multi-keyboard studio. With All selected as an input, you can play any MIDI device in your studio and have it recorded to the track, without having to change your input selection.

* Each input device you've specified in your MIDI setup will appear as an input option. You can choose a single device or even a specific MIDI channel on a given device as an input for your track. This is useful in multi-keyboard setups in which you have multiple musicians playing simultaneously. You can assign multiple tracks to accept input from specific MIDI sources, isolating each musician's performance to separate tracks.

3 **Select** the **input** that suits your situation.

4 **Click** on the **Output button**. The Output menu will appear.

5 **Select** the **device** and **MIDI channel** that are routed to the device you want to use for this track.

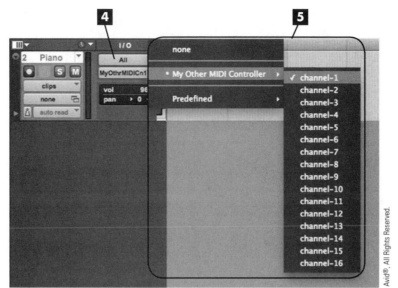

❄ USING MIDI CONTROLLERS

With MIDI, the device you physically play does *not* necessarily have to be the device that you hear. In these cases, where the performance device and the device making the sound are different, the device you actually play is called a *MIDI controller*.

Now your MIDI track is set up to route MIDI data from a source (for example, a MIDI controller) to a destination (for example, an external sound module). When you play your MIDI instrument, you should see an indication on the destination device that it is receiving MIDI data. At this point, that device should respond to the MIDI data by making sound.

Occasionally, you'll need to adjust your MIDI track's volume. This is also a straightforward process:

1 **Click and hold** on the **volume display area**. A small fader box will appear.

2 Still holding down the mouse button, **drag** the **fader** in the fader box to adjust the volume to suit your session.

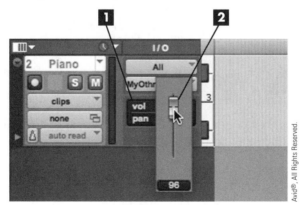

❄ ❄ ❄

Similarly, you can adjust a track's pan settings:

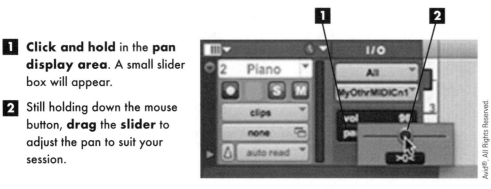

Avid®, All Rights Reserved.

1 **Click and hold** in the **pan display area**. A small slider box will appear.

2 Still holding down the mouse button, **drag** the **slider** to adjust the pan to suit your session.

Setting Up an Aux Track to Monitor Your MIDI Gear

Chapter 3 discussed the idea of Aux tracks (or, more formally, Auxiliary Input tracks). Aux tracks are the track type of choice when you need to manage an audio signal, but you don't need to record audio to your hard drive. In this example, you'll use an Aux track to hear an external MIDI sound module through Pro Tools.

Once you've connected the audio outputs of the MIDI sound module to the appropriate audio input(s) of your Pro Tools interface, follow these steps.

1 **Create** a **new Aux track** and **assign** it a descriptive **name**. (This is the track you'll use to hear your MIDI device.)

2 **Assign** the **input** of this Aux track to match the audio inputs to which your external MIDI sound module is attached.

3 **Assign** the **output** of this Aux track to the audio outputs to which your monitor speakers are attached.

4 **Adjust** the **volume** of the Aux track to suit your session.

At this point, you've completely configured your MIDI signal flow, as well as the audio signal routing that will enable you to listen to your sound-producing device. When you play your controller device (with the MIDI track record armed), you will trigger your slave device (with MIDI data traveling through the MIDI track and recordable on that track) and listen to the audio output of your sound module through the Aux track.

Using Virtual Instruments

A relatively recent addition to the world of music creation, virtual instruments have really boosted the power of the modern DAW. Virtual instruments are real-time plug-ins, but whereas most plug-ins *process* sound, virtual instruments *make* sound! Think of them as the marriage between software plug-ins and MIDI synthesizers, giving you the best of both worlds. With virtual instruments, you not only have the power of a MIDI synth without the bulk of physical hardware, you also have the ability to automate its parameters just like any plug-in. (Don't worry; I'll talk more about that in the next chapter.)

The secret to using virtual instruments is in the setup, which is really just a variation of the traditional MIDI setup that you learned in the previous section. Here again, you can use two tracks to get MIDI and sound to work together within Pro Tools—a MIDI track (for the MIDI data) and an Aux track (for your virtual instrument).

1 **Create** a new **stereo Aux track** and **assign** its **output** to your system's monitor speakers.

2 Because you'll be using a plug-in, and because plug-ins are used via inserts, you'll want to make sure you can see an Inserts column in your Edit window. If you're not seeing an Inserts column, **click** the **Edit Window View button** and **choose** an **inserts view** from the list. (In this image, I'm showing Inserts A–E.)

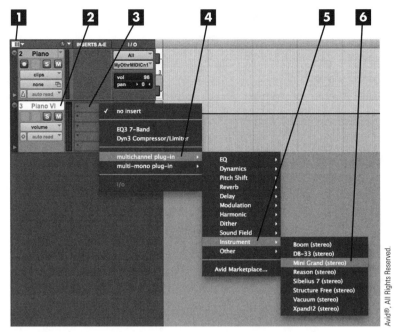

3 **Click** on an **Insert button**. A menu will appear.

4 **Select** either **Multichannel Plug-In** or **Multi-Mono Plug-In** (based on the kind of instrument you want to use; I've chosen Multichannel Plug-In). A submenu will appear.

5 **Choose Instrument.** Yet another submenu will appear.

6 **Choose** your desired **virtual instrument**. (In this image, I've chosen the Mini Grand plug-in.) The plug-in's window will appear.

7 Next, you'll need to create a MIDI track (if you haven't already) and set up the output to be routed to your new virtual instrument. **Click** on the MIDI track's **Output button**. A menu will appear.

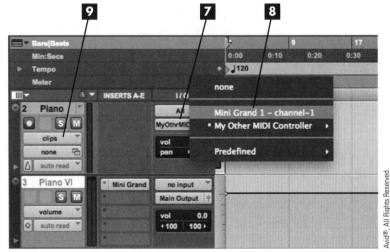

8 After you've launched a virtual instrument plug-in, it will appear as an output option for your MIDI track (in addition to your physical MIDI outputs). **Select** the **instrument** you want to control from the Output drop-down menu.

9 Now let's test your setup. **Click** the MIDI track's **Track View button** (which will initially read "Clips"). A menu will appear.

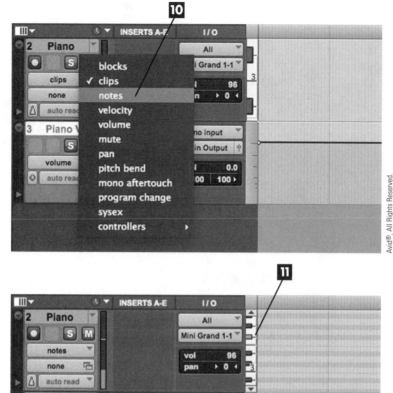

10 The Track View menu will show you the available view options for this track, with the currently active view indicated by a checkmark. **Choose Notes** from the menu.

11 **Click** on any **note** on the mini keyboard to the left of your MIDI track's playlist area. If everything is set up properly, MIDI data will be created, the data will be sent to the virtual instrument, and the instrument will sound.

❄ MIDI METERING

As you click on the mini keyboard, you will see activity in your MIDI track's level meters. What you're seeing is *not* audio, but rather control data (note messages) being sent to the virtual instrument on your Aux track. The levels you see on the Aux track's meters are the audible signal being routed to your monitor speakers.

Instrument Tracks

Instrument tracks are real timesavers for MIDI production, combining the power of a MIDI track *and* an Aux track in a single unit. Let's delete the two tracks you created in the previous virtual instrument scenario and redo the whole job with just one track.

1 **Open** the **New Tracks dialog box** and **create** a stereo track. (Refer to Chapter 3 if you need a refresher on how to do this.) From the Track Type menu, **select Instrument Track**. When you click Create, a new Instrument track will be created.

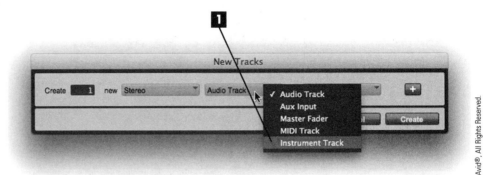

Avid®, All Rights Reserved.

2 **Assign** your track a descriptive **name**. Below the track name, you'll see some familiar-looking buttons:

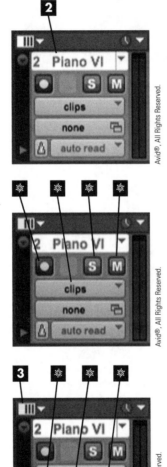

Avid®, All Rights Reserved.

- Track Record Enable
- Solo
- Mute
- Track View Selector

- Patch Select
- Timebase Selector
- Automation Mode Selector (I'll discuss this in the next chapter.)

Avid®, All Rights Reserved.

Avid®, All Rights Reserved.

3 If you're not seeing the Instrument column, **click** the **Edit Window View button** and **choose Instrument**. (Visible columns will be indicated by checkmarks.) The Instrument column mirrors the functionality of a MIDI track's I/O column.

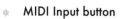

- ❋ MIDI Input button
- ❋ MIDI Mute button
- ❋ MIDI Output button
- ❋ MIDI volume display area
- ❋ MIDI pan display area
- ❋ MIDI Level Meter

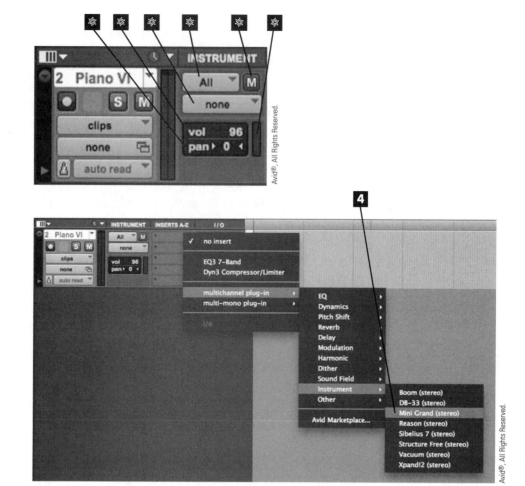

4 The Inserts column of an Instrument track functions just like the Inserts column of an Aux track. Simply **choose** the desired **virtual instrument plug-in** on this track, just as you did before with an Aux track. Your plug-in will launch, and the plug-in window will be displayed. As soon as your virtual instrument is launched, the MIDI Output button of the Instrument track automatically changes to match the plug-in, making an Instrument track even more convenient. If you need to change that MIDI output for any reason, you can do it easily by clicking the MIDI Output button.

5 The I/O column of an Instrument track is identical to the I/O column of an Aux track, and you'll use it the same way. **Set** the **output** of the Instrument track.

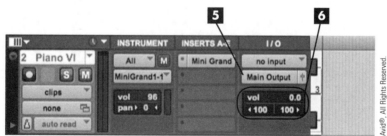

6 Last but certainly not least, **adjust** your track's **output level and pan** as needed. Note that it is standard practice to control the volume level of an Instrument track from the *audio* volume fader rather than the MIDI volume fader.

❋ ❋ ❋

Your track should look something like the image shown here. Initially, the Instrument track view will be set to Clips (similar to the MIDI track you worked with earlier), but as with a MIDI track, you can change the view to Notes and click your mini keyboard to test your setup, as you did in the previous section of this chapter.

MIDI and Instrument Tracks in the Mix Window

The Mix window is well suited to the task of routing and combining individual signals to achieve a pleasing total mix. You'll take a closer look at mixing in the next chapter, but for now let's explore how MIDI and Instrument tracks appear in this environment.

First, you need to make sure you're seeing the appropriate aspects of each track strip in the Mix window:

1 Click the **View menu**.

2 Choose **Mix Window Views.** A submenu will appear.

3 Displayed elements of your session's tracks will be indicated by a checkmark. If the Instruments menu item isn't checked, **click it** now.

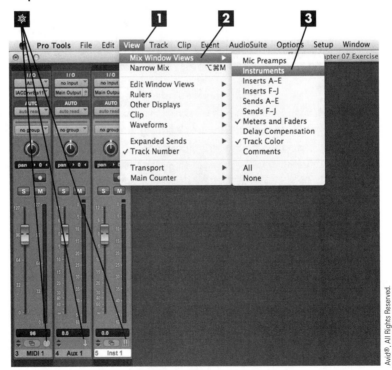

❋ The icons at the bottom-right corner of each channel strip indicate track type (a MIDI plug for a MIDI track, an arrow for an Aux track, and a keyboard for an Instrument track).

❄ The Instrument row (at the top of the channel strip) mirrors the functionality of the Instrument column that you saw earlier in the Edit window (MIDI input, output, volume, pan, and mute). Note that the area is blank in any track other than an Instrument track.

❄ The I/O section of a MIDI track enables the user to choose the MIDI input and output assignments. The I/O section of an Instrument track is the same as the I/O section of an Aux track, and it is here where you will set up your audio ins and outs.

❄ The bottom section of each of these track types enables you to adjust positioning with pan controls and includes Record (when applicable), Solo, Mute, and volume controls.

Recording MIDI

The process of recording MIDI is similar to audio recording in many respects, but with some additional flexibility.

Choosing a Sound

Usually, your first step is to pick a sound that you want to use. How you do this varies slightly, depending on whether you're using an external MIDI device or a virtual instrument plug-in. Let's start with the external device.

Choosing a Sound for an External Device

To choose a sound for an external device, follow these steps:

1 **Click** on the **Patch Select button**. (Conveniently, it's in the same position on MIDI tracks and Instrument tracks.) A dialog box containing a patch list for the MIDI device will open. Depending on the device you configured in your MIDI setup, the patch list displayed will consist of numbers and/or text names.

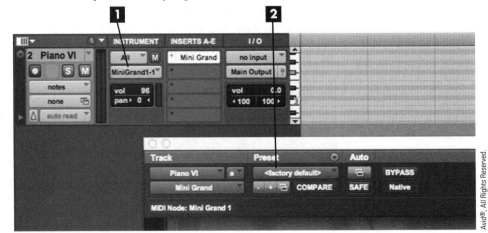

2 **Click** on the **patch** you want to use.

3 **Click** on the **Done button**. The dialog box will close, and the program number or name will appear on the Patch Select button.

Choosing a Sound for a Virtual Instrument

If you're using a virtual instrument (such as Mini Grand), you'll need to choose a sound directly from the plug-in's window:

1 If the plug-in window isn't open already, **click** on the virtual instrument's **Insert button**. The Insert button will be highlighted, and the plug-in window will open.

2 **Click** the **Librarian Menu button** (which will display the currently active sound). A menu of available sounds will appear.

3 **Choose** the desired **sound** from the menu. The menu will close, and your choice will be applied.

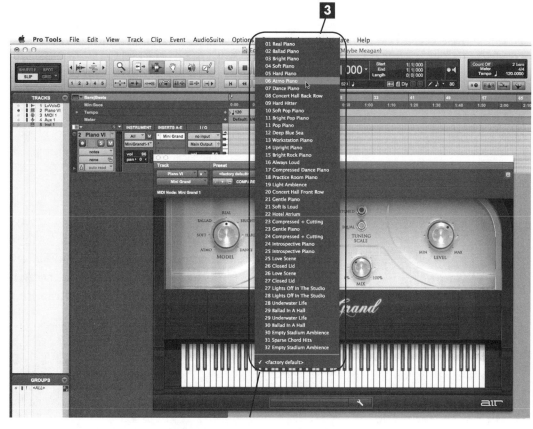

1 **Click** the **Plug-In Settings Select button**. The plug-in settings window will open.

2 If your plug-in presets are organized into submenus, **click** the **Folder menu**. The subfolder hierarchy will be displayed. **Select** the desired **subfolder** from the list that is displayed. When you make your selection, the programs in that subfolder will be displayed in the window.

3 **Select** the desired **sound**.

4 **Click** the **Done button**.

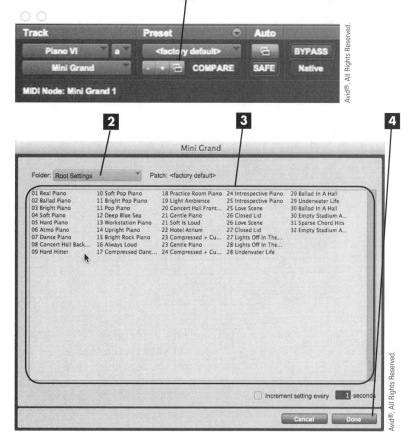

❋ **INCREMENT PATCH**

If you're searching for just the right sound, the Increment Setting Every *n* Seconds checkbox (in the bottom-right corner of the plug-in settings window) can come in handy. Just enable the feature to cycle through all the sounds in this window automatically, allowing you to keep playing while the patches change.

❋ **HEY, I'M NOT HEARING ANYTHING!**

If you're playing your keyboard but can't preview sounds, just record-enable the track. This will route incoming MIDI data to the appropriate instrument.

Basic MIDI Recording

Before you start recording, you might want to set up a click track (which you learned about in Chapter 4, "Recording Audio"). Remember to click on the Metronome icon to enable your click track. Now it's time to actually record the MIDI. The process of recording MIDI is nearly identical to recording audio.

1 **Click** on the **Track Record Enable** button to arm the track for recording.

2 **Click** on the **Record Enable button** in the Transport window (or in the transport controls at the top of the Edit window).

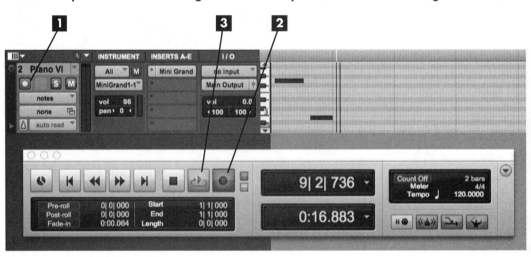

3 **Click** on the **Play button**. Recording will begin. It operates the same as when you record audio, with pre-rolls, post-rolls, and so on.

❋ Here's a nifty feature: MIDI Merge enables you to record on a MIDI track without overwriting any pre-existing MIDI data. It's an especially useful feature when you're working in Loop Playback mode.

❋❋❋

When you're finished, you'll have a clip, as you did when you recorded audio. This time, however, you'll see MIDI note data within the clip rather than audio waveforms!

Recording MIDI Instruments to Audio Tracks

Suppose you've created a killer track using your favorite MIDI hardware, and you want to send the session to a friend so that he can lay down tracks of his own. There's a potential problem: If your friend doesn't have the same MIDI hardware (or virtual instrument) that you have in your studio, he won't be able to hear your killer track the way it's meant to be heard. The solution is to record your MIDI instrument to an Audio track and then send your session out for collaboration.

The process is simple enough. You'll use a bus to connect the output of your MIDI instrument's Aux or Instrument track to the input of an Audio track to which you'll record.

1 Assign the **output** of your instrument's Aux or Instrument track to an available bus. (In this image, I've chosen Bus 1–2.)

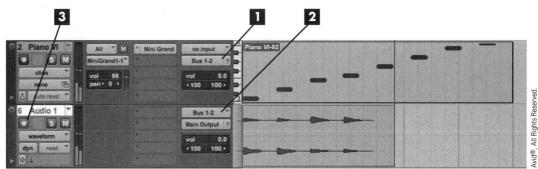

2 After creating an Audio track to record to, **assign** the **input** of that track to the same bus that you chose for the output of the Aux or Instrument track (again, Bus 1–2 in this example).

3 Now that you have your signals routed properly, you can **record** your **Audio track** normally (which I covered in Chapter 4). You'll see that the level meters of the two tracks are identical.

> ✳ **TRACK OUTPUT**
>
> Pro Tools 9 introduced a very useful track-output feature, enabling you to choose either an existing or a new track as an output destination. This can be especially useful when recording virtual instruments to Audio tracks, and is a feature you'll dig into in Chapter 9, "Finishing Touches."

> ✳ **WATCH OUT!**
>
> Back in Chapter 2, "Getting Around in Pro Tools," you learned about a new feature in Pro Tools 11 called Transport Fade-in. While it's a great feature in many cases, you'll definitely want to have it turned off while recording from your Instrument track to an Audio track. If it's left on, you'll record with the fade-in!

Managing a MIDI Session

Here are a few more MIDI operations that will help you work with MIDI. These processes will not only serve you directly if you're a MIDI musician but will also help non-MIDI users work with MIDI projects that come into their studios.

❋ USING THE EXERCISE SESSION

The images in this chapter are based on a project I did some years ago, for a talented American musician named William Brooks. He gave me a vocal and guitar performance of a song (named "Maybe Meagan"). I added MIDI instruments to the live tracks before moving on to the mixing stage.

The Chapter 07 Exercise Session (Maybe Meagan) file is a snapshot of the production process. What you'll see when you download and open the session is a single Audio track, plus a number of empty Instrument tracks. Your job is to get MIDI into the session and use some basic editing tools. For information on downloading this book's exercise materials, please refer to the "Setting Up Your Session" section of the introduction.

Importing and Exporting MIDI Data

One of MIDI's greatest advantages is its broad compatibility. Nearly every MIDI application can utilize MIDI's Standard MIDI File (SMF) format, and Pro Tools is no exception. That means you can easily bring in MIDI data from other applications, as well as send MIDI information *to* other applications.

❋ IF YOU'RE USING THE EXERCISE MATERIALS...

Among the download materials, you'll find a folder called "Chapter 07 Source MIDI," and within that folder, a single MIDI file named "Chapter 07 – Maybe Meagan MIDI." Let's start by bringing that MIDI into the session.

Importing MIDI Data from the File Menu

Just as you can import an audio file to an Audio track, you can import a standard MIDI file to one or more MIDI tracks in your session.

1. **Click** on **File**.

2. **Choose Import.**

3. **Choose MIDI.** The Open dialog box will appear.

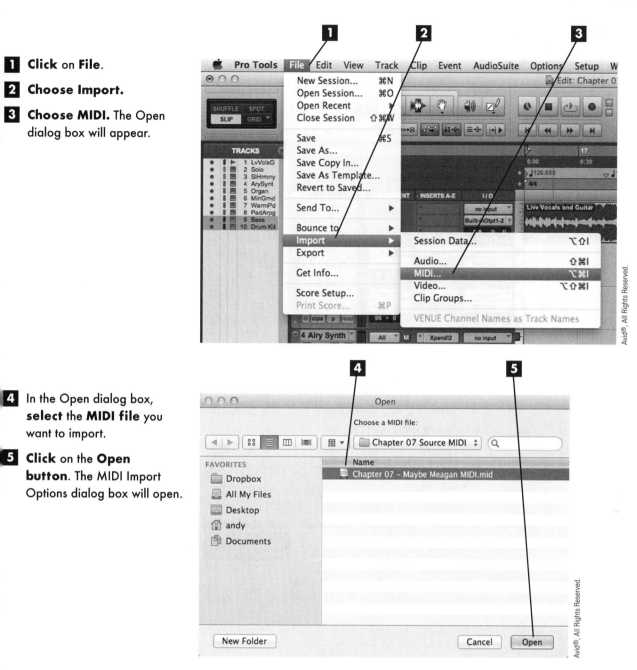

4. In the Open dialog box, **select** the **MIDI file** you want to import.

5. **Click** on the **Open button**. The MIDI Import Options dialog box will open.

⁕ The Destination section of the MIDI Import Options dialog box will enable you to choose whether the imported MIDI data will go to a new track (or tracks) or simply be added to the Clips list.

MIDI Import Options

Destination
○ New Track
● Clip List

Location: Session Start

☐ Import tempo map from MIDI File
☐ Import Key Signature from MIDI File
☐ Remove existing instrument tracks
☐ Remove existing MIDI tracks
☐ Remove existing MIDI clips

Cancel   OK

⁕ The Location drop-down menu will let you choose where the clip will be deposited on the timeline. In this image, the new MIDI data will begin at the session start, but you also have the option of choosing the song start (if it's different from the session start), the beginning of a selection, or a specific spot in your session. (The same Spot dialog box that you use in Spot mode will appear.)

⁕ You have the option of also importing that MIDI file's tempo map or key signatures. Be careful, though—importing these will overwrite the existing Tempo or Key Signature rulers in your session.

⁕ You have the option of removing any existing Instrument tracks, MIDI tracks, or MIDI clips in your session.

6 When you've chosen the options that work best, **click** on the **OK button**. The MIDI will be immediately imported into your session according to your settings.

MIDI Import Options

Destination
○ New Track
● Clip List

Location: Session Start

☐ Import tempo map from MIDI File
☐ Import Key Signature from MIDI File
☐ Remove existing instrument tracks
☐ Remove existing MIDI tracks
☐ Remove existing MIDI clips

Cancel   OK

Importing MIDI Data from the Workspace Browser

Just as you can import audio from the Workspace Browser with ease, you can also import MIDI. When it comes to importing MIDI, though, the news gets even better, because you can import an entire song's worth of material with just a click and a drag. Here's how:

1 **Click** on **Window**.

2 **Choose Workspace.** The Workspace Browser will appear, as you saw in Chapter 3.

3 **Drag** the desired **MIDI file** into your Edit window's playlist area, just as you did with audio files. (You can also drag to the Clips or Tracks list if you like.) When applicable, the MIDI Import Options dialog box will appear, as you saw earlier in this section. According to your import options, the individual MIDI tracks included in the SMF-format file will be created in your Edit window, and the appropriate clips will be created.

❄ AFTER YOU IMPORT

Keep in mind that even after you import your MIDI data, you'll still have to set your MIDI output and Aux track(s) before you can play and hear your MIDI data through the Pro Tools Mixer.

❄ IF YOU'RE USING THE EXERCISE MATERIALS...

If you're using the Exercise session, import or drag the MIDI into your Clips list. Once you have all the MIDI clips in your list, just drag the clips onto the corresponding Instrument track so that the clip begins at the beginning of the timeline. (Tip: Shuffle mode makes this easy!)

Exporting MIDI Data

When you save your session, your MIDI data will automatically be saved in that session file. There's usually no need to save your MIDI data as a separate file. However, from time to time, you may need to save the MIDI portion of your session to an SMF-format file so that you can open it in a different program.

1 **Click** on **File**.

2 **Choose Export**.

3 **Choose MIDI.** The Export MIDI Settings dialog box will appear.

4 Before you can choose where you will save your SMF-format file, you'll need to make a few choices in the Export MIDI Settings dialog box. **Click** on the **MIDI File Format menu** to choose what kind of SMF-format file you'll be creating. You have two options:

* Select the 0 (Single-Track) option to save all your data as a single MIDI track, regardless of how many MIDI tracks you may have in your session. (This is commonly used in multimedia applications.)

* Select the 1 (Multitrack) option to preserve the multitrack organization of your MIDI data. This is the type of SMF-format file most commonly used in professional circles, enabling your tracks to be re-created in any program that supports Type 1 SMF-format files.

5 **Click** the **Apply Real-Time Properties checkbox** to "print" any real-time properties you may have in your session to your new SMF-format file. (For more information on the MIDI Real-Time Properties feature, see Appendix A.)

6 When you're finished, **click** on the **OK button**. A standard Save dialog box will appear, enabling you to choose the name and location for your new SMF-format file. All tracks that are not muted will be exported.

Here's a way to export MIDI on a track-by-track basis:

1 **Right-click** on the desired **track name** (in either the track itself or the Tracks list). A menu will appear.

2 **Choose** the **Export MIDI menu item**. The Export MIDI Settings dialog box will appear, just as you've seen before.

3 In the Export MIDI dialog box **make your choices, click** on the **OK button**, and save your file—easy!

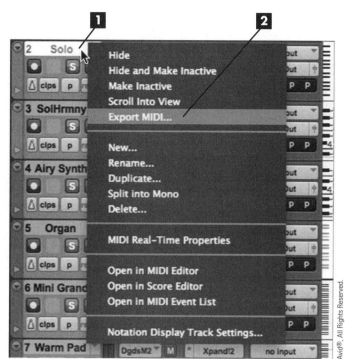

Avid®, All Rights Reserved.

Editing MIDI

There are a number of ways to edit MIDI data, giving you a greater degree of control over specific notes than you might have when working with Audio tracks. Of course, you'll still have all the clip-editing tools that you've come to know in the previous editing chapters; Selector, Grabber, and Trim (including the TCE Trim tool) work with MIDI clips in the same way they work with audio clips. In the interest of efficiency, I won't rehash these basic (but powerful) ways of working in the Edit window, but do take some time to reacquaint yourself with these tools when you get the opportunity.

The interesting thing about working with MIDI is the specificity of control you have over your tracks. You can go beyond the relatively large clip level and work with individual notes themselves, and beyond. Even at these deeper levels, you still have use of the editing tools that are already familiar to you, although their behavior will be somewhat different. The first thing to do, though, is to change your Edit window's view so that you can actually see what you're working with.

✳ ✳ ✳

1 **Click** on the **Track View Selector button** on the desired track. (In this example, I've chosen the Airy Synth track.) The Track View menu will appear.

2 The Track View menu enables you to choose the kind of data you will view and manipulate. Because this is an Instrument track and contains MIDI data, the menu will display all editable aspects of MIDI in Pro Tools, including controllers and system-exclusive data. You'll be working on note data first, so **click** on the **Notes menu item**.

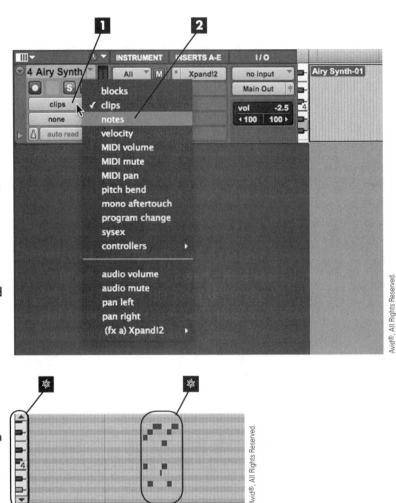

❋ The clip's color will disappear, and a series of blocks will gain prominence. Each of these blocks represents a MIDI note.

❋ On the left edge of the MIDI track's playlist area, you will notice an image of a piano keyboard. This side-facing keyboard indicates the pitches of the MIDI notes on the track.

Depending on the kind of track you're working with, your next step is to get your MIDI data into easy view. There are a few ways to do this, using some familiar tools:

❋ Use the horizontal zoom buttons to see more or less of your timeline.

* Use the MIDI Zoom buttons to zoom *vertically* on your MIDI data. Note that the keyboard image to the left of the playlist area will expand and contract accordingly.

* Click on the arrow at either end of the keyboard image to scroll the register of the track up or down.

The Grabber Tool

The Grabber tool does just what it says: It enables you to *grab* data objects in the Edit window and move them. Because you're working with a MIDI track in Notes view, the "objects" in this case are individual notes.

> ❋ **IF YOU'RE USING THE EXERCISE MATERIALS...**
>
> On the Airy Synth track, the higher note at the beginning of measure 25 is a half step too high. You'll use the Grabber tool to bring it down from one pitch to another.

1 If the Grabber tool isn't already selected, **click** on the **Grabber tool** to activate it.

2 **Click** on a **single note** in your track. The note will be highlighted, indicating that it has been selected and is ready to be moved.

3 **Drag and drop** the **note** to a different pitch or timing, as desired. If you're using the exercise session, take the upper note at measure 25 of the Airy Synth track and lower it by one half-step (from F4 to E4, to be specific), as shown here.

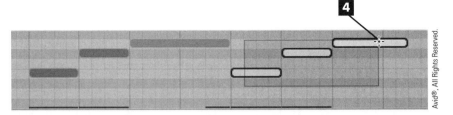

4 If you want to move more than one note at a time, just **click and drag** a box around the **notes** you want to change (again, using the Grabber tool). The group of notes will be high-lighted, indicating that they are selected.

5 **Drag and drop** the **group of notes** in the same manner that you moved a single note.

❋ SELECTIVE SELECTING

There's another way to select a group of notes that you want to move: Just hold down the Shift key while clicking the notes you want to move. The selected notes will be highlighted.

❋ SELECTING A SINGLE PITCH

Here's a quick way to select *all* the notes of a given pitch on a MIDI or Instrument track: Just click on the desired note on the keyboard at the left of your track's playlist area. All the notes of that pitch will be selected. This is particularly useful when you are dealing with MIDI drum tracks (which typically use repeated notes of identical pitch)!

The Trim Tool

The Trim tool enables you to adjust the beginning and/or end of MIDI notes in much the same way you've changed clip boundaries when working with Audio tracks.

❋ IF YOU'RE USING THE EXERCISE MATERIALS...

The last note of the Solo track (played at measure 81 | 1 | 000) is way too long. Use the Trim tool to make the note shorter. If you're not in Slip mode, now would be a good time to switch to it, so that you can change the note length freely.

1 If the Trim tool isn't already selected, **click** on the **Trim tool** to activate it.

2 **Click** on **either end** of a note in your track. The note will be highlighted, indicating that it is selected.

3 **Drag** the **end** of the note as desired. A note can be length-ened or shortened using the Trim tool.

The Pencil Tool

The Pencil tool might just be the most useful of all the MIDI editing tools. Using the Pencil tool, you can create a MIDI note (or another type of MIDI data) and then modify it after the data is created.

The Bass track needs a little work, and the Pencil tool is well suited to helping you fix it. The first problem: The first note is missing, and you'll need to add it! If you're not viewing your Bass track in Notes view, now's a good time to set things up.

In Slip mode, you can create your data anywhere, but in this case, I want to create a 1/4 note right on the first beat of measure 39. To make the job easier, let's switch to Grid mode and set a grid value of 1/4 note. (For a review of this process, refer to Chapter 5, "Editing.")

1 If the Pencil tool isn't already selected, **click** on the **Pencil tool** to activate it.

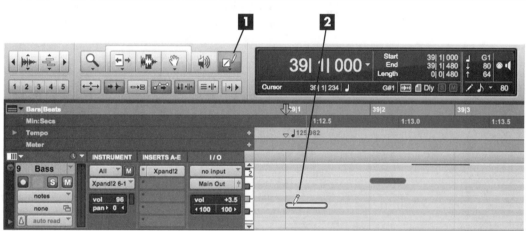

2 **Click** on any **open area** of your track. Wherever you click, a MIDI note will be created. Since I've put myself in Grid mode with a grid value of 1/4 note, the note will be placed directly on the beat. If you're using the Exercise session, place a G1 1/4 note at 39|1|000.

Setting Note Duration and Velocity

In Pro Tools, the Pencil tool defaults to creating notes whose duration follows the current grid value. However, you have the ability to choose a separate default note duration and MIDI velocity value for notes created with the Pencil tool, making the Pencil tool even easier to use.

❋ ❋ ❋

1 **Click** on the **Note Duration down arrow**, located in the lower-right area of the Counters and Edit Selections section of the Edit window. The Note Duration menu will appear.

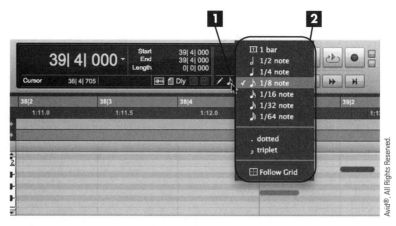

2 **Choose** the desired **note duration** from the list. (The currently selected duration will be indicated by a checkmark.) Choosing the Follow Grid option will change your duration to continually match your grid settings (regardless of whether Grid mode is active). If you're using the exercise session, **choose 1/8 Note**.

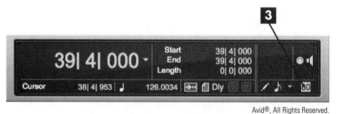

3 **Click** on the **MIDI Velocity indicator** (the value will be highlighted, as shown here) and **type** the desired default MIDI **velocity**. To confirm your value, **press** the **Return key (Mac) or Enter key (PC)**.

Creating a Series of Notes with the Pencil Tool

Creating a string of notes quickly can come in very handy, particularly when you're working with drum tracks. The Pencil tool makes it easy, if you use the Line version of the tool. (The spacing of the string of notes is based on your grid setting.)

❋ **IF YOU'RE USING THE EXERCISE MATERIALS...**

If you listen to the song play through, there is one place that still sounds a little off. The Bass track seems to drop out completely during measure 96. Your job: Use the Line mode of the Pencil tool to write a string of four notes. Our grid setting is 1/4 note, so our notes will follow that spacing. You just set the duration of notes that will be created as 1/8 notes.

1 **Click and hold** on the **Pencil tool**. A list of Pencil tool options will appear.

2 This list of drawing shape variations will come in handy in a variety of situations (particularly when mixing, which you'll explore in the next chapter). In this instance, you'll want to use the Line variation of the tool, so **select Line** from the list.

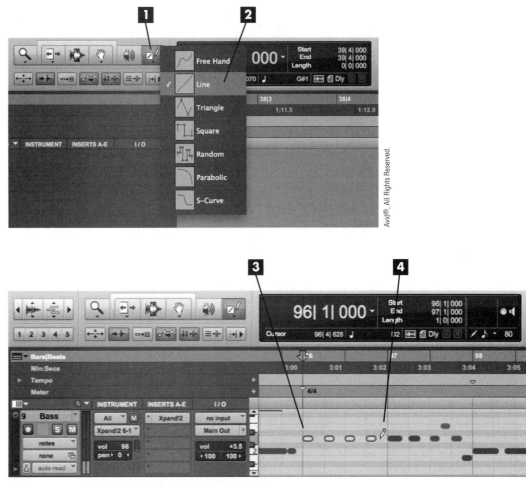

3 **Click and hold** with the Pencil tool at the point where you want to *begin* entering new MIDI note data. If you're using the Exercise session, you'll want to begin your series of notes at 96|1|000 at a pitch of D2.

4 **Drag** the **Pencil cursor** left or right to create a string of notes. Note that in this example, the duration of each note is an 1/8 note (based on the note duration), and the spacing is every 1/4 note (based on the grid value).

❄ MORE POWER WITH THE PENCIL TOOL

The Pencil tool is great for quick MIDI work—not only for its ability to create new notes, but also for its other functions. If you click in the body of an existing note, the Pencil tool will take on the function of a Grabber (enabling you to quickly move the note). If you move the Pencil tool to either end of an existing note, it will become a Trim tool (enabling you to adjust the beginning or end of the note).

❋ PLAYING MIDI NOTES WHEN EDITING

Sometimes it is very convenient to hear notes as you move or tab through them, and sometimes it can be a distraction. Either way, Pro Tools makes it easy to work the way you want.

❋ Click on the Play MIDI Notes When Editing indicator to toggle the feature on and off.

Changing Tempo

As you learned in Chapter 6, "...And More Editing," your session's Bars|Beats time scale and your MIDI tempo settings are interrelated and form the timing basis for your tick-based tracks. You can control tempo quickly and easily from the Tempo ruler or even enter values numerically.

❋ For your session to follow the Tempo ruler (as opposed to the static tempo displayed in the MIDI Controls section of the Edit and Transport windows), you'll need to have the Conductor Track button enabled in the MIDI controls section of the Transport or Edit window.

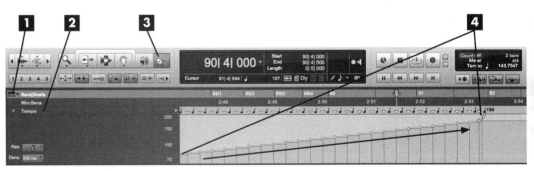

1 If you're not seeing your Tempo ruler, you'll need to reveal it in your Edit window now. **Click** on the **Ruler Menu icon** and **choose Tempo** from the menu. Another way to select it is to **click** the **View menu**, **select** the **Rulers menu item**, and **choose Tempo**.

2 **Click** on the **Tempo Editor Expand/Collapse triangle** to reveal the expanded Tempo ruler.

3 **Click** on the **Pencil tool** (in this example, with the Line option selected).

4 Changing tempo is very simple—just **click and drag** to create tempo-change data.

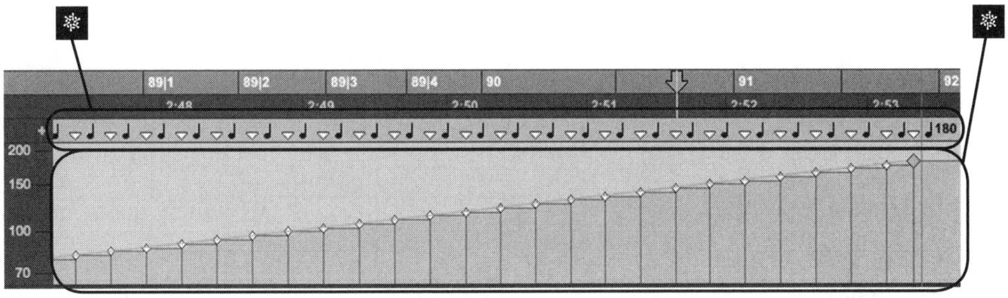

Editing MIDI

Avid®, All Rights Reserved.

❄ The tempo change is represented as a straight ramp (because I used the Pencil tool in Line mode), from 79 beats per minute up to 180 beats per minute in this example. With the Pencil tool, you can write (and overwrite) tempo changes with the Freehand, Line, Parabolic, and S-Curve settings.

❄ The tempo changes are also shown as a series of triangular value changes. You can also edit these values by clicking and dragging or even double-clicking and typing a specific tempo value, although the more graphic tempo display described earlier is far easier for many Pro Tools users to work with.

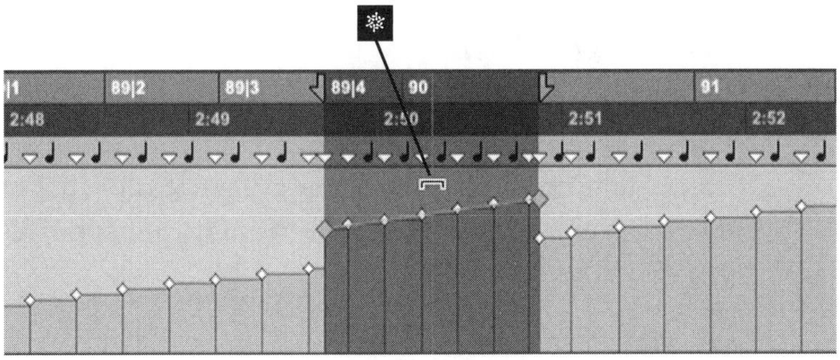

Avid®, All Rights Reserved.

❄ Although changing tempo with the Pencil tool might be the easiest method, it's not the only way. By using the Trim tool (shown here), you can scale tempo up or down as desired. (Note that the Trim tool points down when editing tempo, as opposed to the normal horizontal facing of the tool when trimming clip boundaries.)

You can also create a tempo change by choosing specific times and values.

1 **Click** on the **Event** menu and **choose Tempo Operations**. A submenu appears with options to create a tempo change in a variety of shapes. **Choose** the **option** you want. The process is similar regardless of the shape you've chosen.

Avid®, All Rights Reserved.

295

2 Enter the **start** and **end points** for your tempo change.

3 Select the **tempo value(s)**.

4 Click on the **Apply button**. Your tempo change will be applied.

> ❋ **IF YOU'RE USING THE EXERCISE MATERIALS...**
>
> If you're using the tutorial session, you'll want to undo the tempo changes you've made in this section.

The Event List

Most longtime MIDI users are familiar with the traditional MIDI Event list, a simple yet powerful window in which you can type exact values for your MIDI data. Although it is among the oldest of all MIDI editing environments, it can come in very handy when you want to get specific with your MIDI. Here's how to use it in Pro Tools:

1 Click on the **Window menu**.

2 Choose **MIDI Event List**. The MIDI Event List window will appear.

❋ The button in the upper-left corner of the MIDI Event List window indicates the name of the MIDI track being viewed. Clicking this button will reveal a drop-down menu of all MIDI and Instrument tracks, from which you can choose different tracks.

❋ The Start column shows the beginning time for each event, listed sequentially.

❋ The Event column indicates the type of individual events (note, pan, and so on), as well as their value.

❋ The Length/Info column shows more specific information about each event.

So how do you tweak this data? Easy: Just double-click on the value you want to change, type the new value, and press the Return key (Mac) or Enter key (PC)!

Click the Event List down arrow button to reveal more event-related options.

The Event List pop-up menu will give a variety of viewing options, as well as enable you to create new MIDI events (using the Insert function).

Removing Duplicate MIDI Notes

From time to time, a MIDI note can be doubly triggered during the recording process. (In my personal experience, this has happened mostly with MIDI drum controllers.) Occasionally, these duplicate notes can result in erratic behavior from your MIDI devices—notes being cut off prematurely and so on. To handle this, Pro Tools includes a Remove Duplicate Notes operation.

1 Select the **MIDI data** that you want to clean up through the removal of duplicate MIDI notes.

2 Click on the **Event menu**.

3 Choose **Remove Duplicate Notes.** The duplicate MIDI notes will be removed—you're finished!

Panic!

Reality check: Sometimes things go wrong. Worse yet, sometimes the things that go wrong can be audible, as in the case of a "stuck" MIDI note that never ends. When that happens, the most important thing to do is to stop the data and turn off those notes!

1 Click on the **Event menu**.

2 Choose **All MIDI Notes Off** (quickly!). A MIDI note-off command will be sent on all channels, on all ports of your MIDI interface, and through the four virtual MIDI connections.

✳ PANIC SHORTCUT

The fastest way to trigger the All MIDI Notes Off function is to use the shortcut keys: Shift+Command+. (period) will do it on the Mac, and Shift+Ctrl+. (period) will do it on the PC.

✳ MORE ABOUT MIDI

As mentioned at the beginning of this chapter, the discussion here is limited to the sorts of basic MIDI skills that might be expected of any well-rounded Pro Tools user (even if MIDI isn't his or her thing). The Pro Tools MIDI arsenal includes a whole world of additional—and more powerful—MIDI tools. In fact, in recent versions, Pro Tools has made great strides in the world of MIDI music creation and has established itself as a serious competitor in the world of MIDI music creation and production. All these new features are beyond the scope of a basic book like this (and would take more than a few extra pages). Does that mean you're left high and dry? Heck no! Appendix A will deal with these new features, including advanced MIDI editing and timeline operations, production tips, and an introduction to the powerful MIDI and Score Editor windows. Enjoy!

✳ CHECKING YOUR WORK

As mentioned, this exercise session is a snapshot in time, early on during the arranging process. There are some questionable notes still left in there for you to ferret out, and the mixing process hasn't begun in any real sense at this stage of production. A version of the session, with the steps outlined in this chapter completed, is included with the downloadable materials.

Next stop: mixing!

8 } Basic Mixing

When it comes to DAWs, there are two schools of thought on mixing: mixing inside the box and mixing outside the box. Mixing *inside* the box refers to making use of your DAW's virtual mixer and virtual effects entirely within the Pro Tools environment. When mixing inside the box, you will listen to a summed (for example, stereo) output of your mix through your audio interface, with all the required processing being performed by your computer (the "box"). Mixing *outside* the box refers to the practice of assigning individual tracks to individual outputs of your audio interface and from there to individual channels on a separate physical mixing board. The mixing and automation are performed by this external mixer, and Pro Tools is reduced to a recording, editing, and playback device (still playing critical roles in any production workflow).

There is lively discussion (and I'm being polite here) within the professional community regarding the virtues of mixing outside the box versus inside the box. There are valid points on both sides of the debate, but for the end user, it all boils down to this essential truth: Great work is being done using both methods, and individuals should follow the path that best enables them to realize their creative vision.

This book will explore the world of mixing inside the box—a method that has been used on countless professional projects. In this chapter, you'll learn how to:

* Work with the specific layout and function of the Mix window.
* Use fader groups.
* Use file-based and real-time effects.
* Work with traditional mix routing.
* Use subgroups and track-output features to speed up the mixing process.
* Make the most of Pro Tools 11's enhanced insert and send management.

More Signal Flow

When you're talking about mixing, what you're essentially talking about is signal flow. The more complex your mix gets, the more complex the routing of those signals can be. Even the most complex mixes, however, can be reduced to a few simple elements. The following list will go through the order of audio signal flow through those elements within an Audio or Aux track.

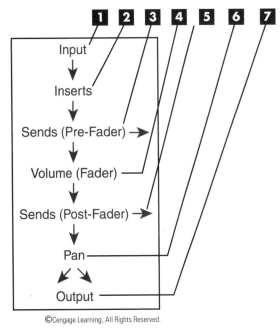

©Cengage Learning, All Rights Reserved.

1 **Input.** On an Audio or Aux track, input can be from an interface input, a bus, or in some cases a plug-in.

2 **Inserts.** Inserts are most commonly used as holders for effects. One-hundred percent of your signal passes through your insert.

3 **Sends (Pre-Fader).** A send makes a copy of the signal to be routed to another destination. A *pre-fader* send makes that copy before the signal hits your volume fader. The destination of this send can be an interface output or a bus.

4 **Volume (Fader).** This is where you control the output volume of the track.

5 **Sends (Post-Fader).** This kind of send makes a copy *after* the signal has been altered by the volume fader. As with a pre-fader send, the destination can be an interface output or a bus.

6 **Pan.** Panning comes next and allows the level of the signal to be varied between a number of outputs (left and right, in the case of a stereo mix). This is how you can create a stereo mix of several mono or stereo tracks. If, on the other hand, you route your track to a single output, no pan slider will be needed, and you won't see one in the channel strip.

7 **Output.** After all these stages are passed, the signal goes to the Pro Tools mix engine and out of an interface output or bus.

❈ **A WORD ABOUT FADERS**

Remember that the volume fader on a track *only* controls the output of that track. That means the fader has absolutely no effect on the *input* coming to the track. The net effect is this: If you're bringing audio into a track (either by recording or internal routing), and you see your levels clipping, turn down the level of the signal source. Changing the fader on a destination track will not fix level clipping.

❈ **SETTING THINGS UP**

To follow along with the illustrations in this chapter, use the Chapter 08 Exercise Session (Shady Grove) file included with this book's downloadable materials. For information on downloading this book's exercise materials, please refer to the "Setting Up Your Session" section in the introduction.

Exploring the Mix Window

You've visited the Mix window before (way back in Chapter 2, "Getting Around in Pro Tools"), but now it's time to dig deeper. If you're not looking at it already, the first thing to do is to switch over to the Mix window (which you also learned how to do in Chapter 2). Depending on how you left the Mix window last time, the channel strips might appear rather narrow. Although the Narrow Mix view can certainly be useful in some situations, you'll be able to see more information with Narrow Mix view turned off. Here's how to check which view you're in and disable Narrow Mix view if it's currently enabled.

1 **Click** on the **View menu**. If the Narrow Mix option is active, the menu Narrow Mix menu item will be indicated by a checkmark, as shown here.

2 **Click** on **Narrow Mix** to uncheck it. The channels will be shown in their normal mode.

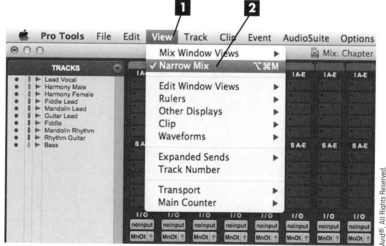

❈ ❈ ❈

Basic Mixer Terminology

Before you progress further, let's review the basic layout of the Mix window:

❄ **Tracks list.** As in the Edit window, a dark dot will appear to the left of shown tracks, and highlighted track names indicate selected tracks.

❄ **Groups list.** Mix groups will be shown here. (You'll learn how to use them later in this chapter.)

❄ **Channel strips.** There is a separate vertical channel strip for each shown track.

Now take a look at the different sections of a basic Audio track's channel strip. These sections can be shown or hidden from the Mix Window Views menu, covered in Chapter 2:

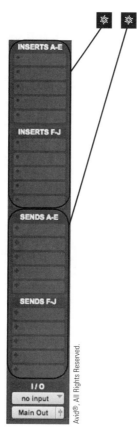

❊ At the top of the channel strip are the Inserts sections. There are 10 inserts for you to use, divided into two sections of five. All audio passing through a channel strip will be routed through the inserts first, in descending order. It is here that you will launch plug-in effects and virtual instruments.

❊ Next are the sends. Like inserts, you have 10 sends, divided into two sections of five. You'll use sends to route a copy of your track's processed audio to another destination. Sends are commonly used in conjunction with other tracks to create more complex effect situations or to create cue mixes in recording situations. (I'll discuss this further in Chapter 10, "Moving to the Next Level: Tips and Tricks.")

❊ MIDI TRACK SIGNAL FLOW

MIDI tracks have no inserts or sends, as inserts and sends can route only audio data.

Moving down the channel strip, the next section looks and functions just like the I/O column of a track in the Edit window.

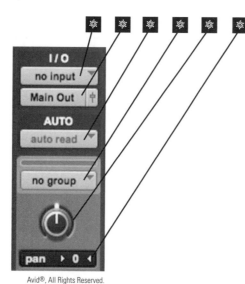

❊ Input Path button

❊ Output Path button

❊ Automation Mode button (covered later in this chapter... finally!)

❊ Group ID indicator

❊ Pan knob

❊ Pan indicator

The bottom section of an Audio track's channel strip may look a bit different from what you've seen in the Edit window, but these buttons' functions should be old hat by now.

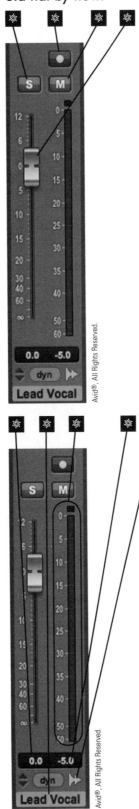

* Record Enable button
* Solo button
* Mute button
* Volume fader

* Volume Level meter
* Volume indicator
* Headroom indicator (this indicates the last registered peak level)
* Track Type icon
* Track name

Longtime Pro Tools users are used to always seeing faders and meters in the Mix window, but that no longer has to be the case. With Pro Tools 11, the main fader and meters section of the Mix window can be shown or hidden from the Mix Window Views menu (covered in Chapter 2).

❄ TRACK TYPE ICONS

If you're using the exercise session, you're just working with a number of Audio tracks. However, as your mix grows, you'll be adding different types of tracks. The Track Type icon at the bottom-right corner of each channel strip will indicate the type of track it is:

Avid®, All Rights Reserved.

  ❄ A waveform indicates an Audio track.

  ❄ An arrow signifies an Aux track.

  ❄ A sigma marks a Master Fader track.

  ❄ A MIDI plug indicates a MIDI track.

  ❄ A small musical keyboard is shown on an Instrument track.

The same icons can be found to the left of each track name in the Tracks list.

❄ IS IT MONO OR STEREO?

You can easily tell whether the track is stereo or mono by taking a look at the volume meters. One volume meter indicates a mono track; a stereo track will have two volume meters.

Track Colors

In Chapter 2, you learned a little about track coloring—small colored tabs at the top and bottom of each channel strip. Although their function is purely visual, you'll find that using track colors is pretty handy. You've learned how to access track colors via the Mix Window Views menu; now let's learn another way to open the Color Palette window:

❄ IF YOU'RE USING THE EXERCISE MATERIALS...

If you're using the exercise session, you'll see that your color tabs have already been set up for you. If you don't like the colors, they're easy to change. Let's try changing the color of the Bass track.

1 **Select** the **track(s)** whose colors you want to change.

2 **Double-click** the track's color tab. The Color Palette window will appear.

3 The Apply to Selected menu will enable you to change the color of different parts of your session. In this image, the changes you make in this window will be applied to the selected tracks in your session. If the menu button does *not* read "Tracks," **click** on the **menu button**.

4 In the Apply to Selected menu, the session element targeted for change will be indicated with a checkmark. Because coloring the track is the job at hand, **choose Tracks**.

5 From this point, it's simple: **Click** on the **color tile** that you want to assign to your selected tracks. In this example, I want my Bass track to be colored blue. After you click on the desired color, the tracks' color will change accordingly.

Track coloring isn't limited to the small tabs at the top and bottom of each channel strip. You also have the ability to apply track colors to the entire channel strips, radically changing the look of your Mix window.

✳ You can toggle channel strip colors on or off by clicking on the Apply to Channel Strip button. When active, the button will be colored blue, and you'll see the track color applied throughout the channel strip.

❄ Once you've activated your channel-strip colors, you then have the ability to adjust the saturation, or intensity, of the colors. The farther you move the slider to the right, the stronger your channel-strip colors will become.

❄ Regardless of whether you're using channel-strip coloring, you have the ability to adjust the brightness of your Mix window. Used in combination with the Saturation slider, you'll be able to tweak your Mix window to suit your taste.

❄ If you ever want to assign the same color to multiple elements (such as multiple tracks or tracks and clips), the Hold button will come in handy. Just choose the color you want to use and then click on the Hold button. The color will remain selected as you navigate different tracks and other session elements until the Hold button is again clicked.

❄ Each track type has a default color code. For example, a new Audio track will be colored blue, a new Aux track will be green, and so on. If you want to set a track's color back to its default value, just click on the Default button.

❄ If you want to remove all coloring from a selected track (or tracks), click on the None button.

Mix Groups

One of the neatest things about mixing in Pro Tools is that you can link faders (and more) together—something Pro Tools calls a *mix group*. With mix groups, moving one fader will move all the faders in that linked group. This is particularly useful in cases where you have a good relative blend between a number of tracks (for example, a nice balance between all the individual drum tracks), and you want to change the volume of those tracks without changing the blend.

To start off, let's get a feel for what a mix group can do. As luck would have it, Pro Tools automatically creates a group (named All) that always includes all the tracks in your session. Take a look at what it does:

1 Before you can use a mix group, that group must be active (indicated by the group's name being highlighted). If the All group name is not highlighted, **click** on **All**. The group name will be highlighted, and the group (which in this case includes all the tracks in your session) will be active.

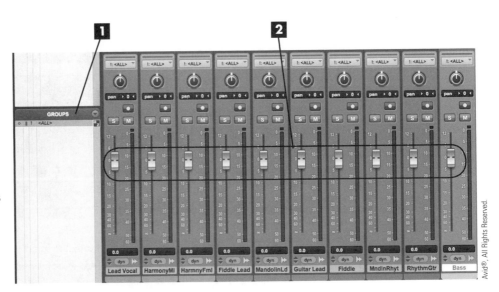

2 **Click** on any **volume fader** and **drag it** to change the volume of the track. Because the All group is currently active, the volume controls for all the tracks will move proportionally.

❋ **GROUP ICONS**

Above each track's pan knob, the Group ID indicator indicates mix group activity on a track-by-track basis. When a group is activated, the group ID letter and name will be shown on the member tracks.

Creating a Mix Group

Of course, you can also create new mix groups of your own. For example, in this session, I have three vocal tracks to group together:

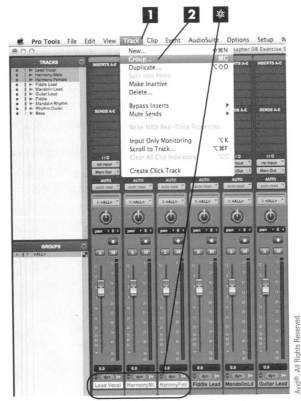

❋ Although it's not strictly necessary at this point, selecting the tracks you want to group together will make the process easier. (In the example shown, I've selected the three vocal tracks in my session.) When that's done, you can open the Create Group dialog box in one of two different ways. Here's one:

1 **Click** on the **Track menu**.

2 **Select Group.** The Create Group dialog box will appear.

❋ ❋ ❋

❄ Mix Groups

Here's another way to launch the Create Group dialog box:

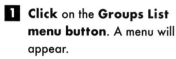

1 **Click** on the **Groups List menu button**. A menu will appear.

2 **Select New Group.** The Create Group dialog box will appear.

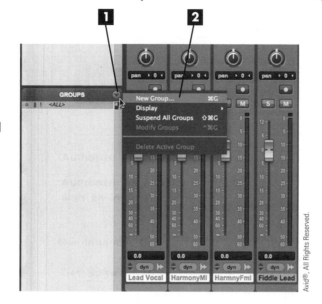

Avid®, All Rights Reserved.

❄ NEW GROUP SHORTCUT

Here's an even quicker way to get to the Create Group dialog box: Press Command+G (Mac) or Ctrl+G (PC).

With the Create Group dialog box open, follow these steps:

1 **Type** a **name** for your new group in the Name field.

❄ By default, new groups are created as both edit and mix groups, meaning the group will be accessible from both the Edit and Mix windows. (This default behavior works well in most situations.) If you choose, you can click on either the Edit or the Mix option button to limit the group to a single window.

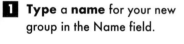

Avid®, All Rights Reserved.

❄ Tracks that are grouped together are always grouped together as far as main volume faders are concerned, but you have the ability to group other aspects together as well. By clicking the appropriate checkboxes, you can group mutes, solos, send levels, and send mutes.

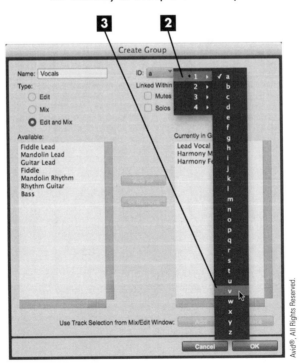

❄ You can choose the members of your group by populating the Currently in Group area. Initially, your selected tracks will be placed in this area, but if you want to add more tracks to your group, just select the desired tracks in the Available field and then click on the Add button. If you want to remove a track from the group, just select the track in the Currently in Group area and then click on the Remove button.

❄ If, after making changes to your group's membership, you want to once again add the selected tracks to the group, you can click on either the Add button (to add the selected tracks to any tracks in the Currently in Group field) or the Replace button (which will clear the Currently in Group area and replace it with the selected tracks).

2 Pro Tools will automatically assign a letter to your group for labeling purposes (in this image, it's currently assigned to group a), but let's change that group ID assignment. **Click** on the **ID menu**. A list will appear.

3 The ID list is divided into four banks of 26 group letters (for a grand total of 104 user-defined groups). **Choose** a **group letter** from this list. Because this is a group named "Vocals," I've chosen the v group letter from the first bank.

4 **Click** on the **OK button**, and your group will be created.

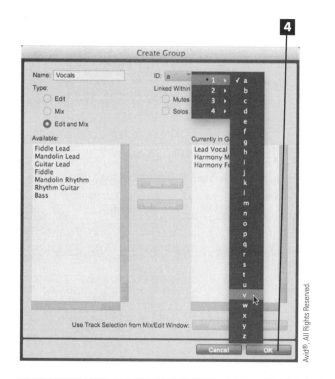

❋ **IF YOU'RE USING THE EXERCISE MATERIALS...**

If you're following the exercise session, you've just created a group of the three vocal tracks (Lead Vocal, Harmony Male, and Harmony Female). Now, create two new groups: a Leads group (composed of the Fiddle Lead, Mandolin Lead, and Guitar Lead tracks) and a Rhythm group (including the Fiddle, Mandolin Rhythm, Rhythm Guitar, and Bass tracks).

Active mix groups are shown by colored group indicators in member tracks' channel strips (showing the group ID letter and group name). You can activate or deactivate any group by clicking on the group name in the Groups list. When a group is deactivated, you will be able to change individual track settings without changing the other members of the group.

Here's where the care you took in choosing group ID letters is going to pay off: When you're in the Mix window, you can use your computer's keyboard to activate and deactivate mix groups by simply pressing the appropriate group ID letter. The way you've set up the session in this example, you can now toggle the Vocals group by just pressing the V key on your keyboard. (Pressing L will toggle the Leads group, and pressing R will toggle the Rhythm group.) I think you'll find that these shortcuts greatly speed up your mixing!

Using Mix Groups

There's just a little more to learn about mix groups before you continue. For this example, I've created a group with a Mandolin Rhythm track and a Rhythm Guitar track (I've named the group "Mandolin and Guitar Rhythm" and assigned it to group ID M), which is a subset of the Rhythm group (referred to as a *nested fader group*). Let's take a look:

❄ A lowercase ID letter in the Group ID indicator indicates that the track is a member of only one active (highlighted) mix group.

❄ An uppercase ID letter means that the track is a member of more than one currently active group.

❄ You can click on a track's Group ID indicator button to reveal a menu of all the active groups of which that track is a member.

❄ In this example, the Rhythm Guitar track is a member of two active groups: the Rhythm group and the Mandolin and Guitar Rhythm group. If you move your mouse over either group name, a submenu will be shown, including an additional submenu that lists all member tracks of that group (shown here).

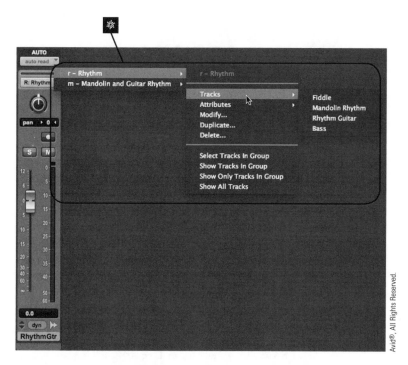

This Group Options menu deserves a closer look. You can display this menu either by clicking on a track's Group ID indicator or by right-clicking a group's name in the Groups list. (This method works for both mix and edit groups.) Here's how the different options work:

❄ **Tracks.** Clicking on Tracks will display a list of all the member tracks of the group.

❄ **Attributes.** Clicking on Attributes will display a list of the different mix parameters (volume, solo, mute, etc.) that are grouped together in the group.

❄ **Modify.** Clicking on Modify will open the Modify Group dialog box (very similar to the Create Group dialog box). Here, you can change group members or any group attribute except the group ID assignment.

❄ **Duplicate.** The Duplicate menu item will open the Create Group dialog box, with initial settings identical to the selected group.

❄ **Delete.** The Delete menu item will remove the group (but not the member tracks).

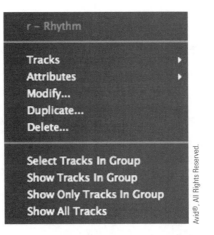

❋ **Select Tracks in Group.** Clicking on Select Tracks in Group instantly selects all the tracks in that group. Only the group's member tracks will be selected.

❋ **Hide/Show Tracks in Group.** Clicking on Hide/Show Tracks in Group will hide the group's tracks if they are currently being shown. If the tracks are hidden, this menu item will show them.

❋ **Show Only Tracks in Group.** Clicking on the Show Only Tracks in Group menu item will hide all non-member tracks.

❋ **Show All Tracks.** Clicking on the Show All Tracks menu item will show all the tracks in your session.

❋ **SELECTING GROUP MEMBERS**

Another quick way to select all the members of a group is to click to the left of the group ID in the Groups list.

❋ **SHOWING ONLY TRACKS IN GROUP**

Another quick way to select only the members of a group is to Control-click (Mac) or Start-click (PC) the group name in the Groups list.

There's one final menu to take a look at before moving on. You've already seen that the Groups List menu button can be used to create a new group, but there are more options available to you:

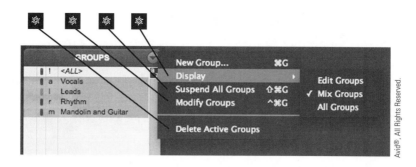

- ❄ **Display.** The Display option shows a submenu (shown here) from which you can choose to see your session's mix groups, edit groups, or all groups in the Groups area of your Mix window.
- ❄ **Suspend All Groups.** The Suspend All Groups option renders all groups inactive. (The group names will be grayed out.)
- ❄ **Modify Groups.** The Modify Groups option opens the Modify Group dialog box.
- ❄ **Delete Active Groups.** The Delete Active Groups option removes all active groups from your session.

At this point, you have a good sense of the Mix window's layout, and you know how to set up mix groups, which puts you in good shape to start doing a rough mix. Generally speaking, the first draft of a mix consists of simple volume and pan adjustments (which you'll tweak to perfection as your mix evolves). You'll find that the mix groups you've created will serve you well here, especially with larger, more complex sessions.

❄ **IF YOU'RE USING THE EXERCISE MATERIALS...**

If you're following along with the tutorial session, you should take some time to get a good rough mix. Once you have a good blend of volume and pan, you'll probably want to add some effects. Read on!

Using Effects

Many software applications use plug-ins—bits of programming designed to operate within a host program. With word processors, plug-ins can be editing tools or macros; graphics applications have visual-effect plug-ins, and so on. Pro Tools is no exception, and Pro Tools plug-ins include all manner of effects processors and virtual instruments. Because they're software (and not hardware), they have great flexibility and can even save you money and rack space in your project studio! In a Pro Tools 11 system, plug-ins fall into two categories: file-based plug-ins (called *AudioSuite*) and real-time plug-ins. First, let's tackle AudioSuite.

❄ ❄ ❄

AudioSuite Plug-Ins

Generally speaking, AudioSuite plug-ins are the most basic of Pro Tools effects. They work directly on files, and this is *not* done in real time as your session plays. That means AudioSuite plug-ins cannot be automated in your Pro Tools session. It also means these plug-ins won't consume your session's valuable real-time resources, making AudioSuite plug-ins well worth exploring. Here's how they work:

❋ **IF YOU'RE USING THE EXERCISE MATERIALS...**

If you're using the exercise session, you'll note that the last clip on the Lead Vocal track is un-usually low. This wasn't the way that the audio was originally recorded but rather a change that I made to the session for educational purposes.

The effect you'll use for this section is a handy little plug-in called *Normalize*. This process is a level adjuster that will bring up your entire selection so that the loudest part of the selection matches the value you set. The simplicity of the effect window makes it an obvious choice for tutorial demonstrations. Normalize can be very useful in some circumstances, but beware of routinely using it to compensate for low recorded levels! Although the volume will be brought up, it will bring up ambient noise levels as well. The bottom line is to record at healthy levels so you won't need to use normalization too often!

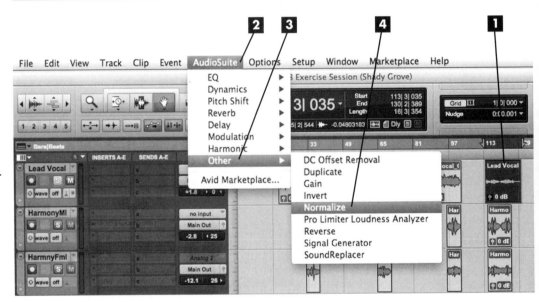

1 **Select** the **clip** or **area** that you want to process. If you're using the exercise session, choose the final clip on the Lead Vocal track.

2 **Click** on the **AudioSuite menu**. A list of plug-in categories will appear.

3 **Choose** the desired **category** of effect. A submenu will appear, showing all the plug-ins of that type. If you're following along with the exercise session, **choose** the **Other** category.

4 **Choose** the desired **plug-in**. The plug-in's window will appear. If you're using the exercise session, **choose Normalize**.

When looking at an AudioSuite plug-in window, it's important to make a distinction between the *function* of some of the buttons and the *labels* they may display at any given time. The buttons at the top of every AudioSuite window show their currently selected settings (as opposed to their function) for quick visual reference.

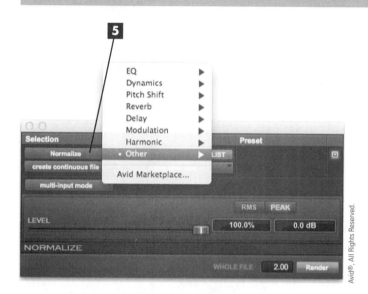

5 Although different effects will differ in appearance and parameters, they all share some common elements. For example, the Plug-In button (which displays the name of the current plug-in, such as Normalize) will enable you to change effects without closing the window. Just **click** on the **Plug-In button**, and a list of AudioSuite plug-ins will appear, identical to the list you saw when you clicked the AudioSuite menu.

6 **Click** on the **Selection Reference button** (which reads "Playlist" in this image) to determine what will be processed. A menu with two options will appear:

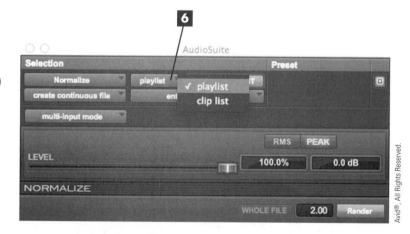

❋ **Playlist.** When Playlist is selected, the plug-in will process the selected area in your track(s).

❋ **Clip List.** Choosing the Clip List option directs the plug-in to process the currently selected clips in the Clips list.

❋ ❋ ❋

7 **Click** on the **Use in Playlist button** if you want the processed audio to appear in your tracks (and in the Clips list). When activated, the button will be blue.

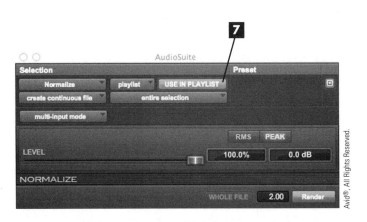

> ✻ **USE IN PLAYLIST**
>
> If the Use in Playlist button is not active, the processed audio will appear only in the Clips list, and the clips in your track will remain unchanged.

8 **Click** on the **File Mode button** (which reads "Create Continuous File" in this image) to determine how audio will be processed. A menu will appear, showing three different processing options:

- ✻ **Overwrite Files.** With this option chosen, the selected audio file(s) will be processed directly and *destructively*.
- ✻ **Create Individual Files.** This mode is *nondestructive* and will create separate audio files for each selected clip. If multiple clips are selected, multiple files will be created.
- ✻ **Create Continuous File.** This mode is also nondestructive, but in this case, it will create a *single* new audio file, regardless of the number of clips that are selected.

9 **Click** on the **Processing Input Mode button** (which reads "Entire Selection" in this image) to determine how your clips will be analyzed prior to processing. A menu will appear, showing two options:

- ✻ **Clip by Clip.** With this option chosen, each selected clip will be individually analyzed and processed.
- ✻ **Entire Selection.** All selected clips will be analyzed prior to being processed.

✻ ✻ ✻

❄ **CLIP BY CLIP AND NORMALIZE**

The Clip by Clip option is commonly used when normalizing multiple clips of different volumes (different sound effects, for example). With this mode selected, each selected clip will be analyzed and processed individually, resulting in multiple clips that all have identical peak volume levels.

10 When the behavior of your plug-in has been determined with the settings at the top of the window, it's time to get to work. **Adjust** the **parameters** in the plug-in window's main section. These parameters will vary greatly from plug-in to plug-in. If you're following the exercise session, **choose** a level of −**4.0 dB** and **select** the **Peak button**, as shown here.

11 **Click** on the **Render button** to apply your effect.

Here's what you'll end up with:

❄ Because the Use in Playlist button is enabled, a new clip has been created to replace the selected clip in the track.

❄ This new clip has also been added to the Clips list and has been named "Lead Vocal-NORM_01-01," indicating that it was created by the Normalize AudioSuite plug-in.

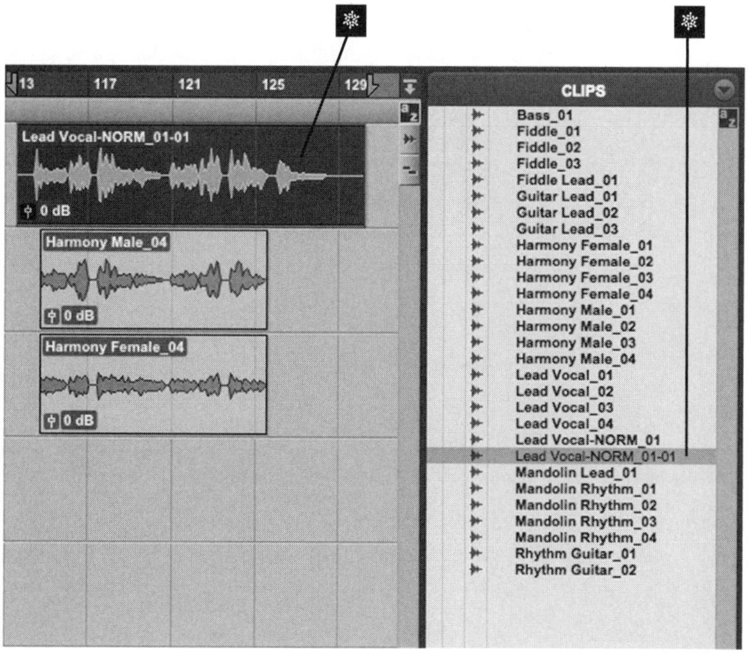

❄❄❄

❊ AUDIOSUITE VARIATIONS

The controls discussed here are basic AudioSuite options common to all AudioSuite plug-ins. Different kinds of effects may have additional features relating to their function.

❊ AUDIOSUITE PREVIEW

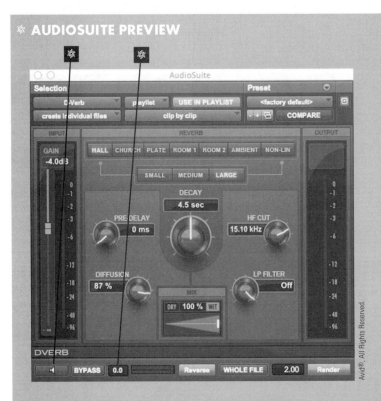

Many AudioSuite plug-ins (like the D-Verb shown here) provide the option of previewing your changes prior to applying them. These preview controls are located at the bottom-left of the AudioSuite window.

Additionally, there are level meters and volume controls available. Just click on the volume-level indicator to reveal a fader you can use to change your preview levels.

❋ REVERSE INTEGRATION

AudioSuite plug-ins are especially good for doing things that are impossible to do in real time. One of those things is reversing a sound. In fact, the Reverse plug-in is one of the most popular of the AudioSuite plug-ins, used in combination with a number of other effects to create interesting sounds.

Because Reverse is used frequently with reverbs and delays, the good folks at Avid have made it even easier for you. At the bottom of the window, you'll see a Reverse button. This button actually enables you to complete an entire workflow with a single click. First, the selected area will be reversed. Next, the plug-in (Reverb or Delay) will be applied to that selection. Then, the selected area will be reversed *again*. Give it a try, and you'll immediately recognize the result! Here's a tip: Make sure that you select an area that extends sufficiently outside the clip to allow for the reverb to (reverse) decay.

❊ AUDIOSUITE HANDLES

In previous versions of Pro Tools, AudioSuite processes were applied only to the selected area or clips, creating a single whole-file clip. While that was all well and good, it also meant that you couldn't use the Trim tool to expand the boundaries of a clip. This also presented certain limitations when crossfading clips created by AudioSuite processing.

Starting with Pro Tools 10, the problem is addressed through the addition of handles—additional processed audio beyond the selected area. That means that two clips are created—a subset clip on your timeline, plus a whole-file clip that is longer than the selected area by some amount. This means that, although your timeline's clip will still be the same length as your selected area, you will now have the ability to trim the clip out or crossfade the clip.

There are two ways to control the handles created by an AudioSuite plug-in:

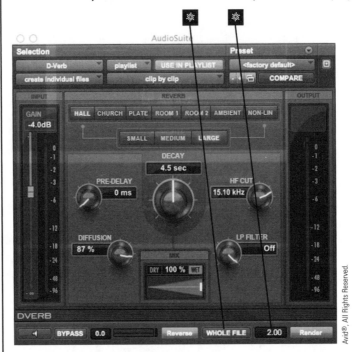

- ❊ By default, a two-second handle will be appended to the beginning and end of the rendered file, but you can change that value to anything you like. Just click on the handle value you wish to change (as shown here) and type the desired value in seconds (up to one minute).

- ❊ Alternatively, you can choose to render the entire file with which the selection is associated, creating a new processed file that is equal in length to the original whole file. To do this, click on the Whole File button. (When active, the button will appear blue.)

Real-Time Plug-Ins

The next evolutionary step in the world of Pro Tools' plug-in effects was the addition of *real-time* plug-ins. Instead of processing audio on a file basis, as is the case with AudioSuite, real-time plug-ins reside on a track's insert and process an incoming signal as the session is played (in real time).

Two huge benefits come with using real-time plug-ins. First, because the audio is being processed in real time, the audio files on your hard drive won't be changed. This enables you to experiment freely with different plug-ins and settings without worrying about filling your hard drive with processed files. Also, as a result of these plug-ins' real-time operation, you can automate the parameters of your plug-in (something I'll cover later in this chapter), meaning your effects can change dynamically over time.

> ### ❋ RTAS AND AAX PLUG-INS
>
> In older versions of Pro Tools, the real-time plug-in format used on host-based system was called "Real-Time AudioSuite," or "RTAS" for short. Pro Tools 10 witnessed the introduction of a new plug-in format called "Avid Audio eXtensions," commonly called "AAX." AAX were designed to be 64-bit compatible, in preparation for Pro Tools 11's 64-bit redesign. AAX plug-ins are the only real-time format supported by Pro Tools 11.

> ### ❋ IF YOU'RE USING THE EXERCISE MATERIALS...
>
> One of my personal favorites in the world of Pro Tools real-time plug-ins is a free plug-in called "Channel Strip." This single plug-in includes dynamic control as well as EQ control and is a great way to sculpt the sound of a track in a single environment. If you're using the exercise session, you'll add the Channel Strip plug-in to the Lead Vocal track.

Launching Real-Time Plug-Ins

Launching (or *instantiating*) a real-time plug-in is easy once you know the steps. In this example, I'm going to add some compression and EQ to the Lead Vocal track to have it stand out in the mix a bit.

1 **Click** on an unused **Insert button** on the track that you want to affect (if you're working with the tutorial session, the Lead Vocal track). A menu will appear.

Avid®, All Rights Reserved.

> ### ❋ ADVICE ON INSERTS
>
> Because inserts are processed in series from top to bottom, the order in which effects are placed in your tracks is significant. For example, a virtual amplifier placed before a reverb will sound a good deal different from an amplifier placed after a reverb. The good news is, it's easy to change the order (or even the track assignment) of a real-time plug-in simply by dragging and dropping the insert icon to a new location in your mixer.

2 **Click** on **Plug-In**. A list of plug-in categories will appear.

3 **Click** on the desired **category** of effect (in this case, **choose EQ**). A submenu will appear, showing all the specific plug-ins of that type.

4 **Click** on the desired **plug-in**. The plug-in's window will appear. (In this image, I've chosen the Channel Strip plug-in.)

The plug-in window will vary, depending on the effect, but just as with AudioSuite plug-ins, there are some common buttons at the top of the plug-in window that you should understand.

Avid®, All Rights Reserved.

1 **Click** on the **Track button** (which shows you the track you're currently working with) to display a list of available tracks in your session. From this list, you can select another track and instantly open an Insert window for that track.

2 **Click** on the **Insert Position button** (a small lettered button to the right of the Track button) to indicate the position of the insert on the track. If you click on this button, a list of all 10 insert positions will appear. From this list, you can select any position and jump to that insert immediately.

3 Finally, **click** on the **Plug-In button** (which shows you the plug-in you're using) to reveal a plug-in menu, from which you can select a different effect without closing the plug-in window.

Recalling Settings

In addition to instantiating plug-ins with ease, you can recall previously created settings (often called *presets*). Here's how to recall a good preset for the Channel Strip plug-in you just launched. (These steps also work with AudioSuite plug-ins.)

1 **Click** on the **Librarian Menu button**. A list of available presets will be displayed.

2 Any factory presets for the plug-in will be shown in this menu, plus any presets saved in your session's Plug-In Settings folder (something you'll learn more about in Chapter 9, "Finishing Touches"). If you're using the tutorial session, I've placed a good preset in your session's Plug-In Settings folder, so **click** on the **Session's Settings Folder menu item**. A list will appear.

Avid®, All Rights Reserved.

3 If you're using the tutorial session, you'll see that there's only one preset in the Session's Settings Folder submenu—appropriately named "Chapter 08 Lead Vocal," created by yours truly. **Select** this **preset**, and the parameters will be applied to your plug-in.

There are a couple other ways presets can be accessed. (Again, these work for both AudioSuite and real-time plug-ins.) Here's one:

❆ Click on the plus (+) or minus (−) button to increment or decrement through the available presets.

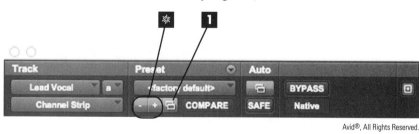

Avid®, All Rights Reserved.

Here's another:

1 **Click** on the **Plug-In Settings Select button** to reveal the Plug-In Settings dialog box.

2 **Click** on the **Folder button** to reveal a list of all preset folders, and **click** on the desired **folder** to display the presets in the dialog box's main area.

3 **Click** on the desired **preset**, and your settings will be immediately applied.

4 **Click** on the **Increment Setting Every __ Seconds checkbox** to automatically cycle through the available presets according to the value entered in the Seconds field. (In this image, presets will change every three seconds.) This is a handy way to preview effect settings while your session plays, especially when there is a large number of presets to choose from.

5 When you settle on the desired setting, **click** on the **Done button**, and the plug-in setting dialog box will close.

❋ NEW IN PRO TOOLS 11: RIGHT-CLICK PRESET POWER!

Starting with Pro Tools 11, you now have one more way to access plug-in presets. It's as easy as right-clicking on the plug-in button in the Inserts section of the Mix window!

Right-click any plug-in button to reveal a list of useful functions (many of which I'll go into later in this book), including submenus of user presets and session presets.

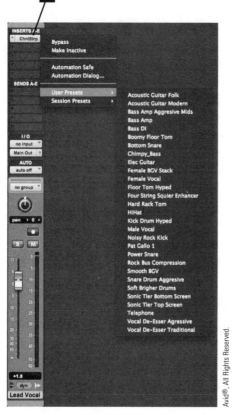

Digging Deeper into Real-Time Plug-Ins

So far, it's been pretty straightforward, but things will get a little more complicated as you go on. For example, when you open a plug-in on a stereo track, you have the option of choosing between a multi*channel* and a multi-*mono* effect. Simply put, a multichannel plug-in is a single plug-in that is designed to process more than one audio stream. Choosing to use multi-mono will open multiple mono plug-ins in a single plug-in window. Confused? Read on!

For this example, let's set up a multi-mono delay on a stereo Aux track.

✻ SETTING THINGS UP

To follow along with these steps, create a stereo Aux track and name it Delay Aux.

1 On a stereo track (in this case, a stereo Aux track named Delay Aux), **click** on an available **Insert button**.

2a **Click** on **Multichannel Plug-In**. In the case of a stereo track (as shown here), a list of stereo plug-ins will appear.

OR

Avid®, All Rights Reserved.

2b **Click** on **Multi-Mono Plug-In**. A list of mono plug-ins will appear.

3 For the purposes of this example, **choose Mod Delay III (mono)** from the multi-mono plug-in family (as shown here). The plug-in will be instantiated, and the plug-in window will open.

When you choose multi-mono on a stereo track, the mono plug-in you select will be opened twice, although only one plug-in window will be shown. A multi-mono plug-in window has several unique features:

❊ The Link button is unique to multi-mono plug-ins. When this button is selected, all channels of the multi-mono plug-in will share the same parameter settings. (In the image shown here, changes made to the left side will be mirrored in the right side.) When Link is disabled, both sides are independently configurable, enabling you to set different delay settings for the left and right sides.

Avid®, All Rights Reserved.

❊ The Channel button will indicate the channel of the multi-mono plug-in you're presently viewing (something that's really only necessary when the Link is disabled). Just click on this button to reveal a list of available channels from which you can choose. (In this example, clicking on the Channel button will enable you to switch from the left plug-in to the right plug-in.)

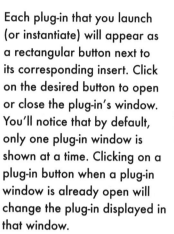

❊ Each plug-in that you launch (or instantiate) will appear as a rectangular button next to its corresponding insert. Click on the desired button to open or close the plug-in's window. You'll notice that by default, only one plug-in window is shown at a time. Clicking on a plug-in button when a plug-in window is already open will change the plug-in displayed in that window.

❊ What if you want to view more than one plug-in window at a time? That's when the Target button comes in handy. The rule for the Target button is simple: Only one plug-in window can be "targeted" at a time. If you click on a plug-in window's Target button to deactivate the target (the button will turn gray), you'll be able to open another plug-in window. The next plug-in window you open will have an active Target button.

Traditional Effects Techniques

The goal of the mixing process is to achieve the perfect blend of audio elements in your session. Over the years, certain conventions have evolved to help mixing engineers reach this goal, and these conventions have become something of a tradition. Before leaving this discussion of effects, let's take a look at some traditional ways to use them—although these are certainly not the *only* ways they can be used!

Using Dynamic-Based Effects

Effects tend to fall into one of two categories: dynamic-based effects and time-based effects. Let's begin with dynamic-based effects. Dynamic-based effects change the volume level of the audio (or a portion of the audio) without changing its duration in any way. Some of the most common examples of dynamic effects are equalizers, compressors, and limiters.

Setting up dynamic-based effects is very easy. In fact, you've done it once already with the Lead Vocal track (if you've been following along with this chapter's tutorial session). Typically, you'll want dynamic effects to process 100 percent of the track's audio, so you'll simply place the effect on an insert of the track you want to change.

1 Click on an **insert** on the desired track and **select** an **effect** (such as the EQ shown here). The plug-in window will appear.

2 Adjust the **parameters** of the effect to suit your mix's needs.

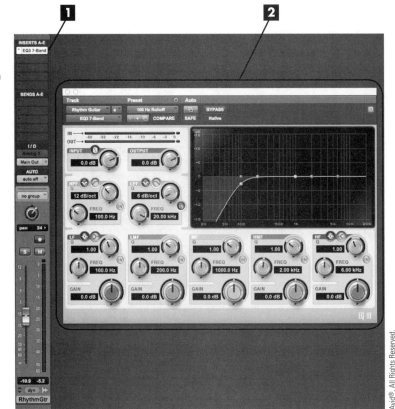

When you're finished tweaking the effect, you're done!

❊ IF YOU'RE USING THE EXERCISE MATERIALS...

Everyone has their own commonly used techniques, and here's one of mine: I typically use an EQ to cut the low end of my guitars and make sonic space for my bass and kick drum. I find that a low-end roll-off at around 100 Hz (shown in the example here) typically is a good place to start.

If you're following the tutorial session, I've even saved these settings as a plug-in preset in the Session Settings folder, named "100 Hz Rolloff." Just launch the EQ3 7-Band plug-in on the Rhythm Guitar track, choose the preset, and you should be all set. For good measure, repeat the process for the Mandolin Rhythm, Mandolin Lead, and Guitar Lead tracks as well.

Using Time-Based Effects

Time-based effects *do* affect the duration of the sound beyond that of its original waveform. Effects such as reverb, delay, and echo would fall under this classification. In these cases, you typically will want to have some sort of a wet/dry mixing scenario (*wet* meaning an effected signal and *dry* referring to an un-effected signal). The generally preferred way to mix these two signals is to use two separate tracks, so that you have the ability to adjust the wet/dry balance with faders in your Mix window.

> ❊ **IF YOU'RE USING THE EXERCISE MATERIALS...**
>
> If you've been following along with the tutorial session, let's go through this process and add a little reverb to the Lead Vocal track.

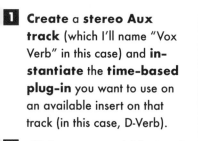

1. **Create** a **stereo Aux track** (which I'll name "Vox Verb" in this case) and **instantiate** the **time-based plug-in** you want to use on an available insert on that track (in this case, D-Verb).

2. **Click** on any available **Send button** on the "dry" track (in this case, the Lead Vocal track). A menu will appear.

3 Because you'll be routing audio from one track to another within the Pro Tools environment, you'll want to use a bus. **Click** on **Bus** in the menu of output options.

4 **Select** an **unused stereo bus**. (We're using stereo buses because the signal will be sent to a stereo track.) Buses already being used in the session will be shown in a bold amber font.

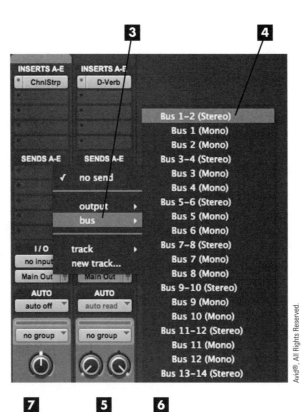

5 To complete the signal-routing process, you'll need to **set** the **input** of the Aux track to match the same stereo bus you chose for the Audio track's send.

6 **Drag** the **volume fader** on the send's output window (if you're not seeing this window, just click on the Send button to reveal it) and increase the volume to an appropriate level. At this point, it's a good idea to play your session to test your setup. If you've routed the audio signal correctly, it will appear in the send's output window and the Aux track's main level meter.

7 On the Aux track, **drag** the **volume fader** to achieve the desired blend of wet and dry sound. (The original Audio track is the dry part of the mix, and the Aux track is the wet part.) It's often useful to solo both tracks when adjusting this blend, at least in the initial stage.

❊ **LEVEL SHORTCUT**

Here's a quick way to move a volume fader (either the main fader or a send fader) to 0 dB (also called *unity*): Just hold down the Option key (Mac) or Alt key (PC) and click on the fader. The fader will immediately jump to the unity position.

❊ **SOLO-SAFE**

When you solo a track, all other tracks will be muted, including the Aux track with your reverb. Of course, you can always solo that reverb track, but that can be a time-consuming annoyance. Pro Tools allows you to *solo-safe* a track, meaning it won't be muted even if other tracks are soloed. To solo-safe a track, just hold down the Command (Mac) or Ctrl (PC) key and click on the Solo button on the track you want to solo-safe.

❊ When the PRE button is highlighted on the send's output window (as shown here), the send is known as a *pre-fader send*, meaning the output of the send will not be affected by the track's main volume fader or Mute button. When the PRE button is not highlighted (the default state of sends in Pro Tools), the send is a *post-fader send*, and the volume fader and Mute button of the Audio track will affect the volume going out of the send.

❊ ❊ ❊

☀ PRE- VERSUS POST–FADER SENDS

Although post-fader sends are generally more commonly used, both pre- and post-fader sends have their uses. It all depends on the results you want. Choose post-fader (the Pro Tools default) if you want your dry track's level to affect the wet track's output. This way, when you raise and lower the volume fader on the dry track, you'll raise and lower the signal being routed to the Aux, maintaining a consistent blend of wet and dry. This is the most common choice when setting up time-based effects (which you did in the previous section). If, however, you want the wet and dry track levels to be completely independent, use a pre-fader send. Because signal will be routed to the Aux track *before* the dry track's fader, a full signal will be sent to *both* faders, allowing more flexibility with the wet and dry balance. (This is commonly used when setting up cue mixes, which I'll discuss in Chapter 10.) Experiment!

☀ THE MIX PARAMETER AND TRADITIONAL TIME-BASED ROUTING

Most time-based plug-in effects have a Mix parameter in the plug-in window that enables you to blend a dry and a wet signal within the plug-in itself. Usually, this setting defaults to 100-percent wet, but not always. Be sure to check your plug-in's Mix parameter; in the traditional mixing workflow you just learned, you'll want that Mix parameter to be 100-percent wet so you can adjust the wet and dry levels using the tracks' faders.

☀ There's one more send-related button to talk about: The FMP button (which stands for *Follow Main Pan*) makes panning your sends much easier. Frequently, it's preferable to have the send's pan mirror the panning of the track as a whole. That's just what FMP does. Simply click on the FMP button in the send's output window, and the send's pan will follow the panning that you choose for your track's output. You can tell whether your send is set to follow the main panner by the lit FMP button and the grayed-out panner in the send's output window.

☀ FMP can be automatically enabled on newly created sends. To do so, open the Preferences dialog box, click on the Mixing tab, and check the Send Pans Default to Follow Main Pan checkbox. (You can access the Preferences dialog box from the Setup menu.)

Here's a variation on the traditional time-based effect workflow—and one that can make production much simpler and boost the performance of your DAW in the bargain!

❄ A bus can have multiple sources and destinations. That means you can create sends on a number of tracks and assign them all to the same bus(es). In this image, I've created sends on all the vocal tracks (Lead Vocal, Male Harmony, and Female Harmony tracks) and assigned all those sends to buses 1 and 2.

❄ All these signals can be combined and routed to a single Aux track, as shown here. Remember that you must set the input of the Aux track to match the buses you're using on your source tracks (in this image, buses 1 and 2). The Aux track will contain the effect you want to apply to your tracks (in this example, a reverb).

❄ It's worth noting that you can independently control the levels and panning of each of your sends via the send output window, enabling you to individually set the level of each source track going to the effect.

That's it! Now you have dry faders (the Audio tracks) and a wet reverb track (the Aux track), and you can adjust the levels to suit your mix.

❄ MOVING AND COPYING IN THE MIX WINDOW

Want to move a plug-in or send from one track to another? No problem. Just click on that plug-in or send and drag it to any available track. To copy, rather than move, a plug-in or send, just hold down the Option key (Mac) or Alt key (PC) as you click and drag! There's only one limitation to this flexibility: Multichannel plug-ins can be moved only to tracks of the same output format. For example, you can drag a stereo plug-in to another stereo track, but not to a mono track.

New in Pro Tools 11: More Mix Control

By now, you've learned a bit about the power that inserts and sends can give you when creating that perfect mix. The good news doesn't stop there—Pro Tools 11 has introduced some very useful new features that will help you work quickly and efficiently!

Bypassing Plug-Ins

If you take a look in the upper-right section of a real-time plug-in, you'll see a button named "Bypass." When a plug-in is bypassed (indicated by the Bypass button being colored amber, as shown here), the plug-in will allow the signal to pass through unaffected. For example, if you have a Channel Strip plug-in on the exercise session's Lead Vocal track and click the Bypass button, you'll hear the track *without* any of the compression, expansion, and EQ that the plug-in would otherwise add to the track.

Bypassing plug-ins is a commonly used and powerful tool for the mix engineer, and the ability to more quickly manage plug-ins in this way is a fantastic new addition to Pro Tools' arsenal. Let's take a look at how you can easily bypass a number of plug-ins simultaneously:

1 **Select** the **tracks** that contain the plug-ins you want to bypass. In this example, I'm selecting my three vocal tracks and the Vox Verb Aux track.

2 **Click** the **Track menu**.

3 **Move the cursor** to the **Bypass Inserts menu item**. A submenu will appear.

❋ The Bypass Inserts submenu will give you control over the plug-ins on your selected tracks:

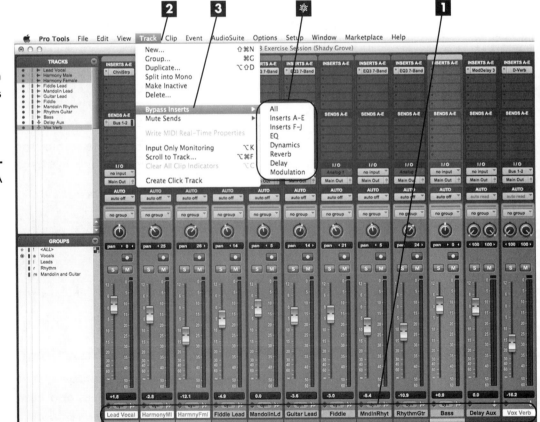

- ❄ Choosing All will bypass all plug-ins on your selected tracks.
- ❄ Choosing Inserts A–E will bypass all plug-ins in the Inserts A–E section on your selected tracks.
- ❄ Choosing Inserts F–J will bypass all plug-ins in the Inserts F–J section on your selected tracks.
- ❄ Choosing EQ will bypass all EQ plug-ins on your selected tracks. In cases where a plug-in includes more than just EQ properties (as is the case with the Channel Strip plug-in), only the EQ section will be bypassed.
- ❄ Choosing Dynamics will bypass all dynamic plug-ins on your selected tracks. In cases where a plug-in includes more than just dynamic properties (as is the case with the Channel Strip plug-in), only the Compressor and Expander sections will be bypassed.
- ❄ Choosing Reverb will bypass all reverb plug-ins on your selected tracks.
- ❄ Choosing Delay will bypass all delay plug-ins on your selected tracks.
- ❄ Choosing Modulation will bypass all modulation plug-ins on your selected tracks.

This feature, as with so many tools in Pro Tools, is also accessible via shortcuts:

- ❄ Pressing Shift+A will bypass all plug-ins on your selected tracks.
- ❄ Pressing Shift+1 will bypass all plug-ins in the Inserts A–E section on your selected tracks.
- ❄ Pressing Shift+2 will bypass all plug-ins in the Inserts F–J section on your selected tracks.
- ❄ Pressing Shift+E will bypass all EQ plug-ins on your selected tracks. In cases where a plug-in includes more than just EQ properties (as is the case with the Channel Strip plug-in), only the EQ section will be bypassed.
- ❄ Pressing Shift+C will bypass all dynamic plug-ins on your selected tracks. In cases where a plug-in includes more than just dynamic properties (as is the case with the Channel Strip plug-in), only the Compressor and Expander sections will be bypassed.
- ❄ Pressing Shift+V will bypass all reverb plug-ins on your selected tracks.
- ❄ Pressing Shift+D will bypass all delay plug-ins on your selected tracks.
- ❄ Pressing Shift+W will bypass all modulation plug-ins on your selected tracks.

Both the menu item commands and the shortcuts act as toggles—for example, bypassing all plug-ins on the selected tracks can be undone by selecting the menu item (or using the shortcut) again.

At this point, being able to identify which plug-ins are bypassed in your session becomes important! It's easy to visually check the state of any plug-in, even if that plug-in window is closed:

❄ A non-bypassed plug-in is indicated by dark text against a light gray background in the inserts section of your Mix window.

A bypassed plug-in is indicated with light text against a dark background. If the plug-in is completely bypassed, the background is a dark blue. If only part of a plug-in is bypassed (such as the EQ section of the Channel Strip plug-in), the background is a dark purple.

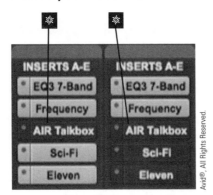

Before you move on, there are a couple more ways to toggle bypass:

Command-click (Mac) or Ctrl-click (PC) an insert to bypass (or un-bypass) an individual plug-in. This is not new in Pro Tools 11, but it is tremendously useful.

Control-click (Mac) or Start-click (PC) to bypass not only that plug-in but all plug-ins below that insert position as well. For example, if you use this technique and click on insert C, plug-ins on inserts C–J will be bypassed.

> ❋ **MULTIPLE MODIFIERS**
>
> One of the most important modifiers in Pro Tools is the Option (Mac) or Alt (PC) key. Among other things, it has the ability to apply certain changes made on one track to all tracks in your session. Want to set all the outputs of your track to the same output path? Just hold down the Option or Alt key and change the output of one track, and you've just done the job in one operation.
>
> This modifier works very well with the two methods of toggling bypass. Command+Option-click (Mac) or Ctrl+Alt-click (PC) an insert to bypass (or un-bypass) an individual insert on all tracks. Control+Option-click (Mac) or Start+Alt-click (PC) to bypass not only that plug-in on all tracks but all plug-ins below that insert position as well. This is a great way to quickly bypass all plug-ins in your session.

Muting Sends

If you take a look just below the pan controls of a send's output window, you'll see a button named "M," for "mute." When a send is muted (indicated by the M button being colored amber), the send will not pass signal on to the send's destination.

Like bypassing plug-ins, muting sends is an important part of the mixing process. Pro Tools 11 gives you new control over this process:

1 Select the **tracks** that contain the plug-ins you want to mute. In this example, I'm selecting my three vocal tracks.

2 Click on the **Track menu**.

3 Move the cursor to the **Mute Sends menu item**. A submenu will appear.

❄ The Mute Sends submenu will give you control over the plug-ins on your selected tracks:

　❄ Choosing All will mute all sends on your selected tracks.

　❄ Choosing Sends A-E will mute all sends in the Inserts A-E section on your selected tracks.

　❄ Choosing Sends F-J will mute all sends in the Inserts F-J section on your selected tracks.

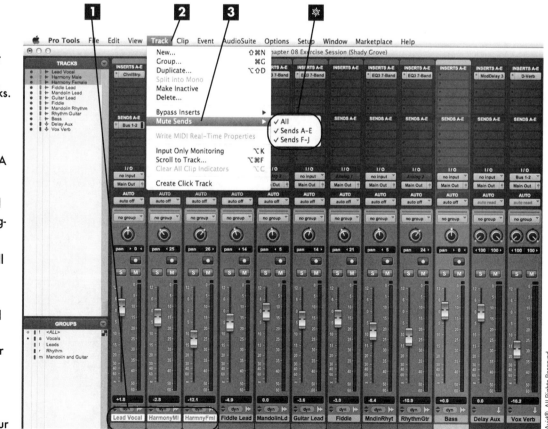

This feature, as with so many tools in Pro Tools, is also accessible via shortcuts:

* Pressing Shift+Q will mute all sends on your selected tracks.
* Pressing Shift+3 will mute all sends in the Inserts A–E section on your selected tracks.
* Pressing Shift+4 will mute all sends in the Inserts F–J section on your selected tracks.

Both the menu item commands and the shortcuts act as toggles. For example, muting all sends on the selected tracks can be undone by selecting the menu item (or using the shortcut) again.

At this point, being able to identify which sends are muted in your session becomes more important! It's easy to visually check the state of any send, as it was with plug-ins, even if that send's output window is closed:

* A non-muted send is indicated by dark text against a light gray background in the inserts section of your Mix window.
* A muted send is indicated with light text against a dark blue background.

Before you move on, there are a couple more ways to toggle muting sends:

* Command-click (Mac) or Ctrl-click (PC) a send to mute (or un-mute) an individual send. This is not new in Pro Tools 11.

* This next bit *is* new: Control-click (Mac) or Start-click (PC) to mute not only that send, but all sends below that send position as well. For example, if you use this technique and click on send C, sends C–J will be muted.

> ☀ **MULTIPLE MODIFIERS**
>
> As with bypassing plug-ins, the Option and Alt keys work well when muting sends. Command+Option-click (Mac) or Ctrl+Alt-click (PC) a send to mute (or un-mute) an individual send on all tracks. Control+Option-click (Mac) or Start+Alt-click (PC) to mute not only that send on all tracks, but all sends below that insert position as well.

Expanded Sends View

As you work more and more with sends, you'll gradually realize two things. First, you'll recognize that being able to view and control send levels is central to the mixing process. Second, having to click the send to open the output window and then position that window every time you want to adjust your send is a royal pain. Fret not, because Pro Tools has another way to view sends: Expanded Sends view.

When you're looking at a send in Expanded Sends view, here's what you'll see in your Mix window's sends area:

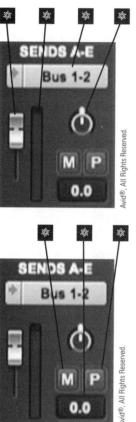

* Send button (This will be visible, allowing you to quickly access the send's output window.)
* Send level meter
* Send pan controls
* Send fader

* Send Mute button
* Send Pre/Post Fader button
* Send Level indicator

There are a few ways to put a send into Expanded Sends view. Let's start off by using Pro Tools' View menu:

1 **Click** the **View menu**.

2 **Move the cursor** to the **Expanded Sends menu item**. A submenu will appear.

❄ The Expanded Sends submenu allows you to activate Expanded Sends view for all sends, none of the sends, or individual sends from A–J. Sends that are in Expanded Sends view will be indicated in this menu with a checkmark.

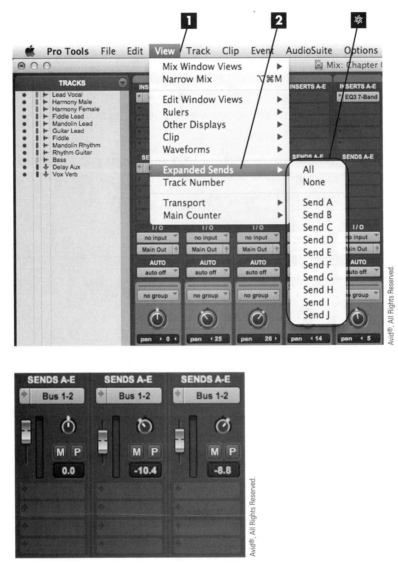

Once you've selected a send to be shown in Expanded Sends view, all sends in that position will be shown in the view. It's a global change in your session. In this example, this is the view you'd see if you selected send A to be shown in Expanded Sends view.

To this point, this is roughly the way that Pro Tools has operated in the past, but with previous versions there was a significant limitation: Only one send per bank could be in Expanded Sends view at a time. In other words, send A and send G could be simultaneously in Expanded Sends view, but not send A and send B.

With Pro Tools 11, however, you can have all 10 sends in Expanded Sends view, giving you a comprehensive view of any of your sends. Taken to extremes, here's what you might see if you used Expanded Sends view for sends A, B, E, F, G, and H:

And of course, there's a way to do it without going to menus—but in this case, you've got to be specific where you click!

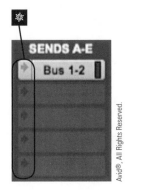

❋ On the left side of each send position, you'll see a small arrow icon (this is true for positions with active sends on them as well as empty slots). Command-click (Mac) or Ctrl-click (PC) to toggle individual positions between normal and Expanded Sends view.

Making the Most of Tracks

Here are a few tips to help you with track navigation, routing, and balance!

Scroll into View

Often, when mixing, you'll run across a track that could use a little editorial tweaking, requiring you to move from the Mix window to the Edit window. That's easy enough, but in cases when you're working with a large number of tracks (more than can be shown in your Mix or Edit window at once), you might find yourself spending a lot of time scrolling through your Edit window to find the track you want! The Scroll into View function does that work for you.

1 **Right-click** on the desired **track name**. (This works in either the Mix or the Edit window.) The track's menu will appear.

2 **Choose** the **Scroll into View menu item**. Two things will happen:

* The Mix window will scroll so that the track will appear on the left-most side (or as left-most as possible).

* The Edit window will scroll so that the track will appear at the top of the window (or as high as possible).

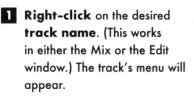

There are a couple other ways to scroll a track into view:

❋ Right-click on the desired track name in the Tracks list (in either the Edit or Mix window) and choose Scroll into View from the menu that appears.

❋ From the Track menu, choose Scroll to Track. You'll be prompted to enter the track number that you want to scroll into view.

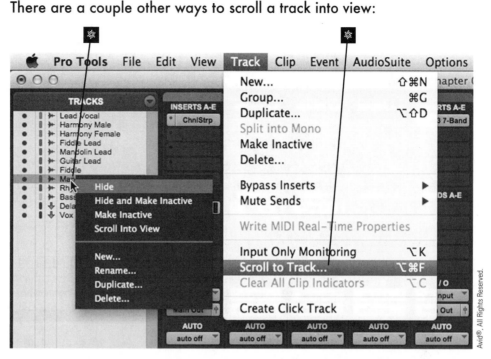

❋ TRACK NUMBERS

The Scroll to Track feature really only works well if you're able to see your track numbers, which can be easily enabled or disabled from the View menu.

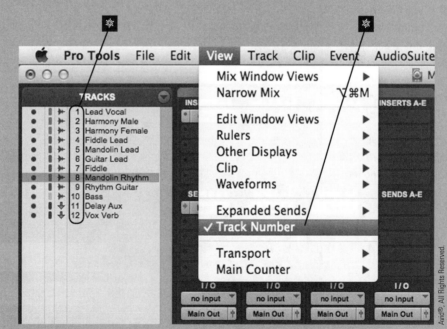

❋ From the View menu, you can enable and disable track number displays. When Track Number view is enabled, the menu item is indicated with a checkmark.

❋ Once the track number display is enabled, you'll see numbering to the left of track names in the Tracks list. These are the numbers you'll refer to when using the Scroll to Track feature.

> ❋ **HEY, THIS DOESN'T WORK!**
>
> The Scroll into View (or Scroll to Track) feature only works (and is only really needed) when you're working with sessions where you can't see all of your tracks simultaneously in the Mix and Edit windows. Additionally, tracks that are near the bottom of the Edit window or the right of the Mix window will only move to the extent possible.

Toggling Groups

Here's a way to change the balance of a mix (fader) group without the hassle of first having to deactivate the group! In this example, there are three vocal parts that are grouped together in an active fader group.

> ❋ **MY FAVORITE MIX WINDOW SHORTCUT**
>
> While I'm on the topic of groups, here's a useful shortcut, especially for those complex sessions with many groups: To quickly show only the tracks in a given group, hold down the Control key (Mac) or the Start key (PC) and click on the name of the group that you want to see in the Groups list. (This works in either the Mix or the Edit window.) All tracks that are not members of that group will be hidden.

1 Press and hold the **Control key (Mac) or the Start key (PC)**, and then **click and drag** the **fader** you want to change. Note that although the group is still being shown as active in the Groups list, you can change individual tracks without affecting the rest of the group.

2 Release the **key**. Your group will be re-enabled, and the tracks' faders will move as a group.

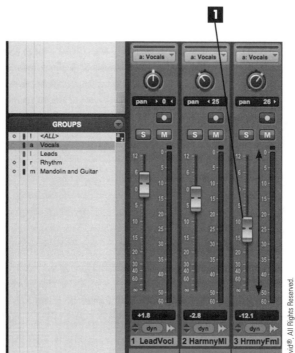

Subgroups

What's a subgroup? Simply put, a *subgroup* is an arrangement whereby the output of a number of tracks is routed to the input of a single track (usually a stereo Aux track). This has the effect of funneling the audio through this single track (often referred to as a *subgroup master*), making levels and effects easier to manage. Take a look:

Avid®, All Rights Reserved.

1 **Create** an **Aux track** to be your subgroup master (in this case, I've chosen to create a stereo Aux track) and **name it** appropriately.

2 Because you'll be using internal routing in this sort of situation, **choose** available **buses** for the input of the subgroup master. (In this image, I've chosen buses 3 and 4.)

❈ ❈ ❈

3 **Assign** the **outputs** of the tracks to be grouped (in this example, I've chosen all the vocal tracks in this session, including the reverb Aux track) to the same buses as you've chosen for the input of your subgroup master.

❋ Your subgroup master track's fader is now in control of the overall volume of your subgrouped tracks. If you're using the exercise session, note that as you adjust the fader, the relative blend of the vocals remains consistent, and the subgroup master controls the overall output.

Avid®, All Rights Reserved.

❋ **ANOTHER USEFUL MODIFIER**

Earlier in this chapter, you learned that the Option key (Mac) or Alt key (PC) is an easy way to make changes to all the tracks in your session. Here's a variation of that modifier key: Shift+Option (Mac) or Shift+Alt (PC) will make changes to all *selected* tracks. This is a great shortcut to use when assigning a number of tracks to the same bus.

In addition to making levels more manageable, subgroups can also help you work more efficiently with plug-ins. For example, if you want to apply a compressor to your drums (a very common thing to do), you *could* instantiate a compressor on each of the tracks. That, however, would be unwieldy to work with and wasteful of your limited processing resources. Instead, just launch *one* compressor effect on an insert of the subgroup master. There's only one plug-in to adjust, and it's thrifty use of your CPU!

Track-Output Options

Earlier in this chapter, you routed a send to the input of an existing Aux track as a part of traditional time-based effects routing. In the previous section, you routed the outputs of a number of tracks to the input of an Aux track to create a mix subgroup. Although neither of these operations is particularly difficult, they do take some time (and are common tasks when it comes to mixing). Fortunately, Pro Tools includes a few output options that can greatly streamline these workflows!

In addition to an interface or bus output, you also have the option to choose a track (new or existing) from the Output menu. What this does is automate many of the steps you've had to deal with up to now. Let's start off by looking at how track outputs can speed up time-based effects routing.

Track Output and Time-Based Effects Routing

In this scenario, I have a single Audio track, and I want to add some reverb. Using the new Track Output option, the job gets much quicker!

❊ **IF YOU'RE USING THE EXERCISE MATERIALS...**
To start out, let's add some reverb to the Fiddle Lead track.

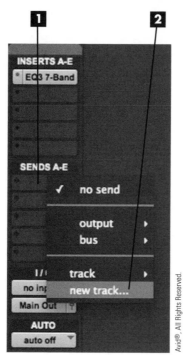

1 **Click** on any available **Send button** of the track that you want to send from (in this case, I'm using the Fiddle Lead track). A list of output options will appear.

2 **Choose** the **New Track menu item**. The New Track dialog box will appear.

349

❊ ❊ ❊

3   **4**

New Track

Width: Stereo   Type: Aux Input   Time Base: Samples   Name: Lead Verb

☑ Create next to current track

Cancel   Create

3 Although not identical to other dialog boxes you've seen, this New Track dialog box should look familiar. Here, you can choose the format and name for your new destination track. As it happens, the default format in this dialog box is to create a stereo Aux track, which is perfect for your purposes. All you have to do is **type** a descriptive **name** in the Name field. This is a fairly important step, so it's best not to skip it.

4 **Click** on the **Create button**. Here's what you've done, with one click of a button:

❆   **5**   ❆

* A new stereo Aux track has been created, named "Lead Verb."

* The output of the send has been set to a new bus, called "Lead Verb." (Pro Tools created this new bus at the same time the track was created.) You'll note that this same bus is the input of the newly created Aux track. Basically, your routing has been done for you (although you will still need to bring up the level of your send)!

5 Although your track and the routing have all been done for you, you'll still have to **choose** a **plug-in** for the track. (In this example, I'll choose a reverb.) At this point, you're ready to blend your wet and dry signals and get back to mixing!

There's more to track outputs than just creating new tracks. You can also route the output of a send to an existing Audio or Aux track.

❆❆❆

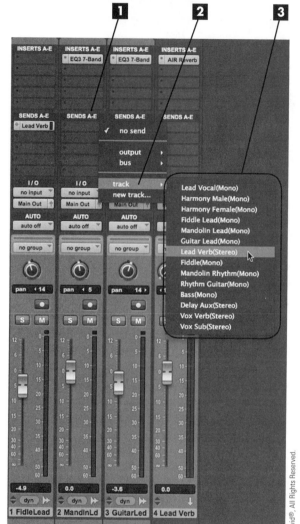

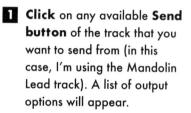 **Click** on any available **Send button** of the track that you want to send from (in this case, I'm using the Mandolin Lead track). A list of output options will appear.

2 **Move the cursor** to the **Track menu item**. A submenu will appear.

3 The track submenu is a list of all tracks that may be the recipient of a send (tracks that are already assigned to in interface input will not appear on this list). **Click** the **track** that you want to send to. (If you're using the exercise session, choose the Lead Verb track.) A send will be created, with the correct routing already done for you!

Track Output and Subgroups

Next, let's take a look at how this same feature can be used to quickly create a subgroup. In this situation, I've got a number of solo tracks, and I want to group their outputs for easy level management.

1 **Select** all the **tracks** you want to be a part of the new subgroup.

2 Now it's time to use the shortcut you used earlier in this chapter: **Hold down the Shift+Option (Mac) or Shift+Alt (PC) keys** and **click** on the **Track Output button** of one of your selected tracks. A list of output options will appear.

3 **Choose** the **New Track menu item**. The New Track dialog box will appear.

4 In the New Track dialog box, **choose** the **default track settings** (the default stereo Aux track works best in the majority of cases) and **name** the **track "Lead Sub."**

Here's what you'll wind up with:

You'll see that, once again, you've created a new stereo Aux track, except in this case, the outputs of the selected tracks have been routed through a stereo bus to the input of the new track.

❋ OUTPUT TO TRACK

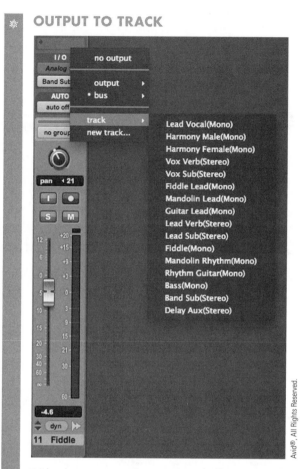

With subgroups as well as time-based effects routing, there's more to track outputs than just creating new tracks. You can also route the output of a track or a send to an existing Audio or Aux track. From the Output menu, choose Track as an output option (as opposed to New Track, as you did previously), and you'll be able to choose a destination track from a menu of available tracks.

❋ IF YOU'RE USING THE EXERCISE MATERIALS...

Before moving on to the next (and last) section of this chapter, use the Track Output feature to create a subgroup of the remaining tracks (Fiddle, Mandolin Rhythm, Rhythm Guitar, and Bass), and name the subgroup track "Band Sub."

Bus Interrogation

Up to now, you've gone through a number of traditional routings, from setting up time-based effects like reverbs to creating subgroups to make your mixing more efficient. As your mix becomes increasingly complex, you may occasionally want to know where a track's input is coming from or where its output is routed to. Pro Tools' track interrogation will let you do just that!

1. **Right-click** on the input or output that you wish to interrogate. (In this case, I've chosen an input.) The following interrogation options will appear:

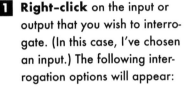

* **Select Assignments to [path name].** Any track that uses the path will be selected.
* **Show Assignments to [path name].** Any track that uses the path will be shown.
* **Show Only Assignments to [path name].** Any track that uses the path will be shown. All other tracks will be hidden.
* **Restore Previously Shown Tracks.** If you've hidden a track by using the Show Only Assignments to [path name] option, this will restore the previous track show/hide state.

Remember, *all* the static parameters you've just set up (send levels, Aux track levels, plug-in parameters, and so on) are simply a starting point, setting the stage so you can go on to tweak your mix further. That's where automation comes in....

Now that you've got the basics of signal flow, it's time to practice and explore. Mixing is perhaps the most subjective and personal aspect of the entire production process, so take time to see what you can accomplish with the tools and techniques you've learned so far. A "Finished" version of the exercise session has been included for you to refer to, but remember that this is merely a snapshot of a work in progress—one that we'll continue in the next chapter.

Next stop...the mixdown!

9 } Finishing Touches

Now that you're at the threshold of finishing your first project, it's interesting to look back at all you've accomplished to get here, from setting up your system to recording, to editing (and more editing), and on to mixing. Now you're moving to the final stages of creating a deliverable product. Good job!

Okay, enough reminiscing. Break's over.

Before you can truly consider a project finished, there's usually some tweaking to be done with the mix. Then, when you're satisfied with everything, it's time to do a final mixdown to a file or number of files that you can listen to on something other than your Pro Tools rig. In this chapter, you'll learn how to:

- ❋ Use basic automation techniques.
- ❋ Tweak your mix automation in the Edit window.
- ❋ Use clip-based gain to manage levels.
- ❋ Use Master Fader tracks.
- ❋ Bounce to disk in a CD-ready format.

❋ USING THE TUTORIAL SESSIONS

If you'd like to follow this chapter's examples, please download the Chapter 09 Exercise Session file. Alternatively, if you worked with the tutorial session for Chapter 8, "Basic Mixing," and you like your mix, you can continue working with that session instead. For information on downloading this book's exercise materials, please refer to the "Setting Up Your Session" section of the introduction.

Automating Your Mix

Automation is one of the coolest things about mixing in a DAW, and in my opinion, nothing beats Pro Tools' automation features. If the term is new to you, *mix automation* refers to the ability to change aspects of your mix (such as volume, for example) over time and to have those changes written to your session. Once those changes have been written, they can be adjusted and played back automatically (hence the term *automation*), giving you the ability to control multiple parameters in real time as your session plays.

> ❄ **RECORDING VERSUS WRITING**
>
> Before I start dealing with mix automation, I should cover some basic terminology. Audio and MIDI data are recorded, but automation is written. When your session plays back, the *written* automation can be read. This might seem like a matter of semantics at this point, but it'll help keep things clear as you work with automation (and these are the standard industry terms).

The Automation Modes

There are five automation modes, which determine the way your fader, pan, and other parameters will be written. Each automation mode is unique, to fit a wide variety of mixing situations. Understanding the distinction between these modes is the best way to start learning about automation.

1 You can set the automation mode for any track, whether you're in the Mix window or the Edit window. **Click** on the **Automation Mode button** on the track that you want to automate (which in this image reads Auto Off or Off). A menu of the five automation modes of Pro Tools will appear.

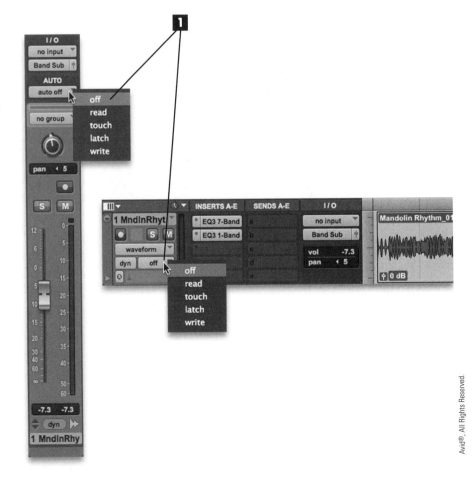

- **Off.** Using this mode, automation will neither be written nor played back. This is a good way to suspend automation on a track that has automation.

- **Read.** Automation cannot be written in this mode, but previously written automation will be played back. Use this mode to play back your automated tracks without running the risk of overwriting that automation.

- **Touch.** The track will read previously written automation until a parameter is touched (clicked with your mouse or using a control surface), at which time automation will be written for that parameter. When the parameter is released, it will return to its previously written automation.

- **Latch.** This mode is similar to Touch. Only when a parameter is touched will automation be written. When the parameter is released in Latch mode, however, it will remain at the last value and continue to write automation at that position until you stop playback.

- **Write.** In this mode, automation will be written on all enabled parameters, regardless of whether the parameter is being touched.

❋ AUTOMATION ON A TRACK-BY-TRACK BASIS
You can choose a different automation mode for each track.

❋ A WORD ABOUT AUTOMATION WORKFLOW
With the Touch, Latch, and Write modes, automation will be written during playback, and writing will stop when playback is stopped (or, in the case of Touch, when you let go of the parameter you're automating).

Write Mode
Let's start by using Write mode to change the volume of a track.

❋ IF YOU'RE USING THE EXERCISE MATERIALS...
In this example, the Mandolin Rhythm track, which sounds fine during the introduction, is a little too loud when the first verse starts. In this section, you'll use Write mode to change the volume of that track at the right time.

❋ SETTING THINGS UP
You can (and often will) do your automation work in the Mix window, but for purposes of visualization, the screenshots in this section will use the Edit window.

❋ ❋ ❋

1 First, let's set things up so you can see the changes you make. **Click** on the **Track View button** to change the data shown on your track.

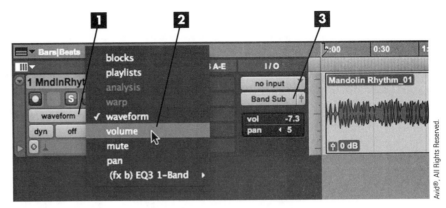

2 **Choose** the **track parameter** you want to view. In this example, I'll choose Volume. You'll see the Volume automation playlist indicated by a horizontal line in your track.

3 If you're writing volume automation in the Edit window, you'll find that the Output window will be a convenient way to access the track's main fader controls. Just click on the **Output Window button** to reveal the track's Output window.

❄ IF YOU'RE USING THE EXERCISE MATERIALS...

If you're using the exercise session, you'll see that the word "Volume" in the track view button is grayed out and in italics (indicating that it's inactive). That's because you're in Auto Off mode. Once you switch over to any of the other automation modes, the automation will become active.

---

4 **Choose** the **Write automation mode** from the Automation Mode menu.

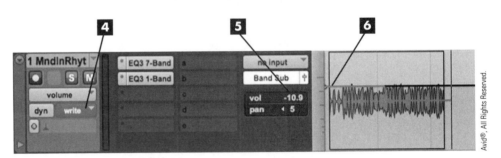

5 Because Write mode will begin writing automation as soon as playback begins, you should **set** your **initial levels**. (In this example, I'll set my initial level at −4.6 dB.) Then **move** the **timeline insertion** to the point at which you want to start writing automation (in this case, I've placed the timeline insertion at the beginning of the session).

6 **Start playback.** Automation will be written for all enabled parameters. As your automation is being written, you will see the data represented as a red line in the track's automation playlist. If you're using the exercise session, bring down the volume at the beginning of the first verse, which starts at about 37 seconds. When you're finished writing automation, **stop** your session's **playback**.

❊ WRITE WARNING

Be careful of following a Write pass with another Write pass. This generally leads to problems. Remember, Write mode is *always* writing on all mix parameters. Touch and Latch, on the other hand, are common choices to follow a Write pass (for reasons that will become apparent shortly).

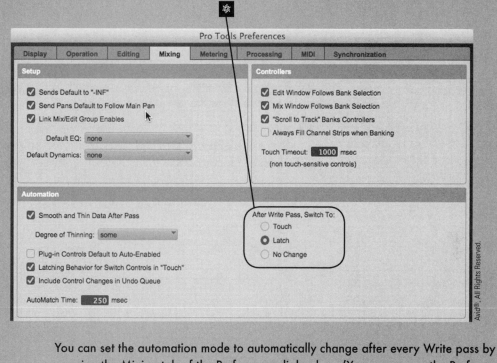

You can set the automation mode to automatically change after every Write pass by opening the Mixing tab of the Preferences dialog box. (You can access the Preferences dialog box from the Setup menu.) In the After Write Pass, Switch To section, you can choose Touch, Latch, or No Change.

When you stop playback, you'll see that the volume line has changed shape to match the fader move that you performed during playback. As soon as playback stopped, the automation stopped as well. However—and this is important—with Write mode, you were also writing automation on other enabled parameters, even if you didn't touch any other controls!

The strength of Write mode is that it writes on all enabled automation parameters (volume, pan, sends, etc.), whether you touched those parameters or not. That makes it a choice for many for first passes at automation. That said, it's rarely used to tweak individual parameters. For that, you'll use Touch and Latch modes.

Touch Mode and Latch Mode: The Update Modes

Although Write mode is certainly powerful, it's not well suited to making specific adjustments on a single automation parameter. For that kind of work, you'll want to use either Touch or Latch mode, collectively known as the "update" modes.

Touch and Latch modes are largely similar, but their few differences are significant ones. Let's take a look at them one at a time:

1 **Select** the **Touch automation mode** from the Automation Mode menu.

2 **Play** your **session**. As long as you don't click on any parameters, your automation will be read back, and the appropriate controls will move.

3 When you want to make a change in your automation, just **click** on the appropriate **control** and **adjust it**. Let go of the control when you want to stop writing, and you'll see your parameter move back to the previously written automation line.

Using the Mandolin Rhythm track, here's what I got with a typical Touch automation pass:

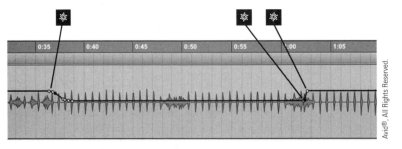

❋ Automation was played back as originally written until this point, when I began moving the volume fader. In this example, I lowered the fader at about 37 seconds (where the first verse began).

    ❋ Here, I released the fader. Because I was in Touch mode, the fader began to move back to the previously written automation playlist. In this case, I released the fader at about 1 minute and 2 seconds (where the first verse ended).

    ❋ Touch mode will take a little time to go back to the previously written automation (a parameter called AutoMatch Time, which you can adjust from the Mixing tab in the Preferences dialog box).

As playback continues, nothing further will be written unless the parameter is once again moved.

The other update mode, Latch, is written using essentially the same steps you took in writing with Touch mode, but the mode's behavior is a bit different. Here's how a similar update pass might look with Latch mode:

❋ ❋ ❋

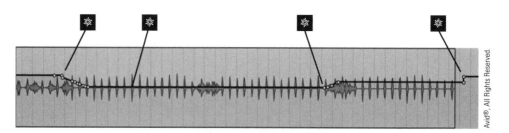

❋ Automation was played back as originally written until this point (the beginning of the first verse, if you're using the exercise session), when I began moving the volume fader. So far, this is the same behavior as you saw with Touch mode.

❋ At this point, I released the fader. Because I was in Latch mode, the fader stayed put instead of going back to previously written automation, as you saw in Touch mode.

❋ I once more moved the fader (to bring the volume up a little bit more for the first chorus) and again let go of the fader control. The level value continued to be written even after I let go of the fader.

❋ When playback stopped, the writing of automation stopped as well.

❋ AUTOMATION INDICATORS

You might have noticed that the track's Automation Mode button turned red as soon as you moved the volume fader. What's up with that? The track's Automation Mode button will turn red when any kind of automation data is being written to it. When using Write mode, the Automation Mode button will always appear red.

❋ IF YOU'RE USING THE EXERCISE MATERIALS...

This section was designed to show the behavior of the different automation modes. Unless you've done some especially cool automation writing, you can safely undo the steps you've done in this section before continuing on.

The Automation Window

The Automation window enables you to have a different kind of control over mix automation, allowing you to choose what types of data can be automated in your session.

1. **Click** on the **Window menu**.

2. **Choose Automation.** The Automation window will appear.

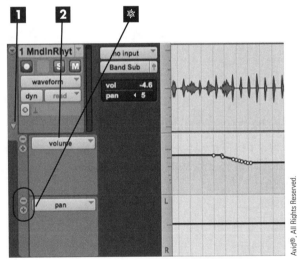

❄ If you click on the Suspend button, all automation (writing and playback) will be disabled.

❄ The seven Write Enable buttons represent automatable mix parameters: volume, pan, mute, plug-in, send volume, send pan, and send mute. An enabled parameter is indicated by a red button. If you click on a given button (removing the red highlighting), the parameter will be rendered unwriteable (although written automation will still be read).

Automation Lanes

You've already seen track lanes (playlist lanes for track comping). Let's take another look to see how track lanes can be used to view multiple mix automation parameters.

1 Click on the **Show/Hide Automation Lanes button** to reveal (or hide) a track's additional lanes.

2 Choosing a lane's view is very similar to what you've done already in the main body of the track. Just **click** on the **Lane View button** and **choose** the desired **automation type** from the list. As with the main Track View menu, the currently visible automation type is indicated by a checkmark and will be shown in the Lane View button itself.

❄ You can add an automation lane by clicking on the Add Automation Lane Below This One button, which is indicated by a plus (+) icon. To remove one, click on the Remove This Automation Lane button, shown as a minus (−) icon.

Plug-In Automation

Virtually every knob or button of a plug-in can be automated, enabling you to change tonal color, ambience, and more!

Enabling Plug-In Parameters: Method One

Here's one way to enable plug-in parameters:

1 **Click** on the **Plug-In Automation Enable button.** The Plug-In Automation dialog box will open. The Plug-In Automation dialog box is structurally similar to the Create Group dialog box that you worked with earlier, with a list of available parameters on the left side of the window and a list of enabled parameters on the right.

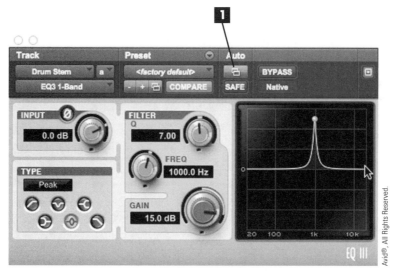

❋ ❋ ❋

2 **Click** on the **effects parameter(s)** that you want to automate. (If you're working with the tutorial session, you'll want to automate the plug-in's Frequency parameter.) Selected parameters will be highlighted. Holding down the Shift key as you click will enable you to select a range of parameters, and holding the Command (Mac) or Ctrl (PC) as you click will allow you to select multiple parameters, one at a time.

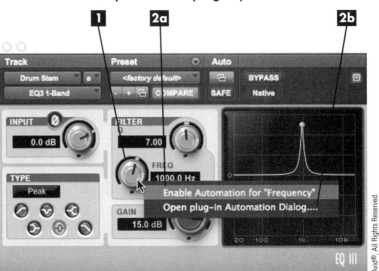

3 **Click** on the **Add button**. The selected parameter(s) will move from the left list to the right list.

4 When you're finished, **click** on the **OK button**.

> ❄ **DISABLING A PARAMETER**
>
> You can disable a plug-in parameter using similar steps: Just select the desired parameter(s) in the list on the right and then click on the Remove button.

Enabling Plug-In Parameters: Method Two

Here's another way to enable plug-in parameters:

1 **Press and hold** the **Control+Option+ Command keys (Mac)** or the **Ctrl+Start+Alt keys (PC)** and **click** on the **parameter** you want to automate (in this case, FREQ). A menu will appear, giving you two options.

2a **Click** on **Enable Automation for <parameter name>** to immediately enable the parameter for automation.

OR

2b **Click** on **Open Plug-In Automation Dialog** to open the Plug-In Automation dialog box that you saw in the previous section. At this point, you can follow steps 2 through 4 from the "Method One" section.

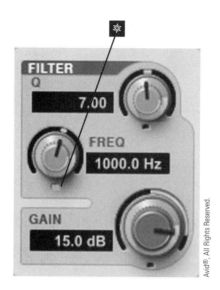

❄ Parameters enabled for automation will be indicated visually. Sometimes it's an outline, sometimes it's a box, and sometimes, as in this image, it's a small light beneath the parameter. This indicator will typically be a cool color (blue, green, etc.) when you're in Read mode, indicating that the parameter will play back written automation, or a warm color (red, yellow, etc.) when you are in Touch, Latch, or Write mode. When working in Off mode, there will be no indicator.

❄ ENABLING ALL PLUG-IN PARAMETERS

Here's a quick way to enable all the parameters on a specific plug-in: Press and hold the Control+Option+Command keys (Mac) or the Ctrl+Start+Alt keys (PC) and click on the plug-in window's Plug-In Automation Enable button. You can also automatically enable all parameters for automation as soon as a plug-in is instantiated, through the Preferences dialog box. Just go to the Mixing tab and check the Plug-In Controls Default to Auto-Enabled checkbox. Once this checkbox is checked, all plug-ins created from that point on will have all their parameters enabled for automation.

Writing Plug-In Automation

Plug-in automation is largely similar to any other kind of automation, but before I close this discussion, let's take a quick look at how you can view plug-in automation data.

❄ Once a parameter is enabled for automation, the plug-in and parameter will appear as an option when you click on the Track View button. Just choose the desired plug-in (which will reveal a submenu) and then choose the specific parameter that you want to view. (This can be shown in track lanes as well.)

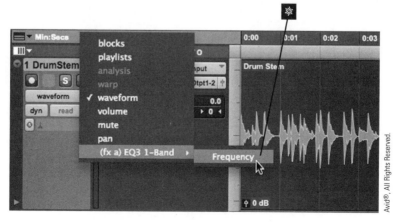

❄ ❄ ❄

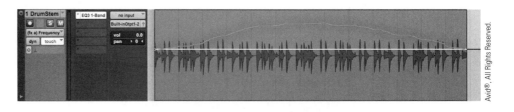

From this point, plug-in automation is identical to other kinds of automation: Choose your automation mode, begin playback, and change the parameter to start writing automation!

Making the Most of Automation

Being able to create mix automation by manipulating knobs, sliders, and faders is a fantastic advantage of using a DAW, but it'll only take you so far. When you need to get really specific with your automation, sometimes the only place to do that is back in the Edit window.

Automation and the Pencil Tool

As you've learned, you'll see a line that represents any parameter movements that have been written to the track. If you haven't done any automation passes, the automation playlist will appear as a straight line.

You've already tried using the different automation modes to write automation. Now let's create some new automation data using the Pencil tool.

> ❄ **IF YOU'RE USING THE EXERCISE MATERIALS...**
>
> If you're using the Chapter 09 Exercise Session–Part 2 session, please go to Memory Location #2–Pencil Tool Automation. Here, you'll use the Pencil tool to write pan automation in different ways.

1 If you're not already there, **switch** to the **Edit window**.

2 **Click** on the **Track View button** of the track you want to work with and **choose** the **data** you want to edit. (In this example, I've chosen to view pan automation on the Blorp track.)

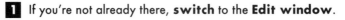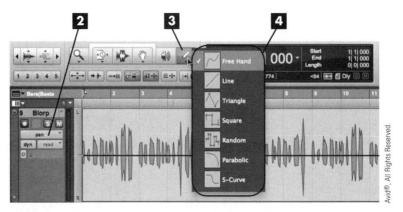

3 To view the different drawing options available to you, **click and hold** the **Pencil Tool button**. A menu will appear.

4 Just like the Trim and Grabber tools, the Pencil tool has some useful variations. For this example, let's **stick with** the default **Free Hand mode**.

5 Click and hold the **Pencil tool** at the point at which you want to begin writing new automation.

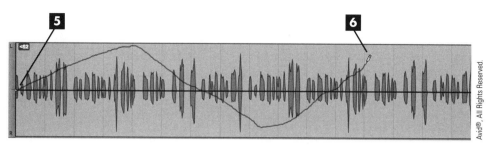

6 **Drag** the **mouse** to the place where you want to stop writing new automation. The Pencil tool will progressively write over pre-existing automation.

7 **Release** the **mouse button**. Your new automation will be written.

The Pencil tool's Free Hand mode is well suited to some kind of work but is perhaps not the best choice for other kinds of automation changes. Want a smooth transition from one parameter value to another (like a smooth increase in volume, for example)? The Line mode of the Pencil tool makes it easy.

There are other useful Pencil shapes as well. Let's try writing some pan automation on the Blorp track that ping-pongs from left to right:

1 Click and hold the **Pencil Tool button**. Again, the Pencil tool options will appear.

2 This time, **click** on the **Triangle menu item**.

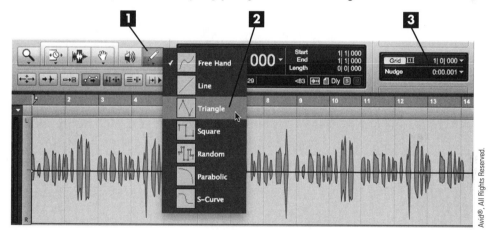

3 When you're dealing with the Triangle, Square, or Random Pencil tool options, the grid setting will determine the frequency of the automation changes (even if you're not in Grid mode). In this case, to pan from side to side every measure, **choose 1 bar** as the grid value, as shown here.

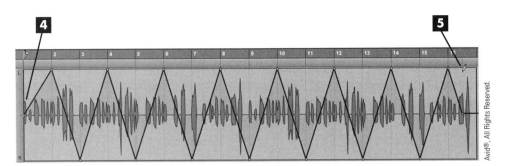

4 **Click and hold** the **Pencil tool** at the point at which you want to begin writing automation. This time, as you drag horizontally, a triangle wave will be drawn across the track. The speed of your panning will be the determined by your grid value. (In my case, it's one measure.) You can change the height of the wave by moving your mouse vertically as you drag. In the case of pan automation, a higher and lower triangle wave will translate into a more extreme pan from left to right.

5 When you're finished, **release** the **mouse button**. The pan automation will be written to your track.

> ❈ **AUTOMATION AND GRIDS**
> Although a triangle wave can be drawn in any of the edit modes, if you want the apex of the triangle wave to fall on a grid line, you must be in Grid mode.

Automation and the Grabber Tool

You may have noticed that your automation line is composed of a number of small dots. These dots are called automation *breakpoints* and define the shape of your automation line. You've seen how useful the Grabber tool can be when working with clips. Here's how you can use it to create, modify, and even delete automation breakpoints.

> ❈ **IF YOU'RE USING THE EXERCISE MATERIALS...**
> Please go to Memory Location #3–Grabber/Trim Tool Automation.

1 To create an automation breakpoint, use the Grabber tool to **click** on the **point in time** in the track where you want it to be.

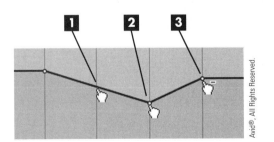

2 To change the time or value of an existing automation breakpoint, **click and drag** the **breakpoint** to the desired location.

3 To delete an existing automation breakpoint, **hold down the Option (Mac) or Alt (PC) key** and **click it**. The cursor will be shown as a pointing hand with a minus (−) sign next to it.

Automation and the Trim Tool

When the Trim tool is moved into a selected area of automation, it will be shown as downward facing, enabling you to drag your mouse up and down to increase or decrease the level of the automation in that selected area (while maintaining the shape of the automation line).

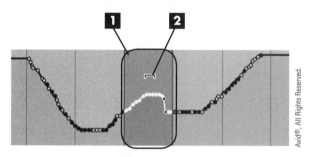

1 Using the Selector tool, **select** the **area** that you want to change.

2 **Move** the **Trim tool** into the selected area. The Trim tool will be shown downward facing, indicating that it's ready to change your automation.

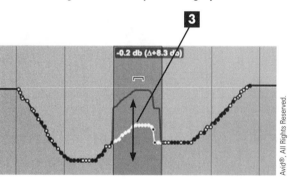

3 **Click and drag** your **mouse** up or down to adjust your automation proportionally.

4 **Release** the **mouse button**. The automation will be proportionally changed in the selected area.

Note that when you use the Trim tool to change volume automation, there will be a small box at the top of the selected area that will not only show you the level of your new automation, but also show a delta value (indicated by a triangle) when adjusting volume. This delta value lets you know the amount of change you're applying.

Copying and Pasting Automation

If you've got a segment of automation that you like, you can cut and paste that automation from one location to another. It's easy!

1 Using the Selector tool, **select** the **area of automation** that you want to copy, just as if you were selecting a segment of audio.

2 **Click** on the **Edit menu** and **choose** any of the basic **editing functions** you've used before (such as Cut, Copy, Paste, or Duplicate). One thing to keep in mind: This will not affect any audio clips or any automation parameters other than the one(s) you have selected.

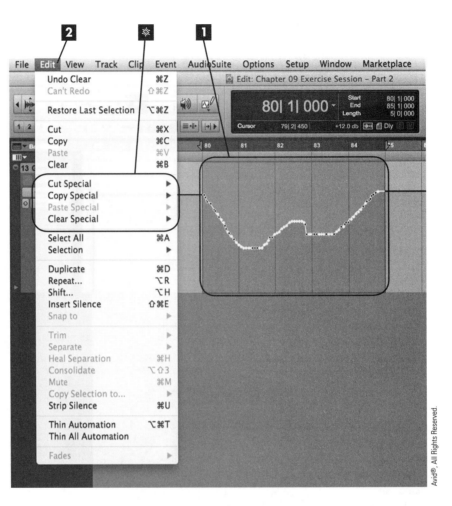

Avid®, All Rights Reserved.

※ Clicking the special editing items (including Cut Special, Copy Special, Paste Special, and Clear Special) will reveal a submenu that will enable you to edit all automation, only pan automation, or visible plug-in automation. (It will also allow you to edit clip-based gain—something I'll talk about later in this chapter.)

 SHORTCUT REMINDER
You can use the regular Cut, Copy, and Paste editing shortcut keys instead of going to the Edit menu. If you're using a Mac, the shortcuts are Command+X, Command+C, and Command+V, respectively. If you're on a PC, the shortcuts are Ctrl+X, Ctrl+C, and Ctrl+V.

Automation Follows Edit

When you move a clip, do you want the automation within that selected area to follow the clip, or do you want it to stay put? Either way, Pro Tools has you covered.

※ IF YOU'RE USING THE EXERCISE MATERIALS...
Please go to Memory Location #4–Automation Follows Edit.

1 **Click** on the **Options menu**.

2 The feature you're looking for is Automation Follows Edit. When active, the menu item will appear with a checkmark. To enable or disable this behavior, **click** the **Automation Follows Edit menu item**.

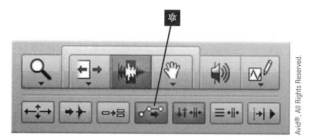

❋ You have an additional way to control this feature, such as clicking on the Automation Follows Edit button in the edit tools cluster. When active, the button will be blue. When inactive, the button is a bright orange, letting you know that your automation will not move with your clips.

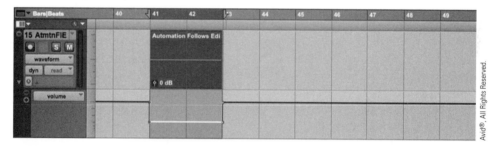

The best way to understand how this feature works is to see it in action. This image shows an example of an unmoved clip, with pan automation in an automation lane below the main playlist. Now, let's say that you move the clip. What will happen to the automation?

❋ If Automation Follows Edit is enabled, the automation will be moved along with the clip.

❋ ❋ ❋

* If Automation Follows Edit is disabled, the automation will not be moved along with the clip. Instead, it will remain in its original position.

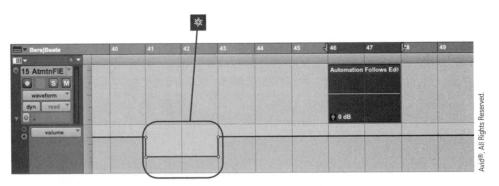

❅ SEPARATING CLIPS WHILE VIEWING AUTOMATION

If you want to separate a clip, but you are currently in an automation view on the main playlist, it's no problem. Just use the Selector tool to place your cursor where you want to split the clip and separate the clip as usual using the processes you learned in Chapter 5, "Editing." Your clip will be separated, just as if you were in Waveform view.

❅ SELECTING CLIPS WHILE VIEWING AUTOMATION

If you want to quickly select an area of a clip, but you are currently in an automation view on the main playlist, just double-click on the clip with the Selector tool (just as if you were in Waveform view). The time corresponding to your clip will be selected.

Momentary Switches and How to Use Them

Volume, pan, and plug-ins aren't the only aspects of your mix that can be automated. Switch-style controls (those that have only an on or off state) can be automated as well. In particular, mute and bypass (for plug-in effects) are often automated to get even more control over your mix.

Typically, these controls latch—that is, if you click on the button once, it will change the state of the parameter until the button is clicked again, like a light switch. You might find, however, that changing the behavior of these switches so they don't latch—in other words, the state of the switch will change only while you're clicking and holding the button—opens new creative possibilities. This non-latching kind of switch is called a *momentary* switch and is quite useful for adding delay or reverb to individual words or notes but leaving the rest of the track dry.

❅ IF YOU'RE USING THE EXERCISE MATERIALS...

Please go to Memory Location #5–Momentary Switches. This is the Japanese vocal for "Listen." Your job is to add some delay, but only to the second syllable of each word. Using momentary switches will make that job *much* easier!

In this scenario, you have a single vocal track, with a send from that track going to a reverb. You also have another send going to a delay (and that delay also being sent to the reverb). Delays can be tricky things and can muddy up a track very easily. To get the sound you want, you want to put a delay only on the second syllable of each word. The way you'll accomplish this is to keep the send to the delay muted, except for the specific times that you want a syllable to have that effect.

1 In the Preferences dialog box (which you can access from the Setup menu), **click** on the **Mixing tab**.

2 **Uncheck** the **Latching Behavior for Switch Controls in "Touch" checkbox** to make the switch momentary.

3 **Click** on the **OK button** at the bottom of the Preferences dialog box.

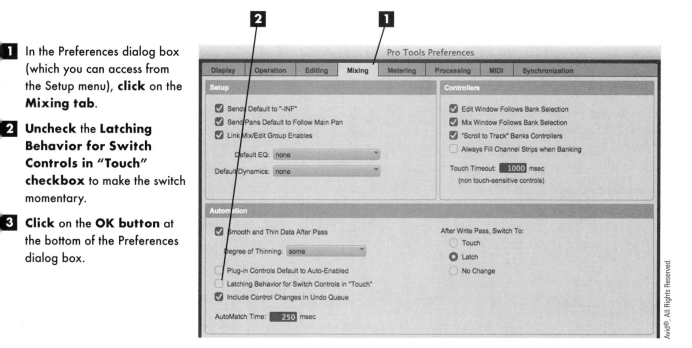

Just put your track in to Touch mode, mute your delay send, and you're ready to rock. After you start playback, click and hold on the send's Mute button (which you'll see in the send's Output window) during every second syllable. As soon as the syllable is finished, release the button; this will put the send back its initial muted state.

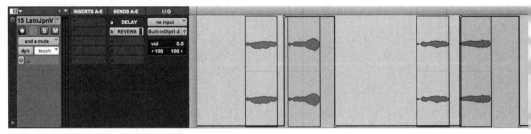

Although it might take a couple attempts to get it right, here's what you should wind up with. If you look at your send's mute automation playlist, you will see your send alternately mute and unmute. When the send is unmuted, signal will be sent to the Aux track, and you'll hear the reverb.

This technique is known in some circles as a *dub hit*, and it can be used on any kind of track, from beats to vocals. Now that you understand how the effect is achieved, you'll hear it in all sorts of modern music. The most obvious example is a vocal in which some individual words have reverbs (or echo or delay) but others are relatively dry.

New in Pro Tools 11: Write Automation While Recording!

In previous versions of Pro Tools, it was not possible to write automation while recording. This was sometimes a frustration for recording engineers who wanted to get a head start on the mix process by creating a rough mix during the tracking session.

There will be times when you want to take advantage of this added functionality and times when you won't, so Pro Tools gives you the ability to activate and deactivate the feature via the Preferences window:

1 **Click** on the **Setup menu** and **choose Preferences**. The Preferences dialog box opens.

2 **Click** on the **Operation tab**.

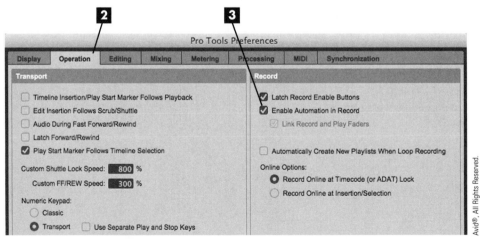

3 **Check** the **Enable Automation in Record checkbox** (by default, this option is disabled). Note that the Link Record and Play Faders option will be grayed out. Linking the two faders isn't possible (or desirable) when writing automation during recording.

Clip-Based Gain

Perhaps the most significant improvement introduced in Pro Tools 10 was clip-based gain. Put as simply as possible, this is a second level of volume automation for audio clips—one that isn't tied to a track but is instead part of the clip itself. This enables you to gain-match clips prior to mixing a track. Although this is aimed more at audio post-production (for video), it really can be used in any kind of situation.

Sound confusing? Let's take a look!

❊ IF YOU'RE USING THE EXERCISE MATERIALS...

Please go to Memory Location #6–Clip-Based Gain. The clips shown here are a voiceover for a video you'll watch later. The problem with it is that the middle of the Control Tower 2 clip is a little quiet in relation to the rest of the track.

The Basics of Clip-Based Gain

In its simplest sense, clip-based gain will enable you to change the volume level of a clip independently of the volume of any track that the clip may be on. It couldn't be simpler:

1 Before you can work with clip-based gain, you'll have to be able to see the controls. If they are not visible, **click** on **View**, **choose Clip**, and **choose Clip Gain Info**.

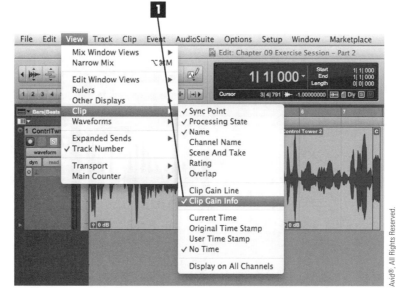

2 In the lower-left corner of a clip, you'll see a small fader icon and a gain value (which will initially read 0 dB). **Click and hold** on this **icon** to reveal a small volume fader.

3 **Adjust** the **fader** to change the gain of the clip. As you change the gain, you'll see the waveform within the clip change accordingly—something decidedly different from volume automation you've created up to now!

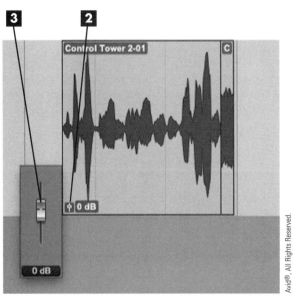

Avid®, All Rights Reserved.

✳ The dB value in the lower-left corner of the clip will reflect the changes you've made, as will the visual representation of the audio within the clip. (In this image, I've decreased the gain by 10 dB for visual effect.)

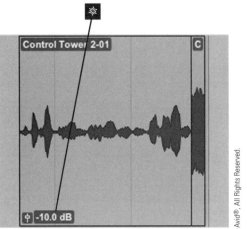

Avid®, All Rights Reserved.

✳ In addition to the value indicator in the bottom-left corner of the clip, you can also view the gain as a line within the clip itself. To do so, click on View, choose Clip, and choose Clip Gain Line.

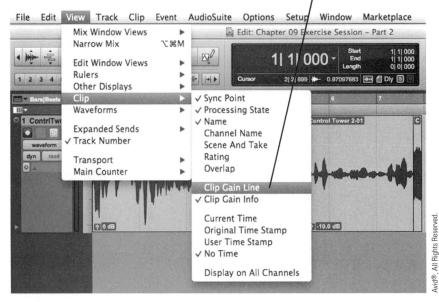

Avid®, All Rights Reserved.

❅ ❅ ❅

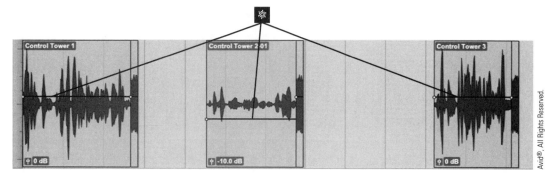

❈ The gain for each clip will be shown as a line within the clip. Initially, this is a straight line, but in the next section, you'll see that it doesn't have to be!

Editing Clip-Based Gain

You've probably noticed that the clip-gain line looks an awful lot like a volume automation line—and that's essentially what it is, except that it affects the clip as opposed to the track's volume fader.

Let's put this into more of a real-world situation. If you take a look at the Control Tower track in the tutorial session, you'll see that the audio in the middle section of the second clip is a bit low. In the previous section, you learned how to adjust an entire clip; now let's adjust a section within the clip using the Trim tool.

> ❈ **IF YOU'RE USING THE EXERCISE MATERIALS...**
> If you've made any gain changes to the second clip in the Control Tower track, please undo those changes before proceeding.

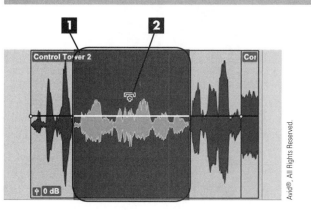

1 Using the Selector tool, **select** the **area** that you wish to change (in this case, the quieter middle section of the second clip). If you're following with the tutorial session, Slip mode will serve you best in making this selection.

2 Using the Trim tool, **move** your **cursor** into the selected area, toward the clip-gain line. The icon for the Trim tool will become downward facing with a small fader icon, as shown here. Next, **drag** your **cursor** up or down to adjust the gain of the selected area.

You'll no doubt have noticed that this editing of clip-based gain is virtually identical to the editing of volume automation on a track. Given this, it's not surprising that the Pencil and Grabber tools can similarly be used to change a clip-gain line.

❈ ❈ ❈

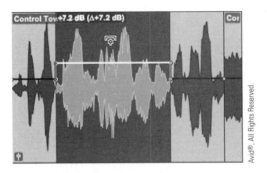

Editing clip gain using the Trim tool.

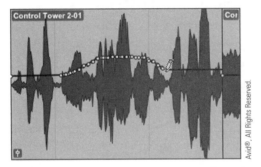

Editing clip gain using the Pencil tool.

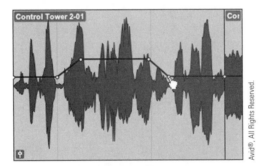

Editing clip gain using the Grabber tool.

※ **CLIP GAIN SHORTCUT**

Here's a nifty shortcut for readers who have a mouse with a scroll wheel: Hold down the Shift+Control keys (Mac) or Shift+Start keys (PC) and move your scroll wheel to raise or lower the gain within a selected area.

Clip-Based Gain Tools

Before you leave this very exciting new feature, let's take a look at a few more ways to work with clip-based gain.

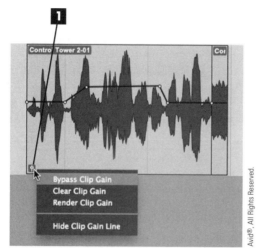

1 **Right-click** the **Clip-Based Gain icon** in the lower-left corner of a clip. The following options will appear:

Avid®, All Rights Reserved.

❊ **Bypass Clip Gain.** Any clip-based gain will be suspended (until un-bypassed). The clip-gain line will be gray, and the waveform view of the clip will revert to its original state.

❊ **Clear Clip Gain.** All clip-gain changes will be removed, and the clip-gain line will be reset to a flat line at 0 dB.

❊ **Render Clip Gain.** Clip gain is a real-time process, meaning that the changes are non-destructively applied to an audio file. If you choose to render clip-based gain, the changes you have made will be applied, and a new audio file will be created. In the track, a new clip will replace the original clip, and the clip-gain line will be reset to a flat line at 0 dB, enabling you to make further changes if you wish.

❊ **Show/Hide Clip Gain Line.** Depending on whether your clip-gain line is shown or hidden, this option will enable you to change the view state of the clip-gain line. (This affects all clips in your session.)

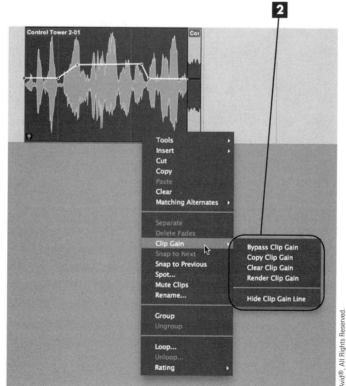

2 **Right-click** any **audio clip**. Within the menu of clip-related functions, you will find a section on clip gain, with similar commands and an added Copy Clip Gain option.

Avid®, All Rights Reserved.

✻ Clip gain can also be selectively imported (or not) in the Import Session Data dialog box. Just click on the Track Data to Import button and choose Clip Gain to select or deselect it for import.

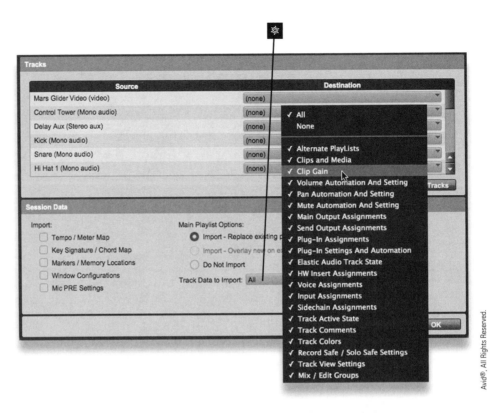

✻ CLIP-BASED GAIN AND CLIP GROUPS

When it comes to clip groups and clip-based gain, the news is all good. Not only is clip gain preserved by the clips within a clip group, but additional clip-based gain can be applied to the entire clip group!

✻ CLIP-BASED GAIN AND SIGNAL FLOW

Although clip-based gain might look like volume automation, from a signal-flow perspective, it's quite different. When you're talking about volume automation, you're talking about making a change *after* the signal has gone though a track's inserts. For example, raising the volume on a track won't change the level of the signal that is being received by a compressor plug-in. In contrast, clip-based gain is *before* the insert stage, so the changes that you make using clip-based gain *will* affect the signal that is going to your plug-ins. This can be a huge advantage in creating consistent levels for compression, expansion, or limiting.

✻ IF YOU'RE USING THE EXERCISE MATERIALS...

The "Shady Grove" session, which you used earlier in this chapter, has a number of opportunities for using clip-based gain (which I actually used in the production of the tune, but stripped away for use as an exercise session). As always, let your ears be your guides, and have fun!

Plug-In Power

Throughout the production process, plug-ins usually require some tweaking to get just the right effect. Top pros know that the ability to recall their favorite plug-ins and plug-in settings is a real timesaver, drastically cutting down the time spent fiddling with parameters! This section discusses three ways to manage your plug-in effects, saving time and boosting creativity!

Creating Presets

Suppose you created the *perfect* EQ for your favorite bassist, and you'd like to use the same settings in future projects. No problem—saving a preset is an easy process! Before you go further, though, there's a setting that you should check—one that will affect where your preset will be stored.

1 Click on the **Settings menu button** (the small circular button immediately to the right of the word "Preset"). The Settings menu will appear.

2 Choose Settings Preferences. A submenu will appear.

3 Choose Save Plug-In Settings To. Another submenu will appear, giving you two options:

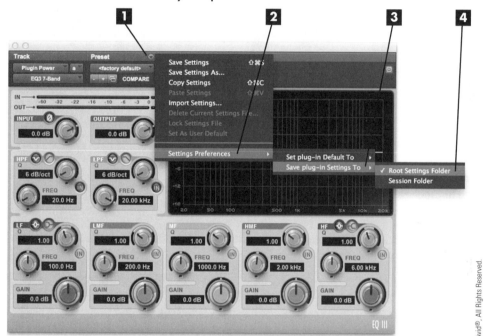

Avid®, All Rights Reserved.

❊ **Root Settings Folder.** Choose Root Settings Folder to save your preset to your host computer's Plug-In Settings folder (typically on your computer's primary hard drive). With this option selected, you'll be able to recall your saved presets quickly in any sessions you create or open on this computer.

❊ **Session Folder.** Choose Session Folder to save your preset to the Plug-In Settings subfolder of the session in which you're currently working. If you choose this option, the plug-in presets will travel with your session folder, and this preset will be recallable on any computer you use to open the session.

4 If you're following along with the exercise materials, **choose Root Settings Folder**.

5 **Adjust** the **settings** for your effect until they're just right.

6 **Click** on the **Settings menu button** and **choose Save Settings As**. The Save dialog box will appear.

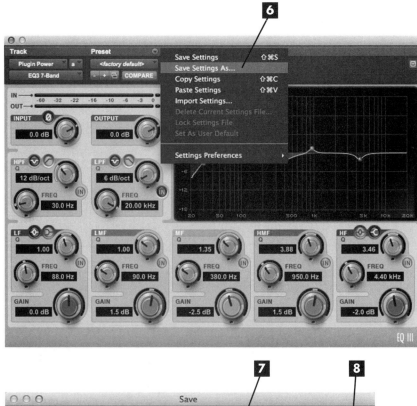

Avid®. All Rights Reserved.

7 **Type** a descriptive **name** for your preset (such as "Andy's Funk Bass," as I've done here, though that probably only makes sense if your name is also Andy!).

8 **Click** on the **Save button**.

Avid®. All Rights Reserved.

※ Your saved preset will be added to the list of available presets for that plug-in. The more presets you save, the longer that list will become!

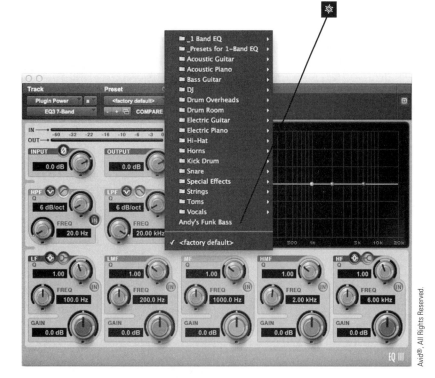

Setting Up Default Plug-Ins

As you gain experience, you might find that you have some favorite EQ and dynamic effects that you use time and time again. Setting them up as default plug-ins will help you recall them quickly.

You'll need to go to your old friend, the Preferences dialog box, to set things up:

1 **Click** on the **Setup menu**.

2 **Choose Preferences.** The Pro Tools Preferences dialog box will appear.

3 **Click** on the **Mixing tab**.

4 In the Setup section, you'll see two options enabling you to select a default EQ and default dynamics plug-in. Let's begin by choosing a favorite EQ. **Click** on the **Default EQ button**. A menu will be displayed.

5 **Move the cursor** to the **Plug-In menu item**. A submenu will appear, listing all the EQ plug-ins installed in your system.

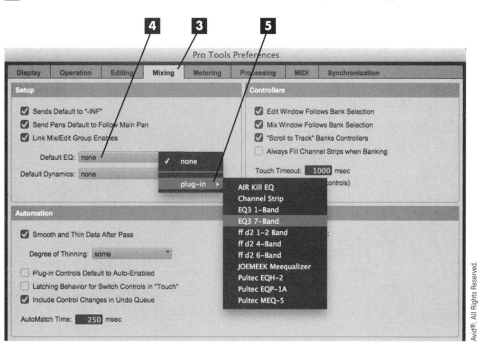

383

※ ※ ※

6 **Click** on your favorite EQ **plug-in**. (In this image, I've chosen the EQ3 7-Band plug-in.) Your choice will be set as the default EQ for Pro Tools.

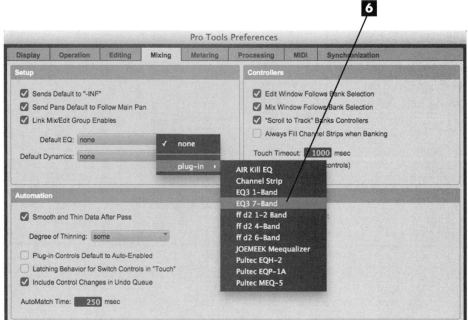

7 Now let's choose a default dynamic plug-in. **Click** on the **Default Dynamics button**. A menu will be displayed, as shown here.

8 The process for selecting a default dynamic plug-in is identical to the steps you took in choosing a favorite EQ. Just **move the cursor** to the **Plug-In menu item** and **choose** the desired **plug-in** from a list of options. (In this image, I've chosen the Dyn3 Compressor/Limiter plug-in.)

9 **Click** on the **OK button**.

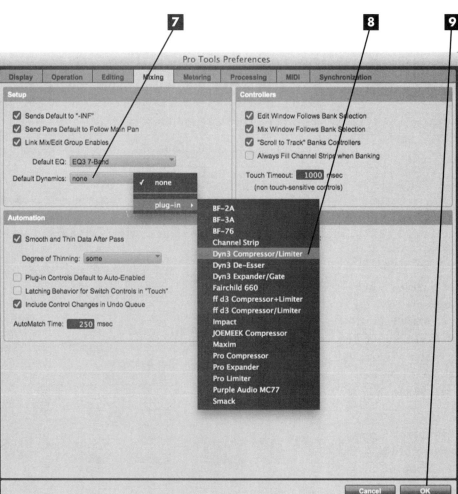

Here's the payoff: Now, when you click on any Insert button, your default plug-ins will appear at the top of the list, easily accessible.

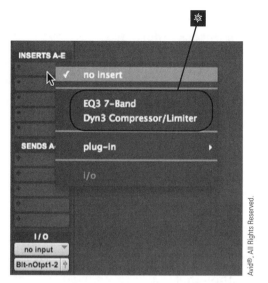

Using the Workspace Browser with Plug-Ins

You've used the Workspace Browser before and seen how easy it is to import audio files and sessions. Did you know that you can also use the Workspace Browser to import plug-in settings?

The first step is to locate your desired plug-in preset in the Workspace Browser. Use the Search function (which you learned about back in Chapter 3, "Getting Started with Audio") to make the job easier.

To refine your search, enter a specific name and specify the kind of file in the Workspace Browser's advanced search fields.

SEARCHING FOR SETTINGS

If you *don't* type in a name, and you only search by the plug-in settings file kind, Pro Tools will show *all* your plug-in settings files.

The only thing you need to do is drag your desired plug-in settings file into an insert position on a track. There are two ways to do it:

❄ If you drag the plug-in preset onto an insert that contains a plug-in (making sure the plug-in setting matches the plug-in that you're dragging to), the preset will be loaded in the plug-in.

❄ If you drag the plug-in preset onto an unused insert, Pro Tools will instantiate the plug-in and load the preset automatically. Job done!

Using Master Fader Tracks

There's one more track type left for you to explore: the Master Fader track. Although it looks similar to an Audio or Aux track, its function is substantially different from anything you've seen up to this point. A Master Fader track is a way to control output, and it is commonly used to control the output of an interface channel (although it can also be used to control the output of buses in more complex mix situations). With this simple but powerful track, you can control the entire level of your session.

Creating a Master Fader Track

First things first: You need to *create* a Master Fader track before you can use it!

1 **Click** on the **Track menu**.

2 **Choose New.** The New Tracks dialog box will open.

3 Using the techniques you learned in Chapter 3, **create** a **stereo Master Fader track**. (You'll find Master Fader listed in the Track Type menu, as shown here.) The new Master Fader track will be created after the last selected track in your session.

The Master Fader track looks similar to any other track, but don't be fooled—it's significantly different!

Avid®, All Rights Reserved.

You'll notice that the area on the channel strip that would normally display an Input button is conspicuously blank. That's because there is no input on a Master Fader track; it is only a way to control an output.

Notice also that there are no sends on a Master Fader track.

If you take a look at a Master Fader track in the Edit window, you'll see that you can't place clips on this track. In this regard, it's similar to an Aux track.

1 **Click** on the **Output button** and **select** the **interface output** you're using to listen to your mix (if it's not already shown on the button). With this output selected, the Master Fader track is in its common role of controlling the output of your entire mix.

Controlling Your Mix with a Master Fader Track

Now let's use your Master Fader track to control your entire mix. Let's start by creating a linear fade-out for your entire mix in one easy process.

❋ **SETTING THINGS UP**
For this section, switch to the Edit window if you're not viewing it already.

1 **Select** the **Pencil tool** and **choose** the **Line option** to create a straight fade-out.

2 **Write** a **linear decrease** in volume automation on the Master Fader track, just as you would on any other kind of track. Because this Master Fader track is controlling the output of your entire mix, you'll hear a linear change in the volume of all your tracks, starting at the point at which the Master Fader track's automation begins.

❋ IF YOU'RE USING THE EXERCISE MATERIALS...

If you're using the exercise session, Chapter 09 Exercise Session–Part 2, write a decrease in volume starting at measure 13 and ending in silence at measure 17. Working in Grid mode will help with this!

❋ AUTOMATION AND MASTER FADER TRACKS

If you want to write automation onto your Master Fader track in the Mix window, it's no problem. Simply write automation just as you would on any other type of track, using any of the automation modes.

❋ 64-BIT MIXERS VERSUS 64-BIT APPLICATIONS

When working with a DAW, it's important to draw a distinction between a 64-bit application and a 64-bit mix engine. A 64-bit application (of any type) has the ability to address more system memory than a 32-bit application. Pro Tools has historically been a 32-bit application but breaks into the 64-bit application world with Pro Tools 11. A 64-bit mix engine, on the other hand, is something that Pro Tools has had for some time and is in many ways more significant than Pro Tools being a 64-bit application. The 64-bit mix engine has an immense internal dynamic range, meaning that it is virtually impossible to overload. That's not to say that you shouldn't watch your meters for clipping, though. With the power of Master Fader tracks (which directly access the Pro Tools' 64-bit mix engine), you'll be able to effectively manage your session's levels.

Basic Mastering Techniques Using a Master Fader Track

Mastering is a post-mix process that further refines a piece of work to a professional quality. It's such a detailed and important process that an entire segment of the professional audio community is dedicated to the specific task of mastering other peoples' mixes. These mastering engineers are dedicated to techniques and processes that are quite outside the realm of normal production, and a good mastering engineer can do things with your final mix that border on the miraculous. The bottom line (at least as I see it): The task of professionally mastering a mix is certainly not recommended for the non-specialist.

You might, however, want to try your hand at a little basic mastering to punch up your mix for your own enjoyment or to make an evaluation mix a little more palatable for your client. Here's where Master Fader tracks can really come in handy, due to another interesting difference between a Master Fader track and any other track—one that may not be initially apparent. This difference is in the area of signal flow—the inserts are *after* the fader in the signal chain. Read on....

❄ ADVICE ON MASTERING

The discussion in this section relates to the process of mastering a mix on your own (as opposed to having your mix professionally mastered by a dedicated mastering engineer). If and when you decide to have your mix professionally mastered, the mastering engineer will want to do the entire job himself or herself (usually with highly specialized and costly gear specific to the process of mastering), so you won't need to go through the steps outlined here. That being said, it's always a good idea to consult with your mastering engineer *before* submitting your mix so you can find out exactly what he or she needs from you.

Using Dither

In overly simplistic terms, *dither* is a very low-level noise that is added to digital audio to offset some of the negative effects of reducing bit depth. For example, if you're working in a 24-bit session but will be creating a 16-bit file for an audio CD, you can improve the quality of your audio by instantiating a dither plug-in on a Master Fader track.

❄ WHEN NOT TO USE DITHER

Dither should be considered only when the final product is to be at a lesser bit depth than the original session. For example, if you have a 24-bit session and will make a 16-bit final mix, you should absolutely add dither. If, however, your final mix is to remain 24 bit, you shouldn't. Sample rates, file formats—all these things have no bearing on dither.

1 On an insert on the Master Fader track, **select** a **dither plug-in** (in this example, I've chosen POW-r Dither) from the Multichannel Plug-In menu. The plug-in's window will appear. (Tip: I usually put this plug-in on an insert other than my first few insert slots, in case I want to add any other plug-ins to the Master Fader—it's important that dither is the last process in your mix.)

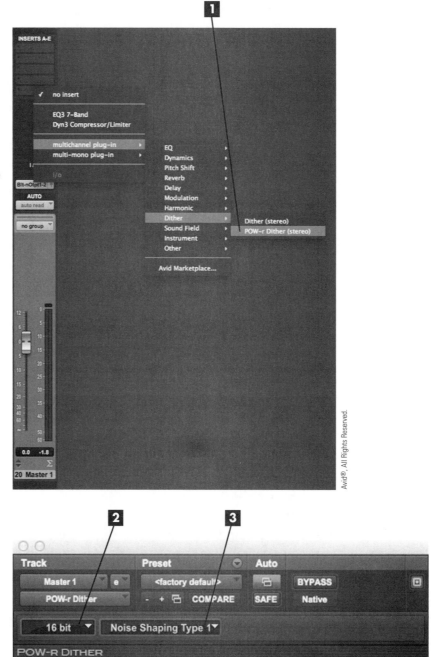

2 **Click** on the **Bit Resolution button** and **choose** the **final resolution** for your mix from the list that appears. For example, if you want to make a Red Book audio CD of your mix (assuming that your session was at 24 or 32 bits), you would choose the 16-bit option.

3 Noise shaping can help make dither "noise" even less audible than it normally is. **Click** on the **Noise Shaping button** and **select** a **noise-shaping type** from the list. For now, you can safely stick with the default shaping, but be sure to listen to different mixes with different noise shaping later to determine which one is best for you.

Punching Up Your Mix with Compression: Two Ways

Another common step in the mastering process is the application of *compression* to the entire mix. This is a tried-and-true method employed to narrow the dynamic range of your audio, thereby maximizing its overall punch. Here's one easy way to get it done:

1 On your Master Fader track, **instantiate** a **compressor plug-in** on an insert before (above) the one you used for dither. The Compressor plug-in window will appear.

2 **Adjust** your compressor's **parameters** to punch up your mix to suit your taste. Of course, it'll take some experimentation to find the best settings for any given situation, but you can start with a preset configuration like the one shown in this example.

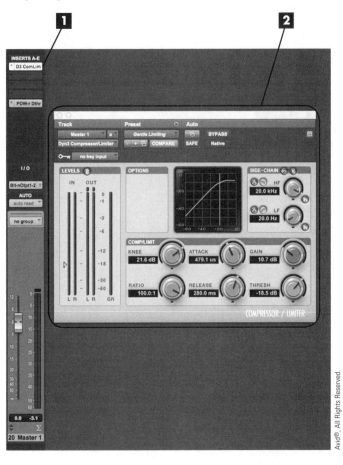

❄ COMPRESSORS AND DITHER

If you're using both dither and a compressor on a Master Fader track, you'll need to arrange your inserts so that the dither is the last plug-in in the insert signal flow (that is, on the lowest insert). Don't worry if your dither is currently on the top insert; you can use your mouse to drag it down to a lower insert position (and thus later in the insert's signal path) and then launch your compressor in an insert above it.

Those of you with mixing experience might notice a problem with this sort of routing. As you know, a compressor operates by attenuating (or reducing) any level above a certain threshold, which you set up in your plug-in window. Any incoming signal below that threshold will not be affected by the compressor. As long as you don't use your Master Fader track for fade-ins or fade-outs, there's no problem with using a compressor on the Master Fader track. If you *do* use the Master Fader track for any kind of volume automation, however, you might hear your compressor kick in or out, depending on whether you're fading in or out.

(The inserts on a Master Fader track are *post*-fader.) How do you get around this problem? I'm glad you asked!

1 **Reassign** the **output** of all tracks previously assigned to your monitors to an available pair of buses. I think you'll find that track interrogation (which you learned about in Chapter 8) is an excellent way to locate these tracks. Your session should now be completely inaudible—but wait!

2 **Create** a stereo Aux track and **assign** the **input** of that track to the same pair of buses that you used as an output for your other tracks. Essentially, you're creating a huge subgroup. Then **drag** the **compressor plug-in** from the Master Fader track (with its post-fader inserts) to the new Aux track (which has *pre*-fader inserts).

✳ The output to which this Aux track is assigned (in this image, Main Out) is still ultimately controlled by the Master Fader track, making it an ideal place to apply dither. Because the inserts of the Aux track are pre-fader, the signal going to the compressor will be affected by neither the Master Fader track nor the Aux track's output level, meaning you can apply your global fade automation on either track without losing that punchy sound. That's it!

 USING TRACK OUTPUT

As mentioned, what you're essentially doing in this second method is creating a huge subgroup. You can use the New Track Output option to simultaneously create the track and routing you need for this sort of work.

❄ **MASTER FADER TRACKS AND METERING**

There's one more very important function of a Master Fader track—one for which it is uniquely suited due to its post-fader inserts. Master Fader tracks are great for monitoring the overall levels of your mix. In addition to the track's own level meters, there is a variety of metering plug-ins available to you.

New in Pro Tools 11: Metering Enhancements

As you've probably noticed while reading this book, there have been some improvements in terms of metering, an aspect of mixing that becomes increasingly important as the mixing process nears its completion. You've already seen output metering built into the Edit and Transport windows. Let's take a look at a couple more gems:

Your sends have small meters in the Send button. These are not high-resolution meters, but they are more than enough to keep track of what your sends are doing as your mix plays.

Avid®, All Rights Reserved.

Perhaps one of the more interesting improvements in metering is the choice that you now get in viewing the level meters on your tracks themselves. There are a number of ways to access this new flexibility. Here's one:

1 **Right-click** a track's **meter**. A menu will appear, giving you control over your tracks' metering.

✳ The selection you make in this menu will affect all of your Audio, Aux, and Instrument tracks in your session:

✳ Choosing Sample Peak (the default metering for Pro Tools) will show sample-by-sample dynamics levels.

✳ Pro Tools Classic is similar to the Sample Peak, but with a linearity more commonly found with older Pro Tools systems.

✳ Venue Peak is identical to Sample Peak, but with a scale that extends to +20 dB.

✳ Venue RMS represents the same scale as Venue Peak but shows average loudness (root mean square) over time rather than absolute sample values.

✳ The Show Send Assignment Level Meter option toggles the display of meters in the Send buttons, as shown earlier.

You have the ability to set independent metering in your Master Faders (you will get the same set of choices in the Meter menu). For example, you could have Sample Peak metering in the Audio, Aux, and Instrument tracks and Venue RMS metering in the Master Faders.

There are other ways to access control over your meters. One is through the Metering tab of the Preferences window:

1 **Click** on the **Setup menu** and **choose Preferences**. The Preferences dialog box opens.

2 **Click** on the **Metering tab**.

❊ The Track and Master Meter Types section allows you to choose the metering types for your tracks, with a checkbox in the upper-left corner allowing you to link your Track and Master Fader meter types.

Pro Tools Preferences

| Display | Operation | Editing | Mixing | **Metering** | Processing | MIDI | Synchronization |

Track and Master Meter Types

☐ Track and Master Meter Types Linked

Track Meters: Sample Peak

Master Meters: VENUE RMS

Advanced Meter Type Settings

Meter Type: VENUE RMS

Decay: 60.00 dBs in 1.00 sec

0 dB = -20 dBFS

Integration Time: ms

Color Break High: 0 dB

Color Break Low: -20 dB

Reset

Peak / Clip

Peak Hold:
- ◉ 3 Seconds
- ○ Infinite
- ○ None

Clip Indication:
- ○ 3 Seconds
- ◉ Infinite
- ○ None

Display

☑ Show Send Assignment Level Meter

❊ The Advanced Meter Type Settings section allows you to customize your meter types in terms of decay, scale, and color levels. If you customize your settings beyond all recognition, don't worry—there's a Reset button to get you back to a more standard view!

❊ Though it's not new in Pro Tools 11, the Peak/Clip section is useful, allowing you to choose how clips are displayed.

❊ Finally, the Display section allows you to show (or not) Send button meters.

❊ MORE METERS!

If you want even more metering choices, Pro Tools HD software might be just what you're looking for. Pro Tools HD software includes 17 different metering options, plus a number of ways of viewing gain reduction.

Bouncing to Disk

When you're working with a Pro Tools session, you're in a multitrack environment. (You probably already knew that.) Even though you may be listening through stereo monitor speakers, you're actually hearing many component tracks, artfully combined by Pro Tools' software mix engine. From a production standpoint, it's a very cool way to work, but if you ever want to hear your song *outside* the Pro Tools environment, you'll have to render the mix down to a format that is compatible with the outside world.

The Bounce to Disk function will enable you to mix down your session to a final format—for example, a stereo file that can be played on an MP3 player. It's a simple process but an important last step that demands some attention to detail, so I'll go over each step carefully. For the purposes of demonstration, here's how to go about bouncing to disk so you can create a file that you could burn onto an audio CD (i.e., in Red Book format):

1 Using the Selector tool, **select** the **area** of your session you want to bounce to disk in the ruler area. (In this example, I'll select from the beginning of my session to the end of my Master Fader track's fade-out.)

2 **Click** on the **File menu**.

3 **Choose Bounce To.** A submenu will be displayed.

4 **Choose Disk.** The Bounce dialog box will appear.

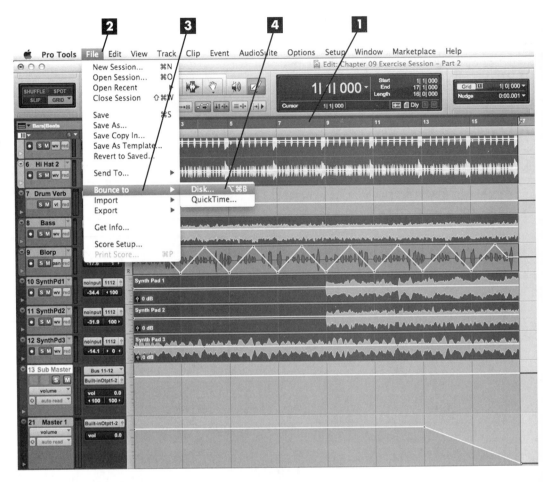

❋ BOUNCE TO DISK SHORTCUT

The shortcut for opening the Bounce to Disk dialog box is Command+Option+B (Mac) or Ctrl+Alt+B (PC).

5 At the top of the Bounce dialog box, you'll see the Bounce Source setting. (The button will display the currently selected bounce source.) To change the source, **click** on the **Bounce Source button** and **select** the **output path** you're using to listen to your mix. Clicking the Bounce Source button will reveal a menu allowing you to choose the desired bus, output path, or physical output for your bounce. (In this case, I want to choose the built-in output 1–2, because that's the path that is connected to my monitor speakers.)

❉ **BOUNCE TROUBLESHOOTING**

If you bounce to disk and later find that your bounce is a silent audio file, you've probably chosen the wrong bounce source.

6 The File Type button will display the type of file you will be creating. (In this example, you'll be creating a WAV file.) If you want to change the file type, just **click** on the **File Type button** and **choose** the desired **type** from the list of available file types (WAV, AIFF, or MP3).

7 The Format button will display the channel format of the file(s) you will be creating with your bounce. If you want to change the format, just **click** on the **Format button** and **choose** the desired **format** from the list. The formats are as follows:

  ❉ **Mono (Summed).** With this option selected, your session will be mixed down to a single mono file (even if it's a stereo session).

  ❉ **Multiple Mono.** When this is chosen, your stereo mix will be output to a pair of mono files—one for the left channel (with a .l after the filename) and one for the right (with a .r after the filename). This is particularly useful for bounces that you intend to import into another Pro Tools session.

  ❉ **Interleaved.** Your mix will be rendered to a single stereo file.

8 The Bit Depth button will display the bit depth of the file you will be creating. To change the bit depth, **click** on the **Bit Depth button** and **choose** the desired **setting** from a list of available resolutions. (In this example, you'll be creating a 16-bit file.)

9 The Sample Rate button will display the sample rate of the file you will be creating. If you want to change the setting, **click** on the **Sample Rate button** and **choose** the desired **sample rate** (16-bit, 24-bit, or 32-bit float).

RED BOOK CD SETTINGS

If your bounced file is going to be put onto a Red Book audio CD, the bit depth should be set to 16, the sample rate should be 44.1 kHz, and the format should be interleaved.

- Next, you have some options as to what will be done with your bounced file.
  - **Enforce Avid Compatibility.** Choose this option if your audio will be used in an Avid video editing system.
  - **Import After Bounce.** Clicking the Import After Bounce checkbox will import your bounced file back into your session on an Audio track or to the Clips list.
  - **Add To iTunes Library.** After your file is bounced to disk, it will be imported into iTunes (if it's installed) the next time iTunes is launched.

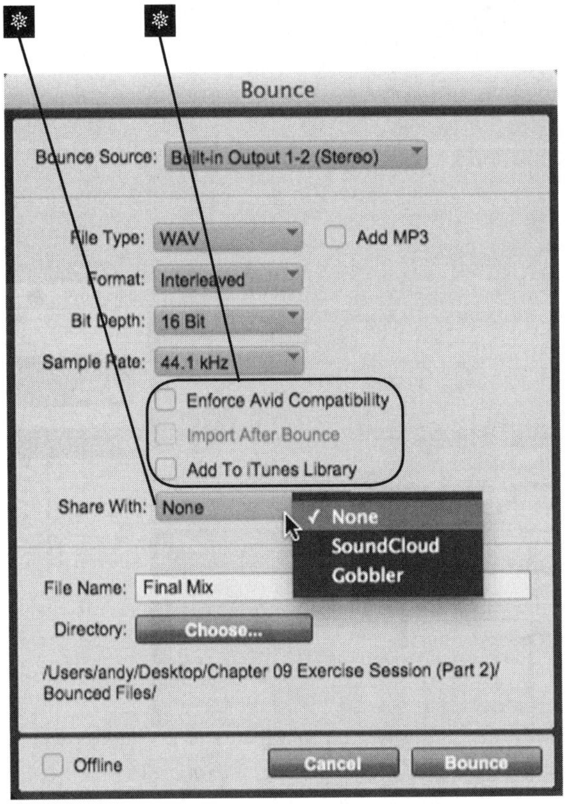

- In addition to iTunes, you have the ability to share your mix with two leading social platforms:
  - **SoundCloud.** SoundCloud (www.soundcloud.com) is a great way to share your mixes with listeners, allowing them to comment on your mix.
  - **Gobbler.** Gobbler (www.gobbler.com) is more of a creatively collaborative environment, often used to share not only final mixes, but entire sessions.

10 **Type** a descriptive **filename** for your bounced file.

11 **Click** the **Choose button** to change the destination location for your bounced file.

12 **Click** the **Bounce button**. Your bounce will begin.

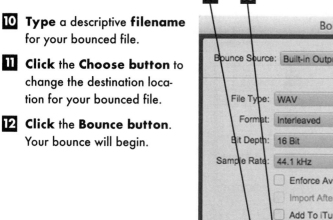

❄ THE IMPORTANCE OF GOOD FILE MANAGEMENT

At this point, I want to emphasize again how important it is to know exactly where and under what name your files are saved. (This goes for session files and other audio files as well.) You can save your bounced file anywhere you choose in your system, but with this great power comes the added responsibility of using it wisely. Make sure you can find your files when you need them!

Bouncing to Disk...

Time Remaining: 0:22

(type Command-period or Escape to cancel)

Your session will begin playing, and a small countdown window will indicate that bouncing is occurring in real time. Once your selected area has played to completion, your bounced file will be created.

❄❄❄

Bouncing to a QuickTime Movie

Because this session happens to have a Video track included in it, you also have the option of bouncing your work to a QuickTime movie file. The process is nearly identical to bouncing to disk.

1 Using the Selector tool, **select** the **area** of your session you want to bounce to disk in the ruler area. (When you're bouncing to a QuickTime movie, a good rule of thumb is to select an area equal to the length of the clip on your Video track.)

2 **Click** on the **File menu**.

3 **Choose Bounce To.**

4 **Choose QuickTime Movie.** The QuickTime Bounce dialog box will appear.

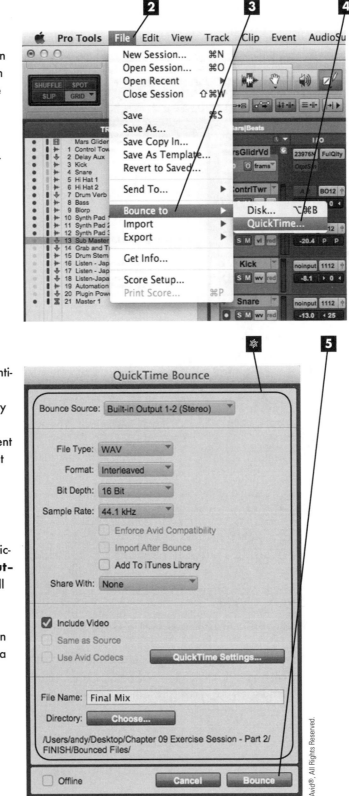

❀ This dialog box is nearly identical to the one you encountered when you bounced only your audio. You may notice, though, that you have different options with regard to format and sample rate, as well as a button you can click to change your video's QuickTime settings.

5 After you've made your choices, **click** on the **Bounce button**. The bounce process will continue just as it did when you were using the Bounce to Disk feature, except that in this case, you'll be creating a QuickTime movie file.

400

❀ ❀ ❀

New in Pro Tools 11: Bounce Two Files Simultaneously!

In previous versions of Pro Tools, you could create only one bounced file at a time. In other words, if you wanted a WAV file and an MP3 file, you needed to perform two separate bounces. Now that's no longer a limitation—you can easily choose to create an MP3 file along with any other bounce that you create.

1 In the Bounce dialog box, **check** the **Add MP3 checkbox**.

❋ Before your bounce starts (after you click the Bounce button in the Bounce dialog box), you'll be presented with the MP3 dialog box, where you can choose standard parameters for your MP3 file.

2 After you've made your choices, **click** on the **OK button**. The bounce will begin.

New in Pro Tools 11: Offline Bounce!

Ironically, perhaps the biggest new feature in Pro Tools is also one of the smallest checkboxes! In previous versions of Pro Tools, all bounces were done in real time. If you had a 20-minute television show soundtrack, the bounce took 20 minutes to complete. On the positive side, it was always good to listen to your mix once more before sending it off, but jeez, it would sure be nice to have a faster than real-time option!

With Pro Tools 11, this long-time request is a reality. By simply checking one box in the Bounce dialog box, you'll be able to create your final bounce just as quickly as your computer can process the file. (The rapidity of the bounce will depend on the power of your computer's CPU.)

Changing your bounce from real-time to offline is very easy:

1 Click the **Offline check-box**.

Avid®, All Rights Reserved.

After you click the Bounce button, instead of seeing a countdown window, you'll see a progress indicator of your bounce. The number in parentheses to the right of the window indicates how quickly your mix is rendering compared to a real-time bounce.

Avid®, All Rights Reserved.

WHEN OFFLINE BOUNCE IS NOT AN OPTION

There are certain cases in which an offline bounce is not possible:

* If hardware inserts are used (outboard effects can't operate in non–real-time modes)
* If external MIDI sound devices are being used
* If any external device (such as a tape deck) is synchronized with Pro Tools

NEW IN PRO TOOLS 11: MIX CONSISTENCY

In the past, there were slight differences between internal bounces (recording from one track to another within Pro Tools) and bouncing to disk. To be sure, the differences were small, but differences were there. Now, with Pro Tools 11, all automation is timestamped and sample accurate, which means that whether you bounce internally, bounce to disk, bounce real-time, or bounce offline, all of your mixes will be identical.

IF YOU'RE USING THE EXERCISE MATERIALS...

Over the last two few chapters, you've worked with a number of different kinds of music, from electronic Japanese to traditional Americana. Before you practice your bounces, now's a good time to indulge your creativity and apply the mixing techniques you've learned so far. I've included some "finished" versions of the exercise sessions for you to check out if you're so inclined!

Whether you're bouncing audio or video, enjoy your final mix—you've earned it!

10 } Moving to the Next Level: Tips and Tricks

Pro Tools is a complex, professional application, and mastering it requires dedication, inspiration, and time. This book is meant to provide you with a solid basic understanding of how to use this powerful product—a foundation upon which to build greater knowledge as you gain experience. Through your study and understanding of this book so far, you've attained that basic understanding. Good on ya!

This chapter is a varied list of next-level functions, designed to enable you to be even more productive. In this chapter, you'll learn how to:

* Get the most out of your system.
* Make the most of your recording sessions.
* Edit with more efficiency and flexibility.
* Understand and use Elastic Audio.
* Use Automatic Delay Compensation.
* Import and use movie files.

Boosting Performance with Disk Allocation

When starting out with Pro Tools, many beginners record to their sole system drives. Although this will work for relatively simple sessions, you may eventually find that a single hard drive—especially if it's your system drive—just doesn't cut it. Here are a few things that can place added stress on a hard drive:

* **High Audio track count.** More Audio tracks requires more streams of communication to and from your hard drive.

* **High-resolution audio or video.** Higher-quality files require a greater bit rate and more of a hard drive's limited bandwidth.

* **Edit density.** The term *edit density* refers to the frequency with which your session needs to retrieve new audio from your hard drive during playback. Each time you create a clip boundary in a track, you require Pro Tools to access a specific location on your hard drive. The more clips you have in a given time, the higher your edit density becomes and the harder your drive has to work to provide uninterrupted audio playback. Aside from general editing practices, there are a few features that tend to increase edit density in a session, including using Beat Detective and Strip Silence—two tools I'll talk about later in this chapter.

One solution to hard-drive/bandwidth problems is to distribute audio playback among *multiple* hard drives, and that's just what the Disk Allocation dialog box lets you do. But first, let's take a quick trip to the Workspace Browser's Volumes view to set up different drives for different jobs:

* To control the role of your individual drives, you'll need to see the Permissions column of the Volumes view of the Workspace Browser. If you're not seeing that column, right-click the menu bar and choose Perm. from the list of viewable options. Visible columns will be indicated with a checkmark.

* In the Perm. column, you'll see a letter next to each drive in the Workspace window. Click the letter in the Perm column that corresponds with the drive you want to configure. (In this case, I want to change the behavior of my system drive.) A menu will appear.

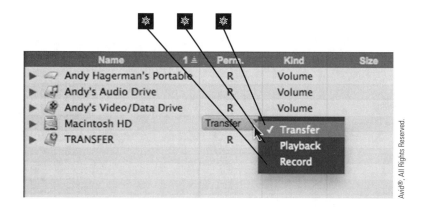

✻   If you set up a drive to be a transfer volume (as I have here), your Pro Tools session will not be able to record or play back audio and video files with that drive. Essentially, the drive is off limits to Pro Tools as far as audio and video files are concerned (although it is worth noting that you can audition audio files that are stored on transfer drives). System drives are commonly set up as transfer volumes, assuming there are dedicated hard drives for audio/video recording and playback.

✻   A playback volume will enable Pro Tools to play back audio and video files, but you may not record to this type of volume. This is a common setting for archive drives, enabling you to listen to your backed-up sessions but not to inadvertently record to that hard drive.

✻   Finally, a record volume is fully functional with regard to audio/video files and Pro Tools, which means you can record to it and play back from it. A typical audio or video drive is set up as a record volume.

Here's a common setup for a Pro Tools system with two dedicated audio drives and a dedicated video drive:

✻ My portable drive is set up as a playback drive only, since I don't record to that particular drive, only play back from it.

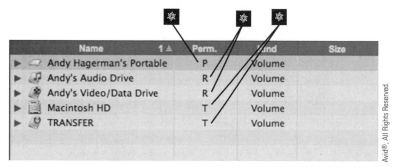

✻   My two audio and video drives have been set as record drives, so that Pro Tools has complete access to them.

✻   Finally, my system drive and transfer drive, which serve important functions not related to audio and video files, have been set as transfer volumes.

When the behavior of the drives has been squared away, it's time to do some disk allocation. In this session, I've created 10 pretty generic tracks, and I'm almost ready to do some recording. This is just the time to set up disk allocation—*before* you record any new audio.

1 **Click** on the **Setup menu**.

2 **Click** on **Disk Allocation**. The Disk Allocation dialog box will appear.

3 In the Disk Allocation dialog box, you'll see a list of all the Audio tracks in your session. The track names will be in the left-most column, and the location to which audio files will be recorded will be shown in the column to the right. From this dialog box, you'll be able to assign individual tracks to available hard drives on a track-by-track basis. Just **click** and **hold** on the **Root Media Folder** column for a track you want to set up. A menu will appear.

4 From this menu, you'll be able to choose which drive will store the audio recorded on that track. (Note that you only see drives that you've configured as record drives in this menu.) You can **choose** one of the **drives** and let Pro Tools create the appropriate folder for you or **click** on the **Select Folder option** to choose a specific location.

When dealing with large numbers of tracks, the basic goal when assigning disk allocation is to balance the session's audio workload as evenly as possible between the audio drives that you have in your system to ensure maximum performance. Here's what I've ended up with:

❄ In this example, I've alternated each track between my audio and video hard drives. Basically, each drive is doing about half the work needed to play and record audio for this session.

❄ Here's a useful feature: If you check the Use Round Robin Allocation for New Tracks checkbox, Pro Tools will automatically cycle through all the record-enabled volumes for your tracks as they are created. The result would be the same as what you're seeing in this image but would have been done automatically by Pro Tools as you added new tracks.

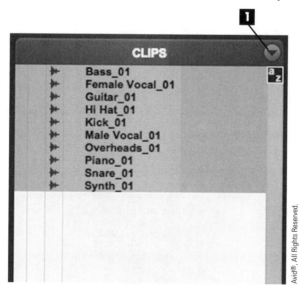

Avid®, All Rights Reserved.

5 Once you've set things up the way you want them, **click** on the **OK button**.

❄ **DRIVE VOLUMES AND ROUND-ROBIN ALLOCATION**

Only the drives that you've designated as record volumes show up in the drive-assignment menu, and they will be the only drives that will be used when the Use Round Robin Allocation for New Tracks checkbox is checked. By setting up your volume designations beforehand, you can make working in the Disk Allocation dialog box quicker, easier, and better.

Now you're ready to record as usual. When you're finished, you'll see clips created in your Clips list. But where have they been recorded to? Let's find out:

1 **Click** on the **Clips List button**. A pop-up menu will appear.

Avid®, All Rights Reserved.

❄ ❄ ❄

2 **Click** on **Show**. A submenu will appear. This menu will enable you to see different aspects of your clips in the Clips list, with displayed information indicated by a checkmark. (You may find showing the full path very useful in tracking down individual files!)

3 In this case, you want to see what disk they've been recorded to, so **click** on **Disk Name**.

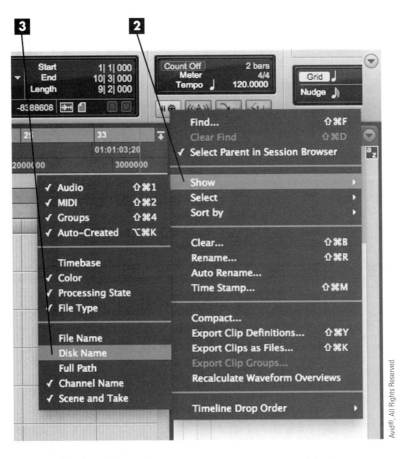

You see both drives represented in the Clips list. That means you're balancing the hard drives' workload and can get extra performance and higher track counts when you need it.

WHEN TO SET UP DISK ALLOCATION

Remember to set up your disk allocation *before* you start recording. Changing your disk allocation *after* your audio has been recorded (and files have been created) will have no effect on the performance of your session.

Recording with Cue Mixes

During the recording process, your artist might want to have a customized mix—
something that's different from what the engineer (that's you) in the control room
is hearing. In cases where there are multiple musicians, for example, each player
will often want his or her *own* personal mix. Not to worry—creating customized cue
mixes is easy to do, using your tracks' sends. Here's a common cue-mix process:

1 Hold down the **Option key (Mac) or the Alt key (PC)** as you **click** on an available **Send button**. (In this image, I've chosen Send A.) Because you're holding down the Option or Alt key, the send you create on this track will be created on all similar tracks.

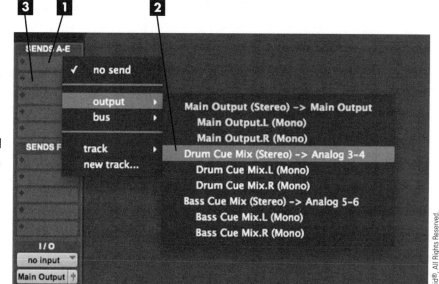

❉ CREATING A SEND ON ALL TRACKS TOO MUCH?

If you've already set up submixes in your session, you might not want to create sends on every track. If that's the case, just select the tracks on which you want to create a send and click on an available send while holding Shift+Option (Mac) or Shift+Alt (PC). A send will be created on all selected tracks.

2 Because the cue mix will be sent out of a physical output, **assign** the send's **output** to an available interface output path. (In this image, I've created a path named Drum Cue Mix.)

3 If you have additional musicians requiring individual cue mixes, you'll need to **repeat steps 1** and **2** for each cue mix. In this example, I have a bassist who wants his own mix, so I'll create my second send at Send B and assign it to interface output path Bass Cue Mix.

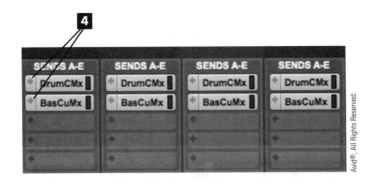

4 If you're following the steps outlined here, when you're finished, you should see one cue-mix send on Send A (for the drummer) and one on Send B (for the bassist). Holding down the Option or Alt key while I was creating the sends made the job easier by creating sends on all the tracks in the session, as opposed to creating sends one at a time. Now, to see the expanded Sends view (you looked at this in Chapter 8, "Basic Mixing"), **hold down** the **Command key (Mac) or the Ctrl key (PC)** as you click on the Send selector button for Send A. Then do the same for Send B.

※ Now that you can see volume, pan, mute, and pre/post controls for each track's sends, you can create a blend of tracks that's suited best to your talent.

5 You will probably want to make sure that changes you make to a track's main fader *don't* affect your talent's headphone mix by changing your cue mix sends to be *pre*-fader. To do so, **click** on the small **P button** in each send. To quickly change this for all similar sends, just **hold down** the **Option (Mac) or Alt (PC)** key as you change one send, and the change will be reflected through all your tracks for that send.

Making the Most of Editing

Let's take a look at some techniques that will make editing even more efficient and fun!

Identify Beat

One of Pro Tools' strengths is its ability to use MIDI and audio in the same environment. To get them to work well together, though, their tempos should agree. That's where the Identify Beat feature comes in. It lets you quickly determine the tempo of a selected area of audio. Once that's set, your tick-based MIDI tracks will naturally follow the tempo of your sample-based Audio tracks.

> ✳ **IF YOU'RE USING THE EXERCISE MATERIALS...**
>
> To follow along with the examples shown in this chapter, launch the session named "Chapter 10 Exercise Session." For information on downloading this book's exercise materials, please refer to the "Setting Up Your Session" section of the introduction.
>
> You'll note that in this session, features are demonstrated through a series of memory locations. You'll note also that even though the session is fairly extensive in its tracks and complexity, it's only using a few different audio files, keeping the overall session folder size small! To follow along with these first steps, go to Memory Location #1–Identify Beat. From the Window menu, open the Memory Locations dialog box, and simply click on location #1–Identify Beat. (For a refresher on how to use memory locations, refer to Chapter 6, "...And More Editing.")

This memory location (#1–Identify Beat) shows a great example of a very common dilemma. Listen to the clip. It sounds like eight full measures of drums, right? Now look at the selection length according to the Pro Tools Tempo ruler. It says that the clip is six measures, one beat, and 741 ticks! Obviously, *your* judgment is correct. Here's how to get Pro Tools to agree with you!

1 Select a specific **musical length**. (In this example, eight measures have already been selected for you.) Use your ears to make a good, loopable selection. *Don't rely on your Bars|Beats ruler.*

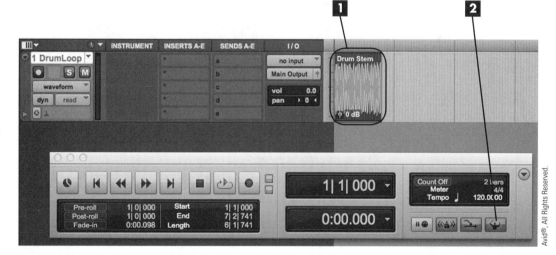

2 Make sure the **Conductor track** is enabled. (You'll find this control in the MIDI section of the Edit window or the Transport window.) When enabled, the Conductor Track button will be colored blue.

3 Click on the **Event menu**.

4 Click on **Identify Beat**. The Add Bar|Beat Markers dialog box will appear.

5 **Type** the musical **location** of the beginning of the selection in the Location text box in the Start area. Again, let your ears be your guide. In this example, because the selection begins at the beginning of the timeline, the beginning should be 1|1|000.

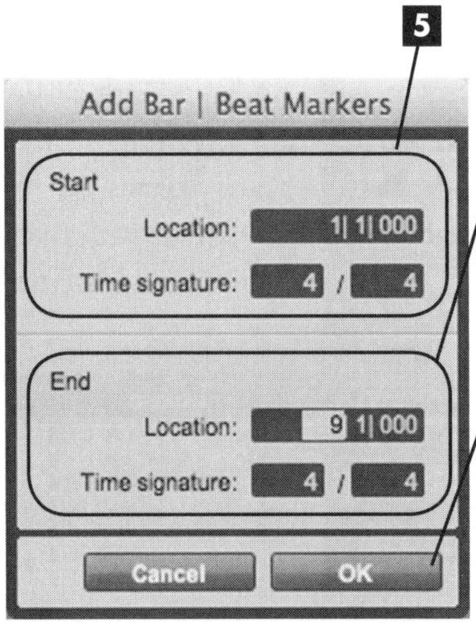

Avid®, All Rights Reserved.

6 **Type** the musical **location** of the end of the selection in the Location text box in the End area. In this example, you are hearing an eight-bar selection, ending at the beginning of bar 9 (9|1|000).

7 **Click** on the **OK button**. The Add Bar|Beat Markers dialog box will close, and your tempo will change accordingly.

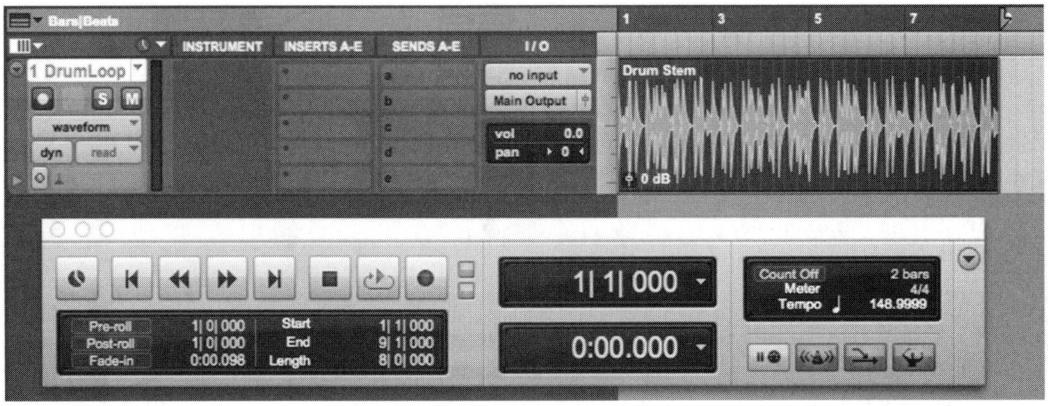

When you're finished, you'll see that your session's Bars|Beats ruler and your ears are now in agreement as to the tempo of the section of audio, as shown here. Now the grid lines will be aligned with the appropriate musical events (assuming your grid scale is set to Bars|Beats), and the selection you made will be correctly displayed in the Edit Selection display (assuming that your main time scale is Bars|Beats).

IDENTIFY BEAT WORKS ANYWHERE!

You can use the Identify Beat function at any point in a session. For example, if you have a live drummer who goes a little faster during the chorus, just select the chorus and enter the correct musical values in the Add Bar|Beat Markers dialog box.

Timeline Versus Edit Selection

Throughout this book, whenever you have made a selection on a track, that selection has been reflected in the ruler area (also called the timeline) and vice versa. Normally, this is the way to work, but these two selections don't *need* to be linked.

1 **Click** on the **Link Timeline and Edit Selection button** (which is normally blue) to deselect it.

2 **Make** a **selection** on any track.

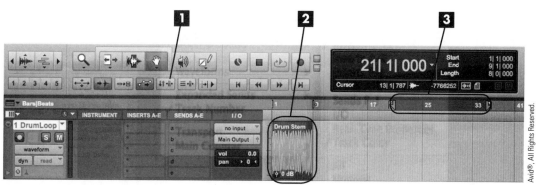

3 Now **make** a **different selection** in the ruler area. Note that the two selected areas do not reflect each other.

It's important to take a moment to see just how Pro Tools acts in this situation. If you try to play your session, what plays back is your timeline selection. In truth, this has always been the case, although many users don't make any distinction between the edit selection and the timeline selection and leave the linking enabled all the time.

Unlinking your timeline and edit selections can be handy when you want to hear a part of your song that's different from the part you're editing. For example, if you want to hear a little *before* the clip you're working with, you can *unlink* your timeline and edit selection and make a timeline selection that reflects what you want to hear. Just be careful to relink when you're finished with this unusual mode of operation!

※ **IF YOU'RE USING THE EXERCISE MATERIALS...**

If you're following along with the tutorial session included with this book, make sure you relink the edit and timeline selections before proceeding to the next section.

Dynamic Transport

You have yet another way to treat your selections and playback independently, through a feature called Dynamic Transport. Dynamic Transport gives you the ability to start playback at any point in your session, regardless of the timeline or edit selection. Take a look:

1 Click on the **Options menu**.

2 Choose **Dynamic Transport**.

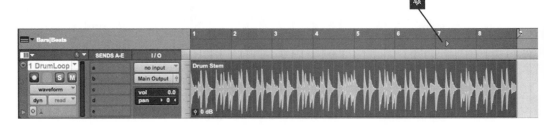

　※　Notice that your main Timescale ruler has gotten twice as tall as any other ruler. In the bottom half of the main Timescale ruler, you'll now see a right-facing blue triangle (the Play Start marker), which indicates where your playback will begin. Just click and drag the triangle to any location on the timeline, and your session will play back from that point. This point can be before a selected area, anywhere within a selection (as shown here), or even after a selected area.

By default, your timeline and edit selections are automatically *unlinked* when you turn on Dynamic Transport. (You can relink them at any time.) When you turn off Dynamic Transport, your timeline and edit selections will be relinked.

Samples Versus Ticks

You learned back in Chapter 6 about the power of *tick-based* Audio tracks. In this section, I'll talk a little bit more about samples and ticks in a Pro Tools session and how they interact.

※ **SETTING THINGS UP**

If you're using the exercise session, go to Memory Location #2–Tempo Operations. Make sure you turn off Dynamic Transport!

MIDI Track Timings

Audio tracks, as you know, are created as *sample-based* tracks, meaning that by default, each clip is anchored to a specific sample (or real-time) location. The upshot of this is that tempo, bar|beat, and meter changes will have no effect on the clips of the track.

Instrument tracks and MIDI tracks, on the other hand, are created by default as *tick-based* tracks, which means clips and notes on these tracks *will* respond to tempo and meter changes. For example, if you increase the tempo of your session, your tick-based tracks will speed up accordingly.

Even though these are the *default* states for each kind of track, there are advantages to working unconventionally!

❄ As you saw in Chapter 6, you can change an Audio track to tick-based timing (indicated by a metronome icon in the Timebase button), enabling you to put your clip timing under the control of your MIDI tempo map. In this example, if you were to change the tempo of your session, your clips would move and change your drum audio's "tempo" as a result.

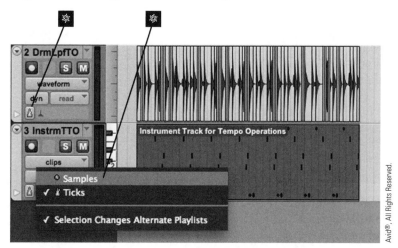

❄ Less common, but no less possible, is the practice of changing a MIDI (or Instrument) track to sample-based timing. To do it, just click on the track's Timebase button and choose Samples from the menu that appears. In this mode, your MIDI track takes on a very interesting behavior, as your MIDI data will not change when you change tempo!

Although sample-based MIDI is somewhat unusual, it opens up interesting opportunities. For example, if you want to use a sampler or other virtual instrument to "play" a sound effect that needs to be synced to video, a sample-based track does the trick nicely. Because MIDI notes on sample-based tracks will ignore tempo changes, you have the freedom to change musical tempo without affecting the timing of these notes, ensuring they remain in sync with the video.

Default Track Timebase

Some users, particularly those primarily doing music production, might want their Audio tracks to be tick based as a general rule.

1 After opening the Preferences dialog box (from the Setup menu), **click** on the **Editing tab**.

2 **Click** on the **New Tracks Default to Tick Timebase checkbox**, located in the lower-left area of the Editing page, to select it. This causes all your new tracks to default to a tick timebase.

3 **Click** on the **OK button** to exit the Preferences dialog box.

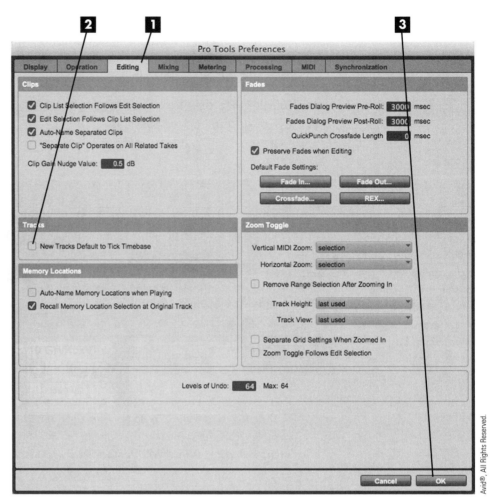

Session Linearity

This next bit can get a little tricky: By default, the rulers of your sessions are evenly spaced (or *linear*) based on real time, which can be broken down into hours, minutes, seconds, frames (in the case of SMPTE timecode), and samples. Another way of saying this is that, by default, Pro Tools uses a linear sample display. This works well in many cases, but from time to time, you might want to look at your timeline in a different way....

> ❋ **SETTING THINGS UP**
>
> If you're using the exercise session, go to Memory Location #3 – Session Linearity.

This image shows a Pro Tools session with a linear sample display. Taking a look at your sample-based and tick-based rulers illustrates this mode well.

❋ Your real-time rulers are evenly spaced.

❋ Your Bars|Beats ruler changes its spacing based on tempo changes in your session. (In this example, the bars and beats get gradually compressed as the tempo increases.)

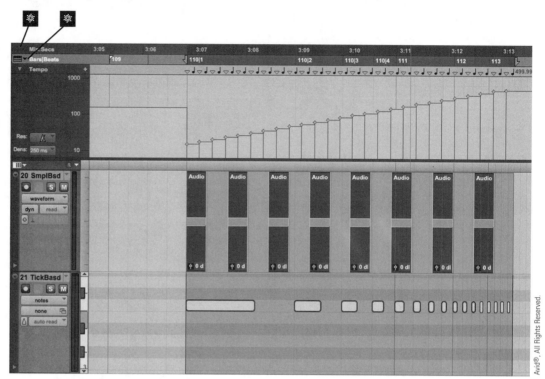

The clips on the Audio track are clearly evenly spaced in real time. The notes on the Instrument track are all 1/8 notes, but the duration and spacing of these notes change due to an increasing tempo. Occasionally, it's desirable to be able to see your notes displayed more consistently, regardless of tempo changes. (I often do this when I'm composing.) It's very easy to do, and it makes quite a difference in your Edit window's view.

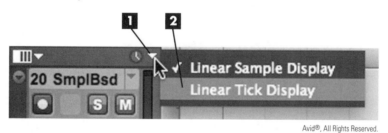

1 **Click** on the **Linearity Display Mode down arrow** (located in the upper-left area of the Tracks column). A menu will appear.

2 **Choose Linear Tick Display.** The Linearity Display Mode icon will change from a blue clock (indicating sample linearity) to a green metronome (indicating tick linearity).

❋❋❋

* Your Bars|Beats ruler is now evenly spaced (despite the tempo change), and the Min:Secs ruler is now unevenly spaced.

* The spacing of both your Audio and MIDI tracks has changed. Note that clips on the sample-based Audio track are now not as evenly spaced as they once were, whereas each 1/8 note in the Instrument track (despite the tempo change) appears at regular intervals.

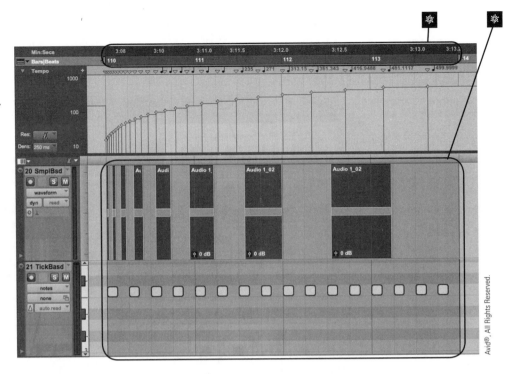

As you listen to and watch the playback of your session, you'll see that the *only* change made to your session has been visual. This change in linearity is simply for ease of use (and can be especially useful when working with MIDI data in sessions with radical tempo changes). Before you go on to the next section, change back to Linear Sample display.

Cool Editing Tricks

We've already covered a bunch of editing processes. Here are a few more for your bag of tricks!

New Ways to Spot Clips

Chapter 5, "Editing," talked a little about the Spot edit mode and how it can make placing clips at specific points in time quick and easy. Spot mode, however, is really only useful if you already know the specific numeric position where you want your clip to go. Many times, you'll want your clip to go to a specific *selected* place in your session. Pro Tools makes this easy as well—especially if you have a mouse with a right-click button!

> **✳ SETTING THINGS UP**
>
> For this section, go to Memory Location #4–Spotting Clips. If you haven't already, please change your session linearity to Linear Sample display.

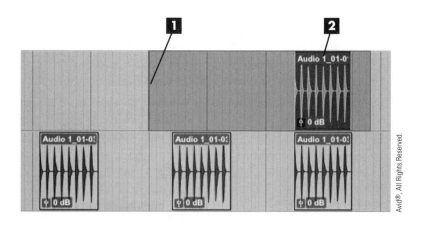

1 Using the Selector tool, **make** a **selection** or **place** your **timeline insertion** at the place at which you want your clip to move.

2 **Command-right-click (Mac) or Ctrl-right-click (PC)** on the **clip** you want to move. A menu will appear. The third segment of the menu will include three clip-moving options:

* **Move Clip Start to Selection Start.** This moves the clip so the *beginning* of the clip aligns with the beginning of the selection or with the timeline insertion.

* **Move Clip Sync to Selection Start.** This moves the clip so the clip's sync point (if it has one) aligns with the beginning of the selection or with the timeline insertion. (I'll discuss sync points in the next section.)

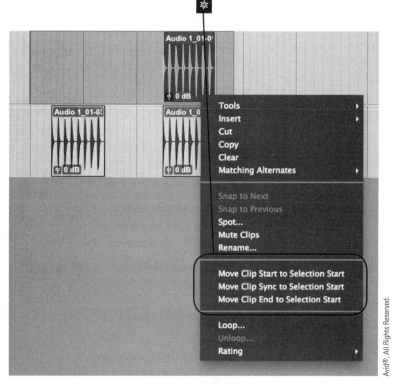

* **Move Clip End to Selection Start.** This move the clip so the *end* of the clip aligns with the beginning of your selection or with the timeline insertion.

If you don't have a mouse with a right-click button, all is not lost. Here are some shortcuts to help you get the job done:

❋ To execute the Move Clip Start to Selection Start operation, hold down the Control key (Mac) or Start key (PC) and click on the clip with the Grabber tool.

❋ To execute the Move Clip Sync to Selection Start operation, hold down Shift+Control (Mac) or Shift+Start (PC) and click on the clip with the Grabber tool.

❋ To execute the Move Clip End to Selection Start operation, hold down Command+Control (Mac) or Ctrl+Start (PC) and click on the clip with the Grabber tool.

Sync Points

So far, I've primarily focused on clip boundaries (beginning and end) when talking about moving clips. Many times, however, the really interesting part of a clip is somewhere *inside* it. For example, within a drum beat, you might have a specific hit that you want to align with another clip, or you might have a specific word in a dialogue clip that is particularly easy to spot. *Sync points* will help you mark these places of interest so that you can align them with your timeline insertion using the techniques discussed in the previous section.

1 Using the Selector tool or the Smart tool, **place** the **timeline insertion** at the point within your clip where you want to create a sync point.

2 **Click** on the **Clip menu**.

3 **Choose Identify Sync Point.** A small green triangle will appear at the bottom of the clip to indicate the position of the sync point.

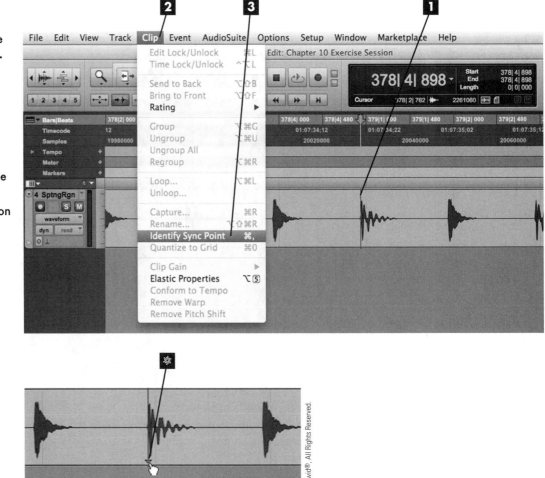

❋ If you need to reposition your sync point after you've created it, the Grabber tool will let you move it. Just move your mouse close to the triangular sync point icon. When the Grabber tool turns into the pointing hand shown here, you're ready to move the sync point; just click, drag, and drop the sync point in its new location.

Now that you've created your sync point, you can utilize the right-click and short-cut commands described in the previous section!

Snapping Clips

Sometimes you'll want a clip to move adjacent to the clip before or after it. Again, the right-click mouse comes to the rescue!

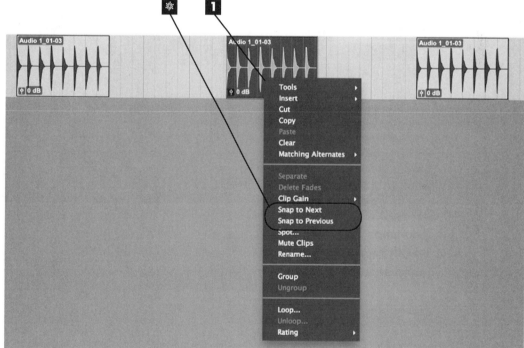

1 **Right-click** on the **clip** you want to move. A menu will appear, with two clip-snapping options:

❄ **Snap to Next.** Choosing this will move the clip so that the *end* of the clip aligns with the beginning of the clip to the *right*.

❄ **Snap to Previous.** Choosing this will move the clip so that the *beginning* of the clip aligns with the end of the clip to the *left*.

❄ ❄ ❄

Using Strip Silence

Strip Silence is a nifty little editing tool that acts upon clips similarly to how a noise gate acts upon audio. When you use Strip Silence, any audio below a specified volume threshold can be removed from your selection, leaving discrete clips that you can move and edit separately. This is a particularly fantastic tool when you work on dialogue tracks!

❋ SETTING THINGS UP

Please go to Memory Location #5–Strip Silence.

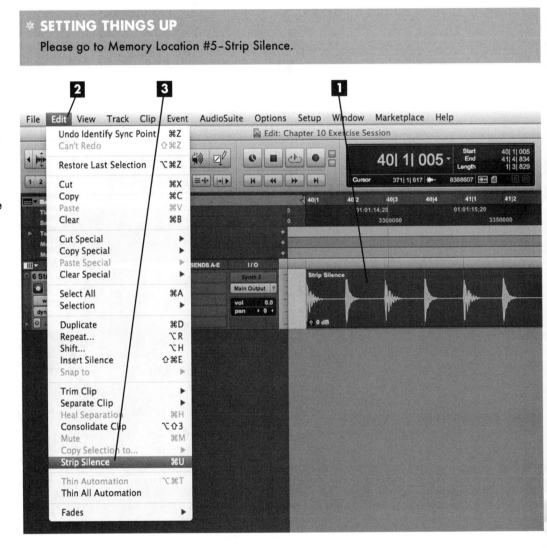

1 Select an **area** in your session that you would like to strip.

2 Click on the **Edit menu**.

3 Click on **Strip Silence**. The Strip Silence dialog box will open.

4 **Adjust** the **parameters** in the Strip Silence dialog box to separate the useful audio from the audio that you don't want to keep. As you adjust these parameters, you will see boxes indicating where new clip boundaries will be created, as shown here. This can take a little time to get just right, as these values are interrelated, so be patient. The four parameters available to you are as follows:

- ❄ **Strip Threshold.** This parameter indicates the minimum volume of the audio that you want to keep (with a range from −96 dB to −0 dB). Portions of audio with volume levels *under* the strip threshold can be stripped from your clip. As you move the fader from left to right, you'll see that you'll be stripping more and more of the audio.
- ❄ **Min Strip Duration.** This value determines the shortest silence Strip Silence can strip out. As you move the fader from left to right, you'll see smaller boxes combine to make larger ones.
- ❄ **Clip Start Pad.** This slider will move the left boundary of each box earlier in time. If you find that by using Strip Silence, you're cutting off the beginning of words or notes, a small amount of clip start padding will fix the problem.
- ❄ **Clip End Pad.** This slider will move the right boundary of each box later in time. If you find that by using Strip Silence, you're cutting off the end of words or notes, a small amount of clip end padding will fix the problem.

5 After you've adjusted these parameters to your liking, **click** on the **Strip button**. Your selection will be chopped into discrete clips, and the unwanted portions of audio will be removed from the track altogether. These newly created clips will be shown in the track and in the Clips list.

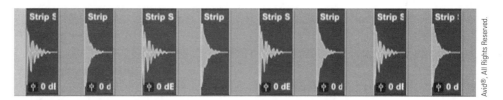

Don't worry; you haven't actually deleted any audio. If you find that you've stripped too much or too little from your track, you can use the Trim tool to adjust individual clip boundaries.

✳ In addition to being able to strip away unwanted audio (by clicking on the Strip button), you have a few other options when using Strip Silence:

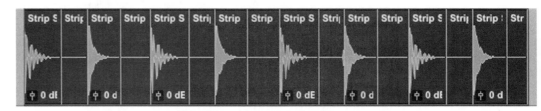

✳ **Extract.** This does the *opposite* of the Strip button, creating clips of audio that are *below* the strip threshold.

✳ **Separate.** This mode will not strip any audio but will only separate your selected area, resulting in alternating clips of sound and silence.

✳ **Rename.** The Rename option will enable you to automatically rename selected clips.

When you click on the Rename button, the Rename Selected Clips dialog box will open.

✳ The Name field will enable you to type a descriptive name for your selected clips.

✳ You can choose a starting number for your clips. For example, in some situations, you might want to have the first clip be numbered 0. In other cases, you'll want to start your numbering with the number 1 (as shown here).

424

The Number of Places field will enable you to set the number of digits that will be used in your clip renumbering. In this example, I've chosen three places, so my files will be numbered 001, 002, 003, and so on.

You may want to add a suffix to your filenames.

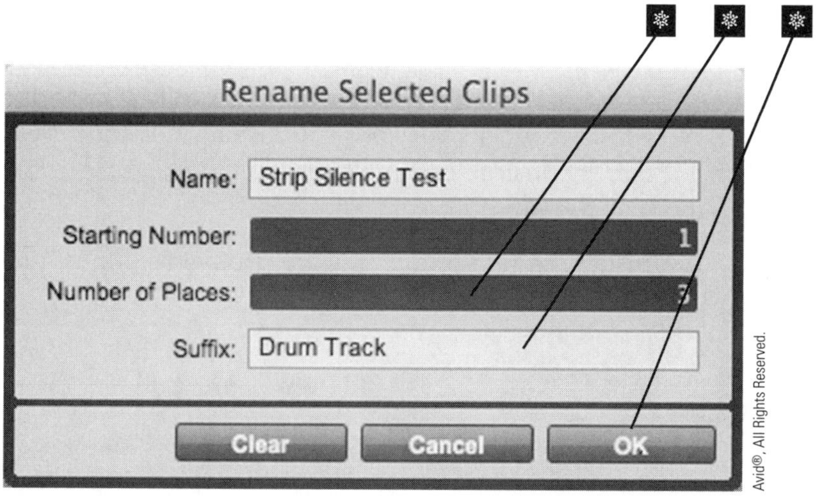

Rename Selected Clips

Name: Strip Silence Test

Starting Number: 1

Number of Places: 3

Suffix: Drum Track

Clear   Cancel   OK

❊ When you've set up your renaming scheme, click on the OK button. Based on the settings shown here, the selected clips will be renamed Strip Silence Test001Drum Track, Strip Silence Test002Drum Track, and so on.

❊ STRIP SILENCE AND PRO TOOLS 11

Strip Silence has always been a valuable editing tool, but with Pro Tools 11, you can use it to get more power out of your Pro Tools system as well. As you learned way back in Chapter 3, "Getting Started with Audio," when you explored the Playback Engine window, Dynamic Plug-in Processing can "turn off" plug-ins whenever there is no audio on a track for them to effect. Using Strip Silence to remove unnecessary audio from your timeline will allow you to make the most of this powerful new feature.

Beat Detective Basics

One of the most interesting music-production tools in Pro Tools' bag of tricks is Beat Detective. Based on the same technology that makes the Tab to Transient feature work so well, Beat Detective can be used in a variety of ways. Essentially, it's used for aligning MIDI and audio. Although it's most commonly used in conjunction with drum tracks, it can be applied to any audio with clearly defined transients (or MIDI). Let's take a look at some basic Beat Detective workflows.

❊ SETTING THINGS UP

If you're following along with the tutorial session, go to Memory Location #6–Beat Detective (pt.1).

❊ TIMELINE AND EDIT SELECTION LINKING

If you've been going through this chapter, you've been linking and unlinking your edit and timeline selection. Going forward, the edit and timeline selections should be *linked*.

The first Beat Detective workflow is based on the idea that, in many cases, a musical groove is *not* mathematically uniform. This "human" element is in opposition to the mathematical precision of a static MIDI tempo. If you're following along with the tutorial session, you'll see just what I mean: Although the Audio track and the Instrument tracks are at the same tempo, they certainly aren't playing well together.

To get the audio and MIDI to groove together, you want to create a complex MIDI tempo map (based on the live drum track). Beat Detective will help you do just that!

1 Select the **segment of drums** that you want to analyze. (If you're following along with the tutorial session, that selection has been made for you.)

2 Click on the **Event menu**.

3 Choose **Beat Detective.** The Beat Detective window will appear.

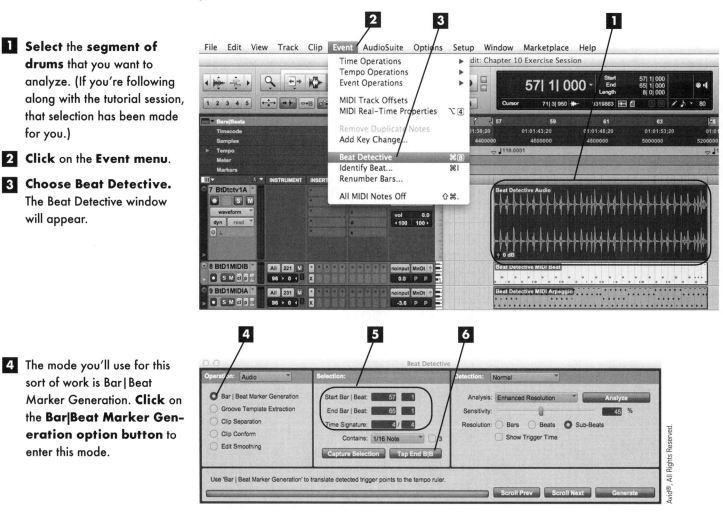

4 The mode you'll use for this sort of work is Bar|Beat Marker Generation. **Click** on the **Bar|Beat Marker Generation option button** to enter this mode.

5 This step is *very* important: **Make sure** the **values** in Beat Detective's Selection area correctly reflect the musical start, end, and meter of your selected area. Just as when you used Identify Beat earlier in this chapter, let your ears be your ultimate guide.

6 **Choose** the smallest **musical note value** of your audio. You'll have to use your ears for this. (In this example, it's 1/16 notes.)

❉ USING CAPTURE SELECTION

Assuming your selection is known to be in agreement with the MIDI Bars|Beats ruler, you can click on the Capture Selection button in the Selection area of Beat Detective. This is an easy way to go with audio in cases where the beat has already been identified.

7 **Click** on the **Analyze button**. Beat Detective will search your selected audio for transient events.

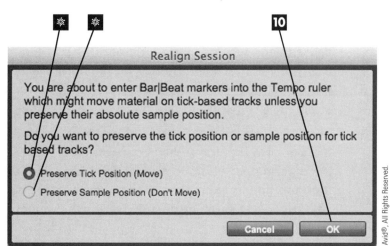

8 Slowly **slide** the **Sensitivity slider** from left to right. Notice that as your sensitivity percentage increases, you will begin to see vertical lines intersecting the transients of your audio. (The loudest transients will be marked first.) When you are satisfied that the important transients have been marked (and no others), stop moving the slider.

9 **Click** on the **Generate button**. The Realign Session dialog box will open. This dialog box is fairly self explanatory. The two option buttons will determine how your tick-based tracks will react to the creation of the new Bar|Beat markers.

❉ If you want the timing of your session's tick-based tracks (such as a drum part on a MIDI track) to move to match the timing of the Audio track, choose Preserve Tick Position (Move). This is what we'll choose in this case, and what is most commonly chosen.

❉ If your tick-based data doesn't need to be matched to your new tempo map, choose Preserve Sample Position (Don't Move). The data on your tick-based tracks will not be changed in any way.

10 When you've made your choice—in this case, choose **Preserve Tick Position**—**click** on the **OK button**.

❉ ❉ ❉

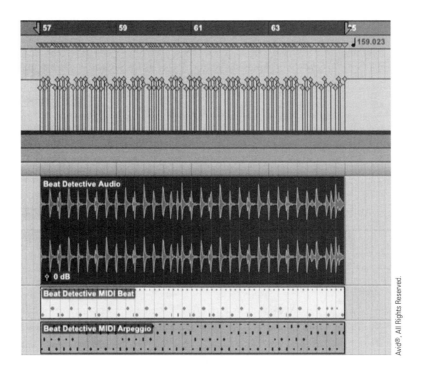

You will see now that a great number of small tempo changes have been added to your Tempo ruler, each shown as a blue triangle in the collapsed Tempo ruler or as tempo events in the expanded Tempo ruler. What you've done is create a tempo map that changes constantly to match the groove of the drum audio, which has effectively created a MIDI grid that also reflects these changes. Because things such as Grid mode and MIDI Quantize rely on this grid for their timing, you can now conform any additional MIDI and audio to this original drum beat, and they will all groove together!

But that's not all that Beat Detective can do—not by a long shot. Let's reverse the process. Suppose that instead of creating a new tempo map based on your Audio track (so that the rest of your session can conform to that audio), you want to conform your audio to the *current* tempo of the session. Beat Detective can do that, too. In this example, you'll conform the same audio clip to the mathematically static tempo of the session, effectively quantizing it to a 1/16-note grid.

❋ WHAT DOES "QUANTIZE" MEAN?

At its most basic level, *quantize* is a MIDI function that aligns the timing of MIDI notes to a grid. It's commonly used to fix timing errors or to create mathematically "perfect" timing when the style of music calls for it. In a larger sense, we use the term to refer to the alignment of audio as well, when using Beat Detective or Elastic Audio (something I'll discuss later in this chapter).

❋ SETTING THINGS UP

Please go to Memory Location #7–Beat Detective (pt.2).

1 **Select** the **segment** of **drums** that you want to analyze. (If you're following along with the tutorial session, that selection has been made for you.)

2 If the Beat Detective window isn't already open, **click** on the **Event menu** and **choose** **Beat Detective**. The Beat Detective window will appear.

3 The first mode you'll use for this sort of work is Clip Separation. **Click** on the **Clip Separation option button** to enter this mode.

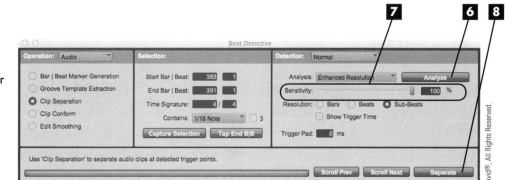

4 Again, **make sure** the **values** in Beat Detective's Selection area correctly reflect the musical start, end, and meter of your selected area. Be careful: Beat Detective does not automatically update its selection values. If you're using the tutorial session, this memory location is at a different section of your session!

5 **Choose** the smallest **musical note value** of your audio (in this example, 1/16 notes).

6 **Click** on the **Analyze button**. Beat Detective will search your selected audio for transient events.

7 Slowly **slide** the **Sensitivity slider** from left to right. Note that as your sensitivity percentage increases, you will begin to see vertical lines intersecting the transients of your audio. (The loudest transients will be marked first.) When you are satisfied that the important transients have been marked (and no others), stop moving the slider.

8 **Click** on the **Separate button**. Your clip will be separated into a number of smaller clips. Not only will you see these clips represented on your track, but they will also be shown in the Clips list.

9 Now that you've chopped up your beat, it's time to get those smaller clips in line. **Click** on the **Clip Conform option button**.

Avid®, All Rights Reserved.

10 **Click** on the **Conform drop-down list**. You'll see that you can move your clips in the standard way (the clips will be quantized to the nearest grid line) or with a groove (using a groove template, similar to MIDI Groove Quantize). For our purposes, **choose** the **Standard mode**.

11 **Click** on the **Conform button**. The clips will move subtly to match the existing tempo map. If you listen to the selected area, you'll hear a change in the feel.

Avid®, All Rights Reserved.

12 As a byproduct of the conforming process, some gaps will be produced between clips. There may also be a few clicks and pops. Beat Detective's final mode will help you clean things up. **Click** on the **Edit Smoothing option button**. The Smoothing section gives you two options:

❋ If there are no problems with clicks or pops, click on the Fill Gaps option button. Clip boundaries will be adjusted to minimize gaps between clips.

❋ If there are clicks and pops, a quick crossfade between clips will fix the problem in most cases. Click on the Fill and Crossfade option button; then set the crossfade length. (This will vary from situation to situation; if you're working with the tutorial session, 5 ms sounds good.)

13 **Click** on the **Smooth button**.

Your audio will now have a significantly different feel and no gaps!

There's one more mode included in Beat Detective, called Groove Template Extraction.

❋ **IF YOU'RE USING THE EXERCISE MATERIALS...**

The next section will extract the groove from the selected drums. Please undo any Beat Detective quantization that you've done so you have a more human groove to extract!

❋❋❋

1 **Click** on the **Groove Template Extraction option button** in the Beat Detective window.

2 Here again, the values you enter in the Selection area of the Beat Detective window are crucial. Once you've done that, **click** on the **Analyze button** and **adjust** the **Sensitivity slider**, just as you've done before.

3 **Click** on the **Extract button**. The Extract Groove Template dialog box will appear.

4a **Choose Save to Groove Clipboard** to immediately use the extracted groove in your session.

4b **Choose Save to Disk** for long-term storage of the groove.

Essentially, what you have done is extract the same sort of timing information you used in Bar | Beat-marker generation, except in this case you've added this information to your list of available MIDI Groove Quantize options. (This is covered in detail in Appendix A, "More MIDI Power.") More simply put, you've given yourself the option to quantize MIDI data (now or in the future) to have the same feel as these drums you've just analyzed!

Beyond the Basics: Multitrack Beat Detective

In the previous section, you learned how to use Beat Detective to align MIDI and audio in a number of different ways. Let's build on that and take a look at how to use Beat Detective when dealing with multiple drum tracks (for example, a recorded drum kit).

Working with Overhead and Room Tracks

Before you get started, there's one thing to look out for: the overhead and room tracks. Very often, when live drums are recorded, microphones are placed above the drum set (overheads) or elsewhere in the drum room (room) to add ambience to the close microphone tracks. Because these microphones are farther from the source of the sound than the close mics, their timing is naturally later than that of the closely recorded tracks.

This is great for ambience but can make things just a little more complicated when working with Beat Detective. Here's the risk: If you analyze the overheads and room tracks along with the other drum tracks, you'll be plagued with a horde of double triggers. Worse yet, if you conform all the tracks together, you run the risk of snapping the individual drum tracks and the ambient tracks, effectively eliminating the natural delay between those tracks and losing your valuable ambience!

The remedy to both these problems is easy. Just follow these steps:

> ❋ **BEAT DETECTIVE PRACTICE**
>
> Don't have any multitrack drums to practice with? No problem. A practice session has been included with this book. Just open the session Chapter 10–Multitrack Beat Detective Practice and go to work! An eight-bar selection (starting at bar 1) has already been made for you. Before you open this session, however, you might want to save the work you've done in the Chapter 10 Session file.

1 **Select** the **desired area** on the close mic tracks *only*. Leave any overhead or room tracks unselected at this point.

2 **Configure** Beat Detective's **Selection** and **Detection sections** as normal.

3 **Click** on the **Analyze** button and **adjust** the **Sensitivity slider** as normal.

4 **Add** the same selected **area** to your overhead and room tracks, while keeping the selected area of the close-mic tracks. (You learned in a previous chapter how to add selections to additional tracks.) When you're finished, you should have *all* your drum tracks selected. You'll note that the Beat markers extend to all the selected tracks.

5 Here's the only tricky part: As soon as you select the additional tracks, you'll see that the Analyze button will again be available to be clicked (re-analyzing this new selection). **Don't click** on the **Analyze button**! The Beat markers will be just a little bit earlier than the transients on the ambient tracks. That's what you want.

6 **Proceed** to the **next step** in the process (which is usually to separate the clips), according to your workflow.

If you separated those selected clips, you'll notice that the clip boundaries on the ambient tracks are a little bit before the transient. Now, when you conform your clips, all the clips will conform uniformly, maintaining the original relative timing differences between the close and the ambient tracks and preserving your sense of ambience while at the same time fixing the timing of the drums!

Collection Mode

In many cases of multitrack drums, musically significant tracks are low in volume in relation to other tracks. A common situation in my experience would be hi-hat cymbals—musically very important, but usually much quieter than kick and snare tracks. When using Beat Detective on multiple tracks, this presents a little bit of a challenge: If you analyze all the clips together, you're likely to create unwanted beat triggers on the louder tracks before you capture the hits you need on the quieter tracks. What you really need here is a way to analyze tracks individually. That's where Collection mode comes to the rescue.

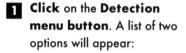

1 **Click** on the **Detection menu button**. A list of two options will appear:

✳ **Normal mode.** This is the mode to use if you want to analyze a number of selected tracks in a single operation. In this case, changes to the Sensitivity slider will affect Beat markers on all tracks simultaneously.

✳ **Collection mode.** This mode enables you to analyze tracks individually and to progressively add Beat markers with each successive analysis.

With these two modes in mind, here are the steps to use Collection mode to its best advantage:

1 With Normal mode chosen, **select** the desired **area** on the first track (let's say the Kick drum track). **Adjust** the **Sensitivity slider** so that you are marking all the important transients.

2 **Switch** to **Collection mode**. You'll see that you have three options:

❄ **Add All Current Triggers to Collection (the Add All button).** Clicking this will add all current beat triggers to the collected analysis.

Use 'Bar | Beat Marker Generation' to translate detected trigger points to the tempo ruler.

Avid®, All Rights Reserved.

❄ **Add Only Unique Triggers to Collection (the Add Unique button).** Clicking this will add all current beat triggers to the collected analysis, except those that duplicate pre-existing beat triggers.

❄ **Clear All Triggers from Collection (the Clear All button).** Clicking this will remove all beat triggers from the collection.

3 Because you're just starting out, **click** on the **Add All button**. You'll see the beat triggers appear in the selected area.

4 **Switch back** to **Normal** mode, and move your selection to the next track (a snare track, for example). **Re-analyze** the **selection** (this is important) and **adjust** the **Sensitivity slider** so that the desired transients are marked.

5 Next, **go back** to **Collection mode**, but this time **click** on the **Add Unique button**. You'll see your current beat triggers added to the ones you collected from the first track.

The rest is pretty straightforward: Just repeat steps 4 and 5 until you've analyzed all the desired tracks. Once you're done with that, you can move on to the next step (creating Bar|Beat markers, extracting groove templates, or separating clips) as normal.

❄ **BEAT DETECTIVE FOR MIDI**

Beat Detective can also analyze MIDI data and perform similar operations. To use Beat Detective with MIDI, just click on the Operation menu button in the upper-left corner (which currently reads Audio) and choose MIDI from the list that's shown. Some subtle changes in the window will appear (and only the first two operation mode option buttons are relevant to MIDI), but the overall workflow is similar to what you've gone through in this chapter.

❄ **FOR MORE INFORMATION...**

The complex applications of Beat Detective go beyond the scope of an introductory book like this one. If you want to go through every button in Beat Detective, you might want to check out a book called *Working with Beats in Pro Tools: Skill Pack*, written by yours truly and published by Thomson Course Technology PTR (2007).

As a general rule, you should check the Ignore Errors During Playback/Record checkbox only when you run into problems in noncritical situations (such as editing). When you're in the important recording or final mixdown stages of your project, remember to uncheck the Ignore Errors During Playback/Record checkbox. You certainly don't want to hear clicks and pops then!

❋ **ONE MORE EDITING SHORTCUT**

Before I close this discussion on editing, here's one more useful shortcut (one that can be used in a variety of situations). On either a Mac or a PC, hold the Shift key while starting playback to play back your session at half-speed. This comes in particularly handy when you're setting punch-in or punch-out points for a particularly tight spot. (Be careful when recording that way, though, as your recorded audio will be twice as fast and twice as high in pitch!)

Elastic Audio

Elastic Audio is a relative newcomer to the Pro Tools arsenal of features, and it's already a favorite for Pro Tools users worldwide. On its face, Elastic Audio enables you to change the timing and pitch of audio in a flexible and non-destructive way and can give you the same kind of control over your audio that you have over MIDI. When you dig deeper, though, you'll see that Elastic Audio can be a tweaker's paradise!

❋ **SETTING THINGS UP**

In the Chapter 10 Session file, please go to Memory Location #8–Elastic Time.

Basic Operation

You can enable, disable, and customize Elastic Audio on a track-by-track basis. To activate Elastic Audio on an Audio track, follow these steps:

1 **Click** on the **Elastic Audio plug-in button**. A menu will appear.

2 **Choose** the appropriate **plug-in** for the job. You have five options:

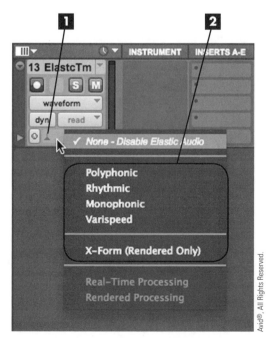

❋ ❋ ❋

- **Polyphonic.** This mode is a good general choice and is well suited for audio in which multiple pitches are being played simultaneously.

- **Rhythmic.** This mode is a good choice for drum tracks and other percussive audio.

- **Monophonic.** This mode is great for Audio tracks in which only one note is being played at a time (for example, wind instruments or vocals).

- **Varispeed.** This mode is fundamentally different from the others. Elastic Audio's other modes maintain the original pitches of your audio regardless of whether they're being sped up or slowed down. Varispeed mode, on the other hand, will raise the pitch of your audio when it is being played faster than normal or lower the pitch when it's being played slower. This is particularly handy for turntable or tape-type effects.

- **X-Form (Rendered Only).** This is a high-quality algorithm and is often my personal choice, but it is only available as a rendered plug-in as opposed to real time. (I will discuss the difference between real time and rendered in a moment.)

> ❄ **IF YOU'RE USING THE EXERCISE MATERIALS...**
> If you're following along with the Chapter 10 tutorial session, you'll note that the track shown is a drum loop, so let's choose the Rhythmic plug-in.

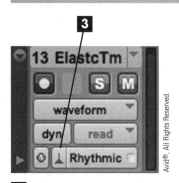

3 You'll notice that once you choose an Elastic Audio plug-in, a button showing your choice will be displayed. Within that button, and next to the name of the algorithm (in this image, Rhythmic), you'll see a small rectangle, which will be either lit with a green color or dark. This will indicate whether Elastic Audio for that track is being processed in real time (green) or in a rendered mode (dark). **Click** on the **Elastic Audio plug-in button** once more so you can take a second look at the Elastic Audio plug-in list.

4 The bottom segment of the Elastic Audio plug-in list will enable you to choose the processing mode for Elastic Audio on that track. (The currently selected mode will be indicated by a checkmark.) **Choose** one of the **options**. (There are two in most cases.)

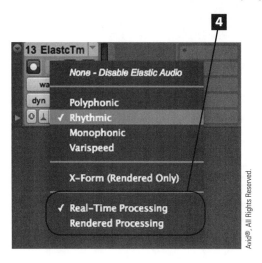

❄ **Real-Time Processing.** Selecting Real-Time Processing will give you the quickest performance, and any changes you make to your audio will be applied immediately. That being said, processing in real time will place an additional load on your computer's CPU, which can be an issue (particularly with less-powerful computers).

❄ **Rendered Processing.** When you choose Rendered Processing, your changes will not be immediately applied. It will take some amount of time (depending on the speed of your computer) to apply the change. During that time, the track will not be audible. Your changes will be written (or rendered) to new files that are saved in your session's Rendered Files subfolder.

❄ ELASTIC AUDIO AND THE TCE TRIM TOOL

One of the first things you'll notice when you enable Elastic Audio on a track is that the TCE Trim tool works a bit differently. When Elastic Audio is set up with real-time processing, instead of creating a new file and clip each time you use the TCE Trim tool, your audio will simply be time compressed or expanded immediately. (New files will *not* be created.) Regardless of the processing mode chosen, you might also notice that as you use the TCE Trim tool repeatedly on the same clip, the clip's audio quality won't progressively degrade (something that can happen with non–Elastic Audio tracks).

Event and Warp Markers (and How to Use Them)

When Elastic Audio is enabled on a track, you'll notice that there are two new track views available to you: Analysis and Warp. Both of these track views have their parts to play. Let's take a look at them one at a time.

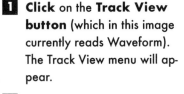

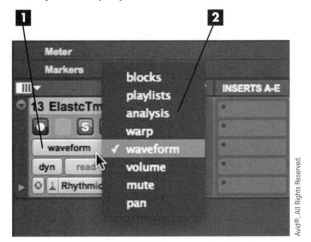

1 **Click** on the **Track View button** (which in this image currently reads Waveform). The Track View menu will appear.

2 **Choose Analysis** from the list of view options.

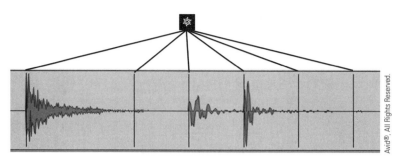

❋ You'll immediately note that there are vertical lines marking transients in your audio—even the very low-level ones. Each of these lines is called an *Event marker*.

Event markers are loosely analogous to the Beat markers you saw earlier in this chapter when you worked with Beat Detective. These markers determine the locations within an audio clip that will move as the audio follows tempo changes or when the audio is quantized, which I'll discuss later in this section.

If you need to, you can move, delete, and add Event markers. The Grabber tool will help you do this. (You can edit Beat Detective's Beat markers in the same way.)

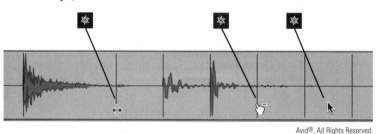

❋ Using the Grabber tool, move your cursor over an existing Event marker. Your cursor will change to the double-arrow shown here. You can click and drag the Event marker to a new location.

❋ You can delete an existing Event marker by holding down the Option (Mac) or Alt (PC) key and clicking on it using the Grabber tool. The cursor will be shown as a pointing hand with a minus (−) sign next to it.

❋ If you want to create a new Event marker, just double-click where you want to create it!

Now, let's move on to the Warp view:

1 **Click** on the **Track View button** and **choose Warp** from the list of options.

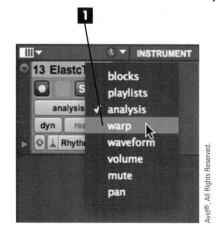

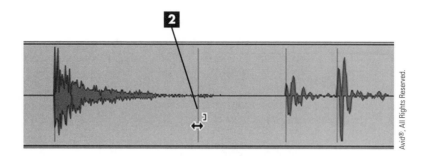

2 Here again, the Grabber tool will be your greatest ally. Move your mouse over any Event marker. (Yes, you can still see your Event markers, even though you're in Warp view.) The cursor will turn into the icon shown here, indicating that you're ready to use the telescoping warp. Just **click** and **drag** to the **left** or the **right** to proportionally compress or expand the entire clip. Markers can be dragged smoothly if you're in Slip, Shuffle, or Spot mode. If you're in Grid mode, you'll see that your marker snaps according to your grid resolution.

Although telescoping warp does have its uses, to really make the most of the Warp view, you'll need to create a new kind of marker, called a Warp marker. Conceptually, you can think of a Warp marker as being a handle that you can grab and move to stretch your audio. Warp markers can be identified by their darker color and the small blue triangle at the base of the marker.

Just as you saw with Event markers, you will find that the Grabber tool helps you get started easily:

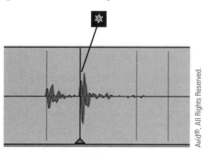

✳ Here's a common starting point: Double-click on an existing Event marker to change it into a Warp marker (shown here).

Here are a few other ways to work with Warp markers:

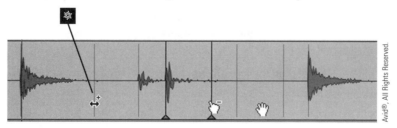

✳ If you have an existing Warp marker to the right of an Event marker, and you want to promote that Event marker to a Warp marker, you'll see a small plus (+) sign next to the cursor. In these cases, a single click will create a Warp marker.

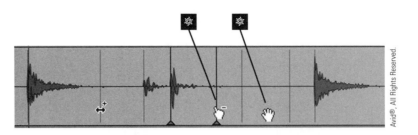

❋ You can remove an existing Warp marker by holding down the Option (Mac) or Alt (PC) key and clicking on it with the Grabber tool. The cursor will be shown as a pointing hand with a minus (−) sign next to it. Double-clicking on an existing Warp marker will also remove it.

❋ If there are no existing Event markers at the location where you want to create a new Warp marker, no problem—just double-click where you want to create one!

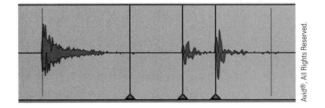

Here's a typical Warp marker setup: The center Warp marker in this scenario is the point of audio that I want to move. The Warp markers to the left and right of the center Warp marker, although they *can* be moved, will act as anchors in this case. Now you're ready to do some serious warping!

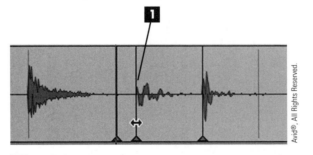

1 **Click and drag** the **center Warp marker** left or right. You'll immediately see that the audio is being pulled like taffy, giving you control over minute aspects of your audio clip, with the adjacent Warp markers acting as anchors.

Here's an even quicker way to create the Warp markers you need for this kind of work:

1 **Hold down** the **Shift key** and **move** your **mouse** over an Event marker that you want to promote to a Warp marker and then move.

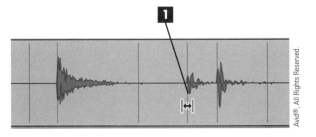

2 **Click** on the **Event marker**.

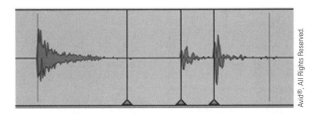

You'll notice that not only has the Event marker you clicked changed to a Warp marker, so have the markers immediately adjacent to it. This puts you in position to adjust the center Warp marker, just as you did earlier in this section.

From time to time, moving a Warp marker can cause audible side effects. While one possible solution is to eschew a given Elastic Audio plug-in for one more suited to the job, you can also tweak the current plug-in a bit to improve its performance.

1 **Click** on the **Elastic Audio Plug-In button** (which in this image reads Rhythmic, the currently selected Elastic Audio plug-in). The plug-in window will appear.

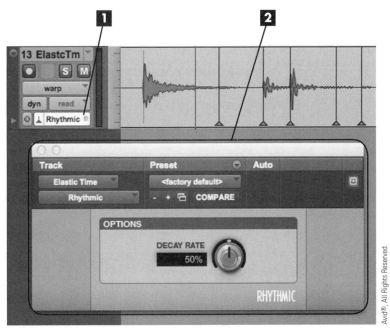

2 The appearance of the Elastic Audio plug-in window will vary, depending on the Elastic Audio plug-in you're using, enabling you to adjust parameters that are most relevant to each one. In the case of the Rhythmic plug-in shown here, you can just **adjust** the **Decay Rate setting**, which can remove unwanted artifacts that sometimes accompany this particular plug-in.

You also have the ability to adjust specific Elastic Audio settings on a clip-by-clip basis.

1 Select the **clip** you want to work with.

2 **Right–click** on the **clip**. A menu will appear.

3 **Select Elastic Properties.** The Elastic Properties dialog box will appear.

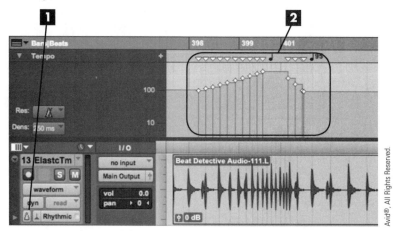

2

Tools
Insert
Add Warp Marker
Remove Warp Marker

Elastic Properties...
Conform to Tempo
Remove Warp
Remove Pitch Shift

Separate
Delete Fades
Clip Gain
Mute Clips
Rename...

Group
Ungroup

Loop...
Unloop...

3

4

Elastic Properties

Clip: ◇   Beat Detective Audio-01

TCE Factor: 100.00 %

Event Sensitivity: 100 %   Reset

Input Gain: 0.0 dB

Pitch Shift: 0 semi   0 cents

4 **Type** new **values** into the appropriate fields. The upper part of the Elastic Properties dialog box will give you overall information about the clip (which will vary, depending on whether the track is sample based or tick based). In the bottom part, you'll see more specific data, including the following:

❊ **Event Sensitivity.** This is similar in function to the Sensitivity slider you worked with in Beat Detective and in this case will allow you to control Event marker placement.

❊ **Input Gain.** You can adjust this downward if you find that your clip clips as a result of warping. A clipping clip will be indicated by a small red rectangle in the upper-right corner of the clip.

❊ **Pitch Shift.** I'll discuss this later in this section.

Elastic Audio and Tempo

This party's just getting started! Let's now set up our Audio track to follow tempo changes.

1 **Change** the **Audio track** from sample based to tick based. (For a refresher on how to do this, take a look at Chapter 6.)

2 Using the Pencil tool, **draw** some **tempo change events** onto the expanded Tempo ruler, as shown here.

1   **2**

Bar|Beats   398   399   401

Tempo

100

Res: ♩

Dens: 50 ms   10

13 ElastcTm   no input

S M   Main Output

waveform   vol   0.0

dyn   read   pan   0

Rhythmic   0 dB

Beat Detective Audio-111.L

If you play back your session, you'll hear that the clip has been compressed or expanded to follow your session's Tempo ruler.

With Elastic Audio, not only do you have the ability to have your audio follow tempo changes, but you can also quantize it as if it were MIDI!

1 **Select** the **area** you want to quantize.

2 **Click** on the **Event menu**.

3 **Choose Event Operations.** A submenu will appear.

4 **Choose Quantize.** The Event Operations/Quantize window will appear.

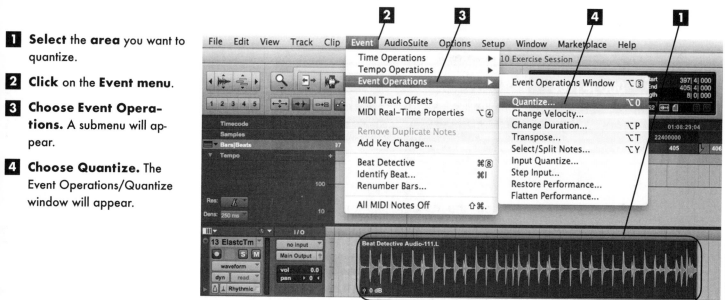

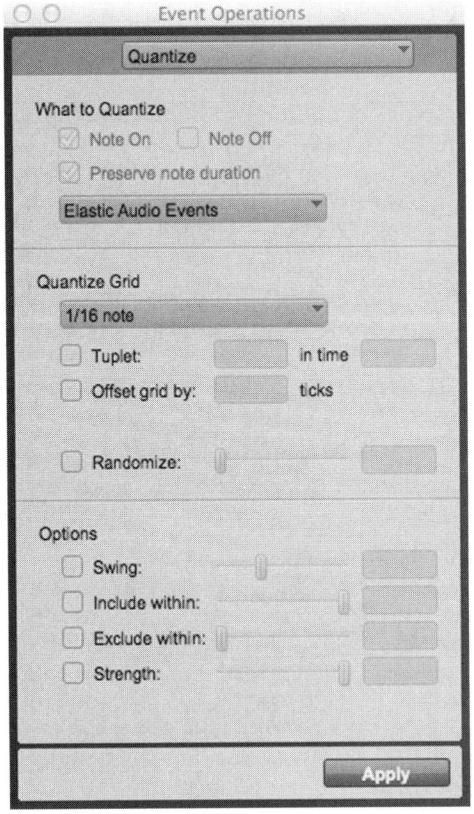

Because you've selected a clip on an Elastic Audio–enabled track (which contains Elastic Audio events, covered next), you have the option of quantizing this drum clip, almost as if it were MIDI! Note that when an Elastic Audio clip is selected, the What to Quantize menu button reads "Elastic Audio Events." You can quantize to either a grid increment (such as 1/16 notes, as shown here) or a groove template when quantizing MIDI.

> ❄ **COMBINING TOOLS**
>
> Now that you have both Beat Detective and Elastic Audio under your belt, you have many ways to get them to work together. Here's one scenario: Suppose you have two drum clips, and you want them to have the same feel. Here's one way to go: Choose the drum clip whose feel you prefer and use Beat Detective's Bar | Beat Marker Generation mode to change your session's tempo map. Just quantize the other drum clip to the new grid (the track needn't be tick based to do this), and you're all set!

Elastic Audio and the Workspace Browser

Elastic Audio is at work not only in your session but in the Workspace Browser as well. Within these browsers, audio files that are analyzed by Elastic Audio and are determined to have a musical pattern (such as a drum beat) are listed as being tick-based files (indicated by a green metronome icon in the Kind column). Files that are analyzed and found *not* to have this sort of pattern (for example, a single drum hit or a spoken sentence) will be listed as being sample based (indicated by a blue clock icon in the Kind column).

1   **2**

Presets: 1 2 3 4 5		0.0	◀ ☖ ▶	9 Items

Locations	Name	1 ▲	Kind	Waveform
▼ 📁 Volumes	🔘 Hi-Hat.wav		🔺 Audio File	◁)
▼ 📁 Chapter 10 Exerci	🔘 Kick.wav		🔺 Audio File	◁)
▶ 📁 Session Audio	🔘 Overheads.L.wav		🔺 Audio File	◁)
▶ 📇 Catalogs	🔘 Overheads.R.wav		🔺 Audio File	◁)
▼ 📁 User	🔘 Room Mics.wav		🔺 Audio File	◁)
▼ 📁 Desktop	🔘 Snare (Bottom).wav		🔺 Audio File	◁)
▼ 📁 Chapter 10	🔘 Snare (Top).wav		🔺 Audio File	◁)
▶ 📁 Audio	🔘 Tom 1.wav		🔺 Audio File	◁)
	🔘 Tom 2.wav		🔺 Audio File	◁)

1   **Click** on the green **Audio Files Conform to Session Tempo button** at the top of the Workspace Browser. Your tick-based audio files will play at your session's tempo (rather than at their original tempo) when previewed. You can **right-click** the **button** to change the Elastic Audio plug-in being used for previewing files in the Workspace Browser.

2   **Click** on the **speaker icon** next to the file waveform that you want to preview. If the file is tick based, the tempo of the previewed audio will match the tempo of your session.

The Audio Files Conform to Session Tempo feature also has an effect on the process of importing files into your session. When the feature is active, a tick-based file will be imported to a tick-based, Elastic Audio–enabled track, with the same plug-in algorithm that you had in your Workspace Browser being applied to that track.

Making the Most of Elastic Audio

For many Pro Tools users, Elastic Audio is an essential production tool, and using it efficiently is a real timesaver. You can tweak the behavior of Elastic Audio through the Preferences dialog box:

1   **Click** on the **Setup menu**.

2   **Choose Preferences.** The Preferences dialog box will open.

3

3 In the Preferences dialog box, **click** on the **Processing tab**. In the Elastic Audio section of this page, you'll see three useful options:

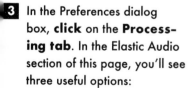

Pro Tools Preferences							
Display	Operation	Editing	Mixing	Metering	Processing	MIDI	Synchronization

AudioSuite

Default Handle Length:
- ◯ Whole File
- ⬤ Length: 2.00 Seconds

TC/E

TC/E Plug-in: Time Shift ▾
Default Settings: <factory default> ▾

Import

- ☐ Convert Imported ".wav" Files to AES31/Broadcast Wave
- ☑ Automatically Copy Files on Import
- ☐ Convert Copied Files to Session Format
- ☐ Don't convert Sample Rate on Import
- ☐ Import REX Files as Clip Groups

Elastic Audio

Default Plug-in: Polyphonic ▾
Default Input Gain: 0.0 dB

- ☐ Enable Elastic Audio on New Tracks

❊ ❊ ❊

❄ **Default Plug-in.** Here, you can choose the initial plug-in used for auditioning files in the browser windows, as well as the plug-in that is initially used if new tracks are created as Elastic Audio tracks.

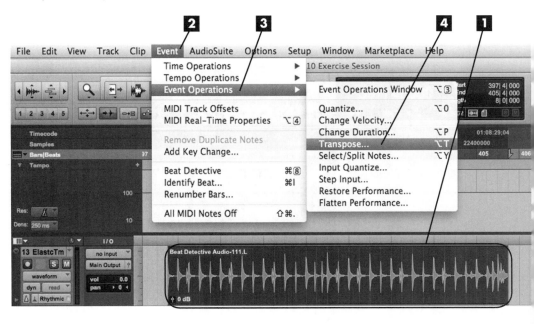

❄ **Default Input Gain.** This will enable you to automatically reduce the volume of Elastic Audio clips to prevent the clipping that can sometimes occur when a clip is warped.

❄ **Enable Elastic Audio on New Tracks.** When this checkbox is checked, new Audio tracks will be created with Elastic Audio enabled (using the default plug-in type).

Elastic Pitch

Elastic Audio can adjust not only the timing of your audio but its pitch as well. Using Elastic Audio, you can easily change pitch on a clip-by-clip basis.

> ❄ **ELASTIC PITCH LIMITATION**
>
> Adjusting pitch with Elastic Audio can be done only when using the Polyphonic, Rhythmic, or X-Form Elastic Audio plug-ins.

There are two different methods by which you can adjust the pitch of a selected clip, each with its own particular advantages. Let's start by looking at a way to transpose a clip.

1 **Select** the **clip** whose pitch you want to transpose.

2 **Click** on the **Event menu**.

3 **Choose Event Operations.** A submenu will appear.

4 **Choose Transpose.** The Event Operations/Transpose dialog box will appear.

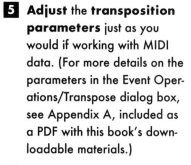

5 Adjust the **transposition parameters** just as you would if working with MIDI data. (For more details on the parameters in the Event Operations/Transpose dialog box, see Appendix A, included as a PDF with this book's downloadable materials.)

6 Click on the **Apply button**, and you're finished!

The previous workflow is very handy in situations when you want to make relatively large changes in pitch. But what if you just want to tweak the pitch of a flat note? No problem. You can make those kinds of fine adjustments in the Elastic Properties dialog box.

1 Right-click on the **clip** you want to change. A list of options will appear.

2 Choose Elastic Properties. The Elastic Properties dialog box will open.

❋ The Pitch Shift controls in the Elastic Properties dialog box will enable you to adjust pitch not only in semitones (something you could also do in the Transpose dialog box), but also in cents, which are very small units of pitch. There are 100 cents in a semitone, or half-step. You will find that by adjusting pitch in terms of cents, you have very fine control over the pitch of the audio.

❋ ❋ ❋

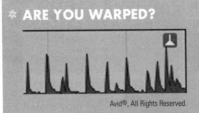
✳ ELASTIC WARNINGS

One final point: From time to time, you might see sections of your audio turn red when dragging Warp markers. Not to worry—Pro Tools is just letting you know that you've applied a good deal of time compression or expansion. Technically speaking, you've gone beyond Pro Tools' recommended limits, but if it sounds good to your ears, go for it!

More Mixing Power

Let's take a more in-depth look at the world of Pro Tools mixing!

✳ SETTING THINGS UP

In the Chapter 10 Exercise Session file, please go to Memory Location #9–Mixing.

EUCON Support

Back in 2010, Avid purchased a company called Euphonix, adding some truly outstanding control surfaces to their product offerings—from the high-end System 5 to the small but powerful Artist series. These control surfaces communicate with Pro Tools (and other DAWs) through a protocol named EUCON (Extended User CONtrol). Here's how to set up your Pro Tools system to communicate via EUCON:

1 Click on the **Setup menu**.

2 Choose Peripherals. The Peripherals dialog box will appear.

3 EUCON is an Ethernet-based protocol, so **click** on the **Ethernet Controllers tab**.

4 **Click** on the **Enable EUCON checkbox**. When enabled, a checkmark will be displayed (as shown here).

5 **Click** on the **OK button**. The Peripherals dialog box will close.

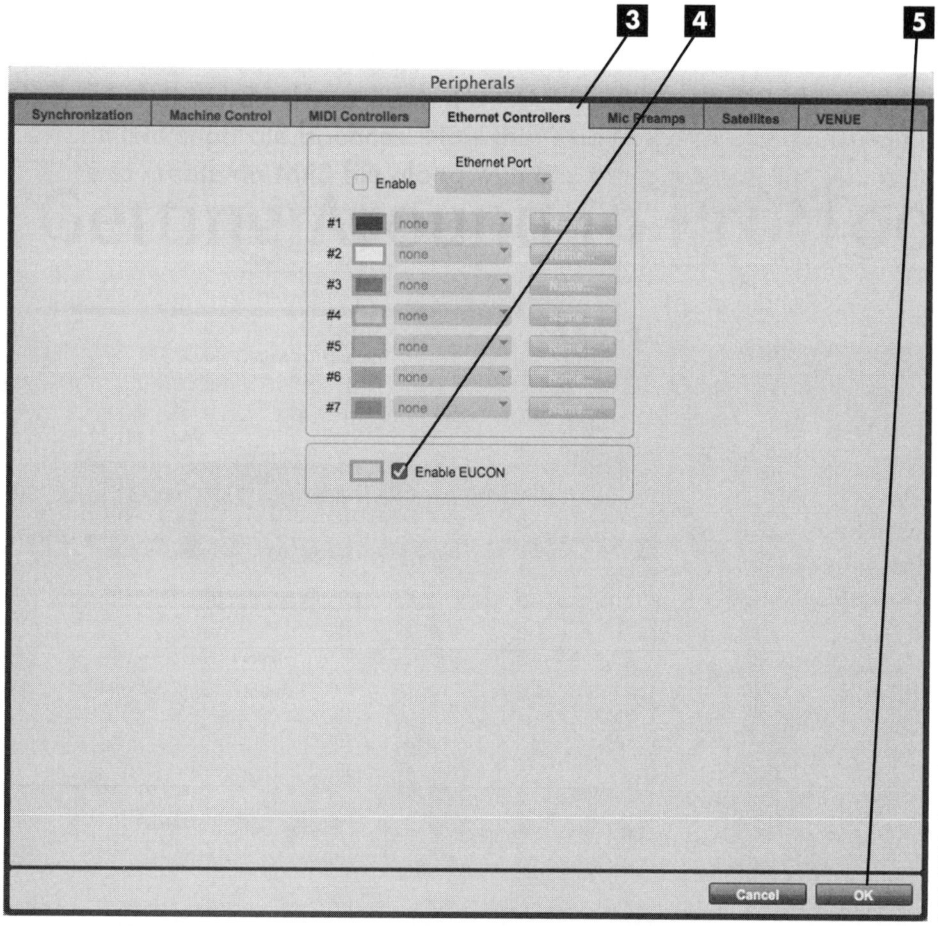

That's it! There are no other Ethernet settings you'll need to worry about in this dialog box (they apply to other kinds of Ethernet controllers). Assuming your control surface is set up (including the installation of the device's EuControl software), you're all set to go!

❋ NEW IN PRO TOOLS 11: EUCON 3

Pro Tools 11 supports the new EUCON 3 protocol, which provides significant improvements in stability over previous EUCON versions. Pro Tools 11 does *not* support previous versions of EUCON.

Pan Depth Options

Okay, this can get a little technical, but hear me out: When identical signals are combined, their levels go up. (Makes sense, right?) Well, that would suggest that when a signal is panned to the center of a stereo pair of speakers, the perceived volume of that signal would be louder than if that signal were panned to the hard left or hard right. Now, if *that* were the case in actual practice, you'd have some pretty serious issues to contend with as you mix, especially when automating things like panning! Clearly, somebody has fixed the problem behind the scenes, and that solution is called *pan depth*.

❋ ❋ ❋

Basically, what pan depth refers to is an attenuation (reduction in volume) of a signal as it is panned to the center so that the perceived loudness stays the same. The problem is that there's no hard-and-fast rule about which amount of attenuation is correct. It depends on a number of factors, including the acoustic quality of the room you're working in. As a result, different mix-console and DAW manufacturers use different pan depths. This can really do a number on a mixer's ears, though—particularly when you mix in different systems with different pan laws. So, Pro Tools gives you the ability to choose the pan depth you prefer!

1 **Click** on the **Setup menu**.

2 **Choose Session.** The Session Setup window will appear. You'll find your session's pan depth displayed in the lower-left corner of the Format section of the Session Setup window.

3 **Click** on the **Pan Depth drop-down list** to display a list of pan-depth options.

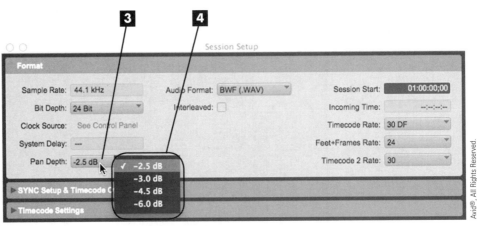

4 You can **choose** a different **Pan Depth setting** for your session from this list (the current setting is indicated by a checkmark). You're sure to find a setting you like—all the standard pan depths are represented here.

Automatic Delay Compensation

When you launch a plug-in, you're effectively adding a mathematical formula to the signal path. Like all math, simple formulae can be processed quickly, whereas more-complex equations take more time. This is as true for computer chips as it is for the human brain. When we talk about delay caused by plug-in math, we call it latency.

You can probably see where this is going. When you're working with multiple tracks, with different kinds of plug-ins on them (different math, and different amounts of latency), your audio can get out of sync. Although this might not sound like a big deal, these small differences in timing can lead to problems of phase alignment and can quickly muddy up your mix.

Pro Tools' Automatic Delay Compensation (ADC) feature fixes this problem by adding varying degrees of latency to each track. It uses the most latent track as a guide so that all tracks share the same amount of latency and are thereby perfectly aligned. Let's take a simple example: Say you have three tracks. One has

100 samples of plug-in latency, the second one has 20 samples of latency, and the third one has zero plug-in latency (there aren't any plug-ins on that track). ADC would add 80 samples of latency to the second track and 100 samples of latency to the third track so that all three tracks have the same amount of latency (100 samples in this case). What's better, ADC is always keeping tabs on how much latency is on each track and maintains sample accuracy between all the tracks, so all you need to do is to turn ADC on and get to mixing!

You can enable and disable ADC from the Options menu:

1 **Click** on the **Options menu**.

2 **Choose Delay Compensation.** When it's active, you'll see a checkmark next to the menu item.

You're pretty much done at this point and can mix secure in the knowledge that your audio is all sample aligned. There are just a few other tidbits that will come in useful:

❋ In the Session Setup window (which you saw in the previous section, about pan depth), you'll see a System Delay value if ADC is active. This value represents the delay caused by ADC plus the delay of your audio interface. This data is invaluable when synchronizing with an external device, like a video tape deck. You can compensate for this delay in the Sync Setup & Timecode Offsets section of the Session Setup window.

❄ By default, your delay values will be shown in Pro Tools in samples, but you have the option of viewing them in milliseconds instead. Just go to the Preferences dialog box (from the Setup menu) and from there to the Operations tab. You'll find the Delay Compensation Time Mode drop-down list in the lower-right corner of this page; just click on the list and choose the time scale you want to use (samples or milliseconds).

Pro Tools Preferences

| Display | Operation | Editing | Mixing | Metering | Processing | MIDI | Synchronization |

Transport

☐ Timeline Insertion/Play Start Marker Follows Playback
☐ Edit Insertion Follows Scrub/Shuttle
☐ Audio During Fast Forward/Rewind
☐ Latch Forward/Rewind
☑ Play Start Marker Follows Timeline Selection

Custom Shuttle Lock Speed: **800** %
Custom FF/REW Speed: **300** %

Numeric Keypad:
○ Classic
◉ Transport   ☐ Use Separate Play and Stop Keys

Record

☑ Latch Record Enable Buttons
☑ Enable Automation in Record
☑ Link Record and Play Faders

☐ Automatically Create New Playlists When Loop Recording

Online Options:
◉ Record Online at Timecode (or ADAT) Lock
○ Record Online at Insertion/Selection

Auto Backup

☑ Enable Session File Auto Backup
Keep: **10** most recent backups
Backup every: **5** minutes

Misc

Delay Compensation Time Mode: Samples

User Library

Root: [Change...]
/Volumes/Macintosh HD/Users/andy/Documents/Pro Tools/

Video

☑ Enable GPU
☑ Prevent Tearing
Play Start Latency: 1 - Shortest

[Cancel]   [OK]

You can easily see what's going on in your session by taking a look at what ADC is doing on a track-by-track basis. There are two ways to show the Delay Compensation view in your Mix window:

❄ From the View menu, choose Mix Window Views. From there, choose Delay Compensation.

❄ Click on the Mix Window View button (in the bottom-left corner of the Mix window) and choose Delay Compensation from the menu that appears.

You'll then see a display at the bottom of each track in your Mix window, with a variety of useful information:

※ The top section will show you the original latency of each track. In this image, the Soprano, Tenor, and Bass tracks have no plug-ins instantiated and therefore no latency. The Alto track, however, has some plug-in latency (quite a bit, actually—1,024 samples!).

※ The middle section enables you to manually add or subtract from this value, effectively nudging the audio forward or backward in time. It's rarely used, but if you need to tweak a particular track's timing, you have the power to do it here.

※ The bottom section will tell you the amount of latency that's been added by the Delay Compensation Engine. In this example, 1,024 samples of latency had to be added to the first, third, and fourth tracks to keep them perfectly lined up with the second track.

※ CLIPPING THE ADC

Pro Tools' ADC can compensate for up to 16,383 samples of latency. Although it's pretty tough to do, it is possible to accumulate more plug-in latency than the Delay Compensation Engine can compensate for. You can see if you're exceeding the capacity of your ADC in two places:

If a track is clipping the ADC, the displays in its Delay Compensation section will appear red.

In the counter display section of the Edit window, "Dly" appears (in the lower-right section) whenever ADC is activated. If the letters are green, all is well. If "Dly" is shown in red type, however, that means you've clipped at least one track, and the Delay Compensation Engine can no longer keep all your audio in perfect synchronization.

❄ DELAY COMPENSATION AND RECORDING

The Delay Compensation Engine operates by adding delay to your session's tracks. When you're recording, you might think this'll create some issues! Don't worry, though—the Delay Compensation Engine is automatically bypassed on recording tracks, and recorded audio and MIDI is time aligned with the rest of the session once a recording pass is finished.

Advanced Resource Management

This section covers yet more ways to view and manage your data!

Inactive Elements

There are two important terms when it comes to resource management—*offline* and *inactive*. An offline clip occurs when source media is not found when you open a session. When that happens, a clip will appear on a track, but that clip will be empty, with the clip name in italics. Inactive elements, on the other hand, are processes that are somehow disabled (either as a result of not having the appropriate plug-in installed on a system or deliberately by the Pro Tools user).

Although an offline clip won't save too much in the way of CPU resources, being able to use inactive tracks and plug-ins will really help you out in a pinch. There are a few good reasons to make a plug-in or track inactive:

❄ Making a plug-in inactive will free up valuable CPU resources while maintaining automation and preset settings.

❄ Making tracks inactive can enable you to work with tracks beyond the Audio track limitation of a given Pro Tools system (although an inactive track will not be audible).

There are two easy ways to make a plug-in inactive. Here's one:

1 Right-click on the **Insert button**. A list will appear.

2 Choose **Make Inactive.**

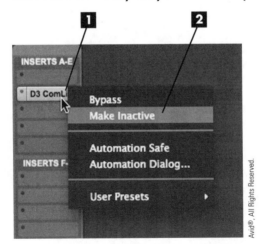

Here's another way to do it:

1 **Press and hold** the **Command+Control keys (Mac) or the Ctrl+Start keys (PC)** and **click** on the **Insert button** for the plug-in you want to disable.

Regardless of the method you choose, here's what you'll see:

❋ The Insert button's text will be italicized, indicating that the plug-in is inactive.

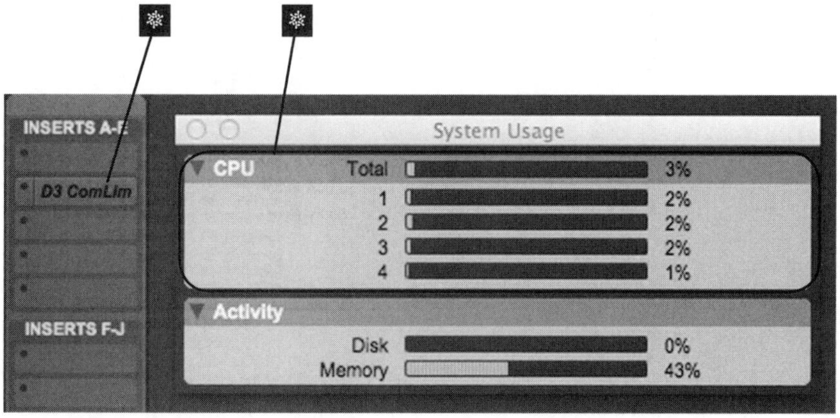

Avid®, All Rights Reserved.

❋ For every real-time plug-in you disable, your CPU usage will decrease (even if only subtly), leaving more processing room for new effects. You can monitor this CPU usage in the System Usage window (which you first saw way back in Chapter 2, "Getting Around in Pro Tools").

❋ OPENING A SESSION WITH PLUG-INS INACTIVE

Holding the Shift key while opening a session will cause the session to open with all plug-ins inactive. This can drastically reduce the time it takes to open many sessions (particularly sessions with a high plug-in count).

Similarly, there are multiple ways to deactivate an entire track:

1 **Select** the **track(s)** you want to deactivate.

2 **Click** on the **Track menu**.

3 **Choose Make Inactive.**

Here's another way to do it:

❋❋❋

1 **Right-click** on the **name** of the track(s) that you want to deactivate. (You can make this selection in the Mix window, the Edit window, or the Tracks list.) A list will appear.

2 **Choose Make Inactive** (or **Hide and Make Inactive**).

And yet one more method:

1 **Press and hold** the **Command+Control keys (Mac)** or the **Ctrl+Start keys (PC)** and **click** on the **track type icon** for the track you want to deactivate.

Here's what you'll get:

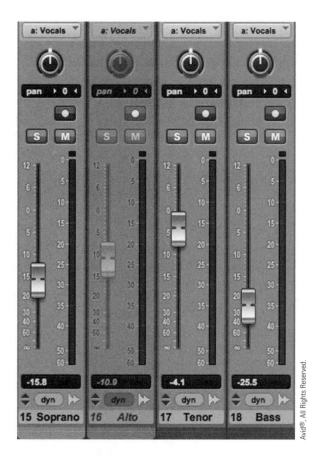

An inactive track's channel strip will be grayed out, and the track name will be italicized. In this case, the Alto track is inactive.

> ### ❋ WORKING WITH HD SESSIONS
>
> When you open a session previously used by Pro Tools HD software, you might find that some of your tracks are inactive because Pro Tools HD supports more active tracks than non-HD software. You can still use them by deactivating any of the currently active tracks and then activating one of the currently inactive tracks.

Edit Density and Consolidation

Edit density refers to the number of times your system must acquire audio data from your hard drive during playback. In extreme cases, high edit density can cause playback problems due to high demands placed on the throughput of your hard drive. The trick in those cases is to decrease the number of clips without changing the sound of your session, and the Consolidate function is the key.

> ### ❋ SETTING THINGS UP
>
> For this demonstration, go to Memory Location #10–Consolidation. You'll see a section of drums to which Beat Detective's Clip Separation feature has been applied, creating lots of clips!

❋ ❋ ❋

1 **Select** a **section** of your session that is particularly dense with clips. (If you're working with the tutorial session, this has been done for you.)

2 **Click** on the **Edit menu**.

3 **Choose Consolidate Clip.** A window will display the progress of the Consolidate function.

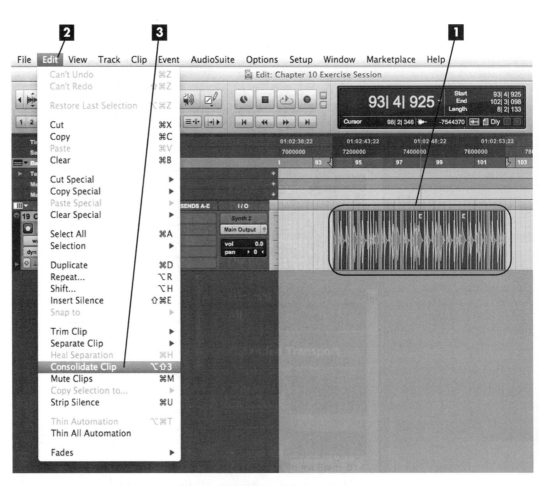

Your selection of multiple clips will be rendered into a single clip (and a single audio file on your hard drive).

✳ CONSOLIDATING SILENCE?

When you use the Consolidate feature, any selected space that is not occupied by a clip will be rendered as silent audio, as will any gaps between clips in your selected area.

✳ CONSOLIDATING MIDI?

MIDI clips can be consolidated as well as audio clips. Note that, although convenient, consolidating MIDI data won't affect your edit density.

New in Pro Tools 11: Freeze Track Workflow

There are a few DAWs on the market that have the ability to render individual tracks within a session—a nifty feature often referred to as "freezing" a track. This ability to render a track in your session has the virtue of "printing" your real-time effects, meaning that you would no longer need to use CPU resources for plug-ins for that track.

Pro Tools doesn't yet have a one-click "freeze track" function, but with the ability to offline bounce, it comes pretty darn close. The good news is that you've already learned the steps to do this. You just need to put them together into a workflow:

1 **Solo** a single **track** that you want to render.

2 **Select** the **area** on the timeline that you want to render.

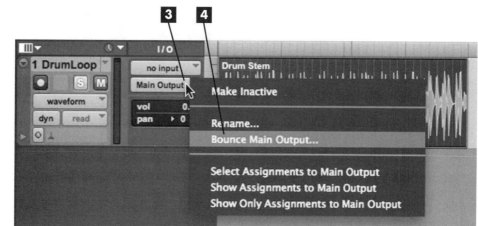
Avid®, All Rights Reserved.

3 This is the only bit that's new: **Right-click** the track's **Output selector**.

4 **Choose Bounce [output path].** The Bounce dialog box will open, with the correct bounce source already configured for you.

5 **Make sure** the **Import After Bounce checkbox** is checked.

6 If the option is available to you, **make sure** the **Offline checkbox** is checked.

7 **Click** on the **Bounce button**. Your track will be bounced and imported into your session.

8 **Deactivate** the **original track**. If you ever need to re-render it, you can always reactivate the track later and repeat the process.

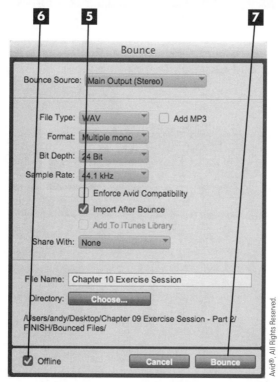
Avid®, All Rights Reserved.

Working with Video

Although Pro Tools is certainly an audio-centric program (as are most DAWs), that doesn't mean you can't incorporate video into your sessions. In fact, working with video in your session is a very straightforward process.

⁕ VIDEO AND PRO TOOLS HD

In a basic Pro Tools 11 system, there are a few limitations with regard to video. For the purposes of this book, we'll limit our discussion on video to basic operations so these limitations won't present a problem. For those of you who need more-advanced video features within Pro Tools, purchasing Pro Tools HD software adds a number of significant features (many of them video related) to your system. You can learn more about Pro Tools HD and what it offers by visiting Avid's website (www.avid.com).

Importing Video

Let's start off with a look at the process of importing a QuickTime movie, which couldn't be easier.

1 Click on the **File menu**.

2 Choose **Import**. A submenu will appear.

3 Choose **Video**. The Open/Select Video File to Import dialog box will appear.

4 Navigate to and **click** on the **file** you want to import. Then **click** on the **Open button**.

⁕ DON'T HAVE ANY QUICKTIME FILES? NO PROBLEM!

If you don't have any QuickTime files to import, you can find some in the Chapter 10 Session folder, inside the Video Files folder.

You can also import video via the Pro Tools Workspace Browser. This is perhaps the quickest and easiest way to bring video into your session.

1 **Locate** the **file** that you want to import.

2 **Drag and drop** the **file** into your session. You can drag it to your session's playlist area, to the Tracks list, or to the Clips list. Regardless of which import method you choose, the Video Import Options dialog box will appear.

3 **Click** on the **Location drop-down list**. You'll be presented with a list of options as to *when* to position your video clip:

❀ **Session Start.** This will place the video clip at the very beginning of the Video track.

❀ **Song Start.** You can set your song to start at a place other than the beginning of your session (something covered back in Chapter 6). If you have done this, you have the option to place your video clip at the song start.

❀ **Selection.** Choosing this option will place your video clip at the beginning of the currently selected area.

❀ **Spot.** Choosing this option will open the Spot dialog box, enabling you to type a specific time location for your video clip.

4 **Click** on the **Import Audio from File checkbox** to also import audio that is included with the video to a new Audio track.

5 To import the video into your session, **click** on the **OK button**.

Although a Video track isn't an Audio track to be sure, you'll still see it displayed in the Edit window. You can arrange the track in the Edit window just as you would any other track, and you can move the video clip just as you would move any audio or MIDI clip.

Viewing Video

You can easily show or hide Pro Tools' Video window:

1 **Click** on the **Window menu**.

2 **Choose Video** to show the Video window (or to hide it, if it's currently being shown).

❀ ❀ ❀

❄ To resize the Video window, just move your cursor to the lower-right corner of the window, click, and drag the window to the desired size. Alternately, you can right-click in the Video window and choose from a list of sizing options that appears.

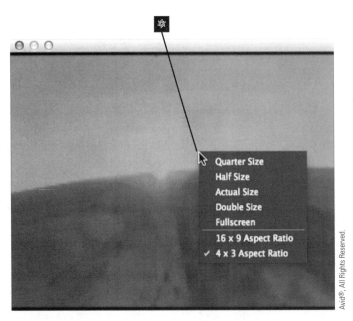

❄ BOUNCING TO QUICKTIME

For information on how to bounce your session to a QuickTime file, refer to Chapter 9, "Finishing Touches," in the section "Bouncing to a QuickTime Movie."

❄ NEW IN PRO TOOLS 11: IMPROVED VIDEO ENGINE

Pro Tools 11, being a fundamental rebuilding of Pro Tools, has significantly increased the power and usefulness of Pro Tools' built-in video engine. Put simply, the video engine that Pro Tools uses is the same as that used in Avid's flagship video applications, such as Avid Media Composer. This means a few things to the Pro Tools user:

   ❄ The ability to view HD MXF video from within Pro Tools

   ❄ Support for Avid HD video peripherals, plus video peripherals manufactured by AJA and Blackmagic

Video playback, especially high-quality video playback, requires no small amount of CPU resources. When working within Pro Tools, those might be resources that you'd prefer were devoted to audio-related tasks. Luckily, Pro Tools 11 gives you the ability to choose the quality of your video playback. Better yet, it's very easy to do:

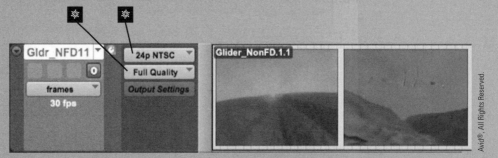

* Clicking the Project Type button allows you to choose the resolution of your video. This is usually not a setting that needs to be changed, but it does allow you to view your video in a number of different formats.

* Clicking the Video Quality button allows you to choose the quality of your video, from Full Quality down to Draft Quality.

✳ **CHECKING YOUR WORK**

To see this chapter's steps in their completed form, check out the Chapter 10 Session-Finished session.

Interoperability: Making Shared Sessions Work

Perhaps the most compelling reason to learn and use Pro Tools is its position as the global standard in the DAW world. From bedroom studios to multimillion-dollar facilities, Pro Tools allows for greater collaboration for amateurs and professionals alike than perhaps any other application. Take your humble author, for example—I wrote a good portion of this book in airports with just a laptop, and I could easily open this book's sessions in any professional studio with a minimum of muss and fuss!

The best way to maximize the interoperability of Pro Tools is to make efforts to ensure that your session can be opened and heard properly on a wide variety of systems and that collaborators can easily understand your work. Here are some recommendations on how to make this happen:

* Name all tracks before recording, in a way that anyone can understand.

* Use the Comments view in both the Edit and Mix windows. The Comments column of every track and the Comment field of memory locations are valuable sources of information to others.

* Use your memory locations. Identify each section of your work and descriptively name it so that anybody can understand the overall layout of your session.

* Internally record (using a bus) all your virtual Instrument tracks to Audio tracks. This ensures that even if your collaborator doesn't have the same virtual instruments installed on his or her system, that person will still be able to hear your session the way it was meant to be heard.

* Use AudioSuite plug-ins when appropriate. Just as with internal recording, this will create a new file that can be played back on any Pro Tools system, even if the actual plug-ins aren't present on that system.

PLAYING IT SAFE...

Before doing AudioSuite processing on a track, create a duplicate playlist so that you'll always have the original regions to go back to you if you need to later.

* Use a click track. Recording a great beat is all well and good, but if you're not in sync with the MIDI tempo of your session, features such as Quantize, Beat Detective, and Grid mode can do more harm than good!

* Before you archive your session or move it from one system to another, do a Save Copy In of your session and click on all appropriate options for saving. This will ensure that all your audio, video, and plug-in settings will be saved in one central location. That's the version you should archive or move to another system for further work. Incidentally, you can also use the Save Copy In feature to save your session as an older version of Pro Tools (if you're collaborating with a user who doesn't have the latest software).

EXPORTING TEXT

If you want a *very* detailed record of all the elements of your session, you can create a text log of your entire session (including the files used and the positions of all clips). Just go to the File menu, then to Export, and then to Session Info as Text. You will be prompted to choose what aspects of your session to include in the text log and where to save the text file.

Good Luck!

Congratulations—you made it! You've gone through a solid introductory tour of Pro Tools' basic operations and features. Although this discussion of Pro Tools is certainly not a comprehensive listing of *everything* Pro Tools can do, you can rest assured that your creative journey has started well. Over time, you'll not only learn more about Pro Tools, but undoubtedly you will find your own working style—a process that will be constantly refined as you gain experience and speed.

❀ **STILL WANT MORE SHORTCUTS?**

Over the course of this book, I've covered a good number of useful shortcuts, but there are still many more for you to discover. Fortunately, there's a resource for your shortcut-browsing pleasure—the Pro Tools Help menu. From the Help menu, choose the Keyboard Shortcuts menu item to view a comprehensive list of shortcuts. You might also want to take a look at the *Pro Tools Reference Guide*, which you'll also find in the Help menu. You can find updated versions of these documents on the Avid website (www.avid.com).

As your skills grow, you may crave more in-depth knowledge. Fortunately, Avid has an excellent training program, offered through the company's worldwide network of training partner schools. Avid's Training and Education Program is a constantly evolving curriculum that can take you from where you are now all the way up to an elite Expert Certification, complete with worldwide listing! For more information, visit www.avid.com/US/support/training.

You've begun a great exploration—and a worthwhile human endeavor, in my humble opinion. I personally believe that artistic pursuits nourish the soul not only of the patron, but of the artist as well. It's my fond wish that this book has served to inspire you to push the limits of your creativity and to share your gifts with others.

Good luck!

} Index

Entries with page numbers such as A1, A2, A3; B1, B2, B3; and C1, C2, C3 refer to material found in Appendix A, Appendix B, and Appendix C, respectively. These materials are available in PDF form on this book's companion website. To access this website, go to www.cengageptr.com/downloads, type Pro Tools 11 Ignite in the Companion Search field, click Search, and click the Pro Tools 11 Ignite link.

❋ ❋ ❋

Like the Book?

Let us know on Facebook or Twitter!

facebook.com/cengagelearningptr

www.twitter.com/cengageptr

Professional • Technical • Reference

BOOKS FOR THE RECORDING MUSICIAN

Cengage Learning PTR offers comprehensive resources for musicians and we cover all music and recording topics. Whether you're looking for a book on music production at home or at the studio or a guide to a popular DAW we've got you covered.

The Guitarist's Guide to SONAR
Craig Anderton ■ $29.99

Designed for guitarists of varying levels of experience with music software, this book covers some of the considerations unique to recording guitar with any computer-based system, and then progresses into guitar-specific techniques for Cakewalk SONAR.

Using Logic Pro's Synthesizers
Kevin Anker ■ $39.99

First, you'll master the simple synthesizers, which will make the essential components of synthesis clear to you. Then, you'll build on that knowledge to learn how to use the more complex synths. In addition, you'll learn about hidden capabilities in the various synths.

Mastering Pro Tools Effects
Getting the Most Out of Pro Tools' Effects Processors
Jeremy Krug ■ $39.99

Offers master-level lessons on using the most essential built-in plug-ins that come with Pro Tools, with detailed descriptions about what each effect is, what each effect does, and how to operate each effect.

Waves Plug-Ins Workshop
Mixing by the Bundle
Barry Wood ■ $29.99

The book on Waves plug-ins! Each chapter introduces the plug-ins in a specific bundle and details how they would be used in a mix.

The Laptop DJ Handbook
Jason Emsley ■ $29.99

Learn to harness all the hardware, software, and musical options available to the modern DJ through helpful explanations, tutorials, and examples.

Pro Tools 101
An Introduction to Pro Tools 11
Avid, Inc. ■ $49.99

This new edition from the definitive authority on Pro Tools covers everything you need to know to complete a Pro Tools project.